The British Isles

English G

Band A6

für das 10. Schuljahr
an Gymnasien
in Bayern

Cornelsen

English G
Band A6 für das 10. Schuljahr an Gymnasien in Bayern

Im Auftrage des Verlages herausgegeben und erarbeitet von
Prof. Hellmut Schwarz · Carl Taylor M.A. · Prof. Franz Vettel

unter Mitarbeit von
David W. Bygott · StD Burkhard Dammann · StD Erich Fleischhack · Dr. James N. Pankhurst ·
StRin Susanne Schroeder-Thürauf · Dr. Angelika Thiele
sowie StD Udo J. Hennig · Karen Carlson-Kreibohm · William C. Flowe · StRin Helga Haubrichs

in Zusammenarbeit mit der Englisch-Redaktion
Michael R. Ferguson (Projektleitung), Eileen Laurie, Jutta Seuren, Hartmut Tschepe (verantwortlich);
John Stevens (Redaktionsdienst Context, Bad Münstereifel)
Assistenz: Jutta Brendemühl, Jenny Dames

Beratende Mitwirkung
John Eastwood M.A. · StD Gerhard Finster

Grafik
Robert Broomfield, David Graham, Gabriele Heinisch, Graham Humphreys, Holger Lipschütz,
Mike Mosedale, Liz Roberts *sowie* Skip G. Langkafel *(Karten und Diagramme)*

Gestaltung und technische Umsetzung
Peter Richter *sowie* Eva Schmidt

Bild- und Textquellen
s. Verzeichnis auf S. 190

Titelfoto: Notting Hill Carnival, London (Mohamed Ansar/Impact, London)

Begleitender Tonträger zu diesem Band:
1 Cassette für Schüler und Lehrer mit einer Auswahl von Texten aus den Units, mit drei Hörverstehenstexten und Teilen der Options 6, 14 und 15. Ca. 90 Minuten. Bestell-Nr. 61205

Ergänzende Grammatik zu diesem Band: ENGLISH G Grammatik. Bestell-Nr. 3728

Begleitende Software zu diesem Band:
English Coach Vokabeltrainer, Diskette zu Band A6, Bayern. Bestell-Nr. 914542 (PC 3,5")

1. Auflage ✔ Druck 4 3 2 Jahr 2000 99 98
Alle Drucke dieser Auflage können im Unterricht nebeneinander verwendet werden.

Druck: Cornelsen Druck, Berlin

ISBN 3-464-07736-5

Bestellnummer 77365

gedruckt auf säurefreiem Papier, umweltschonend hergestellt aus chlorfrei gebleichten Faserstoffen

Contents

Page	Parts of the unit	Main themes/speech functions	Language focus/Grammar revision

Unit 1: Education in Britain and the USA

Page	Parts of the unit	Main themes/speech functions	Language focus/Grammar revision
6	A: **American high schools**	Schulsituation und Schulalltag von	English-German translation I
8	**A German pupil at a British school**	Jugendlichen in den USA und in Großbritannien kennen lernen; über	Common mistakes I
		das deutsche Schulsystem und die	Infinitive and gerund constructions
10	Exercises	eigene Schulsituation sprechen;	Indirect speech
13	English-German translation	über Rolle und Ziele der Erziehung	German 'lassen'
15	Text: **The truancy officer's visit** *(Roger Hall)*	diskutieren	

Unit 2: Great Britain – a multicultural society

Page	Parts of the unit	Main themes/speech functions	Language focus/Grammar revision
19	A: **Who are the British?**	Großbritannien als multikulturelle	English-German translation II
20	**From Empire to Commonwealth**	Gesellschaft kennen lernen; die Lebensweise ethnischer Minder-	Common mistakes II
22	**Post-war immigration**	heiten in Großbritannien kennen	German adverbs and their English equivalents
23	**Keeping the faith**	lernen; Einblicke in geschichtliche	Conjunctions and adverbial clauses
24	Exercises	Hintergründe gewinnen: *Empire* und	Participle constructions
30	Text: **An eye for an eye** *(Carole Boyer/Carl Taylor)*	Kolonialzeit, Unabhängigkeit, Ein-wanderung, *Commonwealth*	Ways of expressing the future
			Prefixes expressing the opposite

Unit 3: The United States – years of growth

Page	Parts of the unit	Main themes/speech functions	Language focus/Grammar revision
33	A: **The frontier**	Das Leben amerikanischer Siedler,	English-German translation III
35	**The railroad/'Wild West'**	Indianer und Cowboys kennen ler-	Common mistakes III
36	**American Indians**	nen, auch im Vergleich zwischen	Modal verbs
38	**The American Civil War**	Mythos und Wirklichkeit; Einblicke in	German 'sollen'
39	**Abraham Lincoln**	die geschichtliche Entwicklung der	Mixed tenses and verb forms
40	Exercises	USA gewinnen: *frontier*, Eisenbah-	Verbs with prefixes and suffixes
45	Text: **"Such is prairie life"** *(Miriam D. Colt)*	nen, Verkehr und Handel, Bürger-krieg, Leben und Wirken A. Lincolns	

Unit 4: Blacks in the USA

Page	Parts of the unit	Main themes/speech functions	Language focus/Grammar revision
48	A: **A historical timeline**	Geschichte und Gegenwart der	English-German translation IV
50	**Black America today**	Schwarzen in den USA kennen ler-	Common mistakes IV
52	**Some statistics**	nen; Statistiken beschreiben und	German 'wollen' · The passive
54	Exercises	auswerten; Gefühle ausdrücken;	Modal verbs
59	Text: **"I have a dream"** *(Martin Luther King)*	Martin Luther King als Persönlich-keit kennen lernen	Conditional sentences
			-ing forms in compounds

Unit 5: The world of literature

Page	Parts of the unit	Main themes/speech functions	Language focus/Grammar revision
62	**Dreams** *(L. Hughes)*	Fiktionale Texte verstehen und mit-	
64	**The moth and the star** *(J. Thurber)*	einander vergleichen; eigene Texte schreiben	
65	**The winner** *(D. E. Westlake)*		
71	**Dreampoem** *(R. McGough)*		
72	**Hidden worlds** *(A. Sillitoe)*		
74	**Playing with language**		
76	**Writing your own literature**		

ministry = Ministerium
combat = bekämpfen
progress = Fortschritt
average = Durchschnitt

Options

Die *Options* ermöglichen eine Erweiterung und Vertiefung von Themen aus den Units. Sie sind einzelnen Units thematisch zugeordnet, können aber beliebig im Laufe des Unterrichtsjahres eingesetzt werden.
Die Cassette zu diesem Buch enthält Aufnahmen zu den Options 6, 14 und 15.

Page

Options mit landeskundlichem/literarischem Schwerpunkt

78 **1** A question of identity (Units 1/3)
From *To live in two worlds* by Brent Ashabranner
81 **2** *The rabbits who caused all the trouble* by James Thurber (Unit 2)
82 **3** An American Indian legend (Unit 3)
83 **4** Slavery in the USA (Units 3/4)
84 **5** Black music (Unit 4)
86 **6** Robert Frost: Poems (Unit 5)
88 **7** Whale nation (Unit 5)

Options zu bestimmten Arbeitstechniken und Fertigkeiten

92 **8** Explaining grammar in English (Unit 1)
94 **9** Using a monolingual dictionary (Units 2/3/4)
96 **10** Using a grammar (Units 1/2/3/4)
98 **11** Presenting a paper (Units 2/4)
100 **12** Literary terms and their collocations (Units 4/5)

Options mit sprachlichem Schwerpunkt

102 **13** Indirect speech/Reported speech (Revision) (Unit 1)
104 **14** What to say in the UK (Unit 2)
109 **15** Varieties of English (Unit 2)
110 **16** What to say in the USA (Unit 3)
114 **17** The passive (Revision) (Unit 3)
116 **18** Conditional sentences (Revision) (Unit 4)
119 **19** Grammar for recognition: special *that*-clauses (Unit 4)

Units and Options at a glance

	'Text' Options	'Skills' Options	'Language' Options
Unit 1	1	8, 10	13
Unit 2	2	9, 10, 11	14,15
Unit 3	1, 3, 4	9, 10	16, 17
Unit 4	4, 5	9, 10, 11, 12	18, 19
Unit 5	6, 7	12	–

120 **Grammar review**

135 **Vocabulary**
155 **Mini-dictionary** (Alphabetical list of words, Books 1-6)
185 **Names**
186 **Grammatical terms** (Books 1-6)
188 **Irregular verbs**
191 **Useful classroom phrases**

Unit 1: Education in Britain and the USA

1

2

3

4

5

6

The Pledge of Allegiance

I pledge allegiance to the flag of the United States of America and to the republic for which it stands, one nation under God, indivisible, with liberty and justice for all.

- Which photos show school in Britain, which in the USA, do you think? Match the photos with these captions: *Football practice – Public school life – Saluting the flag – Morning assembly – Cricket practice – High school graduation day.*
- What do you find interesting in the photos?
- What photos would you choose to show German school life to British or American pupils? Why?

→ Ex 1

American high schools

- What can you remember about life at a US high school from Books 4 and 5, or perhaps from an exchange visit?
- Read this page from the school newspaper of a high school in Dunlap, Illinois. What does it tell you about American high school life?

DUNLAP HIGH SCHOOL NEWS

School info

There will be a Career Day on TUESDAY, April 26. We have invited different speakers to talk about topics from *Biotechnology* to *Working for an airline*. If you are interested in any particular job, you can talk to the individual speakers later.

Erin Spirropoulos, Sarah Cruz and Kevin Metz, Guidance Counselors

I would like to remind all students who drive to school that they must park on the north side of the building. I would also like to remind you again to drive carefully and slowly. And please remember that smoking in the parking lot is not allowed.

Wayne Holmes, Assistant Principal

Father-Daughter Dance

The next Father-Daughter Dance will be held at the Raffestry Center on April 16 from 8:00 to 11:00 p.m. If you can't bring your father, bring an older brother, uncle, etc. Tickets are $10. Soft drinks and snacks will be provided. The couples will dance to music from the 60s.

Your ads

Tired of spending money on car repairs? Join our auto mechanics club. Tuesdays 4-5 p.m. If interested, get info from the office.

I'm quitting my job at the PIZZA PLACE. It's two afternoons a week (Tuesdays and Fridays) from 4 p.m. to 7 p.m. Information is in the office for anybody who is interested.

Craig Rosetti

We regret to say that Debbie Frank is leaving our school, so we need somebody to fill her place as a CHEERLEADER.
If anybody is interested, just come to the gym for a try-out on Tuesday after school when we have cheerleader practice and talk to Joanne Rigby.

From the town paper

DUNLAP GIRLS 71 – O'CONNELL 63

by Pat Lanigan, Sports Editor

The Dunlap girls' basketball team is having a great season under new coach Pam Eastman. The team has won all its games so far. At the start of the season nobody expected them to be very successful, but as Captain Suzie Miller said, "We are not cowards. We play hard and we never give up, no matter what the score is or how good the other team is."

How an American high school is organized

Work with a partner. Read this page and make a list of differences between American high schools and German grammar schools. Make two sections in your list: teaching, and extracurricular activities.

List of activities at school

- Black Students' Association
- Chess Club
- Cheerleading
- Debate
- Drama Club
- French Club
- Math Team
- Music Ensemble
- Newspaper
- Science Club
- Spanish Club
- Yearbook

age	grade		
17	12	seniors	senior high school
16	11	juniors	
15	10	sophomores	
14	9	freshmen	junior high school
13	8		
12	7		
elementary school			

Did you know?

- *Each student in an American high school has his or her own personal schedule. In many schools the schedule is the same every day from Monday to Friday. That means the students do the same subjects in the same order at the same time.*
- *Teachers in an American high school have their own rooms, so students move from classroom to classroom to their different teachers. There are often only three to five minutes between lessons.*
- *Students don't repeat a year as some students have to in Germany, but they can repeat a class in a certain subject. If students fail a subject, they can do additional work in summer school during the summer vacation and then pass the subject.*
- *Subjects are divided into requirements and electives. Requirements are subjects students have to take. Electives are subjects students can choose to take. These are often subjects like Art, Shop, Music, Drama, or Computer Science.*
- *Sports and extracurricular activities are very important in American schools. There is a large choice of activities throughout the year. However, students do different sports in different seasons. Practice takes place after school.*

SPORTS PROGRAM DUNLAP HIGH SCHOOL

FALL	WINTER	SPRING
Cross-country	Basketball	Track and field
Football	Gymnastics	Baseball
Volleyball	Wrestling	Lacrosse
Soccer	Swimming	Tennis
	Hockey	Golf

- What things do you like about the school system in the USA? What do you like about the German system?
- What changes would you like to make in the German system? What would you prefer not to change?

→ Ex 2, 3
→ Option 1: A question of identity

1A

A German pupil at a British school

After his summer holidays 17-year-old Klaus Rösch left his home in Pocking, near Passau, and spent a term as a pupil at Cheney School, a comprehensive school in Oxford, England. At the end of his stay there, *English G* asked him about his experience.

- Find out from the interview what the following words mean: *mixed-ability classes, streaming, community service.*
- What short form of the term 'comprehensive school' does the interviewer use?
- In general, did Klaus enjoy his stay in Oxford?

EG: What kind of school do you go to at home, Klaus?

Klaus: A *Gymnasium.* I'm in Year 11.

EG: So what was it like being at a comprehensive?

Klaus: It was okay. I was a bit surprised that all the children in the area went to Cheney School. They didn't go to different schools like in Germany.

EG: Do you know if Cheney has mixed-ability classes?

Klaus: Yes, it does, but we were put in different groups for maths and English.

EG: That's called 'streaming'.

Klaus: Oh, I didn't know that.

EG: Was there anything you didn't like?

Klaus: Well, in some subjects we had lots of homework. Much more than at home.

EG: Oh really? In Britain people think Germans all work very hard.

Klaus: Some Germans think that, too. *(Laughter)*

EG: What else was new to you?

Klaus: Well, a lot of the pupils were black or Asian, and another thing was the school uniform.

EG: You had to wear one?

Klaus: Yes, it was really funny, you know; our trousers, shirt and pullover all had to be a certain colour.

EG: Tell me, what did you do at Cheney that you wouldn't have done at your school in Passau?

Klaus: Well, the most interesting thing was just before Christmas when I helped with a real live radio show – 'Radio Cracker' – that was run by pupils. I was one of the DJs and played record requests. People who made a request had to pay 50p for charity.

EG: A radio show in school?

Klaus: Yes, they set up a radio station in the school, and we broadcast, just in the Oxford area, from 9 am to 9 pm every day.

EG: So anyone in Oxford could tune in and listen?

Klaus: Yes. The station ran for a week. It was part of a community service project.

EG: I see. Was it easy to make friends?

Klaus: Not at first. Lots of pupils have part-time jobs, usually in shops or supermarkets, so it wasn't easy to meet after school. I was really quite surprised about that, the jobs I mean.

EG: What will you miss when you go home?

Klaus: One thing is the vegetarian food you get at Indian and Chinese restaurants. But I won't miss English bread, not the ordinary 'white, sliced' sort!

EG: Thanks very much, Klaus.

- Read the interview again. List the things Klaus found different from his school in Germany. What was his reaction to them?
- Do you think pupils should be 'streamed' according to their ability?
- Is it a good thing when pupils have part-time jobs? What are the advantages and disadvantages?

→ Ex 4, 5

The following information is from a book for British language assistants who are preparing to teach for a year in Germany.

The German school system

At the age of six, children start primary school, which generally lasts four years. After primary school, pupils attend one of four +types of secondary school, a *Gymnasium* (grammar school), a *Realschule* (sometimes called other names), a *Hauptschule* (secondary modern school), or a comprehensive school. There are certain differences between the 16 federal states. *Gymnasium*, which generally lasts for nine years (years 5 to 13), offers a +broad general education. In the last three years of *Gymnasium* (similar to the 'sixth form' in England and Wales), +conventional classes are replaced by a so-called course system: certain subjects are still +compulsory, but students can choose from a wide range of courses and so can concentrate on certain areas. Subjects are divided into three general +categories: language, +literature and art; the +social sciences; and +mathematics, science and technology.
Each student must take courses from each of these three categories throughout years 11 to 13 and for the *Abitur* examination (similar to A-levels). Secondary +instruction at grammar school ends with the *Abitur* examination, which students take in four subjects. After passing the *Abitur* examination, students are +awarded a +certificate which +entitles them to study the subject of their choice at a university or college of +further education.

Cones filled with sweets – a German tradition on the first day at school

(Based on *Facts about Germany*)

1 Collecting words

Collect the words and phrases from Unit 1 that are related to school and education. Add other words and phrases to do with school and education that you know. What words refer to the UK or the US only?

a **Types of school**
grammar school, …, private school, …

b **Subjects**
English, …

c **Exams**
GCSE, …
sit/pass/fail an exam, …

d **People at school**
pupil/student, sixth-former, …

e **Extracurricular activities**
theatre group, chess club, …

f **Further education**
sixth form, +vocational training, …

g **School in general**
graduation ceremony, streaming, …

2 Words in use

The text above gives a general description of the German school system and is fairly formal in style. Write a letter to a pen-friend about your own school career using a 'neutral' style.

+new word

1 Exercises

1 Calvin and Hobbes

a *Look at the comic strip quickly. What does the boy want?*

b *Use these words to fill in the eight gaps:* for – have to – to – want to – what.

c *Choose one of these sentences for the empty bubble at the end, or, better still, make up your own sentence and read it to the class.*
"Don't you like your teacher?" – "School taught me what I wanted to know." –
"Welcome to the world." – … – …

d *What is the boy's opinion of school? Do you agree?*

In the original the bubble says "Welcome to the world".

2 School and free time

Read the statements on the left by some high school students. How big a role does school play in their lives? Then decide which of the sentences on the right apply to you.

Two days a week I stay at school for cheerleader practice.

Most of my friends are people I know from the basketball team.

My boyfriend at the moment is someone I go to drama club with.

1. Most of my friends are people I know from school.
2. Most people I know in my year have a part-time job.
3. If I go to a party, I usually meet people from school.
4. My boyfriend/girlfriend is someone I know from school.
5. Most of my free-time activities are related to school.

Discuss your answers in groups. How big a role does school play in your lives?

3 A survey of new students

→ Grammar review 12, 13 a/b, 15-18 (pp. 128-130)

a Do you remember how you felt when you started *Gymnasium*? The principal of an American high school asked some new students about their best and worst experiences during their first few days at their new junior high school. *Put in the infinitive (with or without 'to') or the gerund.*

be (2×) be threatened do not have brought eat get lost get up go (2×)
have have to (3×) learn like lose make meet see watch

Seven of the students chose one of their classes as the best thing they had experienced. In particular, before they started junior high school they hadn't expected art (1.) so interesting. One student said (2.) new things was her best experience, while 26 said class was boring. Five students liked (3.) their different subjects in different classrooms, but nine had found you could (4.) in all the different corridors and that was their worst experience.
22 students said the best thing was (5.) new friends and two were happy (6.) that the school was a friendly place although eleven had experienced (7.) or pushed. One hadn't wanted (8.) to such a big school and said he felt safer in the zoo when all the animals were loose. Nine had enjoyed (9.) their new teachers, but four didn't (10.) a certain teacher because she was super boring and got mad when the students fell asleep. Two had liked (11.) to school on the bus. Nine students hated (12.) carry so many books home and back to school.
Nobody voted for (13.) homework as their best experience: twelve people said it was their worst. Many students agreed that they got too much homework and they hardly had any time for (14.) television.
Two had enjoyed (15.) lunch in the cafeteria, but ten had disliked (16.) wait so long in lines that almost reached to the football field. Four of them mentioned (17.) their lunch money on the way to school or (18.) enough and then (19.) owe it to the lady in the cafeteria until the next day. Later it was found they had spent their lunch money on something else.
Five were not looking forward to (20.) in the youngest group in a school again. Finally, two 'worst' votes went to (21.) so early in the morning.

b *List all the verbs in the text that take the gerund as a direct object. What other verbs do you know that can have a gerund as an object?*
Can the infinitive be used after 'to' in 20 and 21? Why?/Why not? → Option 8: Explaining grammar in English

4 Klaus's expectations: In English, please

→ Grammar review 13 a/b (p. 128)

Translate the following sentences into English using the constructions 'expect/want to do' and 'expect/want sb to do'.

1. Klaus wollte ein Trimester bleiben, aber nicht länger. Er wollte nicht, dass die Skisaison ohne ihn anfängt.
2. „Wir erwarten von dir, dass du genauso hart arbeitest wie hier zu Hause", hatten seine Eltern gesagt. Er hatte aber nicht damit gerechnet, mehr Hausaufgaben machen zu müssen als zu Hause.
3. Ein Deutschlehrer an der Cheney School wollte, dass er über das deutsche Schulsystem referiert *(give a talk)*. Klaus hatte nicht damit gerechnet, auch am Deutschunterricht teilzunehmen.
4. „Wir erwarten, dass auch Sie die Schuluniform tragen", wurde ihm gesagt. Klaus hatte nicht damit gerechnet, das tun zu müssen.
5. Er hatte nicht erwartet, dass so viele Engländer so schlecht über Deutschland informiert sind.
6. Er erwartet jetzt, dass seine Englischlehrerin in Passau ihm bessere Noten gibt.

5 What did they say? → Option 13: Indirect speech

Look back at the interview on page 8 and write a short report for the Cheney School magazine. Use indirect speech. You don't have to report every single sentence; your report should read like a real magazine article. You can start like this:
In our irregular series 'Over the fence', James Cox tells us about an interview for *English G* he did with Klaus Rösch, the exchange pupil from Passau in Germany who spent the Christmas term with us. "Klaus told me that at home he goes to a grammar school and that in Germany … . So I asked him … . He seemed surprised that …"

6 'I spy with my little eye …': Common mistakes I → Option 10: Using a grammar

a *The text below has 17 mistakes in it. Try to find them and rewrite the text without them. Explain why you have made the corrections. It may help to consult a grammar and you should also look at pages 121-124 of the grammar review.*

"My name is Norbert Werner. I am born in Augsburg, but I live near Austin, the capital of Texas, since one year.
I am 15 years and I go to the school in Austin. My favorite subjects are biology and history. But the American history is quite hard for me. When I will leave the school, I want to become doctor. That is my wish since I was a boy, because the medicine really interests me. In my free time my main interests are cars and sports. At school I enjoy to take part in track-and-field events. I am also in the drama club. Next month we do a play from Tennessee Williams. We work very hardly on the play in the moment."

b **In English, please** *Be careful not to make the mistakes with articles that you found in the text above.*

1. Don geht nie in die Kirche, obwohl er mit seinen Eltern in einem neuen Haus gegenüber der Kirche an der 77. Straße wohnt.
2. Wenn Don die Schule verlässt, will er an die Universität gehen. Er interessiert sich sehr für die moderne Literatur.
3. Dons Mutter ist Professorin. Sie lehrt an der Universität in Austin. Sein Vater arbeitet als Lehrer.
4. Als Don gestern im Internet gesurft hat *(surf the Internet)*, hat er eine sehr interessante Information über das deutsche Schulsystem gefunden, die er für die morgige Deutschstunde brauchen kann.

7 Don't let them! Make them! (German 'lassen')

Complete these sentences with a form of 'let sb do sth', 'make sb do sth' or 'have sth done'.

1. Some pupils at Cheney School complained that the walls of the school looked boring. They offered to paint pictures on them, so the head teacher …
2. Mrs Jenkins was angry because two or three pupils hadn't worked very well during her music lesson. So she … for an extra ten minutes after the bell had rung.
3. Somebody broke the music room window last week. Mrs Jenkins … at once, of course. But it's just been broken again, so she … again, I suppose.
4. Peter was annoyed when the maths teacher … not … a calculator during the test.
5. The head was pleased with 11B's test results, so he … home early. But 11A's results were so bad that he … the test again.

"Mr Osborne, may I be excused? My brain[1] is full."

[1] brain [breɪn] *Gehirn*

English-German translation

Translating directly from one language into another, word for word, is not usually a good idea, as the cartoon shows.

- The Englishman translated an English sentence word for word. What was the English sentence?
- Look at the examples of possible mistakes below. Did the Englishman make any of these mistakes?

You have been practising translating from German into English for several years now. In this book, we want to focus on the skill of translating from English into German.This is usually a written activity, but in class it serves other purposes too: it helps you to make sure you have understood something; and it demonstrates differences and parallels in English and German grammar, word order, and the way words are used together (collocations).
Doing a good translation demands more than just understanding the text and knowing what all the words mean. On the one hand, you have to keep closely to the English original and convey all the information it contains; on the other hand, the German text should also read well – ideally as if it were no translation at all. Pay special attention to the following points:

- Differences in word order between English and German:

Last year **we went** to Austria. → Letztes Jahr **fuhren wir** nach Österreich.
Mr Green has **been ill**. → Mr Green ist **krank gewesen**.

- English words that have more than one meaning:

I **know** Jack and I **know** where he is now. → Ich **kenne** Jack und ich **weiß**, wo er jetzt ist.

- English grammar structures that don't exist in German, such as contact clauses, and constructions with gerunds and participles:

Is this the book **you lost**? → Ist dies das Buch, **das du verloren hast**?
Instead of sitting there, why don't you help? → **Anstatt** dort **zu sitzen**, …
Having phoned home, he went out with his friends. → **Nachdem er** zu Hause **angerufen hatte**, …

- English words and phrases that are translated with a different German word class (e.g. adverb instead of verb) or a different structure (e.g. active instead of passive):

I **don't like** watching horror films. → Ich schaue **ungern** Horrorfilme.
English **is spoken** here. → Hier **spricht man** Englisch.

- Different collocations in English and German:

I **took** this **photo** last week. → Ich habe dieses **Foto** letzte Woche **gemacht**.
Mrs Green is **popular with** her pupils. → Mrs Green ist **beliebt bei** ihren Schülern.
All over the world people are dying. → **Überall auf der Welt** sterben Menschen.

- Idiomatic expressions that have to be translated as one unit:

Can I **have a word with** you? → Kann ich **kurz mit** Ihnen **sprechen**?
All's well that ends well. → **Ende gut, alles gut.**

Translation

You should never begin to do a translation without first reading through the whole text to find out its general meaning. During this first reading it is better not to think of the translation at all – just try and understand what the text means, using the context and what you know about the world. Then note down the words and phrases that you find difficult. Only during your second reading should you look up words in a dictionary. Your first translation will not be perfect, so go through it again, see that it makes sense, that it contains all the information from the original and that it reads fluently – like a German text. Then make any necessary changes or additions.

Translation practice I

Some time ago Prince Charles gave prizes to some pupils who had done especially well at school. He then gave a speech, which was reported in the press. *Translate this newspaper article into German. Use an English-German dictionary to check any new words.*

Stick to tradition, Charles tells teachers

PRINCE Charles, who dislikes trendy teachers almost as much as trendy architects, yesterday warned the nation to stick to traditional teaching methods." Experience does seem to show that it is the traditional methods that help our children learn more effectively," he told a ceremony[1] in London. The prince said traditional teaching was one of the "foundation stones" of the education system.

His worries about schools have been expressed before. Even the people in his own office could not speak or write English properly, he once complained. "All the letters sent from my office I have to correct myself – because English is taught so bloody badly."

"Poor economic circumstances should not be an excuse for failure," he said yesterday. "As I myself see, visiting schools in some of the poorest and most deprived parts of cities, poverty is not a bar to excellence and achievement."

This word means 'modern' or 'influenced by the most recent trends and ideas'. For Prince Charles it probably means 'unnecessarily modern' or 'too much influenced by recent trends'. How can you express that in German?

Warn can't be translated by 'warnen' here. Check the context to decide on a suitable translation.

In German you'll need an article.

Why is this structure used here? There is a similar way of saying this in German.

Was is not 'war' here. Why?

In German a sentence with an active verb may sound more natural.

This highly informal word is only used in spoken English for emphasis. Some people consider it offensive (= 'anstößig'). Here it is used to stress the adverb *badly*.

Deprived means 'benachteiligt'. But how are you going to translate the superlative *most deprived*?

In German use an adjective + noun.

Why is *does* used here? You'll have to say this differently in German. Try using an adverb.

Another example of indirect speech.

Careful! What part of the verb is this? You'll have to use a clause in German.

You can't translate *poor* by 'arm' here.

A participle structure! Think what it means, then decide how to translate it into German. You will need more than one word in German.

If you look up this word in a dictionary, you'll find it has more than one meaning. Check the context to decide which meaning is suitable here.

[1] tell a ceremony = *bei einer Feierstunde erklären/sagen*

The truancy officer's visit

About 3% (1,200,000) of American schoolchildren and 0.3% (25,000) of schoolchildren in Britain are taught at home, not at school. This is called 'home schooling'. Some parents take their child out of school for religious reasons, others do it because their children have difficulties at school. Whatever the reason, these parents must still see that their children receive an 'efficient full-time education'. The following extracts are from the play Multiple Choice *by Roger Hall. US teenager Paul Hughes has been (illegally) taken out of school by his mother after she had an argument with the principal. In this scene Paul is visited by the truancy officer and has to justify the way he spends his time at home.*

- Before you read the text, discuss what you think of being educated at home. What could be the advantages, disadvantages and the parents' reasons? What could an 'efficient full-time education' at home be like?
- As you read pages 15 and 16, consider these questions:
  - What do you think of Paul and the answers he gives?
  - How might other people react to his answers?

OFFICER: Paul Hughes?
PAUL: Yes.
OFFICER: I rang, but no one answered. The door was unlocked so … School Attendance Officer, District Board of Education. *[PAUL doesn't understand.]* Truancy. You checked out of school three weeks ago. They sent me to see what's going on.
PAUL: Right now it's the housework.
OFFICER: Your mother doesn't do it?
PAUL: She works.
OFFICER: You alone all day?
PAUL: Yes. No. Well, I go down the road, see Mrs. Davidson, help her with her sewing.
OFFICER: Sewing.
PAUL: She makes things for sale. I help her.
OFFICER: You do any school work at all?
PAUL: Yes.
OFFICER: Any math?
PAUL: I do my mother's accounts. Twice a month, I'm presenting her with a statement – what she's spent, all that.
OFFICER: *School* math. What school math did you do yesterday?
PAUL: Yesterday? *[Thinks.]* None.
OFFICER: Day before yesterday?
PAUL: None.
OFFICER: *[Writing]* No math done.
PAUL: Yes, I have.
OFFICER: You just said you didn't.
PAUL: You asked what I'd done yesterday and the day before so I said "none". But Monday, I did ten pages.
OFFICER: You trying to be smart?
PAUL: No. *[Shows him the book.]* Ten pages … sometimes I do more. I reckon I'm about a chapter ahead of class.
OFFICER: Some of these don't show any working.
PAUL: I used a calculator. With problems it's not the working out, it's what to do with the numbers, isn't it?
OFFICER: *[Totally unimpressed]* Calculators aren't allowed in school.
PAUL: They are here. *[Laughs.]*
OFFICER: Geography.
PAUL: We hope to go to Mexico next year. I'm getting all the brochures.
OFFICER: Right now your class is doing Canada.
PAUL: No, no, we don't want to go to Canada.
OFFICER: What's the capital of Saskatchewan?
PAUL: I don't know.
OFFICER: Regina.
PAUL: If I wanted to know, I'd look it up in the atlas. *[Pause.]* What's the capital of Yucatan? *[No reply.]* Merida. One each. *[Laughs.]*
OFFICER: You're breaking the law, you understand? I have to make a report. I have to report back what work you're doing, what books you're reading.
PAUL: I've just started *Foundation* … the Asimov –
OFFICER: Not fiction! What textbooks you're reading. Show me the non-fiction books you're reading right now. And while you're about it, bring me your written work.

Paul: Written work?

Officer: Social studies, history, written expression.

Paul: I don't write it down, I just do it.

Officer: How do we know what you're learning if you don't write it down?

Paul: I wrote a lot of stuff down at school and I still don't know it. They made me write 'separate' a hundred times and I still get it wrong.

Officer: I have to take something back with me. I've got to have something to hold up in front of the Board.

Paul: How about me?! *[Laughs.]*

Officer: *[Stares at Paul with considerable dislike.]* I think pretty soon you're going to find yourself in trouble.

Paul: That's OK – I'm used to it.

Officer: Those the books?

Paul: Yes.

Officer: *[Smiles.]* 'The Chevy Owner's Manual' and 'The Reader's Digest Guide to Sewing'.

Paul's mother is told that her son must go back to school, but she appeals against this decision. She is given a chance to speak to the School Board (four men and a woman) who can decide against her or allow her a special exemption. Then Paul himself has to be interviewed by them …

Harris: Paul, you've been away from school for some time; are there any things that you miss about it?

Paul: The computer. Programming is real neat.

Kramer: So that's one thing straight away you can't get at home.

Paul: I'm going to get one of my own – I'm earning enough to get one.

Sedillo: What would your feelings be if you were told you had to go back to school tomorrow?

Paul: Kinda frustrated, I guess. I mean, I'm just sort of organized now. Earning and learning. Hey, just thought of that, sounds good.

Harris: The thing that concerns the Board, Paul, is what the school attendance officer had to say.

Paul: The who?

Harris: Truancy officer.

Paul: Oh boy, what a weirdo. Like something out of the Gestapo.

Bronski: He said you weren't doing enough work.

Paul: He didn't listen to a thing I said. I tried to tell him all the things I was doing.

Sedillo: Well, tell us.

Paul: It sounds kinda feeble –

Sedillo: *[Kindly]* Go on.

Paul: Car maintenance … handling a bank account and arranging a loan.

Kramer: You don't need to know those things yet.

Paul: I haven't needed quadratic equations either.

Sedillo: Anything else?

[Pause.]

Paul: Sewing.

Before you read on, answer these questions: Why do you think Paul paused before he replied to Sedillo's question? How do you think different members of the Board will react to Paul's reply?

KRAMER: Sewing!

PAUL: I can make a lot of things on the sewing machine …

JULIA: Bravo.

KRAMER: Sewing!!

PAUL: Sell you a neat tote bag for five bucks. Make a great Christmas present. Only joking. It's really interesting ... I've never made things before.

JULIA: Tell us what you think is the most interesting thing you've done since you left school.

PAUL: *[Thinks.]* Collecting the newspaper money. There are some amazing people on my route: a guy who used to run a naval shipyard, a woman who danced with …

BRONSKI: All this is irrelevant! The key point is, you're not keeping up with your school work. At home. Are you?

PAUL: I bet I'm way ahead in science and math. And Spanish.

BRONSKI: But behind in most other things?

[PAUL doesn't reply.]

SEDILLO: Paul, tell me one thing. Are you convinced your mother is doing the right thing?

PAUL: No.

KRAMER: See! Even the kid thinks she's wrong.

PAUL: I didn't say that. I'm not completely convinced she's right … on the whole I think she is. I mean, it wouldn't break my heart if I had to go back to school.

JULIA: But would it hers?

PAUL: Pretty near. I don't see why it's such a big deal, what she's doing. Why are you all making such a big fuss over it?

BRONSKI: Because it's against the law!

PAUL: But it wouldn't be if you gave us the exemption. Why don't you pretend I'm ill … "Allergic to chalk dust" or something. I know you have to work your butt off to get into college. I'm not stupid. I'm not going to let myself get too far behind in things I need. And if I need to go back to school, I will. Any time. All you are saying is you don't trust me. Or Ma. Why don't you just leave us to get on with it?

HARRIS: *[Dismissing PAUL]* Thank you.

[PAUL goes.]

Any further debate? No. All those in favor of granting an exemption?

[JULIA's hand goes up. A pause, and SEDILLO's hand goes up.] Against?

[BRONSKI and KRAMER against.]

Chairman has casting vote. I vote …

Working with the text

a First impressions

Write down your impressions of the School Board. Then compare your ideas with what others in your class have written.

b A closer look at the text

1. What are the most important moments in the above extracts? Why?
2. In informal English people sometimes leave out certain words at the beginning of a sentence if the meaning is clear without them. What examples can you find in the truancy officer's speech? What are the 'missing' words?
3. Why does Paul use phrases like *I guess, I mean, I bet, on the whole I think, kinda (= kind of), sort of* when the School Board interviews him?
4. Say in a few words what makes Paul's case strong and what makes it weak.
5. How do you think the chairman of the Board will vote? Why? How would you vote? Why?

c Beyond the story

1. You have a chance to be educated at home. Write a timetable for your week, then justify it to the class.
2. What is meant by the Latin saying *Non scholae, sed vitae discimus*? Do you think it is true? What is the purpose of education?

Unit 2: Great Britain – a multicultural society

1

1 *Notting Hill Carnival – a street carnival that takes place in London every year*

2 *At a hospital in Birmingham*

3 *Regent's Park Mosque, London*

4 *Diane Abbott – the first black woman MP*

5 *An Asian food shop*

6 *Chinatown in London*

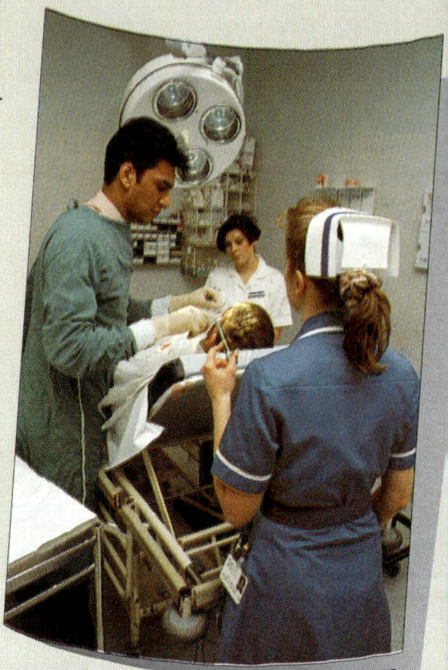

3

4

5

Look at the photos on this page.
What do they show about life in Britain?

Who are the British?

Look at the table on the right:

- What do you understand by the term 'ethnic minority'?
- What percentage of the British population belongs to an ethnic minority?
- What are the three largest ethnic minorities in Britain?

Ethnic group	Number of people	% of total population
White	51,874,000	94.5
Ethnic minorities	3,015,000	5.5
Black Caribbean	500,000	0.9
Black African	212,000	0.4
Black other	178,000	0.3
Indian	840,000	1.5
Pakistani	477,000	0.9
Bangladeshi	163,000	0.3
Chinese	157,000	0.3
Other groups	488,000	0.9

The population of Great Britain by ethnic group (1991)

Where do ethnic minorities live?

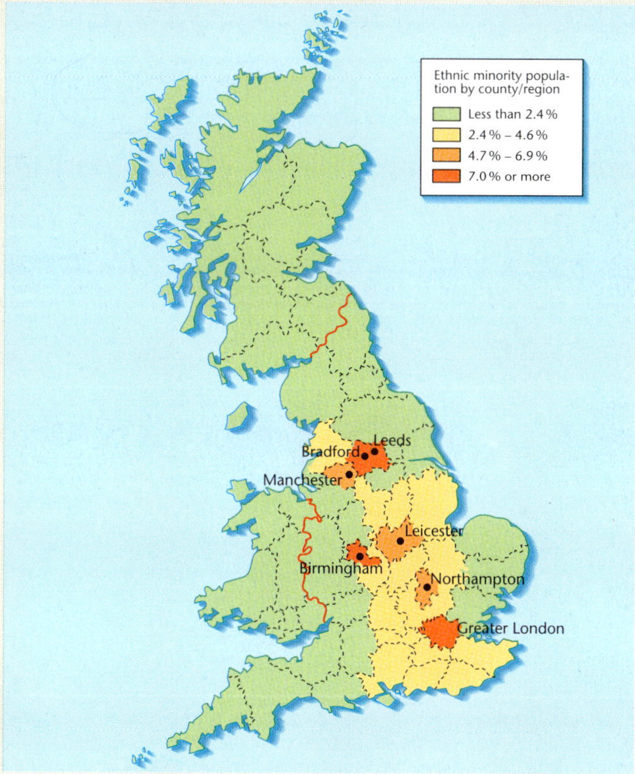

Nearly one half of Britain's ethnic minorities live in Greater London, making up 20% of the capital's population.

- Look at the map. What's the percentage of ethnic minorities in other parts of Britain?
- Why do you think ethnic minorities are rarely found in small towns or rural areas?

Some more facts and figures

Try and fill in these numbers:

9 – 23 – 40 – 53 – 130 – 1000

Then look at the bottom of page 32 and check your answers. Did you guess correctly? Which fact or figure do you find most surprising?

1. ● % of the present black Caribbean community were born in the UK.
2. In London schools there are now children with over ● different native languages.
3. ● % of Britain's doctors were not born in Britain.
4. In 1997 ● of the 659 British MPs were black or Asian.
5. In 1991 ● % of black men between 16 and 34 had a white partner.
6. There are about ● mosques in Britain.

What is meant by the term 'multicultural society'? Have you heard or read about it in the German media?

→ Ex 1-3

2A

Different roles for Britain: from Empire to Commonwealth

Look at the stamps and the coin on the right.
- Where are they from and who do they show?
- What could be the reason for showing 'foreigners' on the stamps or coins of a country?

1985

1895

In order to understand the multicultural nature of Britain today, it is necessary to look back at Britain's past.

Colonies and trade

In the 16th century when travellers to England brought stories of 'new' lands that had been discovered, private companies quickly started to exploit these new sources of raw material and to develop trade. Soon, territories or even whole countries were taken over.
In the 17th and 18th centuries, large profits were made by capturing or buying native Africans and selling them as slaves in the 'New World' across the Atlantic. The loss of the thirteen American colonies in 1783 came as a shock to Britain, but it did not stop the British trading, nor did it stop them settling in new continents. From 1815-60 about 7 million people left the British Isles.

"Rule Britannia"

There were political and economic reasons for colonizing other countries: Britain's population was growing, its social problems at home were increasing, and there was the challenge of greater economic competition from other European nations. Some people also believed it was Britain's duty to bring Christianity and 'civilization' to Africans and Asians.
The Empire was an enormous market for the goods that were produced in Britain's factories.

A British officer relaxing in India in 1900. What does this photo suggest?

It was also a source of raw materials and products such as tea from India and sugar from the West Indies. Trade and industry made Britain a rich and powerful country. Many British people were employed in the colonies – as soldiers, civil servants and traders. The British also introduced their own style of clothes, the English system of law, railways, football and, of course, cricket.
When Queen Victoria died in 1901, her Empire covered a quarter of the world, English was spoken on every continent, and a quarter of the world's shipping and a fifth of its trade were in British hands. Victoria left her son, Edward VII, an Empire 'on which the sun never set'.

- Why did Britain have a policy of acquiring new colonies?
- Why did the sun never set on the British Empire? Have a look at at the world map at the front of the book.

Independence

Gandhi and his followers on a protest march in 1930

After the death of Queen Victoria, most of Britain's colonies continued to be ruled directly from London. Gradually, however, Britain allowed the colonies with the largest white population (Canada, Australia, New Zealand, South Africa) to govern themselves, as long as they accepted the British monarch as head of state. In some other colonies, the inhabitants went on strike or even fought wars in order to win independence. In India the famous Hindu leader and nationalist Mahatma Gandhi led a campaign of non-violent civil disobedience against the British government. In 1947 India finally became independent. By the end of the 1960s most of the other colonies were independent and Britain was no longer a world power.

Find out more about the life and aims of Gandhi and give a talk in class.

→ Option 11: Presenting a paper

The Commonwealth

Meeting of Commonwealth leaders

Several of the colonies that became independent kept the British monarch as their head of state, and nearly all chose to be members of the 'Commonwealth of Nations'. This is a voluntary organization of about 50 independent states, with the British monarch as its symbolic head. The aims of the Commonwealth are to encourage democracy, world peace and cooperation on trade and development and to fight discrimination, oppression and inequality. There have, however, been times when African and Asian members have been angry with British governments for limiting immigration into Britain or for not supporting black people in their demands for justice.

The heads of government of the Commonwealth countries meet every two years to discuss matters of common interest. There are also strong cultural and sporting connections between members. Every four years member states send teams to the Commonwealth Games, a big athletics competition.

- How do you think most people in Britain felt as their Empire grew? And later? And today?
  On patriotic occasions people in Britain still sing the song *Rule Britannia*, which starts, 'Rule Britannia, Britannia rule the waves, Britons never, never, never shall be slaves!'. What feelings does this song express?
- What advantages do you see in being a member of the Commonwealth? Think of the literal meaning of the term 'commonwealth'. Could there also be any disadvantages?

→ Ex 4

Immigration after the war

These photos were taken in Britain in the 1950s.
- What do they show?
- How do you think the people feel?

After the Second World War Britain needed more workers for its factories, hospitals, buses and trains. So the British government encouraged immigration from the Commonwealth nations, particularly from the Caribbean.
However, some British people believed that these immigrants were taking away their jobs or exploiting the social security system. As people from Commonwealth countries were British citizens, they had the right to live in Britain permanently. This changed in 1962, when a new law reduced future immigration: the Commonwealth Immigrants Act.

The new Caribbean and Asian immigrants were often confronted with discrimination and unfair treatment. In 1976 the Race Relations Act was passed. It made it illegal to discriminate against people (because of their colour, race, ethnic origin or nationality) in employment, housing or education. Although the situation has improved, there is still evidence of discrimination against ethnic minorities in Britain.

A victim of racism speaks out

"I have a Saturday job as an assistant in a supermarket. A couple of weeks ago I went to relieve my supervisor from the till and there was a middle-aged white lady waiting to be served next. She had a look of horror when she saw my supervisor getting up to go and realized that I would be the one serving her. She started to shout. She said she didn't want the shopping if she was going to be served by me. At first I was really surprised, but then I became angry when I saw that my supervisor was actually going to serve her instead of letting me do it.

While the lady was packing her shopping, she started to make comments about black people, saying they shouldn't be allowed to work and should all be thrown out of the country.

I was so angry. I'd never experienced racism like that before. I'm really glad I didn't argue with her because I wouldn't want to have given her the satisfaction, but I don't think people should ignore racists either – we should take action and report the problem."

Lisa, 17, Southend

(From: *LET'S BEAT RACISM,* published by *MIZZ* magazine)

Compare the situation of the immigrants from Commonwealth countries with that of the foreign workers who came to Germany in the1960s and 1970s.

- In your opinion, why do people behave in a racist way?
- What can be done to combat racism?

→ Ex 5, 7, 8

Keeping the faith

Ethnic minorities have, by definition, their own traditions and beliefs. There are about 1.5 million Muslims living in Britain – the largest religious group after Christians. Most of them are immigrants from Pakistan and Bangladesh, but there are a growing number of British-born Muslims. How do they practise their religion – Islam –, for example during Ramadan?

Ramadan /ˌræməˈdæn, -ˈdɑːn/ *n* the 9th month of the Muslim year, when Muslims do not eat or drink anything between sunrise and sunset

9 **Nazmin Khanom** is a 16-year-old pupil at a girls' school in east London, and the oldest in a family of five. She was born in England; both her parents are from Bangladesh. She will be fasting this year, and began when she was 13.

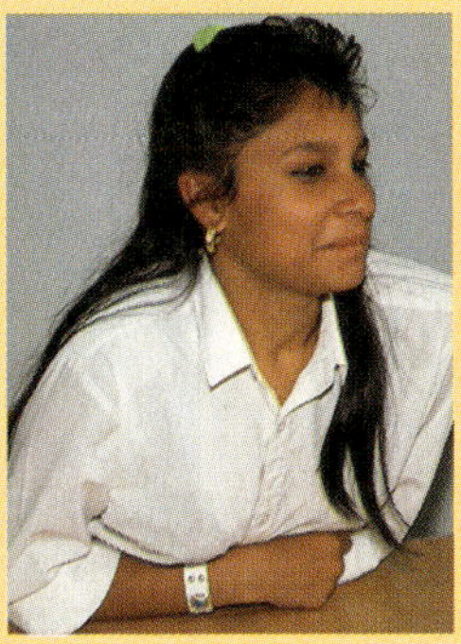

"Fasting is not really hard. You get used to it – and if it gets dark quickly, that's OK. Near the end of Ramadan, the day seems to get longer, though. I do it because I have to – it's part of my religion and Muhammad did it. It's also like having experience of how poor people feel, not having food. And you have to pray as well.

There are a lot of Muslim girls at school, so we have a special room at lunchtime where we can sit without watching others eat.

PE is a real big fuss, though. Some of the girls try to refuse to have a shower afterwards in case water goes in their mouths. But the teachers are strict and we have to do it. So we shut our mouths. I think they should let us off PE because we get thirsty easily and afterwards you feel like breaking your fast.

I usually get headaches in the afternoon during Ramadan. We all do. But it would be very bad to cheat. God can see everything you do, and he will write it down. I look forward to Ramadan, but halfway through I sometimes get fed up. You have to concentrate on your work, and it's hard when you're thinking about food. You think about all the lovely food then, when it's time to eat, you can't eat it.

When you finish keeping Ramadan, you feel proud of yourself, and you know God will be pleased with you.

You feel like you're part of this religion."

(From: *The Times Educational Supplement*, 19.1.1996)

- Why does Nazmin think Ramadan is important?
- Why do some of the Muslim girls not want to take part in PE?
- What does Nazmin find difficult about Ramadan?

At the end of Ramadan Muslims celebrate Id al-Fitr, the festival of Fast-Breaking

→ Ex 6

1 Two famous Britons

Here are some facts about two non-white Britons, Salman Rushdie and Naomi Campbell. Decide which seven facts refer to Salman Rushdie and which other seven refer to Naomi Campbell. Then write short biographies of each of the two. Add any other facts you may know about them.

Has written a detective story about top models (1)

Famous for various novels, e.g. Midnight's Children *about India,* Satanic Verses *about Islam* (2)

British citizen of Caribbean origin (3)

Born and grew up in London, still lives there, but often abroad (4)

Started writing after five years in advertising (5)

Born in Bombay, studied at Cambridge University, then lived in England (6)

'Discovered' as a model at 15 (7)

British citizen of Indian origin (8)

Divides her/his time between Paris, London and especially New York, where she/he also has a home (9)

Has lived in hiding for many years (10)

Sentenced to death (in her/his absence) for blasphemy by the Islamic leader of Iran in 1989 (11)

Born in 1970 (12)

First black model on the cover of Vogue *magazine in 1988* (13)

Born in 1947 (14)

2 Writing a profile

a

"I have a lot of dreams. I hope that one day women and black people will be able to have a fair chance. I hope that I will find a good job. That's difficult these days because unemployment is a real problem where I live. Luckily I'm doing quite well at school. But it would be nice if my school had more computers and if the classes were smaller. One thing that upsets me is that there are so many poor people in London. Maybe I'll try to get a job helping people."

Rebecca Monkton, 17, schoolgirl, South London

Make some notes:

1. What sort of person is Rebecca? What do you think she is like?
2. What are her dreams and wishes? From what you know about Rebecca, can you think of any dreams and wishes she might have but doesn't mention?

You could arrange your notes in the following way:

1.

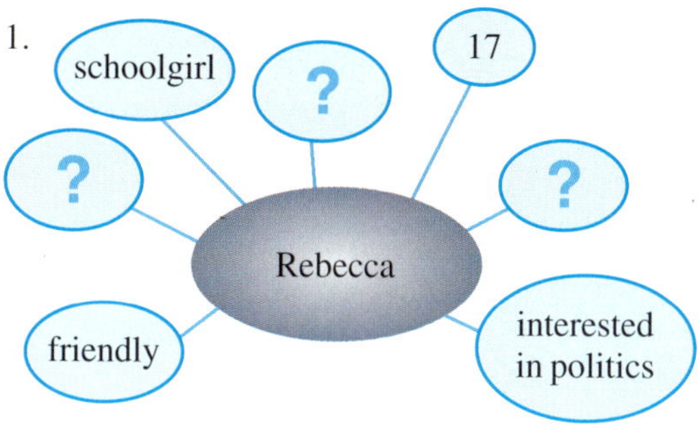

2.

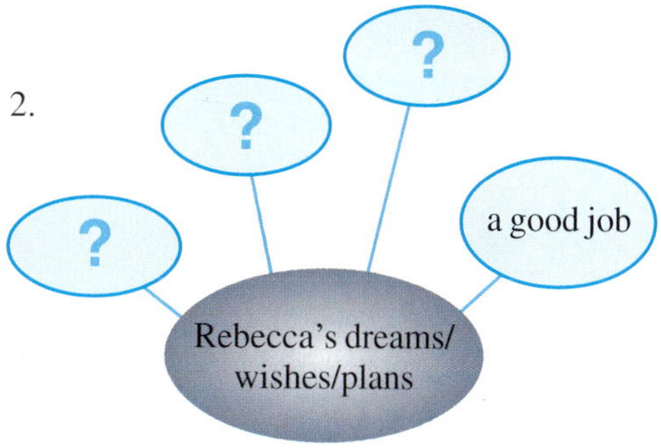

When you have collected enough notes, write a profile of Rebecca as you see her. The following linking words and phrases may help you:

after although because of this before but either … or finally for this reason furthermore however if in order to in spite of this so that

b *Compare your texts. Then make similar notes about a friend or yourself and write another profile.*

› Option 9: Using a monolingual dictionary
› Option 10: Using a grammar

3 'I spy with my little eye …': Common mistakes II

a *The text below has 15 mistakes in it – mainly in nouns, prepositions, adjectives or adverbs. Try to find the mistakes and rewrite the text. Give reasons for your corrections. It may be helpful to consult a grammar or a dictionary.*

A population count, or census, in 1991 founded that 94.5 per cent from the population belonged to the 'white' group while just over three millions people (5.5 per cent) described themselfs as belonging to other ethnic groups. Members of these other ethnic groups are heavy concentrated in urban and industrialist areas. The most highly proportion was in Brent in the north-west London – near 45 per cent. In fifteen year time this figure is expected to go up until 50 per cent. Actual, by then, mostly 30 per cent of London's population will be made up of ethnic minority groups. London will then be the most ethnic mixed capital in the world! The potential problems of this mixture are easily to see and are a challenge to politicians, both now and in the future.

b **In English, please**

Be careful to avoid the mistakes you found in the text above.

Es ist hochinteressant, sich Statistiken zur *(on)* Altersstruktur *(age structure)* ethnischer Minderheiten in Großbritannien anzusehen: 33 Prozent der Angehörigen ethnischer Minderheiten sind unter 16 Jahre. Im Vergleich [dazu] fallen nur neun Prozent der weißen Bevölkerung in diese Altersgruppe. Am anderen Ende der Skala *(scale)* sehen wir ein völlig anderes Bild: Von den drei Millionen Menschen in Großbritannien, die einer ethnischen Minderheit angehören, sind nur drei Prozent älter als 65. In der weißen Bevölkerung sind jedoch 17 Prozent in dieser Altersgruppe. Welche Konsequenzen könnte diese Altersstruktur in einigen Jahren haben?

4 German adverbs and their English equivalents

As you know, there are some German adverbs which are often translated by verbs or verbal expressions in English.

1. Hongkong war **früher** eine britische Kolonie.	Hong Kong **used to** be a British colony.
2. **Hoffentlich** wird es bald ein geeintes Europa geben.	**I hope** there will soon be a united Europe.
3. **Bestimmt/Sicher/Mit Sicherheit** werden die Falklandinseln noch viele Jahre eine britische Kolonie bleiben.	The Falkland Islands **are certain to/are sure to** remain a British colony for many years.
4. Königin Elisabeth II. interessiert sich **bekanntlich** sehr für das Commonwealth.	Queen Elizabeth II **is known to** be very interested in the Commonwealth.
5. Ich war **zufällig** zur Zeit des *Notting Hill Carnival* in London.	I **happened to** be in London at the time of the Notting Hill Carnival.

a *Match the German adverbs and the English expressions. Which expressions are followed by an infinitive, which by a gerund and which by a* (that-)*clause? It may help to consult a dictionary or a grammar.*

hoffentlich vermutlich gern ungern
lieber wahrscheinlich (nicht) leider
bekanntlich bestimmt/sicher/mit Sicherheit
weiter zufällig anscheinend früher

I'm afraid (would) prefer/'d rather seem to
used to be (un)likely to hate I suppose
I hope/Let's hope keep (on) happen to
be certain/sure to like/enjoy be known to

b *Use the right English expressions to complete the two dialogues below.*

... the history of the British Empire? *(gern studieren)*
– .... *(leider nicht)* But ... us to understand the present problems of the old colonies. *(vermutlich helfen)*
Is this topic something that ... in your written exams? *(wahrscheinlich vorkommen)*
– .... *(hoffentlich nicht)* But our teacher ... about the colonies in the oral exam. *(bestimmt fragen)*

◆◆◆

Gibraltar ... a British colony for many years. *(sicher bleiben)*
– You're right. It ... independent. *(wahrscheinlich nicht werden)*
No, although the Spanish government ... the Rock part of Spain. *(bekanntlich machen wollen)*
– My uncle ... in Gibraltar and he says the Gibraltarians will never agree to become Spanish. *(früher arbeiten)*
I know. I recently ... someone who worked there as well, and she also said they would ... part of Spain. *(zufällig treffen – ungern sein)*
– Yes, they all ... a British colony. *(lieber bleiben wollen)* But Gibraltar ... a typical colony. *(anscheinend nicht sein)*

5 Living together in Britain (1) → Grammar review 21-25 (pp.131-132)

Read this short text about a Pakistani immigrant. Complete the sentences with the right participle form of the verbs in brackets, and decide whether you should use one of the following conjunctions before the verbs: after, although, before, when, while.

1. (drop) the remains from the dirty plate into the bucket of uneaten food on his trolley, Mohammed's thoughts were travelling far away to his mother's home. 2. (return) from work at a self-service restaurant at Heathrow Airport the night before, he had found a note on his door (say) that she was on

her deathbed. 3. (deeply shock) by the news, Mohammed had spent the night awake, (wonder) whether he could afford to fly home to Pakistan. 4. "Take that bucket away while I'm eating," a voice next to him said. (hear) this kind of comment on many occasions without getting upset, Mohammed felt deeply (hurt) by it today. 5. He looked up and saw an elegant lady (dress) all in black. 6. (come) to England, Mohammed had never experienced such humiliation. The offer of a job at Heathrow Airport had seemed like a dream come true in Pakistan, where he had been very, very poor. 7. (remember) what he had been told then, Mohammed felt his anger (rise): "Special cheap flights for airport employees." 8. (promise), these flights were not available when he asked this morning – not for another three weeks.

6 A cross-cultural marriage

a

Read the following text carefully, then do the tasks below.

Ann: So your brother is marrying a Muslim girl?
Jill: Yes, and they are going to live next to his wife's parents when they are married, so John will be living in London's Muslim scene.
Ann: And will they be bringing up their children as Muslims?
Jill: I don't know. They aren't talking about children yet.
Ann: And what do your parents think about it?
Jill: They're very happy about it.
Ann: Where will the wedding be?
Jill: Most of Seema's relatives live in Bangladesh, so they are getting married there.
Ann: Are you going to the wedding?
Jill: Oh yes, I think I will … but I'll have to save for the flight, of course.

Look at each verb or verb group, say what tense it is and whether it refers to the present or the future. How many different ways of referring to the future can you find in the text? → Grammar review 3 (pp.122-123)
Translate the text into German. Pay special attention to how you express the future meaning.

b *What do you think about cross-cultural marriages? Ask your partner what he or she thinks.*

7 Listening comprehension: The attack

The Patels, an Asian family, have just moved into their new shop. The family – Mr and Mrs Patel, their daughter Rita and their son Sumit – eat in the shop on this first evening as they haven't yet unpacked everything. Listen to what happens, then answer these questions.

1. What are the Patels doing at the beginning? 2. Why does Mrs Patel send her children upstairs? 3. What's Mr Patel's reaction? 4. Would you describe the police's attitude towards the Patels as helpful? 5. Why do the police officers want to see the Patels' passports?

→ Option 14: What to say in the UK → Option 15: Varieties of English

8 Living together in Britain (2) (Translation practice II)

Read this article about a white family from London, then translate it into German. Before you start, read the general notes about translating on pages 13-14 of Unit 1.
In this text there are some participle constructions. Before you translate them, think about what they mean and remember that in German they are usually translated as subordinate clauses with a conjunction (see part 23 of the grammar review, pages 131-132).
Use an English-German dictionary to check any new words.

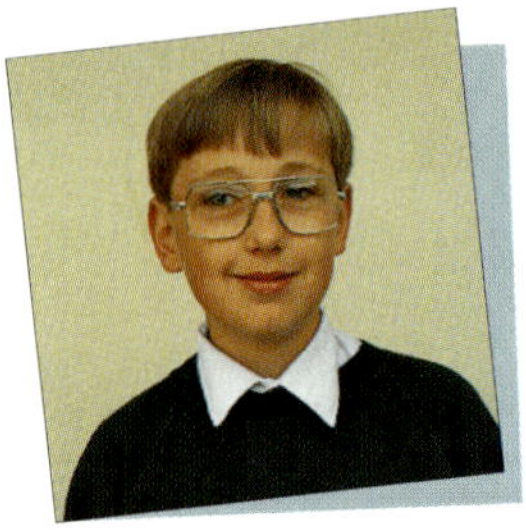

Simon Bradford

New hope for bullied boy

Eleven-year-old Simon Bradford peers round the front door of his parents' first-floor council flat in east London, before skipping down the hall and tucking into a bowl of chocolate ice cream. Ever since moving into the block of flats with his disabled mother Anita, aged 48, and father Raymond, 46, four years ago, Simon has been the victim of bullying and intimidation. He has been hit with a cricket bat more than once. Cycling to school one day, he was knocked off his bike.

Yesterday, the High Court declared that Tower Hamlets was under a legal duty to consider accommodating Simon in a safer place. This ground-breaking decision was the culmination of the family's fight against a neighbourhood "campaign of hatred". Coming home one day in July 1995 to find "white trash" written across their front door, the Bradfords decided to make an urgent application for a new flat. With excrement being regularly pushed through the letter box and the car tyres slashed 18 times, life had become intolerable for the family. Mr Justice Kay has ordered the London Borough of Tower Hamlets to act "as soon as reasonably practicable".

(Based on an article in *The Guardian*, 14.1.1997)

Be careful. This word doesn't mean 'Halle' here.

An adjective is possible here before the noun 'Mutter' in German.

The end of the article explains what this is.

How are you going to translate this collocation?

This does not mean 'in order to find' here. It is the same as 'and finding'.

Choose the right dictionary translation for the context. How will you translate the collocation *make an urgent application for*?

This is used as the title of a judge ('Richter/in') here.

Don't use a preposition here.

This means 'as it is at all possible'.

You'll need more words in German.

A rented flat provided by the authorities.

An informal word for 'eating enthusiastically'.

What tense in German?

This is the highest court of law in England and Wales. Does a corresponding institution exist in Germany? What's its name?

There is a similar compound in German, but with a different noun.

A *neighbourhood campaign* is a campaign carried out by neighbours.

There's a good compound noun for this in German.

This is another word for 'rubbish'. *White trash* is a term of racist abuse.

You'll have to express this participle construction differently in German. What does it mean?

This means 'and (with) the car tyres (having been) slashed'.

You need an article in German.

9 WORDS WORDS WORDS

a **Trouble spot: Phrases with German 'haben'**

Translate the following sentences into English.

1. Dein Vater hatte nicht Recht, als er sagte, es gäbe zwei Millionen Inder in Großbritannien. 2. Was für eine Farbe hatte das Auto? 3. Schau doch mal im Kühlschrank nach, wenn du Hunger hast. 4. Tut mir Leid, aber ich kann nicht länger warten. Ich habe es eilig. 5. Hast du wirklich Angst vor Mäusen? 6. Hast du was Kaltes zum Trinken da? Ich habe einen wahnsinnigen Durst. 7. Ich hätte gern ein Paar Schuhe. – Welche Größe haben Sie? 8. Wer hat Schuld an dem Unfall? 9. Alexander hat seit Wochen keine Arbeit. 10. Anne hat heute Geburtstag.

b WORD BUILDER'S CORNER **Prefixes expressing the opposite**

un-, *in-*, *dis-* and *non-* are the most common prefixes to form the opposite of a word. *un-* is used more often than any other. But it is not possible to predict which prefix is used with a particular word. The correct forms must simply be learned.

un-	**in-**	**im-** (before 'p')	**ir-** (before 'r')	**dis-**	**non-**
unborn	incorrect	impatient	irregular	disadvantage	non-fiction
un-British	independent	impersonal	irresponsible	disagree	non-returnable
undress	informal	impolite		disappear	non-standard
unfamiliar	inhuman	impossible		dislike	non-violent
unforgettable	intolerant	impractical		dissatisfied	
unhealthy	involuntary				

– *Complete the following sentences with suitable words from the list.*

1. I've been waiting for 20 minutes and I'm beginning to get … . 2. I see things differently. That's why I … with you. 3. When the police arrived, the gang had already … . 4. Did you know that *steal* is an … verb? 5. It was a hot day. So when Sarah came home, she … and had a shower. 6. Julia likes her job, but she … getting up so early. 7. No, you don't have to wear a tie. It's just an … meeting with a few friends. 8. The way the prisoners were treated was cruel and … . 9. I'll always remember our holidays in England. They are … . 10. It's 8.30 now, so it's almost … to catch the 8.40 train.

– *Use a dictionary and write down words with the prefix* un- *whose stems you already know. You'll be surprised how many there are.*
Examples: unable – able, uncertain – certain, …

– **In English, please**

Translate the following phrases and sentences and make similar ones using the words from the list above.

1. eine unhöfliche Antwort 2. unzufriedene Kunden 3. eine unbeabsichtigte Bewegung 4. unverantwortliches Verhalten 5. ein unpraktischer Mann 6. eine ungesunde Lebensweise

1. Sein Verhalten ist unbritisch. 2. Gewaltfreie Proteste sind effektiver. 3. Ich finde es unverantwortlich, dass du immer noch Einwegflaschen kaufst. 4. Das Commonwealth besteht aus ungefähr 50 unabhängigen Staaten, die früher Teil des britischen Empire waren.

An eye for an eye

- What do you remember about the Patels from Exercise 7 (p. 27)? What happened during their first night in their new home?
- Look at the first sentence of the text below. Who are 'they'?
- What does the title of the text suggest the text will be about?

They were there again, as they were most evenings. Rita could hear them shouting outside in the dark street, "Pakis out! Pakis out!" She got out of bed and went to the window. Five youths, five stupid ignorant yobs. They were standing on the pavement outside their shop, beer cans in hand, ruining their nights, destroying their lives. Because of them her family was being forced to live in fear and even think of moving away.

She went back to bed. In the next room, behind the thin wall, she heard her younger brother, Sumit.

"Go to sleep," she said.

"I can't," he answered.

"Pull the blankets over your head," she said.

Soon a window belonging to the shop down stairs was broken and she heard her father talking quietly on the phone. "The name is Patel. 26 Redwood Road. A gang of hooligans is attacking our house again. Can you please do something about it?"

Leaving the house the next morning, Rita saw her mother cleaning away the broken glass from the pavement. Their shop, once fresh and blue with its new sign 'Patel & Son, Quality Tailors', was now covered in graffiti; several of the windows were covered with boards where the Patels had given up repairing them.

"There must be something we can do," Rita thought as she walked to school. She had written to the town council, even to her MP, but all she had got back were letters saying that they were waiting for replies from the police, etc. – which meant nobody was doing anything.

In history that morning Rita fell asleep. At the end of the lesson her friend Leela had to wake her up.

"Oh, my God," said Rita. "He sends everybody to sleep. What have we got now?"

"What's wrong with you?" asked Leela. "You look terrible."

Rita sighed. "We've had visitors again."

"Oh no," said Leela, "How long has this been going on?"

"Almost four months."

"Listen," said Leela. "I know some people who can help you."

That evening a group of young men, some white and some Asian, came to their house. They knocked on the door after the Patels had just eaten their evening meal.

"Mr Patel?" said their leader. "We are friends of Leela's. We call ourselves the PAR, People Against Racism. We've heard you are having trouble."

"Yes," said Mr Patel, surprised, not knowing who had asked them to come or why they were there. But the PAR were very nice and friendly, and soon the Patels and the young men were sitting together relaxed in the living-room. For the first time in weeks there was laughter in the Patels' home. It was almost like a party as they drank, ate sandwiches and played cards.

"If you feel tired," said one of the PAR, "you can go to bed. We'll stay all night if necessary."

"But we can't possibly go to bed while you wait here," said Mrs Patel. "It's unfair."

"I shall stay with them," said Mr Patel. "The rest of you can go to bed."

They came at midnight. "Switch the lights off," said Jeff, the PAR leader, as soon as they heard the shouting in the street outside. They had brought a powerful light and together the PAR opened the window and held the light out. The gang stopped. As the light fell on their faces, some turned and ran away.

"Come on," shouted one of the PAR. "Show us who you are." Most had now run away, except one youth who stood alone on the pavement.

"Do you recognize him?" asked Jeff.

"Rita calls him Flatface," said Mr Patel. "He's their leader."

"You," shouted Jeff. "Come on, give us your name!" The youth turned and ran away.

It was over. It had been as simple as that. Rita and her family were suddenly able to sleep. It was a wonderful feeling to lead a normal life again. In the mornings she felt so great she almost ran to school. Her parents became much healthier and argued less. They were happy and friendly, as they had always been before.

Then Sumit was attacked and thrown from a railway bridge on his way from school one afternoon. When Rita found the note at home that he was in hospital, she went there at once. She found her parents sitting at the bed. Sumit was not moving, his head covered in bandages. That night the shouting started outside their house again. Sumit died two days later. A feeling of deep sadness and emptiness entered their home and their lives. The person they had all loved the most had gone for ever. Nobody in the family looked at each other. Nobody talked. The mother moved weakly around the home, like an old woman. "Why didn't I go and meet him that day?" she said again and again.

"You couldn't have done anything," said Rita. "They might have attacked you, too. Take your tablets and go to bed, Mum, please."

"I don't want to take any tablets," said Rita's mother and walked slowly out of the room.

"Why don't you *do* something?" Rita suddenly shouted at her father after her mother had gone to bed.

"What more can I do? I have talked to the police. I have talked to the headmaster, I have talked to the teachers. Nobody saw anything."

"Nobody ever sees anything," said Rita angrily. "Why don't they arrest somebody?"

"They can't just arrest anybody," her father said.

"Dad, they can arrest Flatface."

"There are laws in this country, Rita. The police need proof."

"But those people don't care about laws."

"Rita, *we* cannot behave like them."

"You're useless!" she screamed and ran to her room.

Rita had made her preparations. She waited until her parents were in bed before she left the house. They always came at the same time and from the same direction. At midnight she walked quietly down the stairs and opened the front door. She was carrying a shopping bag. Inside was a piece of cloth from her father's shop, a box of matches, and a bottle filled with petrol. At quarter past, the gang arrived in two cars, music coming loudly from their stereos. They were laughing as they walked along the street, past a row of garages, towards the Patels' house. From the roof of one of the garages, Rita suddenly shouted, "Flatface!"

The gang stopped. Looking up, they saw only a dark figure and a flame coming from a burning cloth. Not understanding what it was, they stopped. At that moment Rita threw the bottle.

(Based on *The Diary of Rita Patel* by Carole Boyer, a film shown on BBC 2, 14. 9. 1988)

2T

Working with the text

a First impressions

1. Write down in no more than five or six short sentences what happens in the story.
2. Compare what different people in your class have written. (If you can't agree on some points, note down the points and check what is right or wrong after you have done task b.)

b A closer look at the story

Try to reconstruct the events that lead to Rita's violent behaviour. Go through the text carefully and make notes for each of the following questions. Then use your notes to retell the story.

1. What has been going on for nearly four months? How has this affected the lives of Rita, her brother and her parents?
2. What has Rita done to try and solve the problem? Has she had any success?
3. How does Rita's friend Leela try to help the Patels? How does the help of the PAR affect the Patels' lives?
4. When and why do things get worse again?
5. Why is Rita so angry with her father?
6. What does she finally do?

c Explaining details

1. *... several of the windows were covered with boards where the Patels had given up repairing them.* (p. 30, ll. 25-27)
   How must the Patels have reacted when the hooligans first broke the windows? Why do you think they have given up?
2. *"We've had visitors again."* (p. 30, l. 40)
   What does Rita really mean and how does she know Leela will understand?
3. *As the light fell on their faces, some turned and ran away.* (p. 31, ll. 10-11)
   Why do some of the hooligans run away?
4. *Nobody in the family looked at each other.* (p. 31, ll. 37-38)
   What do the members of the Patel family express by this behaviour?
5. *"Nobody ever sees anything."* (p. 31, l. 53)
   What does Rita really mean?
6. *"Rita,* we *cannot behave like them."* (p. 31, l. 60)
   Why does Mr Patel say this?

d Looking at Rita's behaviour

1. Describe how Rita's behaviour changes in the course of the story. Go through the text and find out what causes the changes.
2. In what way might her parents', especially her father's, behaviour have influenced Rita's final decision?
3. How might the story end after Rita's attack on the gang?
4. What effect on the family's and on Rita's own life might her violent behaviour have? Was it worth taking "an eye for an eye"?

e What do you think? (Points for discussion)

1. Could this have happened in Germany?
2. How should the state (the police/the government/other citizens) react in the face of racist attacks?
3. What advice would you have given Rita if she had asked you?

→ Option 2: The rabbits who caused all the trouble

The correct figures on page 19 are: (1.) 53 – (2.) 130 – (3.) 23 – (4.) 9 – (5.) 40 – (6.) 1000.

Unit 3: The United States – years of growth

- Look at the three American flags. Compare them. Say what is similar and what is different.
- Decide which is today's flag, which is from 1777 and which is from 1775.
  Why did the American flag change between 1775 and 1777?

From its beginning, America has been a nation on the move. The country began as 13 small colonies on the east coast. But the population of these colonies grew quickly, and after the War of Independence (1775-1783) many Americans started moving west across the Appalachians in search of land, gold, opportunity and adventure. By the 1830s they had started to farm the land east of the Mississippi River.

John Gast, American Progress *(1872)*

- Look carefully at John Gast's painting. Describe what you can see.
  (Here are some words to help you: *stagecoach, buffalo, oxen, telegraph poles, cable.*)
- What do you know about the people and objects shown?
- The name of the picture is *American progress.* How has John Gast shown this 'progress'? What kind of message is there in the picture? What do you think of the name and the message?

3A

The frontier – westward ho!

In the 1840s colonists continued to move west. The furthest point of white settlement was called the frontier. Beyond that, the country was wild and unknown to the settlers. As one frontier region was settled, people moved further west, where land was cheap.
Crossing the American continent was difficult and dangerous. The settlers traveled with horses and oxen in groups of wagon trains which left the East in May in order to reach the West before early October. In winter, crossing the snow-covered mountains was almost impossible. In order to cover about 3200 km in five months, the wagon trains had to travel all day. The greatest danger was illness: cholera and other diseases killed whole wagon trains. Even those settlers who arrived in the West had to fight to survive: starting a new life without any supplies, medical care or schools was a challenge in itself.
As more and more Americans moved west, the idea became popular that the United States should expand all the way to the Pacific Ocean. A newspaper described this belief as America's 'Manifest Destiny': the settlers had been 'chosen' by God to extend the United States to the Pacific Ocean.

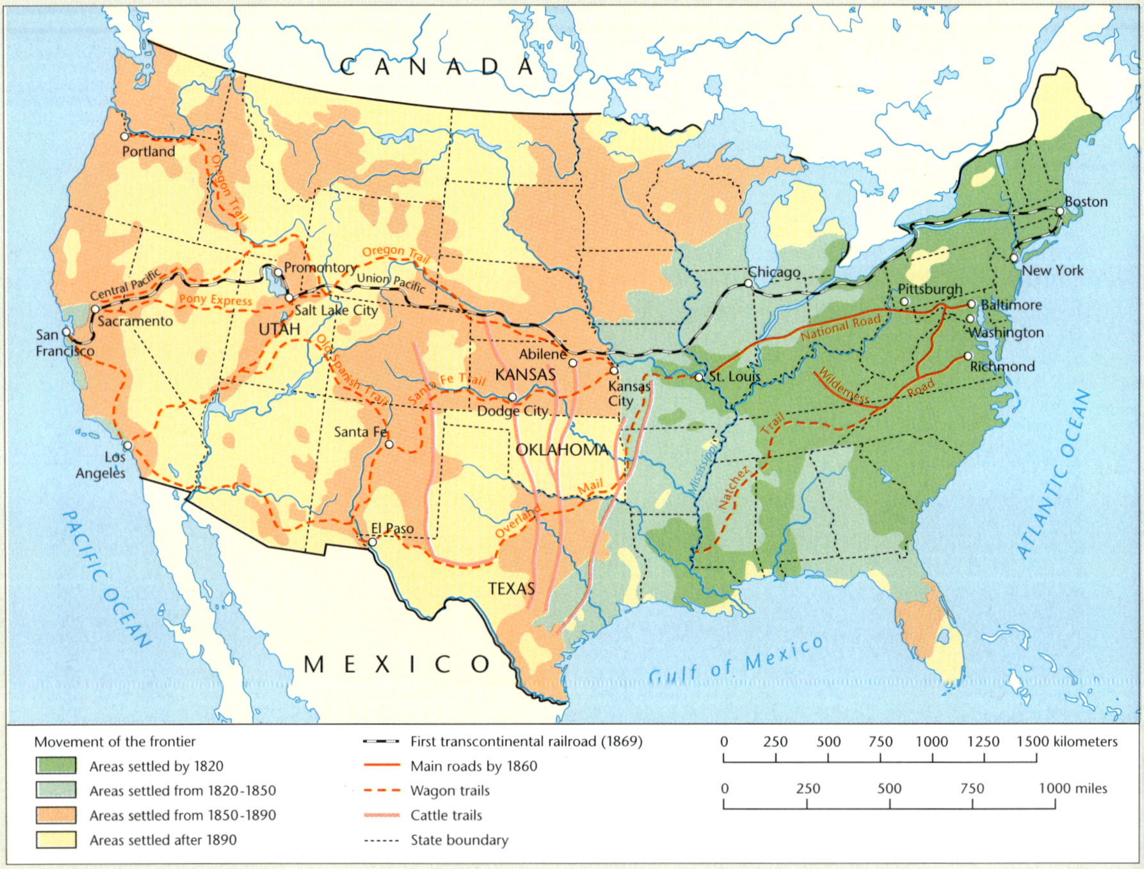

- Study the map and describe how/when the frontier moved west.
- Why did the settlers decide to move west? What difficulties did they face?
- What do you think of the idea of 'Manifest Destiny'?
- American politicians today sometimes call for a new 'frontier spirit'. What do they mean?

East and West united

In 1862 the American government in Washington, D.C. wanted to link the gold-rich settlements along the Pacific Coast more closely to the rest of the USA. Therefore, it gave land to two different companies to build a railroad across the country. One started in the East, one in the West.

Promontory, Utah
Monday, May 10, 1869

Today the last rail was laid. The transcontinental railroad is finished. At quarter to one, in front of a crowd of several hundred workmen, officials and reporters, the Union Pacific Railroad's chief engineer, Grenville Dodge, put in the last spike, and East was united with West. Now passengers from the East can travel by railroad all the way to the Pacific. A journey from New York to San Francisco, which might take up to five months by wagon, can now be made in only eight days. This railroad will provide reliable long-distance transportation and be a lifeline between frontier towns and the markets in the eastern cities. As I write these words, the union of the continent is being celebrated in the whiskey tents

and dance halls of this railroad town. And all America is thinking of us here, as the news spreads of this great moment.

By 1890 the frontier had finally disappeared. What role did the railroads play?

The 'Wild West'

As the railroads were built, cattle ranchers saw a way to make money. They realized they could use the new railroads to transport cattle to the East, where buyers were hungry for meat. They hired men called 'cowboys' to drive their half-wild cattle from Texas hundreds of miles north to the railroads in Kansas. This way the slow-moving herds were fattened up on their way to market. 'Cow towns' on the railroads, such as Abilene or Dodge City, became rich. Very soon meat from Texas was feeding people in Europe as well as those in the eastern United States. Although many people think the life of a cowboy must have been free and exciting, the daily routine usually consisted of dirty and exhausting work, poor food and low pay.
Even so, myths and legends have grown up about cowboys, as can still be seen from many Hollywood productions and from adverts.

Clint Eastwood in Pale Rider (1985)

- What do you know about cowboys? Where does your knowledge come from?
- Why do you think cowboys are still so popular today as a film topic or in advertising?

→ Ex 1, 2

American Indians

Think about the Westerns you have seen. What picture do they give of American Indians? Create a network using your ideas.

Nobody knows exactly, but it is believed that Indians have been living on the American continent for almost 50,000 years. When the first European settlers arrived in America in 1600, there were hundreds of tribes, and they spoke many different languages. They lived all over America: the Hopi lived in the southwest in mud-brick villages called 'pueblos', in the northeast the Iroquois hunted deer and gathered nuts and berries, and the tribes of the Great Plains, for example the Sioux[1] and Comanche, hunted buffalo. Many were excellent farmers.

For a short time the early settlers lived peacefully with the Indians, who even showed them how to grow and use plants like corn and tobacco. But as more and more white settlers moved west over the Great Plains, they took over the hunting grounds of the Plains Indians. Many tribes fought back and tried to stay on their territory. The American government promised that white settlers could not have land without the permission of the Indians, but these promises were often broken. Many Indians were killed or died of diseases that the white settlers had brought with them.

In 1834 the government decided that all Indians living east of the Mississippi would be moved west to an area called Indian Territory. The Indians were forced to leave their homes and move to reservations that were very often on infertile land. One of the saddest experiences was the 'Trail of Tears': in 1838 thousands of Cherokees were driven west to Oklahoma during a bitterly cold winter. The terrible journey lasted almost five months and over 4000 men, women and children died.

Today American Indians make up only 0.8% of the US population.

In your opinion, which of these statements best sums up the main idea of the text? Give reasons.

a) American Indians lived in many parts of America before the white settlers arrived.
b) The American government gave American Indian land to the settlers.
c) The lives of the American Indians changed for ever when the settlers moved onto their land.
d) From 1834, Indian Territory was west of the Mississippi.

The Trail of Tears. Compare this picture with the one on page 33. Describe the atmosphere in each picture.

[1] Sioux [su:]

→ Ex 3, 4 → Option 3: An American Indian legend

Focus on WORDS: Talking about different attitudes and values

The relationship between the American Indians and the European settlers was difficult partly because they did not share the same attitudes and values. The 'frontier spirit' which helped to create the USA was in direct conflict with the traditional American Indian way of life. The settlers came west looking for land to claim and call theirs, but the American Indians did not believe in owning land, for example. For them this idea was as strange as owning the sky.
American Indians today live in a world that is influenced both by Indian tradition and by 'modern' American culture. Of course there are TVs and fast-food places on many reservations nowadays, and many American Indian teenagers have similar or the same values as other American teenagers. But still a lot of American Indians try to maintain their old values.

"Why can't you be like other people?"

1 Arranging words

Here is a collection of words and phrases. Make two lists, one with the items you think belong to the cultural values of 'modern' America and one with the items which you associate with traditional American Indian values. Compare some of your lists in class. Perhaps you'll find that some of the items could be put easily into one of the lists while others cause problems. Discuss why this might be the case.

live	in +harmony with nature each day as it comes
be afraid of	silence age and getting older
believe in	competition youth and youthfulness the future individuality doing things only when they need to be done
believe that	only people are important there is life in all things we have power over nature we are in control of the elements only the +immediate family is important

don't believe in	making plans for the future exploiting the resources of the earth
attach importance to	time material things a person's status somebody's personality large homes patience advice from older people +extended families
share	+wealth with others homes with other people
respect	+elderly people all life on earth individual +achievements

2 Words in use

a Work in groups. Decide which values are typically German, which are British and which are American. Compare your lists and try to identify those values which are most likely to be prejudices.

b Through traveling and reading, you will have come into contact with different cultures. Think of a country you know quite well and talk about those things which you believe travelers to that country ought to be aware of.

c Which things do you yourself value? What about your friends, classmates or older people you know?

d What conflicts may come up when groups of people or individuals value different things?

→ Option 1: A question of identity → Option 16: What to say in the USA

The American Civil War

- Do you think that any one of the German *Bundesländer* has the right to break away from Germany and form an independent state? What would or should the German government do?
- Now read the following text. Find out what happened in the 1860s when 11 states broke away from the US.

In the first half of the 1800s, while the western territories were being settled, the North and South of the original thirteen colonies had developed differently: the South relied on black slaves to work on its many farms and cotton plantations, whereas in the more industrial states of the North slavery was illegal.
By the 1850s the issue of slavery had divided the country: people in the South were afraid that slavery would not be allowed in the new western territories. They believed that they would then totally lose their influence in national government.
When Abraham Lincoln became President in 1860, southerners were afraid that he might abolish slavery altogether. So between 1860 and 1861 eleven southern states left the Union and founded a new nation – the 'Confederate States of America'. But Lincoln was determined to keep the country together. This situation led to war between the North (the 'Union') and the Confederate States of the South.
At first the South won many battles, but by late 1862, the Union began to win the war. To weaken the Confederate States further, Lincoln declared the slaves of the Confederacy free from January 1, 1863. This Emancipation Proclamation gave the North a new purpose in the war: it was now not only fighting to save the Union, but also for the freedom of slaves.
The Civil War finally ended with a victory for the Union in 1865. It ensured that the United States was one nation whose parts could not be separated, and it led to the end of slavery. However, bitter memories survived, as over 600,000 soldiers had died in the war – more than in any other war that the US has fought in. A lot of southern cities, plantations and homes were left in ruins. It took many years for the States to become truly united again.

The eleven Confederate States and their flag. The Confederate flag can still be seen in the South today.

- Why did the South leave the Union?
- What were the major differences between the North and the South? Use the table below to compare their resources and to explain why the North won the war.

Resources of the North and South in 1861	***North***	***South***
Farmland	*105,835 acres (= 65%)*	*56,832 acres (= 35%)*
Railroad track	*21,847 miles (= 71%)*	*8,947 miles (= 29%)*
Value of manufactured goods	*$1,794,417,000 (= 92%)*	*$155,552,000 (= 8%)*
Factories	*119,500 (= 85%)*	*20,600 (= 15%)*
Workers in industry	*1,198,000 (= 92%)*	*111,000 (= 8%)*
Population	*22,340,000 (= 63%)*	*9,103,000 (= 37%)*
		(incl. 3,954,000 slaves)

→ Option 4: Slavery in the USA

Abraham Lincoln

Abraham Lincoln was President of the US during the Civil War. Many people believe his greatest achievement was the abolition of slavery in the USA in 1865, but in fact Lincoln's main aim was to keep the Union together – with or without slavery. He succeeded, but had to pay a high price for it. Only five days after the South surrendered on April 9, 1865, he was killed by a fanatic southerner.

Lincoln Memorial, Washington, D.C.

Abraham Lincoln (1809-1865), born into an illiterate frontier family, was a self-made man, who began with very little. He hardly ever went to school, but had all kinds of jobs as a young man. After much disciplined self-study he became an attorney in 1836. However, it is not as a successful attorney that he is remembered today, but for his achievements in his political career. In 1856 he joined the newly-founded Republican Party, and in 1860 he became the 16th President of the United States of America.

Lincoln is famous for his speeches and his powerful use of language. He made his best-known speech in 1863 at Gettysburg, Pennsylvania, where an important Civil War battle had taken place a few months earlier. In that battle the South had been defeated, but thousands of Union soldiers had died as well.

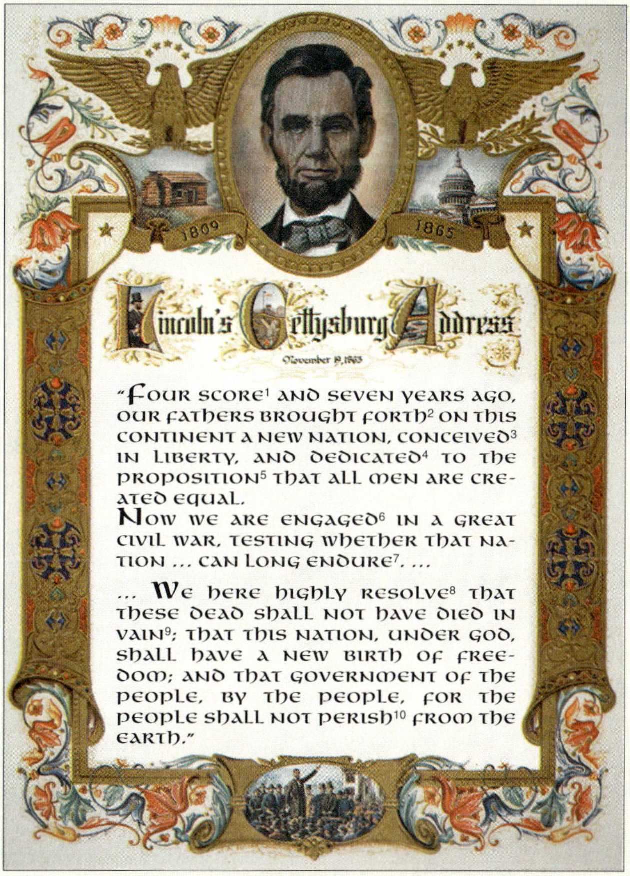

Read the Gettysburg Address on the right and answer these questions:

- What happened "four score and seven years" before the Gettysburg Address?
- According to Lincoln, what are the principles that the soldiers killed in the Civil War died for?
- What is meant by "government of the people, by the people, for the people"?

[1] score [skɔ:] *20* [2] bring forth (fml) *hervorbringen* [3] conceive [kən'si:v] *zeugen;* (fml) *ersinnen, planen* [4] dedicate ['dedɪkeɪt] *widmen* [5] proposition [,prɒpə'zɪʃn] *Behauptung, Auffassung* [6] engaged in (fml) *beschäftigt mit, beteiligt an* [7] endure [ɪn'djʊə] (fml) *Bestand haben, fortdauern* [8] resolve [rɪ'zɒlv] (fml) *den Vorsatz fassen, beschließen, versprechen* [9] in vain [veɪn] *vergeblich, umsonst* [10] perish ['perɪʃ] (fml) *untergehen, verschwinden*

→ Ex 5-7

1 Who said what?

Work in pairs or small groups. Match the people to the quotations: who said what? What do the quotations tell you about the people or their situation?

People

- Robert Whitestone, a settler
- Thomas Jefferson, President of the USA 1801-09
- Amelia Knight, a settler
- An Indian chief
- John F. Kennedy, President of the USA 1961-63
- General Sheridan, US army
- Sacajawea, a female Indian guide

"Our journey with these white men took us many moons. The white men wrote down everything they saw on the journey in many books and gave strange new names to the plants and animals." (1)

"We stand today on the edge of a new frontier. But the New Frontier of which I speak is not a set of promises – it is a set of challenges. It sums up what I intend to ask of the American people." (2)

"The white man will disappear, sooner perhaps than most other tribes. Keep on polluting your [river]beds and one night you will no longer be able to breathe." (3)

"We are creeping along slowly, one wagon after another, out of one mud hole and into another. The men are all soaking wet and look sad and comfortless." (4)

"It will take a thousand years for Americans to populate the vast emptiness of the West." (5)

"Some people here in Oregon are talking about going back to America." (6)

"The only good Indian is a dead Indian." (7)

Example:
It was (perhaps/probably) Sacajawea who said …/who spoke about the journey with the white men. It must have been her because she is the only one who talks about going on a trip with white men. She is obviously talking some time after the journey. She sounds as if she finds the white settlers a bit strange. She wonders why they gave new names to the plants and animals.

2 Stereotypes of the West: Cowboys

→ Grammar review 2, 4 (pp. 121-124)

Read the information in the box below and the text in the speech bubble, then continue the text using the phrases given.

"… The Virginian – come – West – 1870s – where – work – Judge Henry's ranch / he – quiet – strong – honest – peace-loving – and – he – like – by most people / one day, – while – visit – town not far away, – hear – how – Trampas, – strange character, – tell lies – Molly Wood / Molly – our school teacher – who, like the Virginian, – come – from – East / Virginian – force – Trampas – take back – what – say / from then on – Trampas – Virginian's deadly enemy / I could see – clear – how – end – one day: Trampas – provoke – Virginian; – there – be – showdown – which – one of them – die / it – happen – sooner – I – expect / fortunately – Virginian – draw faster / to this day – I – remember – Molly – be shaken – when – find out – that – peaceful life – be – something – you – have to – fight for – in the West / some time later – accept – Virginian's proposal of marriage."

> *Owen Wister's novel* The Virginian: A Horseman of the Plains *was published in 1902. It became a best-seller and sold three million copies. The book served as a model for all the romantic cowboy stories that had little to do with the often miserable life of real cowboys. It was through this book that the cowboy really became a national figure.*

3 Stereotypes of the West: Indians

→ Grammar review 2-4, 24 (pp. 121-124, 132)

Find the right forms for the verbs in brackets.

Even today, there (be) many people who (associate) the word 'Indians' with two types of people they (know) from films and novels.
First, there (be) the bad Indians who (fight) white settlers, who (drink) a lot of whiskey, and you (can/not/believe) a word they (say). If you (look) at pictures of this type of Indian, you (see) them (ride) across the plains, perhaps (attack) some innocent settlers or even (kill) them. This kind of Indian (can/often/find) in 'cheap' books and films.
Then there (be) the good Indians. Karl May's *Winnetou* (be) a typical example. He (see) as a man who always (do) the right thing, who (be prepared/help) the weak and (risk) his life for others.
Until about 40 years ago, American Indians themselves (not/openly/fight) against this black and white picture of their culture. However, during the 1960s, while the civil rights movement in the USA (fight) for the rights of blacks, the Indians, too, (start/tell) the truth about the lives of their ancestors. They (draw) attention to the miserable conditions their ancestors (force/live in). Suddenly a wider public (discover) that the Indian tribes and the early settlers (live) together peacefully before the waves of settlers (arrive). For many tribes, fishing, hunting and farming the land (be) their most important activities.
Since the 1960s more and more American Indians (try/live) according to their old traditions.

*plight [plaɪt] *missliche Lage, Misere*

There is a consonant missing from the caption of this cartoon. Which one? – What do you think of the cartoon?

4 Listening comprehension: The Canyon de Chelly

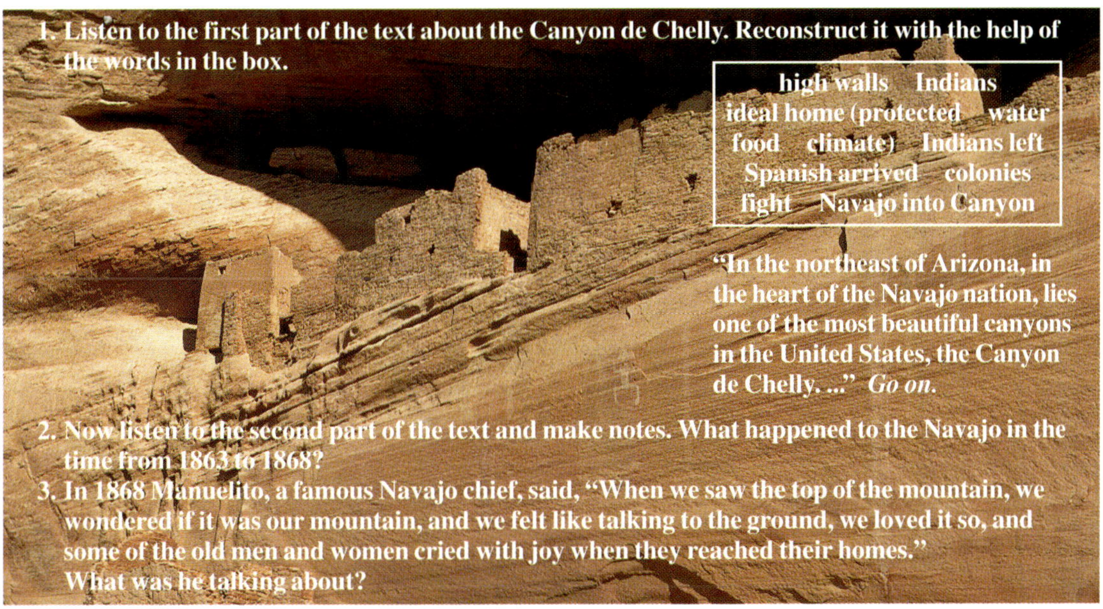

1. Listen to the first part of the text about the Canyon de Chelly. Reconstruct it with the help of the words in the box.

high walls Indians ideal home (protected water food climate) Indians left Spanish arrived colonies fight Navajo into Canyon

"In the northeast of Arizona, in the heart of the Navajo nation, lies one of the most beautiful canyons in the United States, the Canyon de Chelly. ..." ***Go on.***

2. Now listen to the second part of the text and make notes. What happened to the Navajo in the time from 1863 to 1868?

3. In 1868 Manuelito, a famous Navajo chief, said, "When we saw the top of the mountain, we wondered if it was our mountain, and we felt like talking to the ground, we loved it so, and some of the old men and women cried with joy when they reached their homes." What was he talking about?

5 Dances with Wolves
(Translation practice III)

Here is an excerpt from a film guide. Translate the summary of the US western Dances with Wolves ('Der mit dem Wolf tanzt') *into German. Imagine you are translating for the average German reader. Your translation will have to include some additional information here and there to make things clear. See the notes. Use an English-German dictionary to check any new words.*

Kevin Costner as Lieutenant Dunbar in Dances with Wolves *(1990)*

After the Civil War John W. Dunbar, a soldier in the Union Army, is given a remote post in South Dakota. He is alone but not lonely, and basically happy with the situation because he is able to experience the frontier before it disappears. His nearest neighbors are some Sioux. After meeting several times, they slowly get to know each other.

One day the Indians bring along *Stands with a Fist*, a white woman living with the tribe since her family was killed by Pawnee Indians when she was a girl. She remembers a little English and can translate for them. Eventually Dunbar gives up his post and goes to live with the tribe, where he's given the name *Dances with Wolves*. He falls in love with *Stands with a Fist*, eventually taking her as his wife. He hunts buffalo and helps the Sioux in their fight against the Pawnee Indians.

While getting ready to leave with the tribe for its winter camp, Dunbar makes a last trip to his post to get the diary he started when he first arrived there.

Meanwhile some soldiers have arrived, however, and Dunbar is taken prisoner. He refuses to lead the soldiers to the Sioux, and so is sent back to the nearest fort, where they intend to hang him for disobeying orders.

A group of Sioux frees him and Dunbar rejoins his tribe. But knowing the army will search for him, he and his wife just ride away …

Which one? Make it clear to the average reader.

The German word 'Union' may not mean much to the average reader.

'Sich erinnern an' is not really suitable here.

You can't translate this word for word.

Another passive which is expressed by an active construction in German.

What is the German collocation?

Remember to put the subject *Dunbar* in the German subordinate clause.

Translate as 'goes to … one last time'.

What's missing from this contact clause?

What does the prefix *re-* express?

Use 'versetzen auf' or an active construction with a different verb.

Another specifically American term, which you should explain further ('the frontier of the Wild West').

In the German version of the film this name is translated word for word.

Use a relative clause.

This is a false friend. It doesn't mean 'eventuell'.

This participle after the main clause expresses result (German: 'und …').

Which preposition in German?

= 'in order to'

What is the German collocation?

Translate as 'man'.

In German use a phrase with a noun ('wegen Befehls…').

Think of a suitable conjunction to start the translation of this participle construction.

6 German 'sollen'

The German verb 'sollen' can be translated into English in a number of ways.

a

1. What **shall I/we** do now?	Was soll ich/sollen wir jetzt tun?
2. **Shall I** see what's on TV?	Soll ich nachsehen, was im Fernsehen läuft?
3. **Shall we** watch *Independence Day*?	Sollen wir uns *Independence Day* anschauen?

In questions *shall* is used to ask for a suggestion (1), to make an offer (2), or to make a suggestion *('Shall we ...?')* (3).

b

1. You **should** ask/**ought to** ask for permission.	Du solltest um Erlaubnis bitten.
2. I **should have** asked/**ought to have** asked for permission, but I didn't.	Ich hätte um Erlaubnis bitten sollen, aber ich habe es nicht getan.

With the verbs *should* and *ought to* the speaker says what in their opinion is the best or the right thing to do. (1)
should have done/ought to have done often expresses criticism of what has been done wrong, or not done at all. (2)

c

1. The head teacher says you **are to** apologize.	Die Schulleiterin sagt, du sollst dich entschuldigen.
2. Ann **was to** arrive at 10.	Ann sollte um 10 Uhr ankommen.

Be to is used to give or report an order by a person in authority. (1)
Be to is also used to say what is or was expected or planned to happen. (2)

⚠ A special meaning of *was/were to* is to express how something developed or turned out (often differently from the way that was expected):

3. Later they **were to** become great friends.	Später sollten sie gute Freunde werden.
4. It **was to** be the last time they met.	Es sollte das letzte Mal sein, dass sie sich sahen.

d

1. The Rockies **are supposed to** be dramatic.	Die Rocky Mountains sollen dramatisch sein.
2. Lincoln **is supposed to** have said that.	Lincoln soll das (angeblich) gesagt haben.
3. Becker's manager **is said to** have refused.	Beckers Manager soll sich geweigert haben.
4. You **are supposed to** wear a jacket and tie.	Man soll Jacke und Krawatte tragen.

Be supposed to is used to refer to what is generally believed to be true. (1, 2)
News reports often use an expression such as *be said to, be believed to, be thought to*, rather than *be supposed to*, in the sense of 'man sagt, dass'. (3)
Be supposed to is also used to say what people are expected to do or what is the correct thing to do. (4)

e

This text **is meant to** help you understand American history.	Dieser Text soll dir helfen, die amerikanische Geschichte zu verstehen.

Be meant to (or *be intended/designed to*) expresses that there is a particular purpose involved.

f **In English, please**

Im Jahre 1861 brach der [amerikanische] Bürgerkrieg aus. Es sollte einer der blutigsten *(bloody)* Kriege in der amerikanischen Geschichte werden. Über 600000 Soldaten sollen in diesem Krieg gefallen oder an Krankheiten und Epidemien *(epidemics)* gestorben sein. Ein Ziel des Krieges war [es], die Sklaverei abzuschaffen. Den Sklaven sollten Freiheit und Bürgerrechte gegeben werden, obwohl Lincoln einmal gesagt haben soll, dass die schwarze und die weiße Rasse seiner Meinung nach sozial und politisch nicht gleichgestellt sein *(be equal)* sollten. Lincoln wollte aber vor allem die Staaten zusammenhalten. Er meinte, dass alle Staaten in der Union bleiben sollten. „Ein geteiltes Haus kann nicht stehen", sagte er.

→ Option 17: The passive

→ Option 9: Using a monolingual dictionary
→ Option 10: Using a grammar

7 'I spy with my little eye ...': Common mistakes III

The text below has 15 mistakes in it. Find them and correct the text. Explain why you have made the corrections. It may help to consult a dictionary or a grammar book.

Lincolns Gettysburg Address in the November 1863 was held for a terrible speech at first. Even Lincoln was terrible disappointing with it: "I failed, I failed, and that is about all that can be said about it," he shall have said.
The main speaker at that day in 1863 was a man called Edward Everett. He was speaking for two whole hours. The speech he held was quite long, but the hearers loved it. Then it was Lincoln's turn. His speech was only ten sentences long and took only two minutes. It was short, direct and understandabel, but hardly anybody enjoyed to listen to that sort of speech. The most people in Gettysburg that day prefered the speech of Everett.

8 WORDS WORDS WORDS

a Trouble spot: hear/listen (to) – see/look (at)/watch

Fill in the correct verb form to complete the following sentences. Add 'to' or 'at' if necessary.

1. ★★★ where you're going. 2. I could ★★★ the monkeys for hours. 3. Are you ★★★ the radio, or shall I switch it off? 4. Tommy never ★★★ what you tell him. 5. The thief became nervous because he felt he was being ★★★. 6. I'm sure the accident was the driver's fault. He should have ★★★ more carefully. 7. "Steve, ★★★ the board, please," said the teacher. 8. Although we ★★★ carefully, we couldn't ★★★ a sound. 9. ★★★! Somebody is knocking at the door, I think. 10. On our way to the movies we ★★★ Helen on the other side of the street. She was ★★★ us and shouting something we couldn't ★★★ very well. 11. We look forward to ★★★ from you.

b WORD BUILDER'S CORNER — Verbs with prefixes and suffixes

You can understand many 'new' verbs that you have never met before if you can recognize the prefixes and suffixes that have been added:

re- *pref* (used widely with *vs* and related *ns*) again: *reapply ∘ redecoration ∘ re-entered.*

-en *suff* (with *adjs* forming *vs*) to make or become: *blacken ∘ sadden.*

mis- *pref* (with *vs* and *ns*) bad; wrong; not: *misdirect ∘ misconduct ∘ mistrust.*

-ize *suff* (with *ns* and *adjs* forming *vs*) **1** to become or make like: *dramatize ∘ miniaturize.* **2** to act or treat with the qualities of: *criticize ∘ deputize.*

(Examples from *Oxford Advanced Learner's Dictionary*)

re-: rearrange, rebuild, redo, reappear, re-elect, refill, renew, rename, reorganize
mis-: misplace, misuse, mislead, misinform, misbehave, mistreat, misspell
-ize: terrorize, modernize, symbolize, legalize, generalize, nationalize
-en: widen, shorten, deepen, blacken, strengthen, flatten, harden, weaken

Work in groups: Look up the 'new' words in a monolingual dictionary. Check if you know how to pronounce them correctly, then write down their meaning and the examples which show how they are used. Examples:

rearrange: place in a different way or order – *rearrange the furniture*
misplace: put in the wrong place – *misplace one's glasses/keys/a book*
terrorize: fill with terror – *terrorize the neighborhood*
widen: make or become wider – *widen a road/one's knowledge*

"Such is prairie life"

Before you read the text, describe the photo:
- What situation is shown?
- What do the people look like?
- What do you think their life was like?

Most of the settlers who went west believed in the 'American dream', i.e. the idea that everyone had the chance to live in freedom and to become rich, successful and happy if they worked hard enough. But that dream didn't come true for everybody, as is shown by the following extracts from the diary of Miriam Davis Colt, a New York born teacher.
Having lived in Montreal, Canada, for ten years, Miriam and her husband, William, decide to join an experimental settlement in the state of Kansas. After a strenuous journey by rail, boat and wagon, they arrive in Kansas City, Missouri. Then they travel further west through the state of Kansas. With them are their children Willie and Mema as well as William's parents and his sister, Lydia.

Now read what Miriam writes about the first two and a half weeks of pioneer life.
- What problems does she have to face?
- Can you detect any change in her overall mood?

(The footnotes will help you to understand the text. If you need to, you can look up other words in a dictionary.)

April 30, 1856: Here we are, at Kansas City in Missouri, all safely again on *terra firma*, after one week on the water.

May 1: Take a walk outside – view the city, and see that it takes but a few buildings in this western world to make a city. … I review the past pleasant years, and a shadow comes over me, as I try to look away into the future and ask, "What is my destiny?" Ah! Away with all these shadows. We shall be very busy this year in making our home comfortable, so that no time is left for homesickness[1] to take hold of us.

May 2: A lovely day. Our husbands are loading the ox-wagons. … Women and children walk along up the hill out of this 'Great City', wait under a tree – what a beautiful country is before us! Will our Kansas scenery equal this?

May 11: 'Made' but a few miles yesterday across the prairie. Crossed the little Osage[2] river. … Our husbands complained of the great weight of the wagons. Ours has eight trunks[3], one traveling bag, three carpet bags, a box of crackers, 200 pounds of flour[4], 100 pounds of corn meal[5], a few pounds of sugar, rice, dried apple, one washtub[6] of little trees, utensils[7] for cooking, and two more boxes of food. … Arrive at Elm Creek – no house to sleep in tonight – supper cooked on camp-fire, and eaten with appetite, sitting in family groups around the big fire. Some will sleep in wagons, others under the blue heaven.

[1] homesickness *Heimweh* [2] Osage [əʊ'seɪdʒ] [3] trunk *Schrankkoffer* [4] flour ['flaʊə] *Mehl* [5] corn meal *Maismehl* [6] washtub *Waschzuber* [7] utensil [juː'tensl]

May 12: Full of hope as we leave this morning. Expect tonight to arrive at our new home. It begins to rain, rain, rain, like a shower. … We move slowly and wetly into town just at nightfall. … Look around, and see the grounds all around the large camp-fire are covered with tents in which the families are staying. Not a house is to be seen, except one cabin[1], with mud between the logs[2] on the inside, instead of on the outside. We can share it with some other families.

May 15: A cold, drizzling[3] rain. The prairie winds come whizzing[4] in. Have hung up an Indian blanket at the door … . It is dark, uncomfortable and cold inside. Have a fire outside to cook by. … It is not very enjoyable work, cooking out of doors in this windy, rainy weather, or when the burning sun shines. The bottoms of our dresses are burnt full of holes now, and they will soon be burnt off. … Our menu is limited – hominy[5], Johnny cake[6], Graham pudding[7], some white bread, now and then stewed apple[8], a little rice, and sometimes tea for the old people.

May 17: The greater number of the company that came with us, and others that were here, feel so disappointed that they left this morning for Kansas City; and from there they know not where they will go.

Now read the diary entries for the next two months and answer the following questions:
- How does Miriam describe the Osage Indians?
- Why does Miriam describe her family's situation as 'a doomed[9] ship'?

May 19: Have been to the creek[10] and done our last month's washing. Had the trouble of hard water and only a small supply of soap. … A rub[11] through the hand is all our clothes can have.

May 26: Have been washing today, and dried our clothes right out in the burning hot sun. We don't leave them out at night, for fear of the Indians, who come thieving round, taking everything they can lay their hands on. … They are soon going two or three hundred miles west on their buffalo hunt, where they go twice a year, staying three months at a time. These Osage Indians are said to be friendly, but I cannot look at their painted faces without a shudder; and when they come around our cabin, I sit down and take Willie on my lap[12], and have Mema stand by my side, for fear they may steal my children from me. They point to my boy and make signs that he is pretty. … These Indians take life easy, depending upon their hunting tours and their government support money. Some of them dress, others dress only little except a breech cloth[13], moccasins, deer-skin[14] leggings to keep off the snakes[15], and their blankets. They come into our cabin and sit down – while sitting, their blankets fall from their shoulders, showing their large dark brown and nearly nude[16] forms, to the shudder of the unaccustomed[17] observer.

June 3: A most terrible thunderstorm came up last night. … When we heard the storm coming nearer, we dressed ourselves, putting Indian blankets around us, and tried to protect our children from the rain that was then coming through the roof, covering them with our five umbrellas[18]. We all got wet, and had to lie in our wet beds till morning. This morning all was calm; the bright sun rose in a cloudless sky. … But the rain had washed out all the mud, and the wind had blown it into every corner of the house. Have had all our sheets to wash, beds and blankets to dry and clean in the sun, our log walls to brush down, our shelves and dishes to clean, and our own selves to wash. "Such is prairie life," so they say.

June 7: My husband is up at his claim[19] planting corn. Hopeful man! … I have cooked so much out in the hot sun and smoke that I hardly know who I am, and when I look in the little looking glass[20], I ask, "Can this be me?" Put a blanket over my head, and I would pass[21] well for an Osage squaw.

to protect sb. from sth.

1 cabin ['kæbɪn] *Hütte, Blockhaus* 2 log *Baumstamm* 3 drizzle ['drɪzl] *nieseln* 4 whizz [wɪz] *sausen*
5 hominy ['hɒmənɪ] *Maisbrei* 6 Johnny cake *Maisbrot* 7 Graham pudding ['greɪəm ˌpʊdɪŋ] *Brei aus Weizenschrot*
8 stewed apple [stju:d] *Apfelkompott* 9 doomed *verloren, dem Untergang geweiht* 10 creek *Bach* 11 rub *Reiben*
12 lap *Schoß* 13 breech cloth ['bri:tʃ klɒθ] *Lendenschurz* 14 deer-skin *Hirschleder* 15 snake [sneɪk] *Schlange*
16 nude [nju:d] *nackt* 17 unaccustomed [ˌʌnə'kʌstəmd] *(diesen Anblick) nicht gewohnt* 18 umbrella *Regenschirm*
19 claim *Landanteil, Parzelle* 20 looking glass *Spiegel* 21 pass for *gehalten werden für*

June 16: What are we to look for, and what fear next? The mosquitoes have suddenly come upon us. They troubled us very much at the creek today while washing.

June 29: I have fallen victim to the chills[1] and malarial fever, as have several members of our company. ... My head has ached terribly; am glad to get outdoors, breathe a little fresh air, see the sun go down, and ask, "Can this be the same sun that shines on our Northern friends, who are enjoying advantages and comforts they know not how to appreciate?"

June 30: Mr. V. has arranged a passage in an ox-wagon, for himself and wife, to Kansas City; my husband thinks we had better[2] make preparations to leave the territory with Mr. V., and not wait till he and father get sick.

July 1: The water is fast drying up and not fit to drink. Disappointment is on the way again! Am afraid father is going to upset all our plans about getting away. He says, out and out, that he will not go.

July 2: "A doomed ship!" thought I, this morning, as father told mother and Lydia to get in the wagon and said, "I am going to the old Indian house, where I can get some water to drink ...!" The difficult question comes up now to be answered, "What shall we do?"

July 16: I have been writing to friends, sitting on the floor of the old Indian house that we moved into. My husband is lying on our bed of prairie grass; his fever is passing off. Willie lies on an Indian blanket near the door, calling for water. Mother lies on her bed in the other room; seems very sick. Father on a blanket, on the floor; his fever is very high. Lydia has got up and is sitting on her trunk; looks weak and sad. Mema's fever is off. ... Just three months today since we left home; notice the contrast!

Sickness, the loss of their oxen, and threats from the Indians convinced Miriam and William Colt that they should leave Kansas. When they did so in September, they were nearly penniless. A few weeks later, William and Willie died in St. Louis, Missouri, and Miriam and Mema returned to New York. In an attempt to earn money to support herself and her daughter, she wrote Went to Kansas, *which was published in 1862.*

(From: *Women of the West* by Cathy Luchetti and Carol Olwell)

Working with the text

a Understanding the text

1. What are your first impressions of Miriam's new life in Kansas?
2. What do we learn from the text about the everyday life of a woman pioneer?
3. What does the text tell you about Miriam's thoughts and feelings about the Osage Indians?
4. Identify words and phrases that clearly show Miriam's mood on a particular day.
5. What are the reasons for the Colts' decision to leave the settlement?
6. What do you notice about the style and language of the diary?

b Beyond the text

1. Besides writing her diary, Miriam also wrote home to her mother in New York City. Write the letter that she wrote either on May 2, June 29 or July 16.
2. Why do you think Miriam kept a diary? What can you find out from a diary that you wouldn't learn in history books?
3. Do you think life on the frontier was harder for men or for women? What personal qualitites did a person need to live on the frontier?
4. It's the year 1872. John Gast has just finished his painting *American progress (see page 33).* Imagine you are Miriam Colt (who is 55 now) and you get the chance to talk to the artist. Comment on his painting.

[1] the chills *Schüttelfrost* [2] had better *sollte(n) besser*

Unit 4: Blacks in the USA

1619 The first 20 Africans are brought to work as 'servants' in Jamestown, Virginia. During the next two hundred years thousands more are brought as slaves to work on the tobacco and cotton fields in the South.

1808 Congress passes a law making it illegal to import slaves, but it is generally ignored.

1820 Slavery is declared legal in the South, but illegal in all states north of Missouri.

1861 Abraham Lincoln becomes president of the United States. The number of slaves in the USA has reached 4 million. Eleven southern 'slave' states leave the Union, afraid that Lincoln will abolish slavery, which is the basis of their economy. The Civil War breaks out.

1865 The North defeats the South. Slaves are freed throughout the nation.

Free at last

Free at last, free at last,
Thank God Almighty I'm free at last;
Free at last, free at last,
Thank God Almighty I'm free at last.

1. Way down yonder in the graveyard walk,
   Thank God Almighty I'm free at last,
   Me and my Jesus goin' to meet and talk,
   Thank God Almighty I'm free at last.

2. On my knees when the light passed by,
   Thank God Almighty I'm free at last,
   Thought my soul would rise and fly,
   Thank God Almighty I'm free at last.

3. Some of these mornings, so bright and fair,
   Thank God Almighty I'm free at last,
   Goin' to meet King Jesus in the air,
   Thank God Almighty I'm free at last.

1868 Blacks officially become American citizens. But it is made difficult if not impossible for blacks to vote in the South.

- What do you think of the text on the T-shirt? What is it trying to say?
- Using the information on these two pages explain why the 'name' for black Americans has changed so many times since 1619. Which period of African-American history do the words on the T-shirt apply to?
- Read the spiritual 'Free at last'. What does the singer say, directly and indirectly, about his/her situation?

Segregation

1896 The Supreme Court says any state can have facilities for blacks and whites, as long as they are 'separate, but equal'. In some southern states there are separate schools for blacks and whites, separate theaters, restaurants, hotels, taxis, and seats on buses.

1909 The National Association for the Advancement of Colored People (NAACP) is founded by a moderate group of blacks. The NAACP is an organization that wants to create equality and a racially integrated society by fighting racism, segregation and discrimination.

From 1919 on Thousands of blacks move to cities in the North, looking for work.

1954 The Supreme Court changes its 1896 decision: Schools must be desegregated in all states. Some areas in the South don't accept this.

1955 In Montgomery, Alabama, Rosa Parks refuses to stand up and give her seat to a white man on a bus. She is arrested by the police. Blacks protest by boycotting the buses for 382 days.

Rosa Parks

1956 The Supreme Court declares that Segregation on public buses is against the Constitution.

1963 Dr. Martin Luther King leads 250,000 people to Washington, D.C. in the largest protest march in US history up to that date. His speech is the climax of the civil rights movement. Civil rights leaders meet President Kennedy.

1964 Congress passes a civil rights law which makes discrimination illegal in hotels, restaurants and at work.

1965 Congress ends voting discrimination, so that all blacks are finally able to vote.

1967 Carl Stokes of Cleveland, Ohio, and Richard Hatcher of Gary, Indiana, are elected as the nation's first black mayors of major cities.

1968 Martin Luther King is assassinated. Riots break out in many American cities.

Jesse Jackson

1988 Jesse Jackson is the first black with a serious chance of being chosen as a candidate for president.

1989 David N. Dinkins becomes mayor of New York City.

1992 Carol Moseley-Braun becomes the first black woman to be elected to the US Senate.

1993 Writer Toni Morrison is the first black American to win the Nobel Prize for Literature.

→ Ex 1-4 → Option 4: Slavery in the USA

4A

Black America today

- What general impression of the situation of black people in the USA do you have?
- Look at the titles on the right, and the pictures and the captions that go with them. What do you expect the people to tell you?
- Read what Leon Brooks, Gail Rand and Linda Roberts say about themselves and their families. Then work with a partner. Arrange in a network what you find important about 'Black America today'. Compare some of the networks.
- Then turn to the box at the bottom of this page and the newspaper article on p. 51 and add the information you find there to your network.
- One group of black Americans is not mentioned here: the extremely successful. What very successful blacks do you know and what do you know about them?

Some facts and figures

- *Only 12% of the total population of the USA are blacks. About 53% of them live in the eleven southern states. Large numbers live in the big industrial cities of the North, such as Chicago, Detroit or New York.*
- *Black and white Americans have more contact than before, especially at work and at school. However, in their free time they often go their separate ways.*
- *Segregation can still be found in the places where Americans live. One third of all blacks live in neighborhoods which are almost totally black. Six out of ten whites live in mainly white areas.*

Successful, but still not equal

Leon Brooks is a lawyer. His wife Cora is a manager at an electronics company. They have a comfortable home in a mostly black middle-class area in Washington, D.C. Their children can expect to go to college and have successful careers.

Making ends meet

Gail Rand works in a department store in Washington. Her husband Charles is a waiter in a small restaurant. They live in an apartment in northeast Washington.

The poverty trap

Linda Roberts works as a secretary for a Washington company. She has two children aged two and four.

9 "Unfortunately, many whites have not yet gotten used to a successful black middle class. Some feel threatened. They seem to believe that the good life is for whites only. Of course I want to live in a nice area and I want my kids to go to a good school. But the feeling we often have is that we're not allowed to enjoy the things we have worked so hard for. As a successful black I'm also likely to experience annoying insults that few whites will ever face.
Being ignored by taxi drivers as I wait on the street is one example of what can happen when I travel to other cities on business. You have to learn to accept it, and it reminds you that no matter what we achieve as individuals, we will always be judged by what people see first – our color."

"We've come a long way since the civil rights marches of the 1960s. A black president could soon become a reality. But we still have a long, long way to go. If you went into a good restaurant here in Washington, you wouldn't think you were in a city with a population that's 70% black, because you would hardly see any blacks at the tables. Only a minority has really made it. The people who work in this city, the people in the department stores, the people who serve in the restaurants, drive the buses, build the homes – they are all black people.
We couldn't live on what Charles and I earn. We both have second jobs to help pay the bills and make sure we can save enough to send our daughter to college."

"I live with my mother in Anacostia. If she didn't look after my children during the day, I couldn't possibly go to work. There aren't enough day-care facilities for working women in the United States, and I would never be able to pay for private day care. My husband Floyd lives with his mother. He used to work for a construction firm till he lost his job. Now we can't afford the rent for an apartment together. If I didn't have a job, we'd have nothing at all, and I'd have to live on welfare. Although I have a full-time job, the salary I get is so low that I am still living below the poverty line. I worry myself sick about the future of my children, who are growing up in an area like this. There's drug-related crime everywhere. Many of the friends my husband grew up with are already dead or in prison. I don't want that to happen to my kids, but I don't know how to protect them from it, either."

Friday, September 23, 1994
The Washington Chronicle

Rich-Poor Gulf Becoming Wider Among Blacks

By FELICITY BRENNMEIER
Special to *The Washington Chronicle*

WASHINGTON, Sept. 22 – The civil rights movement of the 1960s helped those black Americans who were talented, educated and skilled, or already had qualifications – those who really had been held back by race.

One important development from this period has been the appearance of an authentic black middle class, better educated and better paid than any group of blacks before.

For other blacks who were not in this group, however, very little has happened. In general, black workers are still badly paid even today, and many families need two salaries to survive. Furthermore, as well-off blacks move to better neighborhoods to find a better life for themselves and their children, they have left behind a socially disabled group of poor people who have become the underclass. Once caught in such a situation, it is almost impossible for families to escape.

A major problem in black America and one that contributes to the continuation of the underclass is the huge increase in one-parent households. About 58% of all black households are headed by single black females. Their children often live in poverty. The dangers they face in the ghettos where they grow up are drugs, violence from street gangs, and other crimes.

▸ Ex 5-7

4A

The charts on this page show how the lives of black Americans have changed since the 1960s.

Education and achievement

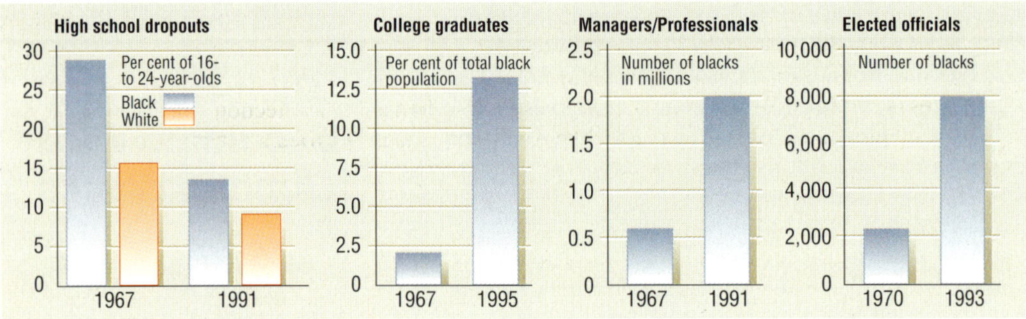

Income and unemployment

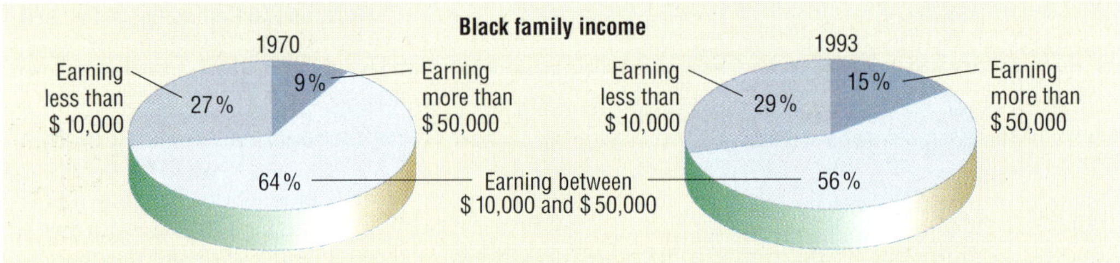

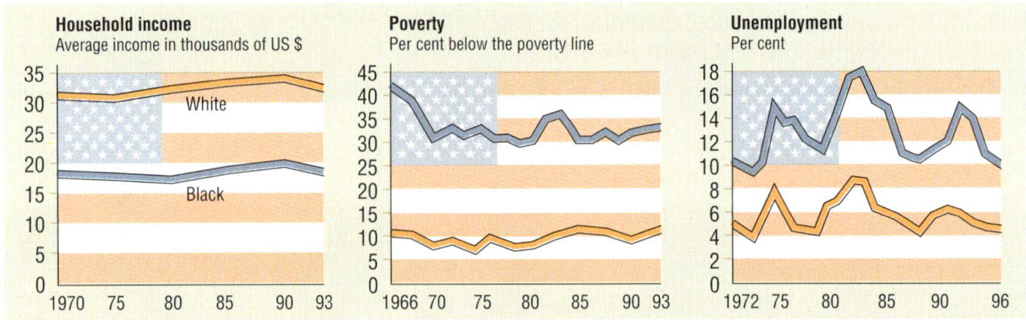

- Write a few sentences about each graph. You can use these phrases.

  The charts illustrate .../deal with .../focus on ...
  The chart on *poverty* gives information about ...
  Between *1967* and *1991*, / From *1967* to *1991*, | there was an increase/a decrease (of ...) in the number of ...
  The percentage/number of ... increased/decreased | by ... (%). / from ... to ...
  The difference(s) between ... and ... (with regard to ...) remained largely unchanged.
  The figures on ... show ...

- Now summarize your findings. How has the situation of black Americans developed since the 1960s? What progress can you see? What can you say about the difference between blacks and whites? Use the notes you have made and prepare a short talk in class or write a short essay.

→ Option 11: Presenting a paper

Focus on WORDS: Talking about feelings and emotions

Linda Roberts has mixed feelings and emotions when she talks about her situation. She feels frustrated that she cannot live with her husband. She is obviously pleased that she still has a job, but she is annoyed that there aren't enough day-care facilities in the United States.

She is quite +fond of her work and she gets a lot of satisfaction from it, but she feels very angry that her salary still leaves her below the poverty line.

Linda loves her family like any mother. She gives her children a lot of +affection, but she is worried that her children are growing up in an area like Anacostia. She is +terrified that her son might join a local gang one day and get into serious trouble.

She tries to look at things positively, but a feeling of helplessness often comes over her when she thinks about what the future might bring.

1 Collecting words

Collect the words which express Linda's feelings and add them to the following word lists. If you go through pages 50 and 51 again, you will find more words. (If they don't fit into one of the groups a-d, why not start a new group?)

a **Words expressing happiness or sadness**
- be/feel happy, pleased, …
- satisfaction, joy, …
- be/feel unhappy, helpless, …
- unhappiness, loneliness, …

b **Words expressing love, dislike or hate**
- like, love, be fond of, …
- love, affection, …
- dislike, be fed up with, …
- hate, …

c **Words expressing worry and fear**
- be/feel afraid, frightened, +scared, …
- +anxiety, nervousness, …

d **Words expressing +anger**
- be/feel annoyed, fed up with, …
- +rage, …

2 Arranging words

a There are several ways to arrange words. You can look for
- word families (to disappoint – disappointing – disappointment – …),
- opposites (boring – exciting; to like – to dislike; love – hate)
- or 'word thermometers' like the one on the right.

Take the 'feeling' words you have collected and try to find other word families, opposites and word thermometers.

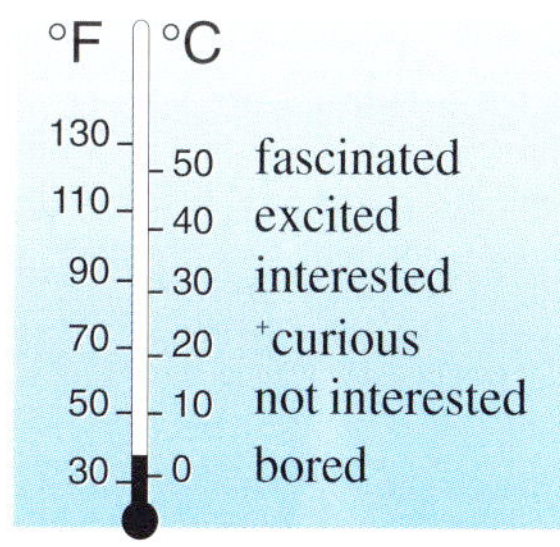

b Make a network of your own free associations. Here is an example of how somebody started such a network. You can either complete the example in your exercise book or choose a different starting word.

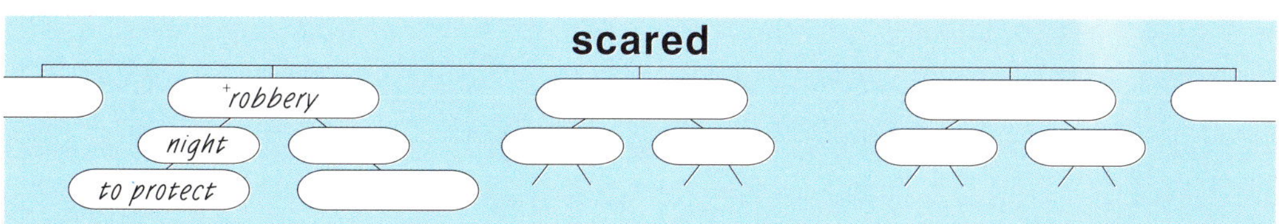

3 Words in use

Ask one of the other people in your class for her/his network and find out together why one word has led to another. (Look at the dialogue in the box for help.)

> Why has *scared* led to *robbery*?
> – Well, you might be scared when you hear there's been a robbery near where you live.
> What about *robbery* and *night*? …

1 Frederick Douglass (1817-1895): From slave to politician

→ Grammar review 2, 4, 9 (pp. 121-124, 126)

a *Put the verbs in brackets into the right form. You will have to make some of them passive.*

In 1877 a family named Douglass (move) into the part of Washington, D.C. which (be) now Anacostia and which (then / call) Uniontown. The fact that today the home of the Douglass family (be) a historical monument which (can / visit) by everybody (show) that somehow they (be) a 'special' family.
From about 1840, Frederick Douglass, the father of the family, (become) known as an author, a fighter for civil rights and a politician. In 1877 he (make) US marshal for Washington, D.C., and later in his life he (have) several other government jobs.
After Frederick's death in 1895, his wife Helen (found) the Frederick Douglass Memorial Association. That is why his name (not forget) up to this day and why important events in his life (can / reconstruct): Douglass (be) a slave, but he (be able to) escape to the North in 1838. In 1845 he (have to / leave) the USA and (go) to England. He (return) after some of his friends (pay) his former owner $710. In his anti-slavery newspaper, The *North Star*, which Douglass (start) in 1847, he not only (continue) his fight for the freedom of black people, he also (fight) for the rights of women. Today Frederick Douglass's work for more equality in American society (recognize) by all Americans. In schoolbooks that (use) all over the USA, Frederick Douglass (mention) next to such a great leader as Martin Luther King.

Statue of Frederick Douglass at Morgan State University, Maryland

b *Now read the text you have written once again, and try to rephrase those parts where a passive verb is used, but without using the passive. Why is it often better to use the passive in these cases?*

2 Different ways of reacting to a statement

→ Grammar review 9-11 (pp. 126-127)

a Depending on the context and on what is important, a speaker can react in many different ways to a statement. *Look at the statement in the middle and read how six different people reacted to it. Put in the correct form of the verbs in brackets, or use the correct form of one of these verbs:*
be able to, be allowed to, have to.

"Since 1965 black Americans (can / vote) in all elections."

1. Who knows? A black candidate (may / soon / elect) President.
2. Until 1965 they (must / pass) tests before they (may / vote) in some southern states.
3. Nobody (be going / can / convince) me to get interested in politics.
4. They (should / may / vote) a hundred years earlier.
5. More support (must / give) to black candidates in elections. There (might / be) many more blacks in important positions years ago if black people (can/ convinced) to use their right to vote.
6. They (must / fight) a long time to get the right to vote.

b *Translate the complete sentences in part* a *into German.*

3 Listening comprehension: The history of the blues

Listen to the cassette and answer the following questions.

1. What do the spirituals and work songs of the slaves have to do with the blues? 2. Why is the guitar such a good blues instrument? 3. How did the blues reach the big cities? 4. How did the topics of the songs change? 5. How is rhythm and blues different from traditional blues? 6. What did Arthur Crudup and Elvis Presley have to do with the history of the blues? 7.Why is the blues still so popular today?

→ Option 5: Black music

→ Option 9: Using a monolingual dictionary
→ Option 10: Using a grammar

4 'I spy with my little eye ...': Common mistakes IV

a *The text below has 14 mistakes in it. Try to find them and rewrite the text. How many different kinds of mistakes did you find? Sort them into groups. It may be helpful to consult a grammar or a dictionary.*

Quite a lot English words are almost certain from African origin and have been introduced into English by black slaves in the 17th and 18th centuries. Under them are *cola, banana, gorilla, zombie* and *boogie-woogie*. However, it was not until middle of the 1940s that people begun studying black speech[1] and her influence on English. Before that, white Americans were simple not prepared to accept that they were using words that blacks had passed on to them. During they had no problem seeing the Dutch, German, Spanish or Italian origin from certain English words, they didn't believe blacks were importantly enough to cause changes in English language. In fact, blacks were not even considered able to speak proper. For example, a 1949 newspaper article described the linguistic[2] ability of blacks on the following absurd way: "The American Negro is not able to pronounce the *r* in *horse* because his lips are too thick."

b **In English, please**

Be careful to avoid the mistakes you found in the text above.

Man darf *(can)* fast sicher annehmen *(assume)*, dass das englische Wort *jazz* afrikanischen Ursprungs ist und durch Sklaven ins Englische eingeführt worden ist, obwohl ein Sprachforscher *(linguist)* namens Krapp noch 1925 behauptete, *jazz* habe seine Wurzeln *(roots)* in einem alten englischen Dialekt. Tatsächlich war diese Art von Aussage bis Mitte des 20. Jahrhunderts nicht ungewöhnlich. Wer wollte [schon] in jenen Jahren zugeben, dass er die Sprache der Sklaven verwendete? Während der afrikanische Einfluss auf die englische Sprache damals ignoriert wurde, wird er heutzutage allgemein anerkannt und untersucht. [So] versuchen Sprachforscher beispielsweise herauszufinden, wo genau der afrikanische Ursprung des Wortes *jazz* liegt. Manche glauben, dass *jazz* von *Chaz* abstammt *(stem from)*, andere, dass es auf *chasse* zurückgeht. *Chaz* war der Spitzname eines afrikanischen Musikers und *chasse* ist der Name eines afrikanischen Tanzes.

"Professor Day, before you read us your paper on 'New ways of solving the country's increasing energy problems by sending special satellites into space which can orbit[3] the earth and transmit[4] energy to us from the sun', would you mind singing us a spiritual?"

[1] speech *Sprache, Sprechweise*
[2] linguistic [lɪŋ'gwɪstɪk] *sprachlich* [3] orbit ['ɔːbɪt] *umkreisen* [4] transmit [trænz'mɪt] *übertragen*

5 If their lives were different

→ Option 18: Conditional sentences

On pages 50-51 you read what Leon Brooks, Gail Rand and Linda Roberts had to say about their situations. *Try to imagine what their lives might have been like in very different circumstances. Here are some suggestions to help you:*

1. If … lived in Germany, he/she would … . 2. If … had/didn't have children, life would be … . 3. If … was/were white, he/she/they … . 4. If … had been born thirty years earlier, … . 5. If … had dropped out of high school, … . 6. If … had a different/no job, … .

6 German 'wollen'

a

1. Jenny **wants** another ice-cream.
2. I **want to** get better at English.
3. Tim offered to take Sue home, but she **didn't want to** go.
4. My mum expects me to play the piano, but I **don't want to.**

When the German verb 'wollen' expresses a wish or willingness, it is usually translated by *want (to)*. The *to* can only be left out if *want* is followed by a direct object (sentence 1).

⚠ Note that 'wollen' can be followed directly by an adverb phrase in German: Ich will heute ins Kino. Er will nach Hause. Ich will hier raus. The English translations need an additional verb: *I want to go to the cinema today. He wants to go home. I want to get out of here.*

5. I **would like to** ask you a question. — Ich will/möchte Ihnen eine Frage stellen.

It is often more polite to use *would like (to)* instead of *want (to)*, which can sound rather abrupt.

6. Do you **want me to tell** you the truth? — Willst du, dass ich dir die Wahrheit sage?
7. I **would like you to come back** tomorrow. — Ich möchte, dass du morgen zurückkommst.
8. The Millers **want their house (to be) painted.** — … wollen, dass ihr Haus gestrichen wird.

Although in German 'wollen' or 'mögen' can be followed by a 'dass'-clause, there is never a *that*-clause after *want* or *would like.* A construction with object + *to*-infinitive is used instead.
If, after an object, the infinitive is in the passive, *to be* is usually left out (sentence 8).

b

My grandparents **are going to** visit us soon. — Meine Großeltern wollen uns bald besuchen.

When 'wollen' expresses an intention or decision to do something, the *going to*-future is used in English.

c

We **would prefer to** go/**would rather** go by train. — Wir wollen/würden lieber mit dem Zug fahren.

The English for 'lieber wollen' is *would prefer to* or *would rather.*

d

1. Sarah just **won't** tell me why she's angry. — Sarah will mir einfach nicht sagen, warum …
2. Tom was late today. His car **wouldn't** start. — … sein Auto wollte nicht anspringen.

Both *won't* and *wouldn't* can sometimes be used as translations for 'nicht wollen', if the sentence expresses the idea that someone or something is/was unwilling or refuses/refused to do something.

e **In English, please**

1. Jeder will etwas von mir. 2. Papa will, dass meine Zensuren besser werden. 3. Meine Lehrerin will, dass ich meine Hausaufgaben mache. 4. Und dann Onkel Willi: „Wann willst du dir die Haare schneiden lassen?“ 5. Mama will, dass mein Zimmer aufgeräumt wird, und mein kleiner Bruder will ständig an meinen Computer. 6. Ich will aber lieber allein an meinem Computer sitzen. 7. Wenigstens meine große Schwester will bald nichts mehr von mir: Sie will nächste Woche ausziehen, weil sie jetzt eine eigene Wohnung hat. 8. Christine, das nette Mädchen aus meiner Klasse, will einfach nicht mit mir ins Kino gehen. 9. Falls sie mich jemals wieder fragen sollte, ob ich bereit bin, mit ihr Mathe zu üben *(do)*, werde ich ihr sagen: „Nein, ich will nicht.“

7 **Malcolm X** (Translation practice IV)

On November 18, 1992 a movie was released in the US on the life and death of the militant black civil rights leader, Malcolm X (1925-1965). Below is part of an article that appeared on the same day in the *Los Angeles Daily News*. The article has been adapted. *Translate it into German. Use an English-German dictionary to check any new words.*

A hero for the nineties

BOSTON In a Roxbury high school near the streets where Malcolm X spent his youth, the 11 teenagers in Steve Grace's history class sat straight and spellbound as the stark image of the African-American Muslim leader spoke from a television set at the front of the class.

The man in the thin tie and glasses was talking to 1960s Harlem about how drugs were destroying the community, how they were flown in by outsiders and how African-Americans needed to unite against the scourge – words that could as easily have been said of 1990s Roxbury.

The teenagers nodded their heads in agreement, then bombarded their teacher with questions and comments. "You look at him, and you see how good a man he was," Orlando Lang, one of the older members of the class said with sadness.

For Spike Lee, whose movie debuts today, Malcolm X may be a career-defining project. But to African-American urban teenagers whose daily routines include avoiding crack dealers and gangs, Malcom X is their folk hero, the resurrected spokesman for an angry generation. "He stood up to the white man and he had dignity doing it," said James Fuller, a third-year student at Fresno State University.

Annotations:

- stark: Careful – this is a 'false friend'. It doesn't mean 'stark' in German, but rather 'schlicht', 'ungeschminkt'.
- 1960s Harlem: This means 'people in Harlem in the 1960s'.
- were destroying: You need the subjunctive ('Konjunktiv') or a form with 'würde' in German to translate indirect speech like this.
- were flown: Indirect speech again.
- outsiders: This is another false friend. It doesn't mean 'Außenseiter', but 'people from outside (Harlem)'.
- needed: It's still indirect speech.
- as easily: This means 'equally', 'just as well'.
- their heads: You don't have to translate this.
- in agreement: Here you need an adverb in German.
- how good a man: Translate 'what a good man he was'.
- debuts: Find the German word for 'showing a new movie for the first time'.
- career-defining project: A project that will be important for his career.
- urban: You can't translate this with 'städtisch'.
- crack: The name of a drug. The same word is used in German, but it may be clearer to say 'Rauschgift' or 'Droge'.
- stood up to: *Stand up* doesn't mean 'aufstehen' here. *Stand up to sb* is a phrasal verb with a special meaning.
- doing it: Use a clause with a conjunction, or think of a freer translation of 'had dignity doing it'.
- third-year: You'll have to express this differently: use a phrase with a preposition.

→ Option 19: Grammar for recognition: special *that*-clauses

8 WORDS WORDS WORDS

a Trouble spot: Words which can easily be mixed up

Choose the correct word from the following pairs of words to complete the sentences.

> foreigner/stranger fault/mistake meaning/opinion boil/cook narrow/small
> murder/murderer check/control become/get grammar school/gym
> take place/sit down strict/strong pension/rent notes/notices

1. I'm sorry I can't tell you the way, I'm a ● here myself. 2. The accident was your own ●. 3. What's your ● of the new history teacher? 4. Didn't you know that water ● at 100 °C? 5. I'm afraid this street is too ● for our lorry. 6. The ● may be sent to the electric chair for his crime. 7. When we crossed the border, our passports were ●. 8. If we don't leave now, we won't ● our train. 9. 'Max-Planck-Gymnasium' is the name of the ● I go to. 10. Teachers who are too ● are usually not very popular. 11. Mrs Potter's ● is not enough to live on. 12. Anne gave a talk on Gandhi with the help of her ●.

Now form sentences with the words you haven't used.

b Trouble spot: Pronunciation

Odd one out. Which word has got a different vowel sound?

1. [ʌ] once – done – gone – worry – enough
2. [e] bed – said – threat – say – men
3. [ɜː] girl – heard – world – hurt – preferred – heart
4. [ʊ] push – butcher – foot – pull – front
5. [ɑː] chance – aunt – laugh – because
6. [ɒ] bottle – comb – watch – cough – cost

c WORD BUILDER'S CORNER *-ing* forms in compounds

Compound nouns from gerunds:

working + clothes → working clothes
gerund + noun → compound noun

Don't forget to bring your **working clothes**.
… eure **Arbeitskleidung** …

Compound adjectives from present participles:

hard + working → hard-working
adverb + participle → compound adjective

Hard-working people often suffer from stress.
Schwer arbeitende Menschen …

Make sensible compound nouns like 'closing time' from the following two word lists. (Some verbs go with more than one noun, and some nouns go with more than one verb.)

> (to) climb (to) close (to) drink (to) drive
> (to) listen (to) read (to) swim (to) train
> (to) wait (to) walk (to) wash (to) write

> boots camp comprehension licence
> machine paper pool room skills
> stick time water

Now invent funny things like 'drinking boots' and explain what they are or what you can use them for.

"I have a dream"

The struggle of black Americans for equal treatment in the 1950s and 1960s is known as the civil rights movement. In August 1963, about 250,000 people, blacks and whites together, took part in a 'March on Washington' to show their support for new civil rights laws.
In front of Washington's Lincoln Memorial (see page 39)*, Dr. Martin Luther King, Jr., a Baptist minister and perhaps the best-known black civil rights leader of the 20th century, delivered his now famous 'I have a dream' speech.*

- The following are quoted or referred to in the speech. What do you remember about them?
  - the Declaration of Independence
  - the Constitution of the US
  - the Emancipation Proclamation of 1863
- Now listen to the first part of King's speech. What does it sound like? How does it make you feel?

(The footnotes will help you to understand the text. If you need to, you can look up other words in a dictionary or in the Vocabulary on p.152.)

Dr. Martin Luther King (1929-1968)
What do you know about his life and death?

"Five score[1] years ago, a great American, in whose symbolic shadow we stand today, signed the Emancipation Proclamation. This momentous[2] decree came as a great beacon light of hope to millions of Negro slaves who had been seared[3] in the flames of withering[4] injustice. It came as a joyous daybreak to end the long night of their captivity[5].
But one hundred years later the Negro still is not free. One hundred years later, the life of the Negro is still sadly crippled[6] by the manacles[7] of segregation and the chains of discrimination. One hundred years later, the Negro lives on a lonely island of poverty in the midst of a vast ocean of material prosperity[8]. One hundred years later, the Negro is still languishing[9] in the corners of American society and finds himself an exile[10] in his own land. So we've come here today to dramatize a shameful condition.
In a sense we have come to our Nation's capital to cash a check. When the architects of our republic wrote the magnificent[11] words of the Constitution and the Declaration of Independence, they were signing a promissory note[12] to which every American was to fall heir[13]. This note was a promise that all men – yes, black men as well as white men – would be guaranteed 'the inalienable[14] rights of life, liberty, and the pursuit[15] of happiness'. …"

- Who is the 'great American' mentioned in l.1?
- Describe briefly what King says about the situation of black Americans in 1963.

[1] score [skɔː] *20* [2] momentous [mə'mentəs] *bedeutsam* [3] sear [sɪə] *verbrennen*
[4] withering ['wɪðərɪŋ] *ausdörrend, vernichtend* [5] captivity [kæp'tɪvətɪ] *Gefangenschaft* [6] cripple *verkrüppeln, lähmen*
[7] manacles ['mænəklz] *Fesseln* [8] prosperity [prɒ'sperətɪ] *Wohlstand* [9] languish ['læŋgwɪʃ] *dahinschmachten*
[10] exile ['eksaɪl] *Verbannte(r)* [11] magnificent [mæg'nɪfɪsnt] *wunderbar* [12] promissory note *Schuldschein*
[13] fall heir to [eə] *das Erbe antreten von* [14] inalienable [ɪn'eɪlɪənəbl] *unveräußerlich*
[15] pursuit of [pə'sjuːt] *Streben, Trachten nach*

Now read or listen to the end of the speech.
Make a list of the places Martin Luther King mentions. Find them on a map of the USA and define the geographical area of oppression according to King.

"I have a dream that one day little black boys and black girls will be able to join hands with little white boys and white girls."

"... Go back to Mississippi. Go back to Alabama. Go back to South Carolina. Go back to Georgia. Go back to Louisiana. Go back to the slums and ghettos of our northern cities, knowing that somehow this situation can and will be changed. Let us not wallow[1] in the valley of despair[2].

I say to you today, my friends – so even though we face the difficulties of today and tomorrow, I still have a dream. It is a dream deeply rooted[3] in the American dream. I have a dream that one day this nation will rise up and live out the true meaning of its creed[4]: 'we hold these truths to be self-evident[5], that all men are created equal'.

I have a dream that one day on the red hills of Georgia, the sons of former slaves and the sons of former slave-owners will be able to sit down together at the table of brotherhood. I have a dream that one day, even the state of Mississippi, a state sweltering[6] with the heat of injustice, sweltering with the heat of oppression, will be transformed into an oasis of freedom and justice. I have a dream that my four little children will one day live in a nation where they will not be judged by the color of their skin but by the content of their character. I have a dream today!

I have a dream that one day, down in Alabama – with its vicious[7] racists, with its governor having his lips dripping[8] with the words of interposition[9] and nullification[9] – one day right there in Alabama, little black boys and black girls will be able to join hands with little white boys and white girls as sisters and brothers. I have a dream today!

I have a dream that one day 'every valley shall be exalted[10], every hill and mountain shall be made low, the rough places will be made plain[11], and the crooked[12] places will be made straight and the glory of the Lord shall be revealed[13] and all flesh shall see it together'.

King says that his own dream is "deeply rooted in the American dream" (ll.10-11). Can you explain this? Remember what the 'American dream' means to Americans.

[1] wallow ['wɒləʊ] *sich suhlen* [2] despair [dɪ'speə] *Verzweiflung* [3] rooted ['ru:tɪd] *verwurzelt* [4] creed [kri:d] *Glaubensbekenntnis* [5] self-evident ['evɪdənt] *offenkundig* [6] swelter *vor Hitze vergehen* [7] vicious ['vɪʃəs] *böse* [8] drip, -pp- *triefen* [9] interposition and nullification [ˌɪntəpə'zɪʃn, ˌnʌlɪfɪ'keɪʃn] = *Einspruch gegen die Anwendung bestimmter Bundesgesetze* [10] exalt [ɪg'zɔ:lt] *erhöhen* [11] plain *eben* [12] crooked ['krʊkɪd] *hügelig* [13] reveal [rə'vi:l] *offenbaren*

This is our hope. This is the faith that I go back to the South with. With this faith we will be able to hew[1] out of the mountain of despair a stone of hope. With this faith we will be able to transform the jangling discords[2] of our nation into a beautiful symphony of brotherhood.
With this faith we will be able to work together, to pray together, to struggle together, to go to jail[3] together, to stand up for freedom together, knowing that we will be free one day. This will be the day when all of God's children will be able to sing with new meaning: 'My country, 'tis of thee, sweet land of liberty, of thee I sing; land where my fathers died, land of the pilgrim's pride; from every mountainside, let freedom ring' – and if America is to be a great nation this must become true.
So let freedom ring from the prodigious[4] hilltops of New Hampshire. Let freedom ring from the mighty mountains of New York. Let freedom ring from the heightening Alleghenies of Pennsylvania. Let freedom ring from the snow-capped Rockies of Colorado. Let freedom ring from the curvacious[5] slopes of California.
But not only that. Let freedom ring from Stone Mountain of Georgia. Let freedom ring from Lookout Mountain of Tennessee. Let freedom ring from every hill and molehill[6] of Mississippi, from every mountainside, let freedom ring.
And when this happens, when we allow freedom to ring, when we let it ring from every village and every hamlet[7], from every state and every city, we will be able to speed up that day when all of God's children – black men and white men, Jews and Gentiles[8], Protestants and Catholics – will be able to join hands and to sing in the words of the old Negro spiritual: Free at last, free at last; thank God Almighty, we are free at last."

Working with the text

a Understanding the text

1. Very briefly, describe Martin Luther King's 'dream'.
2. Match the four quotations marked by ' ' in the text to these sources:
   - the Bible,
   - a patriotic poem written in 1831,
   - the Declaration of Independence (2×).
3. Collect examples of images in the speech that are negative, e.g. 'the flames of withering injustice' (p. 59, l. 6), and examples of positive images, e.g. 'beacon light of hope' (p. 59, ll. 4-5).
4. Why do you think King finishes his speech with a quotation from a Negro spiritual?

b 'I have a dream' as a political speech

1. How does Martin Luther King deliver his speech? Think about the way he uses speed, volume, pauses, emphasis and rhythm.
2. Find examples on page 59 of how King appeals to the patriotic feelings of Americans.
3. Where and why does King refer to great Americans from the past?
4. Why does King use quotations in his speech?
5. Although King says '*I* have a dream', he also uses plural forms, e.g. '*we*'ve come' (p. 59, l. 18), '*our* hope' (p. 61, l. 1). Why?
6. Why does King use repetition in his speech? Find examples.
7. What is the effect on the listener of King's use of imagery? Which metaphors and similes do you find most powerful?

→ Option 12: Literary terms and their collocations

[1] hew [hjuː] *hauen* [2] jangling discords [ˌdʒæŋglɪŋ ˈdɪskɔːdz] *schrille Missklänge* [3] jail [dʒeɪl] *Gefängnis*
[4] prodigious [prəˈdɪdʒəs] *gewaltig* [5] curvacious [kɜːˈveɪʃəs] *geschwungen* [6] molehill *Maulwurfshügel*
[7] hamlet *Weiler* [8] Gentile [ˈdʒentaɪl] *Heide/Heidin, Nichtjude/-jüdin*

Unit 5: The world of literature[+]

Dreams

Hold fast[1] to dreams
For if dreams die
Life is a broken-winged[2] bird
That cannot fly.

Hold fast to dreams
For when dreams go
Life is a barren[3] field
Frozen with snow.

Langston Hughes

DREAM

1 a sequence[4] of scenes and feelings happening in the mind[5] during sleep
2 a state of mind in which the things happening around one do not seem real
3 an ambition[6] or ideal

(adapted from the *Oxford Advanced Learner's Dictionary*)

DREAMS

Everybody has dreams; whether or not the dream is remembered depends on how quickly after it the sleeper wakes up. The new combinations of ideas produced in dreams can be creative and valuable.

(adapted from the *New Webster's Universal Encyclopedia*)

DAYDREAMS

Some psychologists believe that daydreams are a kind of wishful thinking[7] that happens when inner needs cannot be expressed in real behavior. We daydream, they claim, when the world outside us does not meet our needs, or when we are motivated to do something but cannot achieve our goal[8].

(adapted from *Psychology* by Charles G. Morris)

[+] Not all the new words in this Unit are explained, but you should be able to understand the texts. Only the key words are explained at the foot of the page. The new words in the questions can be found in the

[1] hold fast to *festhalten an* [2] wing [wɪŋ] *Flügel* [3] barren ['bærən] *öde, leer, unfruchtbar*

[4] sequence ['siːkwəns] *Reihe, Folge* [5] mind *Geist, Verstand, Gehirn* [6] ambition [æm'bɪʃn] *Wunsch, Ziel*
[7] wishful thinking *Wunschdenken* [8] goal [gəʊl] *Ziel*

Look at the picture on these two pages for a few moments and then, slowly, read the poem[+].

Why do you think this particular picture was chosen to go with the poem?
Who could the speaker in this poem be? Who might she/he be addressing?
What might a possible situation be, quite concretely, in which she/he is saying this?

When I look at the picture, I think .../feel .../have the impression ...; and when I read the poem, I ... .
The speaker could be ... or ... . She/He might be addressing .../Perhaps she/he is addressing ...
I could imagine a situation ...; or maybe ...

Try to read the poem aloud to yourself several times, and then read it to the class.
Listen to different pupils and compare the effect different readings have on you.
What do you think is the function of the repetition in the two stanzas?

I feel the way Y read the poem fits the spirit of the poem very well because .../doesn't fit so well because ... .
Somehow it seems that through the repetition ... .
Langston Hughes might want to stress/show ... .

Look again at the poem and find out what exactly the differences are between the two verses. Pay particular attention to Langston Hughes' choice of words and the central image in each verse.

The first difference is ...; secondly, L. Hughes chose to write ... in the first verse and ... in the second verse.
The image in lines three and four ... . If you compare what the images mean, you could say ...

Looking at the complete poem, what do you think dreams and dreaming mean to different people?
Langston Hughes (1902-67) was a black American. What do you think dreams and dreaming meant to him?
Why does/doesn't the poem appeal to you?

Read the information about dreams and dreaming in the three texts on the left. It might help you when you are talking about the following four texts on pages 64-73.

Vocabulary on pages 153-154.

[+]Words underlined in this Unit are listed and explained in Option 12 (Literary terms and their collocations).

- What do moths normally do when there is a light? What happens to them quite often?
- Look at the illustration. Why does this moth seem to be different from the 'average moth'?
- Read the fable and find out about this moth's life.

The moth and the star

A young and impressionable[1] moth once set[2] his heart on a certain star. He told his mother about this and she counselled him to set his heart on a bridge lamp instead. "Stars aren't the thing to hang around," she said; "Lamps are the thing to hang around." "You get somewhere[3] that way," said the moth's father. "You don't get anywhere chasing stars." But the moth would not heed[4] the words of either parent. Every evening at dusk when the star came out he would start flying toward it and every morning at dawn he would crawl[5] back home worn out with his vain endeavour[6]. One day his father said to him, "You haven't burned a wing in months, boy, and it looks to me as if you were never going to. All your brothers have been badly burned flying around street lamps and all your sisters have been terribly singed[7] flying around house lamps. Come on, now, get out of here and get yourself scorched[8]! A big strapping moth like you without a mark[9] on him!"

The moth left his father's house, but he would not fly around street lamps and he would not fly around house lamps. He went right on trying to reach the star, which was four and one-third light years, or twenty-five trillion miles, away. The moth thought it was just caught in the top branches[10] of an elm[11]. He never did reach the star, but he went right on trying, night after night, and when he was a very, very old moth he began to think that he really had reached the star and went around saying so. This gave him a deep and lasting pleasure, and he lived to a great old age. His parents and his brothers and his sisters had all been burned to death when they were quite young.

Moral: Who flies afar[12] from the sphere[13] of our sorrow[14] is here today and here tomorrow[15].

James Thurber

Working with the text

1. Describe and explain Thurber's illustration. → The illustration shows … At the bottom …
2. What seem to be the 'unwritten laws' to live by in 'moth country'? → If you look at what the mother/father says, one such 'unwritten law' could be …
3. Say how the author characterizes the moth
   – in his younger years,
   – in his later years.
   → In his younger years the moth … Later on … And as the years go by …
4. The star, the street lamps, etc. have 'symbolic qualities': What might they suggest to different readers? → To one reader the star/the … might stand for … … suggests that …
5. Read the moral and say what Thurber thought of the moth's dream. → The moral reveals that Thurber most likely …

---

6. Was the moth's dream worth dreaming?

Useful phrases (see arrows above)

[1] impressionable *leicht zu beeindrucken* [2] set one's heart on – set – set *sein Herz hängen an* [3] get somewhere (infml) *Fortschritte machen* [4] heed *beachten* [5] crawl [krɔːl] *kriechen* [6] vain endeavour [ɪn'devə] (fml) *vergebliche Anstrengung* [7] singe [sɪndʒ] *versengen, ansengen* [8] scorch [skɔːtʃ] *versengen* [9] mark *Markierung, Mal* [10] branch [brɑːntʃ] *Zweig* [11] elm *Ulme* [12] afar [ə'fɑː] *weit (weg)* [13] sphere [sfɪə] [14] sorrow *Kummer, Leid* [15] *eine Abwandlung der Redensart* 'here today and gone tomorrow' *(= von kurzer Dauer)*

→ Option 6: Robert Frost: Poems

Look at the illustration that goes with the following short story. Look at the faces of the two men and at the way they are dressed.

- Who could the men be?
- What might they be talking about?
- Why do you think the younger man is not looking at the older man?

The winner

Wordman stood at the window, looking out, and saw Revell walk away from the compound[1]. "Come here," he said to the interviewer. "You'll see the Guardian[2] in action."

The interviewer came around the desk and stood beside Wordman at the window. He said, "That's one of them?"

"Right." Wordman smiled, feeling pleasure. "You're lucky," he said. "It's rare when one of them even makes the attempt. Maybe he's doing it for your benefit[3]."

The interviewer looked troubled[4]. He said, "Doesn't he know what it will do?"

"Of course. Some of them don't believe it, not till they've tried it once. Watch."

They both watched. Revell walked without apparent[5] haste[6], directly across the field toward the woods on the other side. After he'd gone about 200 yards from the edge of the compound he began to bend[7] forward slightly at the middle, and a few yards farther on he folded his arms across his stomach as though[8] it ached him. He tottered[9], but kept moving forward, staggering[10] more and more, appearing to be in great pain. He managed[11] to stay on his feet nearly all the way to the trees, but finally crumpled to the ground, where he lay unmoving.

Wordman no longer felt pleasure. He liked the theory of the Guardian better than its application. Turning to his desk, he called the infirmary[12] and said, "Send a stretcher[13] out to the east, near the woods. Revell's out there."

The interviewer turned at the sound of the name, saying, "Revell? Is that who that is? The poet?"

"If you can call it poetry." Wordman's lips curled in disgust[14]. He'd read some of Revell's so-called poems; garbage[15], garbage.

The interviewer looked back out the window. "I'd heard he was arrested," he said thoughtfully.

Looking over the interviewer's shoulder, Wordman saw that Revell had managed to get back up onto hands and knees, was now crawling slowly and painfully toward the woods. But a stretcher team was already trotting toward him and Wordman watched as they reached him, picked up the pain-weakened body, strapped it to the stretcher, and carried it back to the compound.

As they moved out of sight, the interviewer said, "Will he be all right?"

"After a few days in the infirmary. He'll have strained[16] some muscles."

The interviewer turned away from the window. "That was very graphic," he said carefully.

"You're the first outsider to see it," Wordman told him, and smiled, feeling good again. "What do they call that? A scoop[17]?"

[1] compound ['--] *Gefängnishof* [2] Guardian ['gɑːdɪən] *Wächter/in* [3] for your benefit *Ihretwegen* [4] troubled *beunruhigt*
[5] apparent [ə'pærənt] *offensichtlich* [6] haste [heɪst] *Eile* [7] bend – bent – bent *(sich) krümmen* [8] as though *als ob*
[9] totter *wanken* [10] stagger *taumeln* [11] manage to do sth *es schaffen, etwas zu tun*
[12] infirmary [-'---] *Krankenstation* [13] stretcher *Bahre, Trage* [14] disgust [-'-] *Empörung, Abscheu*
[15] garbage ['gɑːbɪdʒ] (infml) *Schund, Mist* [16] strain *zerren* [17] scoop *sensationelle Erstmeldung*

"Yes," agreed the interviewer, sitting back down in his chair. "A scoop."

They returned to the interview, just the most recent of dozens Wordman had given in the year since this pilot project of the Guardian had been set up. For perhaps the fiftieth time he explained what the Guardian did and how it was of value to society. The essence of the Guardian was the miniature black box, actually a tiny[1] radio receiver, which was surgically inserted[2] into the body of every prisoner. In the center of this prison compound was the Guardian transmitter[3], perpetually[4] sending its message to these receivers. As long as a prisoner stayed within the hundred-and-fifty-yard range[5] of that transmitter, all was well. Should he move beyond that range, the black box inside his skin[6] would begin to send messages of pain throughout his nervous system. This pain increased as the prisoner moved farther from the transmitter, until at its peak[7] it was totally immobilizing.

"The prisoner can't hide, you see," Wordman explained. "Even if Revell had reached the woods, we'd have found him. His screams would have led us to him."

The Guardian had been initially[8] suggested by Wordman himself, at that time serving as assistant warden[9] at a more ordinary penitentiary[10] in the Federal system. Objections[11], mostly from sentimentalists, had delayed its acceptance for several years, but now at last this pilot project had been established, with a guaranteed five-year trial[12] period, and Wordman had been placed in charge[13].

"If the results are as good as I'm sure they will be," Wordman said, "all prisons in the Federal system will be converted to the Guardian method."

The Guardian method had made jailbreaks[14] impossible, riots easy to quell[15] – by merely turning off the transmitter for a minute or two – and prisons simplicity[16] to guard. "We have no guards here as such," Wordman pointed out[17]. "Service employees only are needed here, people for the mess hall[18], infirmary and so on."

For the pilot project, prisoners were only those who had committed crimes against the State rather than against individuals. "You might say," Wordman said, smiling, "that here are gathered the Disloyal[19] Opposition."

"You mean, political prisoners," suggested the interviewer.

"We don't like that phrase here," Wordman said, his manner[20] suddenly icy. "It sounds Commie[21]."

The interviewer apologized for his sloppy use of terminology, ended the interview shortly afterward, and Wordman, once again in a good mood, escorted him out of the building. "You see," he said, gesturing. "No walls. No machine guns in towers. Here at last is the model prison."

The interviewer thanked him again for his time, and went away to his car. Wordman watched him leave, then went over to the infirmary to see Revell. But he'd been given a shot[22], and was already asleep.

Revell lay flat on his back and stared at the ceiling. He kept thinking, over and over again, "I didn't know it would be as bad as that. I didn't know it would be as bad as that." Mentally, he took a big brush of black paint and wrote the words on the spotless white ceiling: *"I didn't know it would be as bad as that."*

"Revell."

He turned his head slightly and saw Wordman standing beside the bed. He watched Wordman, but made no sign.

Wordman said, "They told me you were awake."

Revell waited.

"I tried to tell you when you first came," Wordman reminded him. "I told you there was no point[23] trying to get away."

Revell opened his mouth and said, "It's all right, don't feel bad. You do what you have to do, I do what I have to do."

"Don't *feel* bad!" Wordman stared at him. "What have *I* got to feel bad about?"

Revell looked up at the ceiling, and the words he had painted there just a minute ago were gone already. He wished he had paper and pencil. Words were leaking out of him like water

[1] tiny ['taɪnɪ] *winzig* [2] surgically inserted [ˌsɜːdʒɪklɪ‿ɪn'sɜːtɪd] *operativ eingesetzt* [3] transmitter *Sender*
[4] perpetual [pə'petʃʊəl] *fortwährend* [5] range *Reichweite* [6] skin *Haut* [7] peak *Höhepunkt, Gipfel* [8] initial [ɪ'nɪʃl] *anfänglich*
[9] warden (AE) *Gefängnisdirektor/in* [10] penitentiary [ˌ--'---] (AE) *Gefängnis* [11] objection [-'--] *Einwand*
[12] trial ['traɪəl] *Erprobungs-* [13] place sb in charge *jm die Leitung übertragen* [14] jailbreak *Gefängnisausbruch*
[15] quell *(Aufstand) unterdrücken* [16] simplicity [-'---] (infml) *hier: die einfachste Sache der Welt*
[17] point out *klarmachen* [18] mess hall *Speisesaal* [19] disloyal [dɪs'lɔɪəl] *illoyal* [20] manner *Art, Auftreten*
[21] commie (infml) *kommunistisch* [22] shot (infml) *Spritze, Injektion* [23] no point *sinnlos*

through a sieve[1]. He needed paper and pencil to catch them in. He said, "May I have paper and pencil?"
"To write more obscenity? Of course not."
"Of course not," echoed Revell. He closed his eyes and watched the words leaking away. A man doesn't have time both to invent and memorize, he has to choose, and long ago Revell had chosen invention. But now there was no way to put the inventions down on paper and they trickled[2] through his mind like water and eroded away into the great outside world. "Twinkle, twinkle, little pain," Revell said softly[3], "in my groin[4] and in my brain[5], down so low and up so high, will you live or will I die?"
"The pain goes away," said Wordman. "It's been three days. It should be gone already."
"It will come back," Revell said. He opened his eyes and wrote the words on the ceiling.
"It will come back."
Wordman said, "Don't be silly. It's gone for good, unless you run away again."
Revell was silent.
Wordman waited, half-smiling, and then frowned[6]. "You aren't," he said.
Revell looked at him in some surprise. "Of course I am," he said. "Didn't you know I would?"
"No one tries it twice."
"I'll never stop leaving. Don't you know that? I'll never stop leaving. I'll never stop being, I'll not stop believing I'm who I must be. You had to know that."
Wordman stared at him. "You'll go through it *again*?"
"Ever and ever," Revell said.
"It's a bluff." Wordman pointed an angry finger at Revell, saying, "If you want to die, I'll let you die. Do you know if we don't bring you back you'll die out there?"
"That's escape, too," Revell said.
"Is that what you want? All right. Go out there again, and I won't send anyone after you, that's a promise."
"Then you lose," Revell said. He looked at Wordman finally seeing the blunt, angry face. "They're your rules," Revell told him, "and by your own rules you're going to lose. You say your black box will make me stay, and that means the black box will make me stop being me. I say you're wrong. I say as long as I'm leaving you're losing, and if the black box kills me you've lost forever."
Spreading his arms, Wordman shouted, "Do you think this is a *game*?"
"Of course," Revell said. "That's why you invented it."
"You're insane[7]," Wordman said. He started for the door. "You shouldn't be here, you should be in an asylum[8]."
"That's losing, too," Revell shouted after him, but Wordman had slammed the door and gone.
Revell lay back on the pillow. Alone again, he could dwell[9] once more on his terrors. He was afraid of the black box, much more now that he knew what it could do to him, afraid to the point where his fear made him sick to his stomach, but he was afraid of losing himself, too, this a more abstract and intellectual fear but just as strong. No, it was even stronger, because it was driving him to go out again. "But I didn't know it would be as bad as that," he whispered. He painted it once more on the ceiling, this time in red.

Wordman had been told when Revell would be released[10] from the infirmary, and he made a point[11] of being at the door when Revell came out. Revell seemed somewhat leaner[12], perhaps a little older. He shielded his eyes from the sun with his hand, looked at Wordman, and said, "Good-bye, Wordman." He started walking east.
Wordman didn't believe it. He said, "You're bluffing, Revell."
Revell kept walking.
Wordman couldn't remember when he'd ever felt such anger. He wanted to run after Revell and kill him with his bare hands. He clenched his hands into fists and told himself he was a reasonable man, a rational man, a merciful[13] man. As the Guardian was reasonable, was rational, was merciful. It required only obedience[14], and so did he. It punished only such purposeless defiance[15] as Revell's, and so did he. Revell was antisocial, self-destructive, he had to learn. For his own sake, as well as for the sake of society, Revell had to be taught.

[1] sieve [sɪv] *Sieb* [2] trickle *tröpfeln, rieseln* [3] soft *leise* [4] groin *Leiste(ngegend)* [5] brain *Gehirn*
[6] frown *die Stirn runzeln* [7] insane *wahnsinnig* [8] asylum [ə'saɪləm] (veraltet) *Irrenanstalt* [9] dwell on *nachdenken über*
[10] release (from) *entlassen (aus)* [11] make a point of doing sth *Wert darauf legen, etwas zu tun* [12] lean *mager*
[13] merciful *barmherzig* [14] obedience [ə'biːdɪəns] *Gehorsam* [15] defiance [dɪ'faɪəns] *Trotz, Widerstand*

Wordman shouted, "What are you trying to *get* out of this?" He glared[1] at Revell's moving back, listened to Revell's silence. He shouted, "I won't send anyone after you! You'll crawl back *yourself*!"

He kept watching until Revell was far out from the compound, staggering across the field toward the trees, his arms folded across his stomach, his legs stumbling[2], his head bent forward. Wordman watched, and then gritted his teeth, and turned his back, and returned to his office to work on the monthly report. Only two attempted escapes last month.

Two or three times in the course[3] of the afternoon he looked out the window. The first time, he saw Revell far across the field, on hands and knees, crawling toward the trees. The last time, Revell was out of sight, but he could be heard screaming. Wordman had a great deal of trouble concentrating his attention on the report.

Toward evening he went outside again. Revell's screams sounded from the woods, faint but continuous. Wordman stood listening, his fists clenching and relaxing at his sides. Grimly he forced himself not to feel pity[4]. For Revell's own good he had to be taught.

A staff doctor came to him a while later and said, "Mr Wordman, we've got to bring him in."

Wordman nodded. "I know. But I want to be sure he's learned."

"For God's sake," said the doctor, "*listen* to him."

Wordman looked bleak. "All right, bring him in." As the doctor started away, the screaming stopped. Wordman and the doctor both turned their heads, listened – silence. The doctor ran for the infirmary.

Revell lay screaming. All he could think of was the pain, and the need to scream. But sometimes, when he managed a scream of the very loudest, it was possible for him to have a fraction of a second for himself, and in those fractions of seconds he still kept moving away from the prison, inching[5] along the ground, so that in the last hour he had moved approximately[6] seven feet. His head and right arm were now visible[7] from the country road that passed through these woods.

On one level, he was conscious[8] of nothing but the pain and his own screaming. On another level, he was totally, even insistently, aware of everything around him, the blades of grass near his eyes, the stillness of the woods, the tree branches high overhead. And the small pickup truck, when it stopped on the road beyond him.

The man who came from the truck and squatted beside Revell had a lined and weathered face and the rough clothing of a farmer. He touched Revell's shoulder and said, "You hurt, fella?"

"Eeeeast!" screamed Revell. "Eeeeast!"

"Is it okay to move you?" asked the man.

"Yesssss!" shrieked Revell. "Eeeeast!"

"I'd best take you to a doctor."

There was no change in the pain when the man lifted him and carried him to the truck and lay him down on the floor in back. He was already at optimum distance from the transmitter; the pain now was as bad as it could get.

The farmer tucked[9] a rolled-up wad of cloth into Revell's open mouth. "Bite on this," he said. "It'll make it easier."

It made nothing easier, but it muffled[10] his screams. He was grateful[11] for that; the screams embarrassed[12] him.

He was aware of it all, the drive through increasing darkness, the farmer carrying him into a building that was of colonial design on the outside but looked like the infirmary on the inside, and a doctor who looked down at him and touched his forehead and then went to one side to thank the farmer for bringing him. They spoke briefly over there, and then the farmer went away and the doctor came back to look at Revell again. He was young, dressed in laboratory white, with a pudgy face and red hair. He seemed sick and angry. He said, "You're from that prison, aren't you?"

Revell was still screaming through the cloth. He managed a head-spasm[13] which he meant to be a nod. His armpits felt as though they were being cut open with knives of ice. The sides of his neck were being scraped by sandpaper. All of his joints[14] were being ground back and forth, back and forth, the way a man at dinner separates the bones of a chicken wing. The interior of his stomach was full of acid. His body was stuck

[1] glare at *wütend anstarren* [2] stumble *stolpern* [3] in the course of *im Laufe von* [4] pity *Mitleid*
[5] inch *sich zentimeterweise (vorwärts) bewegen* [6] approximately [-'----] *ungefähr* [7] visible *sichtbar*
[8] be conscious of sth ['kɒnʃəs] *sich einer Sache bewusst sein* [9] tuck *stecken* [10] muffle ['mʌfl] *dämpfen*
[11] grateful *dankbar* [12] embarrass sb *jm peinlich sein* [13] spasm *Zuckung* [14] joint *Gelenk*

with needles[1], sprayed with fire. His skin was being peeled off[2], his nerves cut with razor blades, his muscles pounded with hammers. Thumbs were pushing his eyes out from inside his head. And yet, the genius[3] of this pain, the brilliance[4] that had gone into its construction, it permitted his mind to work, to remain constantly aware. There was no unconsciousness for him, no oblivion[5].

The doctor said, "What beasts[6] some men are. I'll try to get it out of you. I don't know what will happen, we aren't supposed to know how it works, but I'll try to take the box out of you."

He went away, and came back with a needle. "Here. This will put you to sleep."

"Ahhhhh."

"He isn't there. He just isn't anywhere in the woods."

Wordman glared at the doctor, but knew he had to accept what the man reported. "All right," he said.

"Someone took him away. He had a confederate out there, someone who helped him get away."

"No one would dare[7]," said the doctor. "Anyone who helped him would wind up[8] here themselves."

"Nevertheless," said Wordman. "I'll call the State Police," he said, and went on into his office.

Two hours later the State Police called back. They'd checked the normal users of that road, local people who might have seen or heard something, and had found a farmer who'd picked up an injured man near the prison and taken him to a Dr Allyn in Boonetown. The State Police were convinced the farmer had acted innocently.

"But not the doctor," Wordman said grimly. "He'd have to know the truth almost immediately."

"Yes, sir, I should think so."

"And he hasn't reported Revell."

"No, sir."

"Have you gone to pick him up yet?"

"Not yet. We just got the report."

"I'll want to come with you. Wait for me."

"Yes, sir."

Wordman traveled in the ambulance in which they'd bring Revell back. They arrived without siren at Dr Allyn's with two cars of state troopers, marched into the tiny operating room, and found Allyn washing instruments at the sink. Allyn looked at them all calmly and said, "I thought you might be along."

Wordman pointed at the man who lay, unconscious, on the table in the middle of the room. "There's Revell," he said.

Allyn glanced at the operating table in surprise. "Revell? The poet?"

"You didn't know? Then why help him?"

Instead of answering, Allyn studied his face and said, "Would you be Wordman himself?"

Wordman said, "Yes, I am."

"Then I believe this is yours," Allyn said, and put into Wordman's hands a small and bloody black box.

The ceiling was persistently bare[9]. Revell's eyes wrote on it words that should have singed the paint away, but nothing ever happened. He shut his eyes against the white at last and wrote in spidery letters on the inside of his lids the single word *oblivion*. He heard someone come into the room, but the effort[10] of making a change was so great that for a moment longer he permitted his eyes to remain closed. When he did open them he saw Wordman there, standing grim and mundane at the foot of the bed.

Wordman said, "How are you, Revell?"

"I was thinking about oblivion," Revell told him. "Writing a poem on the subject." He looked up at the ceiling, but it was empty.

Wordman said, "You asked, one time, you asked for pencil and paper. We've decided you can have them."

Revell looked at him in sudden hope, but then understood, "Oh," he said. "Oh, *that*."

Wordman frowned and said, "What's wrong? I said you can have pencil and paper."

"If I promise not to leave any more."

Wordman's hands gripped the foot of the bed. He said, "What's the matter with you? You can't get away, you have to know that by now."

"You mean I can't win. But I won't lose. It's your game, your rules, your home ground, your equipment; if I can manage a stalemate[11], that's pretty good."

1 needle *Nadel* 2 peel off *abschälen* 3 genius ['dʒiːnɪəs] *geniale Schöpferkraft* 4 brilliance ['brɪljəns] *Genialität* 5 oblivion [ə'blɪvɪən] *Vergessen* 6 beast *Bestie* 7 dare *(es) wagen* 8 wind up (at a place) [waɪnd] – wound [waʊnd] – wound (infml) *(irgendwo) enden, „landen“* 9 bare *kahl* 10 effort ['efət] *Anstrengung* 11 stalemate *Patt, Remis*

Wordman said, "You still think it's a game. You think none of it matters. Do you want to see what you've done?" He stepped back to the door, opened it, made a motion, and Dr Allyn was led in. Wordman said to Revell, "You remember this man?"
"I remember," said Revell.
Wordman said, "He just arrived. They'll be putting the Guardian in him in about an hour. Does it make you proud, Revell?"
Looking at Allyn, Revell said, "I'm sorry."
Allyn smiled and shook his head. "Don't be. I had the idea the publicity of a trial might help rid[1] the world of things like the Guardian." His smile turned sour. "There wasn't very much publicity."
Wordman said, "You two are cut out of the same cloth. The emotions of the mob, that's all you can think of. Revell in those so-called poems of his, and you in that speech you made in court."
Revell, smiling, said, "Oh? You made a speech? I'm sorry I didn't get to hear it."
"It wasn't very good," Allyn said. "I hadn't known the trial would only be one day long, so I didn't have much time to prepare it."
Wordman said, "All right, that's enough. You two can talk later, you'll have years."
At the door Allyn turned back and said, "Don't go anywhere till I'm up and around[2], will you? After my operation."
Revell said, "You want to come along next time?"
"Naturally," said Allyn.

Donald E. Westlake

Working with the text

1. Collect what we are told about
   - the main characters and the motives for their behavior,
     → … seem to be the main characters because … On page xx, in line xx, for example, he says …
   - the setting,
     → The action takes place … (and covers a time of about …). We are/are not told in detail what … looks like. But I imagine …
   - the action.
     → The story starts with … The reader learns about/is told … It continues with … This is followed by a (short/longer) passage about …

   Note: Not all important information is expressed explicitly. You will have to infer some information from the context.

2. Try to write down in two or three sentences what you believe is the theme of the story. Compare different answers and decide together on one short text.
   → The story deals with …
3. What has this story got to do with the topic 'Dreams and reality'?
4. How far do you think this story is relevant today?
5. Some suggestions for speculation and for creative writing:
   - What do you think the state is like where the story takes place?
   - Describe the crime which you think Revell must have committed.
   - Write the interviewer's report for a sensational or a serious magazine.
   - Write the speech Dr Allyn made during the trial and present it to the class.
6. Look at the fable on page 64 and this short story. Is it worth 'holding fast to dreams' (p. 62)?

Useful phrases

[1] rid of, -dd- *befreien von* [2] be up and around *wieder auf den Beinen sein*

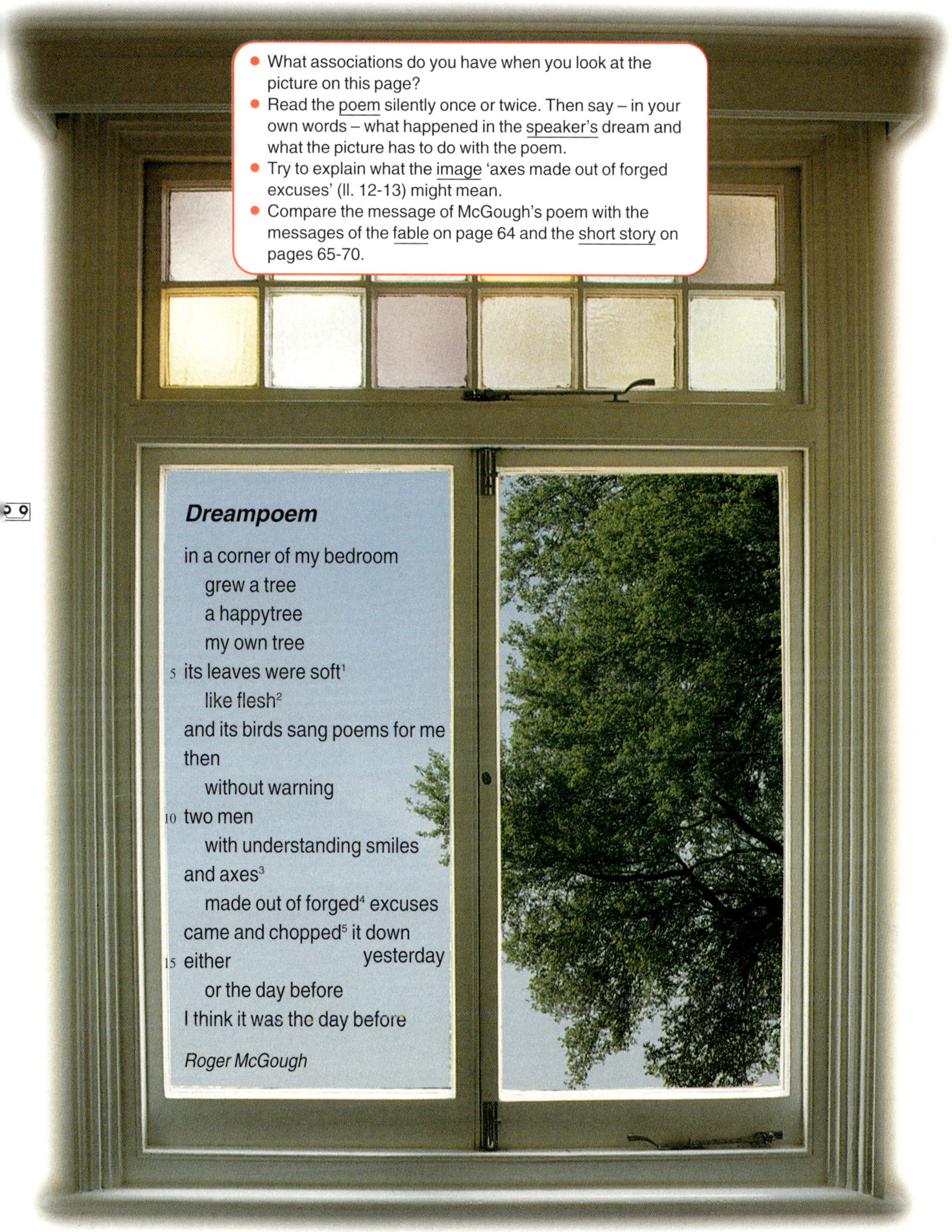

- What associations do you have when you look at the picture on this page?
- Read the poem silently once or twice. Then say – in your own words – what happened in the speaker's dream and what the picture has to do with the poem.
- Try to explain what the image 'axes made out of forged excuses' (ll. 12-13) might mean.
- Compare the message of McGough's poem with the messages of the fable on page 64 and the short story on pages 65-70.

Dreampoem

in a corner of my bedroom
grew a tree
a happytree
my own tree
its leaves were soft[1]
like flesh[2]
and its birds sang poems for me
then
without warning
two men
with understanding smiles
and axes[3]
made out of forged[4] excuses
came and chopped[5] it down
either yesterday
or the day before
I think it was the day before

Roger McGough

[1] soft *weich* [2] flesh *(lebendiges) Fleisch* [3] axe [æks] *Axt, Beil* [4] forge [fɔːdʒ] *schmieden, fälschen*
[5] chop down, -pp- *fällen*

Dreams and reality – an excerpt from a novel

The following text is an excerpt from the novel Key to the Door *by Alan Sillitoe, who was born in Nottingham in 1928. Sillitoe left school at the age of 14 to work in a bike factory. He once said that he started reading serious literature only after the age of 18 while he was in hospital for several months.*
The novel deals with the first 21 years in the life of Brian Seaton. The first part of the novel describes Brian's life as a working-class boy in Nottingham in the 1930s, a time of mass unemployment and great poverty. As Brian's father is unemployed, the Seaton family lives in extreme poverty.

Hidden worlds

A large atlas was opened at a map of the world, surrounded by dictionaries and foreign language books – the only section of the shop that interested him. He went in, and told a brown-dressed girl by the cash-desk[1] that he wanted to buy *The Count[2] of Monte Cristo*, started to explain the simple financial system into which he had entered.
She left him standing with four pink receipts[3] and the final sixpence, and came back with the manager. "I know him," he said. "He's a customer of ours." He turned to Brian, took the receipts and money and spread them on the cash-desk. "*The Count of Monte Cristo*, wasn't it? Go and get it for him, will you?"
The book came, and he had only time to glimpse at the picture-cover[4] of a man holding a sword before it was taken away and wrapped up.
He opened the packet outside, flipped the hundreds of pages through his fingers, from cover to cover and back again. A posh[5] woman's voice said from behind: "You're going to be busy, aren't you?" He turned and said yes, ran his eyes up and down the formidable list of chapter[6] titles. No one was home, and he sat by the fire to read. The room had been scrubbed and the table cleared, and in the congenial emptiness he sped[7] on through the easy prose of the story, had reached Edmond Dantès' betrothal[8] ceremony before his parents came in. They took off their coats.
"That looks like a nice book," his mother said. "Where did you get it from?"
"I bought it from downtown."
"Who gen you all that money?" his father put in.
"It must 'ave cost a pretty penny," his mother said, spreading the cloth for tea.
"Nobody gen me the money," Brian told them, closing the book carefully. "I saved it up." Irritation came into his mother's voice: "How much was it?"
"Half a crown."
"Yer've wasted 'alf a crown on a book?" his father exclaimed.
He'd imagined they'd be pleased at his cleverness in bringing such a thing into the house, but it was the opposite. It was as though he'd been split in half and was bleeding to death. All for a book. "It was *my* money," he cried, anguished[9] and bitter, because instead of buying the book he should have given the money to them.
"You're bloody-well silly about books," his father said, a definite threat in his voice. "You read till you're bloody-well daft[10]." His mother came back from the kitchen: "You stand need to spend half a crown on books, when you ain't got a bit o' shoe to your feet. And you're a sly little swine to 'ave money in the 'ouse all that time when I've often bin wi'out a shillin' ter buy some snap[11]."
"I didn't have the money here," he explained.

[1] cash-desk (BE) *Kasse(ntisch)* [2] count *Graf* [3] receipt [rɪ'siːt] *Quittung* [4] picture-cover *Bildeinband*
[5] posh (infml) *vornehm* [6] chapter *Kapitel* [7] speed (on) – sped – sped *(weiter)jagen, -eilen*
[8] betrothal [bɪ'trəʊðl] (fml) *Verlobung* [9] anguished ['æŋgwɪʃt] *verzweifelt* [10] daft (infml) *blöd(e)*
[11] snap *(im nordenglischen Dialekt) (Mittag-)Essen*

Dreams and reality – an excerpt from a novel

"I took it bit by bit to the bookshop, like a Christmas club." This was even worse, because he'd made sure that, starving[1] or not, they hadn't been able to get their hands on it. "You'd 'ave 'ad more sense[2] to a got yoursen a pair o' shoes," Seaton cried. "I've a good mind to throw it on the bleddy fire."

" 'E's got no more sense than 'e was born with," his mother said. Brian was horrified[3] at his father's threat, saw flames already at their work. "It's *my* book," he shouted.

"Don't cheek[4] me," Seaton said, "or you'll be for it[5], my lad." His tears were open, and they saw it. "I hope there's a war on soon so's we're all killed," he raved[6].

"What a thing to say," his mother said. "I don't know where he gets it from."

A smack[7] across the head from his father. "Say one more word, and I'll show yer what I'll do wi' yer."

"Wait till I grow up," Brian cried.

But Seaton only said: "He'll be a lunatic[8] one day wi' reading so many books."

He sat by the fire while they drank tea, trying to force back the sobs[9], difficult because he saw too easily how he had done wrong. But hatred[10] and pity for himself surmounted[11] this, and so he couldn't stop. Vera passed him some tea: "Come on, it ain't the end o' the world." His eyes were drawn to the book cover, where a brave man held a rapier[12] as if he didn't care for anyone in the world, as though nothing could ever trouble him. And if it did, the face and sword said, it would be an easy matter to fight a duel and dispose[13] of whatever it was.

He ate bread and jam, and went on reading. The story grafted[14] itself to him, slowly becoming him and he becoming it, and he left behind with each second the light and noise in the house, and went on wondering footsteps down into the dungeons[15] of the Château d'If with Edmond Dantès, following the guards and slipping[16] invisibly into the cell[17], and all night long he listened to the tapping and whispers that came from the granite floor, heard the patient scraping[18] and scratching[18] of freedom, was shown that even dungeons and giant prisons were unable to keep men in forever, though fourteen years was longer by four than he had so far lived: he listened to the chipping of home-made tools, and voices whispering as if from the dead, that talked of knowledge and freedom and hidden treasure on the Island of Monte Cristo.

Note on the language:
'Yer' (you), 'yoursen' (yourself), 'bin' (been), 'ter' (to), 'gen' (gave), 'stand need' (don't need/shouldn't), 'to a got' (to have got), 'so's' (so/so that) *are words from the dialect of the English Midlands.*

Note on the British currency up to 1971:
£1 = 20 shillings
half a crown = two shillings and sixpence
1 shilling = 12 pence

For sixpence you could buy a packet of tea in the 1930s; for half a crown you could buy a pair of shoes.

Working with the text

1. How do Brian's parents react when they see that their son has bought a book? Do they react in the same way? How do you explain their behaviour?
2. Why do you think the book means so much to Brian? (You will be able to answer this question best if you take the situation of the Seaton family into consideration and if you find out some more about *The Count of Monte Cristo*.)
3. Talk about the different functions of reading: Consider what reading means to Brian. What might reading mean to different people? What does reading mean to *you*?

1 starve *verhungern* 2 sense *Verstand* 3 horrified at *entsetzt über* 4 cheek sb (BE, infml) *frech sein zu jm*
5 be for it [-'--] (infml) *dran sein, Ärger bekommen* 6 rave *toben* 7 smack *Schlag, Klaps* 8 lunatic ['lu:nətɪk] *Wahnsinnige(r)*
9 sob *Schluchzer* 10 hatred *Hass* 11 surmount [sə'maʊnt] *überwinden* 12 rapier ['reɪpɪə] *Rapier (Fechtwaffe)*
13 dispose of *beseitigen, aus dem Weg schaffen* 14 graft oneself to *sich übertragen auf*
15 dungeon ['dʌndʒən] *Verlies, Kerker* 16 slip, -pp- *schlüpfen* 17 cell *(Gefängnis-)Zelle* 18 scrape, scratch *kratzen*

A baby sardine
Saw her first submarine[1]:
She was scared and watched through a peephole[2].

'Oh come, come, come,'
Said the sardine's mum,
'It's only a tin full of people.'

Spike Milligan

1. Show how Spike Milligan plays with the common phrase 'packed like sardines (in a tin)' by choosing an unusual point of view.
2. What is the rhyme scheme of the poem? How does rhyme contribute to the humorous tone of the poem? Look especially at the 'rhyme words' in lines 3 and 6.
3. Try to write a similar humorous poem from an animal's point of view.

applaws)

"fell
ow
sit
isn'ts"

(a paw s

E. E. Cummings

1. At first glance the poem looks rather strange. But if you read it aloud, very carefully, you will begin to under stand what it says:
   - Make a pause after the first bracket and before the second bracket. What are the words in lines 1 and 6 in 'real' English?
   - Read the four lines in quotation marks fast, linking the 'words' as much as possible. What two 'real' English words can you make of these four lines?
2. Hold your right hand in front of you in the shape of a bracket (as in line 1) and your left hand too (as in line 6). What does this suggest to you?
3. What situation is presented in the poem? Who is the speaker of lines 2-5? What might his/her job be? How is the audience involved in what is going on?
4. Why do you think Cummings gave his poem such a strange form? How seriously does he take the speaker and the audience?

[1] submarine [ˌsʌbməˈriːn] *Unterseeboot* [2] peephole [ˈpiːphəʊl] *Guckloch*

Southbound[1] on the freeway[2]

A tourist came in from Orbitville[3],
parked in the air and said:

The creatures[4] of this star
are made of metal and glass.

Through the transparent[5] parts
you can see their guts[6].

Their feet are round and roll
on diagrams – or long

measuring tapes[7] – dark
with white lines.

They have four eyes.
Two in the back are red.

Sometimes you can see a 5-eyed
one, with a red eye turning

on the top of his head.
He must be special –

the others respect him
and go slow

when he passes, winding
among them from behind.

They all hiss[8] as they glide[9],
like inches[10], down the marked

tapes. Those soft shapes,
shadowy inside

the hard bodies – are they
their guts or their brains[11]?

May Swenson

1. Describe the setting and the point of view adopted by the speaker of the poem.
2. Go through the poem stanza by stanza and explain what is said about the 'creatures' mentioned in the poem.
3. What view of human beings is presented in the last four lines? – What role do cars and people play according to the poem?
4. What other strange things might the 'tourist' have seen from above? Write a short text or poem about one of them.
5. Read all three poems on pages 74 and 75 again. Which one do you like best? Try to give reasons for your choice.

→ Option 7: Whale nation

[1] southbound *in Richtung Süden* [2] freeway (AE) *Autobahn* [3] Orbitville: orbit ['ɔːbɪt] *Umlaufbahn um die Erde, Orbit*
[4] creature ['kriːtʃə] *Geschöpf, (Lebe-)Wesen* [5] transparent [-'--] *durchsichtig*
[6] guts [gʌts] *(pl) Eingeweide, (das) Innere* [7] measuring tape ['meʒərɪŋ ˌteɪp] *Maßband* [8] hiss *zischen*
[9] glide *(dahin)gleiten* [10] inch *Zoll (2,54 cm)* [11] brain(s) *Gehirn*

Reading may also encourage you to write your own literature. These two pages show you three types of 'home-made literature': a story that must include a number of given words, a mini-saga and a clerihew. Each of them has one or two typical characteristics.

The story that must include a number of given words *was made popular through a competition in* The Spectator *magazine a few years ago. People wanting to take part in the competition had to write a story, not too long, which contained twelve words given by the editors of the magazine. The words could be used in any order.*

The official birth of the ***mini-saga*** *was 1982, when the* Sunday Telegraph Magazine *had its first mini-saga competition. Since then, mini-sagas have become very popular. The aim of the mini-saga is to tell a complete story in exactly 50 words. Additionally, the story may have a title consisting of up to 15 more words.*

The ***clerihew*** *is a humorous verse of four lines which serves as a mini-'biography' of a famous person. It was invented by Edmund Clerihew Bentley (1875-1956), whose first such verse appeared in 1905.*

A story with a number of given words

Here are the twelve words for one of the stories in *The Spectator* and one of the winning texts. (Both the words and the text have been slightly simplified.)

classless – leave – mad[1] – Kant – behaviour – carry – spelling – annoying – facilities[2] – goodbye – nature – struggle

"I've decided to leave Paul," Marion said, taking off her hat.
"Are you sure it isn't the other way round?" I asked, remembering how annoying her pedantic husband had found their long conversations, her bad spelling and even worse maths.
"Oh, no," she replied. "It was me. I'd accepted his strange behaviour far too long. First it was his love of philosophy[3]; daily talks on Kant and Hegel nearly drove me mad. Next, he developed an interest in social reform and creating a classless society. Then last summer he decided to go back to nature and move to an old hut which was miles from anywhere and had no facilities. He expected me to struggle through the mud every morning and carry wood up a mountain path. It was either 'Goodbye, Paul' or men in white coats for me."

Now choose one of the two lists below. See if you can write a similar short text in which you use all the words from the list you have chosen.
Or:
Write a list of twelve words. Then get together with a partner, exchange your lists and make up a story which contains all the words given by your partner.

crisis – surprised – caravan – ketchup – giraffe – alcohol – neighbour – introduce – intelligent – emigrate – reorganize – suggest

household – human – amazed – affection – non-returnable – responsibility – recycle – hairdresser – argument – safe – survive – properly

[1] mad *verrückt* [2] facilities *(pl)* *sanitäre Einrichtungen* [3] philosophy [-'---]

Mini-sagas

Just One Of Many Stories In A Park

They were
sitting on a bench[1]
keeping their distances,
nothing to say.
Both reading
their books.

Suddenly her book fell down and he
picked it up. What a nice surprise!
He was reading the same book as her.

They had to go.
They might
see each
other again.
Who knows?

Angeles Manzaneque

Out of the mouths of babes[2]?

"Come and meet my friend on
Sports Day, Mummy."
Sports Day came.
"Where's your new friend, Paul?"
"He's sitting on the front
bench."
There were ten on the front
bench.
"He's wearing red shorts."
There were three boys with
red shorts.
"His hair's curly[3]."
"Oh, the black one,"
said Mummy.

Kathryn Clarke, age 15

Now try to write your own mini-saga. Perhaps you can even have a competition in class.

The clerihew

Look at the illustration and read the 'mini-biography' of E. A. Poe, a famous American writer. Then try to write your own clerihew of a famous person or of one of your friends. – Perhaps you can add an illustration to your verse.

Edgar Allan Poe
Was passionately[4] fond of roe[5].
He always liked to chew[6] some
When writing anything gruesome[7].

[1] bench *Sitzbank* [2] babe *kleines Kind* [3] curly *lockig* [4] passionate ['pæʃənət] *leidenschaftlich*
[5] roe [rəʊ] *Rogen (Fischeier)* [6] chew *kauen* [7] gruesome ['gru:səm] *grausig*

A question of identity

Lynn, an American Indian teenager, has always lived with her family on a Navajo[1] reservation in Arizona. But her life is going to change dramatically …

When Lynn was 16, her teachers told her about a new government program for minority high school students – blacks, Hispanics, American Indians – who were good at school. If they were chosen, these students would be given the chance of going to some of the best schools in the United States, where they could prepare for college.

"We hope that you'll try to win a place in the program," said one of Lynn's teachers. "The competition will be great, but we feel that you have a good chance of being chosen."

Lynn began to feel nervous. "And if I win a place, where will I go? Will it be far from the reservation?"

"We don't know," said another of her teachers. "But most of the schools are in California or on the east coast."

Lynn listened carefully while her teachers explained the program to her. Finally, after talking to her parents, she agreed to apply and take the exam. "I know I won't pass," she thought, "so there's nothing to worry about." A short time later, she took the exam. It was difficult, as she had imagined it would be. She was sure she had done terribly and soon forgot the whole thing.

And then one day, she was called into the principal's office. He smiled when she walked in and held up a piece of paper. "Congratulations, Lynn," he said. "You've been chosen. You're going to Brandermill School in Vermont. It's one of the best schools in the country. You're very lucky."

Lynn suddenly felt weak and afraid. "But it's so far away," she said.

In June there was a special summer program in Texas to prepare the students before they left for their new schools. That gave Lynn just two weeks to be with her family, just two weeks to have a last look at the red earth of the reservation, at the desert, and the wild, strange rocks that the winds and water had made into fantastic figures over thousands of centuries.

During those two weeks, she visited her relatives, sat in her grandparents' hogan[2] and fetched water for them, as they had none in their home. She helped to make bread and look after her grandfather's sheep. And at night she lay on the ground outside and watched the stars in the dark sky, felt the cool wind against her face. "It will be so different," she thought.

Before you read on:

- Look at a map of the USA and find Arizona and Vermont. What is the distance between these two states?
- What kind of problems might Lynn have in her new school?

 [1] Navajo ['nævəhəʊ] *nordamerikanischer Indianerstamm* [2] hogan ['həʊgən] *achtseitige Behausung der Navajo-Indianer*

Brandermill was a school for the children of rich parents. It cost more money to go there than Lynn could imagine. The school could afford the best teachers in the country and the students' results were among the best. Everybody had told Lynn how lucky she was to go to such a school. But two weeks after school had started, Lynn felt completely miserable[1]. She was lonely and homesick[2] for her family and her Navajo friends. She hated September in New England and she missed the warmth of Arizona. How she wished to be home among the great rocks and deep canyons. So Lynn sat quietly in all her classes, afraid of saying the wrong thing; she felt she could not compete[3] with her classmates[4]. They seemed to be so much more intelligent. In English they talked about books and writers she had never even heard of. Lynn was also having problems with her English. On the reservation she had learned both English and Navajo, but she had always thought in Navajo. Now she had to think in English. During the following weeks, Lynn felt that she was surely failing.

And Lynn made no friends. A few of the other students talked with her sometimes, but it was usually about homework. Lynn did not try to make friends either. "I am not part of their world," she thought. "They just don't notice me." By the middle of October Lynn was sure that she should leave Brandermill and go back to the reservation. She went to the counselor to tell him of her decision. He listened quietly while she told him about her problems.

"I'm not good in class," she said. "I can't follow. I'm unhappy with the life here. I'm really a Navajo. I should be back where I belong."

"You *are* a Navajo," said her counselor. "That's right. And right now you belong here."

"But I'm failing," said Lynn.

"Have any of your teachers said you are failing?" the counselor asked.

"No," said Lynn. "I just know it."

The counselor smiled. "You just *think* you know it. I've talked with your teachers and they say you're doing just fine in everything. You have to improve your written English, but you're certainly not failing."

"But I'm not happy," said Lynn.

"That's a different thing," said the counselor. "What you're doing is very difficult. Belonging to two worlds isn't easy. You have come from your own special world into one that is very different. There are few people who could do what you are doing and succeed. That's why you were chosen, because somebody believed you could do it." "But I can't," said Lynn.

The counselor looked at her. "You *can* do it. Believe me. If you go back to the reservation now, you won't feel good about yourself or about leaving here. You'll feel that you've failed. You'll feel that you've let down[5] your tribe, your family, and your friends. Stay here until Christmas. You'll be able to go home then. Don't leave before. Make a calendar, count the days on the wall, do anything, but don't leave now. When you get back to the reservation, then you can decide whether you want to come back to Brandermill. That's the place where you have to make the decision."

[1] miserable ['mɪzrəbl] *traurig* [2] be homesick ['- -] *Heimweh haben* [3] compete [kəm'pi:t] *konkurrieren*
[4] classmate ['klɑ:smeɪt] *Klassenkamerad/in* [5] let down *im Stich lassen*

The conversation with her counselor helped Lynn. She threw herself into her work. She studied harder and spent more time in the library. She forced herself to speak in class, she forced herself to talk to the other students – and some even became more friendly. And time flew by, until suddenly it was Christmas and she was on her way back home.

On her first night at home Lynn sat with her mother and her grandparents in their hogan. During the day she had ridden with her father and grandfather. She had looked again at the mountains and the canyons. She felt at home, felt that these were her people and this was her life. Now a cold winter wind was blowing outside, but inside it was warm and comfortable. Lynn told her family about the school, how big and expensive it was, how good the teachers were – and she talked about her problems. "What if I turn into[1] a white person?" she said. "If I learn white ways and how they think, if I learn their language and read their books, if I spend most of my time with them – won't I become a white person?"
Her grandmother answered in Navajo. "You should learn the ways of the white people. You can help all of us in the tribe by learning the white man's knowledge. But the ways of your own people are deep inside you. I don't think you will forget who you are."
And her mother said, "Nothing can make you a white person unless you want to be one."
In that moment her decision was made.

(Based on 'Lynn, a Navajo' from *To live in two worlds* by Brent Ashabranner)

1. Divide the text into sections that represent stages[2] in the story and give each section a short title, for example 'The exam', … .
2. Summarize Lynn's feelings in each section of the story.
3. "Belonging to two different worlds isn't easy." (p. 79, ll. 49-50) Why did Lynn's teacher say this? What did he want to tell her?
4. Read the poem below by a group of 11-year-old Navajo students. How does it help us to understand Lynn better? Explain the last line of the poem.

It is Not!

The Navajo reservation is a lonesome[3] place?
It is Not!
The skies are sunny,
Clear blue,
Of grey with rain.
Each day is gay[4] –
In Nature's way.
It is not a lonesome place at all.
A Navajo house shabby and small?
It is Not!
Inside there's love,
Good laughter,
And Big Talk.
But best –
It's home
With an open door
and room for all.
A Castle could have no more.

[1] turn into *werden* [2] stage [steɪdʒ] *Stadium* [3] lonesome = lonely [4] gay [geɪ] *fröhlich*

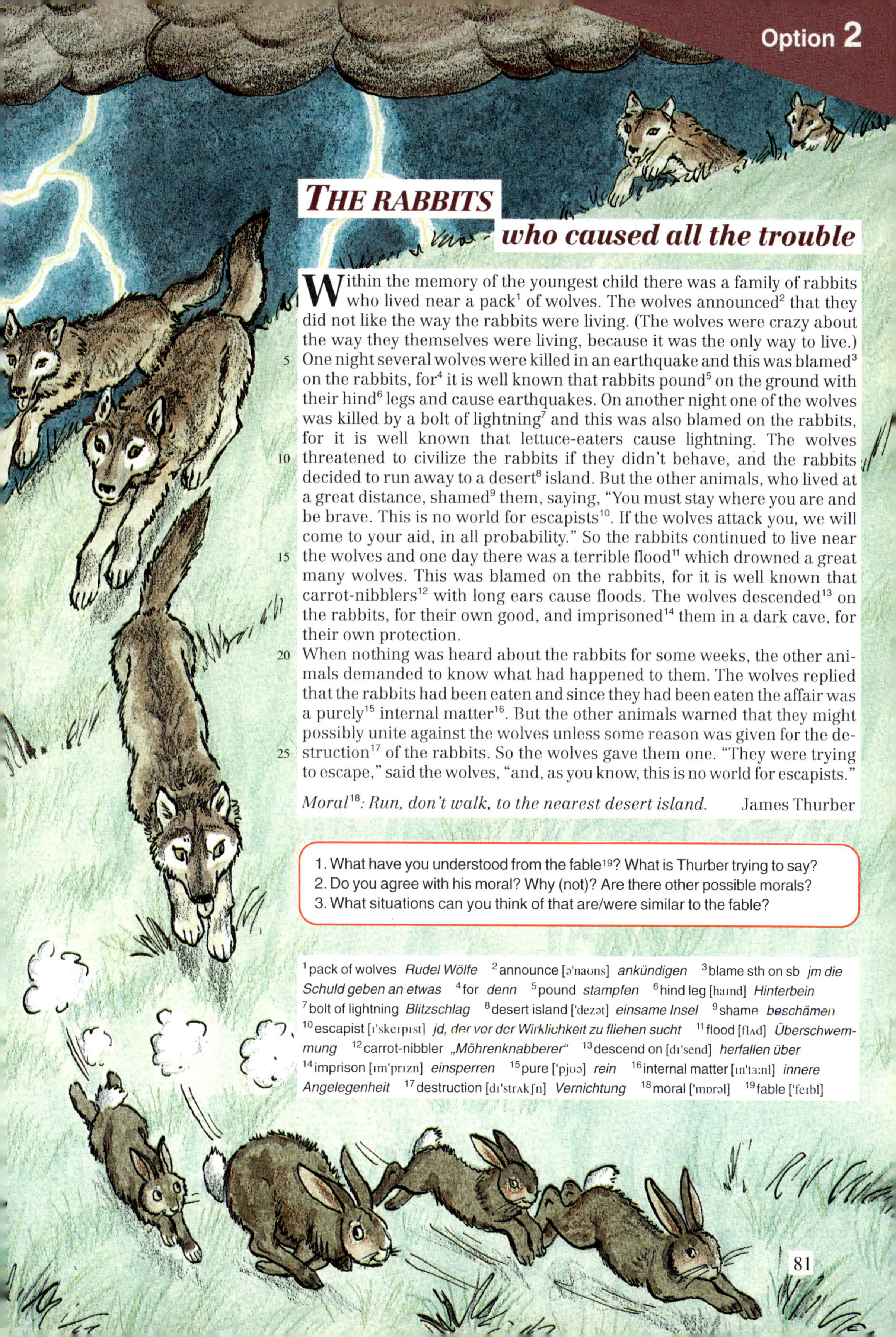

The Rabbits *who caused all the trouble*

Within the memory of the youngest child there was a family of rabbits who lived near a pack[1] of wolves. The wolves announced[2] that they did not like the way the rabbits were living. (The wolves were crazy about the way they themselves were living, because it was the only way to live.) One night several wolves were killed in an earthquake and this was blamed[3] on the rabbits, for[4] it is well known that rabbits pound[5] on the ground with their hind[6] legs and cause earthquakes. On another night one of the wolves was killed by a bolt of lightning[7] and this was also blamed on the rabbits, for it is well known that lettuce-eaters cause lightning. The wolves threatened to civilize the rabbits if they didn't behave, and the rabbits decided to run away to a desert[8] island. But the other animals, who lived at a great distance, shamed[9] them, saying, "You must stay where you are and be brave. This is no world for escapists[10]. If the wolves attack you, we will come to your aid, in all probability." So the rabbits continued to live near the wolves and one day there was a terrible flood[11] which drowned a great many wolves. This was blamed on the rabbits, for it is well known that carrot-nibblers[12] with long ears cause floods. The wolves descended[13] on the rabbits, for their own good, and imprisoned[14] them in a dark cave, for their own protection.

When nothing was heard about the rabbits for some weeks, the other animals demanded to know what had happened to them. The wolves replied that the rabbits had been eaten and since they had been eaten the affair was a purely[15] internal matter[16]. But the other animals warned that they might possibly unite against the wolves unless some reason was given for the destruction[17] of the rabbits. So the wolves gave them one. "They were trying to escape," said the wolves, "and, as you know, this is no world for escapists."

Moral[18]: Run, don't walk, to the nearest desert island. James Thurber

1. What have you understood from the fable[19]? What is Thurber trying to say?
2. Do you agree with his moral? Why (not)? Are there other possible morals?
3. What situations can you think of that are/were similar to the fable?

[1] pack of wolves *Rudel Wölfe* [2] announce [ə'naʊns] *ankündigen* [3] blame sth on sb *jm die Schuld geben an etwas* [4] for *denn* [5] pound *stampfen* [6] hind leg [haɪnd] *Hinterbein* [7] bolt of lightning *Blitzschlag* [8] desert island ['dezət] *einsame Insel* [9] shame *beschämen* [10] escapist [ɪ'skeɪpɪst] *jd, der vor der Wirklichkeit zu fliehen sucht* [11] flood [flʌd] *Überschwemmung* [12] carrot-nibbler *„Möhrenknabberer"* [13] descend on [dɪ'send] *herfallen über* [14] imprison [ɪm'prɪzn] *einsperren* [15] pure ['pjʊə] *rein* [16] internal matter [ɪn'tɜːnl] *innere Angelegenheit* [17] destruction [dɪ'strʌkʃn] *Vernichtung* [18] moral ['mɒrəl] [19] fable ['feɪbl]

Option 3

An American Indian legend

A long time ago a famous hunter was going home with some birds he had shot, and he saw a little snake[1] by the side of the trail. It was a beautifully colored snake, and it looked friendly too. The hunter stopped and watched it for a while. He thought it might be hungry, so he threw it one of his birds before he went home. A few weeks later he was coming past the same place with some rabbits he had shot, and he saw the snake again. It was still very beautiful and seemed friendly, but it had grown. He threw it a rabbit and said "Hello" as he went on home. Some time after that, the hunter saw the snake again. It had grown very big, but it was still friendly and seemed to be hungry. The hunter was taking some turkeys home, so he stopped and gave the snake one. Then, one time, the hunter was going home the same way with two buck deer on his back. By this time, that pretty colored snake was very big and looked so hungry that the hunter felt sorry for it and gave it a whole deer to eat. That night the people were dancing around the fire and singing the old songs when the snake came and started moving around the fire too, outside of where the people were dancing. The snake was so big and long that it stretched[2] all around the people. The snake was covered with pretty colors and it seemed friendly, but it looked hungry too, and the people began to be afraid. They told some boys to get their bows[3] and arrows[4] and shoot the snake. They all shot together and they hit the snake. The snake was hurt. It thrashed its tail all around[5] and killed a lot of people. They say that snake was just like the white man.

1. According to the legend, how do American Indians see their relationship with 'the white man'?
2. Rewrite the legend from the snake's point of view. Include the snake's thoughts and feelings and its view of the hunter and 'the people'.
3. What do the Indian sayings[6] on the right mean?
4. What attitude towards nature do they express?

"The people belong to the land; it's not the land that belongs to the people."

"How can you sell land? Why not sell the clouds – or the ocean?"

greedy = gefräßig, gierig

[1] snake [sneɪk] *Schlange* [2] stretch [stretʃ] *hier: schlängeln, sich erstrecken* [3] bow [bəʊ] *Bogen* [4] arrow ['ærəʊ] *Pfeil*
[5] It thrashed its tail all around [θræʃ] *Sie schlug mit dem Schwanz um sich.* [6] saying *Sprichwort, (Aus-)Spruch*

Slavery in the USA

Why slavery?

The white man's ideal slave

The United States was founded on the idea from the Declaration of Independence that "all men are created equal". However, not all men or women were treated equally. In 1810 there were 7.2 million people in the United States. 1.2 million of these people were black slaves. Why was there slavery in a country that meant freedom for so many? In the southern states many workers were needed to work on the cotton plantations. Free white men and women, who had emigrated to America, could not be forced to stay on the plantations. Even poor whites could move west and farm their own land. African slaves, on the other hand, were actually the property of their white owners, on whom they were completely dependent. From the 16th to the early 19th century slaves were captured and bought in Africa and then transported to the Caribbean and America. The living conditions on the slave ships were so hard that many blacks died of hunger or illness during the long journey. After arriving in the States, most slaves were sold at public auctions[1].

Working in the cotton fields

How slaves lived

Many slave-owners wanted to get the most work possible out of their slaves. Slaves often had to work 16 hours a day. The stronger slaves, including women and children, worked in the fields, ploughing[2], planting and picking cotton. Slavery did not just mean hard work. It also destroyed family bonds[3] and cultural roots[4]. Slaves were given new names, were not allowed to speak their own languages or to practice their traditional religions. Keeping a family together was difficult. The law did not even recognize slave marriages[5] or slave families. Familes could be broken up at any time: husbands, wives and children could all be sold to different owners. Nevertheless[6], family life provided a feeling of pride[7] for slaves. Families tried to spend as much time as possible together. Although they were not allowed to, parents taught their children stories and songs as a way to pass on their traditional heritage[8] and customs. Faith in God also helped slaves cope[9] with the harshness[10] of daily life. Bible stories about how the Israelites were freed from slavery inspired many slave songs. Slavery was finally abolished in 1865, but it took another century before the freed blacks were given equal rights under the law.

1. Why were African slaves needed in the USA?
2. How did the slaves live?
3. Why do you think the slave-owners tried to destroy their slaves' cultural identity?
4. Imagine you are a slave in the 1850s who has escaped from a cotton plantation to the North, where slavery is illegal. A reporter for a newspaper wants to know what your life as a slave was like. Try to write the interview with a partner.

[1] auction [ˈɔːkʃn] [2] plough [plaʊ] *pflügen* [3] bond [bɒnd] *Band, Verbindung* [4] root [ruːt] *Wurzel*
[5] marriage [ˈmærɪdʒ] *Ehe* [6] nevertheless *nichtsdestoweniger, trotzdem* [7] pride [praɪd] *Stolz*
[8] heritage [ˈherɪtɪdʒ] *Erbe* [9] cope with *fertig werden mit* [10] harshness [ˈhɑːʃnəs] *Härte*

Black music

- First look at the two photos on this page: What's going on in each of them? What's similar in the two photos and what's different? Then find out more about these two approaches[1] to music from the introductory text.
- Now look at the illustration on page 85. What do you think it shows? Finally, read texts A-F and match them with the labels[2] 1-7 on the tree.

It all started in Africa, where music played an important part in the religious events of the tribes. Musicians played drums[3] and other instruments, as singers danced and sang. Unlike in 17th- and 18th-century Europe, where the audience[4] sat and listened silently while the musicians played note for note the music of a single composer[5], there was no clear separation between the African musicians and their audience. Musicians and dancers improvised and created as they played. Making music was a social event in which everyone took part. The African approach to music was an important basis for many new genres[6] of music in the New World.

A From rhythm and blues two very popular genres of music developed: **rock and roll** and **soul**. Rock 'n' roll was created when white singers, influenced by black musicians, started to sing rhythm and blues. Soul music is the further development of rhythm and blues.

B **Spirituals** were the first important genre of black music created in the New World. When African slaves were brought to America, they also brought with them their approach to music. They were not allowed to practice their traditional African religions, so they combined their African approach to music with Christian texts. The result was a new genre of music.

[1] approach to [ə'prəʊtʃ] *Herangehensweise an* [2] label ['leɪbl] *Schildchen, Etikett* [3] drum *Trommel* [4] audience ['ɔːdɪəns] *Publikum* [5] composer [kəm'pəʊzə] *Komponist/in* [6] genre ['ʒɒnrə] *Genre, Art, Gattung*

C **Jazz**, the most important music form of the 20th century, developed from blues. Jazz was created when black musicians played together and applied their improvisational approach to the music. They combined European instruments like the trumpet and the trombone[1], for example, with African instruments like drums and the banjo[2]. As jazz evolved[3], it became one of the most complex[4] and expressive[5] forms of music.

D Like jazz, **rhythm and blues ('R and B')** also developed from blues. When musicians, influenced by the blues, formed bands and started to play electric guitars and drums, the music they created was more urban and reached a larger audience of black and white listeners. The songs were often the same songs that the blues singers sang, and they often had the same blues structure.

E Later, **blues** branched[6] off from spirituals and became another important genre of black music. Blues singers, who usually also played guitar, had the same approach to the music as the singers of spirituals. Both types of music are emotional[7], but unlike spirituals, blues texts are not religious.

F From soul, **rap** developed, one of the most important genres of black music today. Rap is often very political, and deals with such topics as racism and life in the inner city. In rap, the meaning of the words and their complex rhythms are very important. Rap artists often see the genre as a source of information for black people.

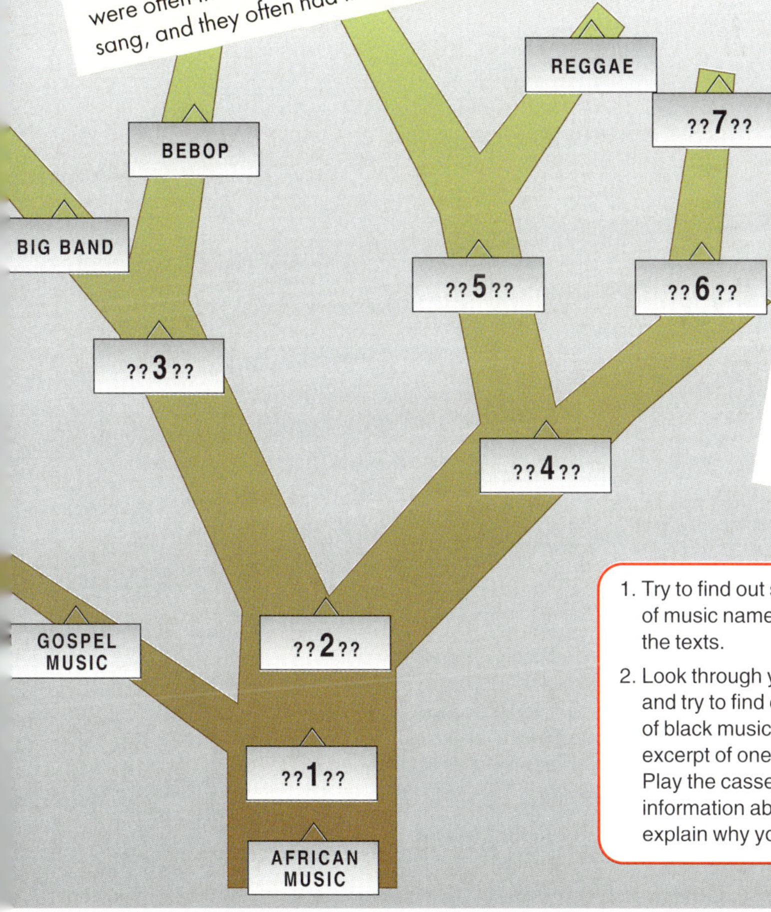

1. Try to find out something about the four genres of music named in the tree but not discussed in the texts.
2. Look through your parents' record/CD collection and try to find examples of the different genres of black music. Record on a cassette a short excerpt of one song you particularly like/dislike. Play the cassette to the class and give some information about the singer(s) or group. Then explain why you like/dislike the song.

1 trombone [trɒm'bəʊn] *Posaune* 2 banjo ['bændʒəʊ] 3 evolve [ɪ'vɒlv] *sich weiterentwickeln* 4 complex ['kɒmpleks]
5 expressive [ɪk'spresɪv] *ausdrucksstark* 6 branch off [ˌbrɑːntʃ_'ɒf] *abzweigen* 7 emotional [ɪ'məʊʃənl] *gefühlsbetont*

Robert Frost: Poems

The poet at the age of 88

At the time of his death Robert Frost (1874-1963) was considered to be the most famous living American poet. He has remained popular till today. Although he was born in California, he has often been called the *poet of New England. He spent many years in the state of New Hampshire, where he tried to make a living*[1] *as a farmer and started writing poetry. Many of his poems comment on scenes or events from rural life in New England. But like all great poems, they convey more than that: Frost's poems increase our awareness*[2] *and understanding of human nature – and of ourselves.*

The telephone

"When I was just as far as I could walk
From here today,
There was an hour
All still
When leaning[3] with my head against a flower
I heard you talk.
Don't say I didn't, for I heard you say –
You spoke from that flower on the window sill[4] –
Do you remember what it was you said?"

"First tell me what it was you thought you heard."

"Having found the flower and driven a bee[5] away,
I leaned my head,
And holding by the stalk[6],
I listened and I thought I caught the word –
What was it? Did you call me by my name?
Or did you say –
Someone said 'Come' – I heard it as I bowed[7]."

"I may have thought as much, but not aloud."

"Well, so I came."

1. Practice reading the poem aloud.
   Before you start, find out which lines are spoken by each of the two speakers.
2. What is 'the telephone'? Explain its function[8] in the poem.
3. The speakers seem to play a kind of game. How does it work? And why do they play it, in your opinion?
4. Try to describe the speakers of this dialogue (young or old, boy or girl …?)
5. Can you see a reason why the poet made lines 15 and 19 as well as lines 17 and 18 rhyme?
6. 'Cool/gentle[9]/(in)formal/ironic[10]/light-hearted[11]/playful/serious/simple/warm' – which of these adjectives would you say describes the tone[12] of the poem best?

1 make a living *sich seinen Lebensunterhalt verdienen* 2 awareness [ə'weənəs] *Bewusstsein* 3 lean [li:n] *sich lehnen* 4 window sill *Fensterbank* 5 bee *Biene* 6 stalk [stɔ:k] *Stängel, Stiel* 7 bow [baʊ] *(sich) verbeugen, verneigen* 8 function ['fʌŋkʃn] 9 gentle ['dʒentl] *zart, sanft* 10 ironic [aɪ'rɒnɪk] *ironisch* 11 light-hearted [,- '--] *unbeschwert, heiter* 12 tone [təʊn] *Ton*

Dust[1] of snow

The way a crow[2]
Shook down on me
The dust of snow
From a hemlock tree[3]

Has given my heart
A change of mood
And saved some part
Of a day I had rued[4].

1. How does the speaker feel before the little event described in the poem?
2. Why does he feel different afterwards?
3. What message does the poet probably want to convey? Write a short text or a poem about a similar experience you might have had.

Stopping by woods on a snowy evening

Whose woods these are I think I know.
His house is in the village, though;
He will not see me stopping here
To watch his woods fill up with snow.

My little horse must think it queer[11]
To stop without a farmhouse near
Between the woods and frozen lake
The darkest evening of the year.

He gives his harness[12] bells a shake
To ask if there is some mistake.
The only other sound's the sweep[13]
Of easy wind and downy[14] flake[15].

The woods are lovely, dark, and deep,
But I have promises to keep,
And miles to go before I sleep,
And miles to go before I sleep.

1. Describe the situation the speaker is in and the atmosphere resulting from it.
2. Why do you think the speaker stops on his way? And why does he decide to go on?
3. Some words in the poem may have certain connotations[16] or perhaps even a symbolic meaning for the reader. Find examples (e.g. in lines 13-16) and say what they mean to you.
4. The poem has an interesting rhyme pattern[17]. What effect does it have? Comment on the repetition in lines 15-16, too.

Nothing gold can stay

Nature's first green is gold,
Her hardest hue[5] to hold.
Her early leaf's a flower;
But only so an hour.
Then leaf subsides[6] to leaf.
So Eden[7] sank to grief[8],
So dawn[9] goes down to day.
Nothing gold can stay.

1. Try to explain the paradoxical[10] statements of lines 1 and 3.
2. What evidence does the speaker give that in nature 'Nothing gold can stay'?
3. Show how the meaning of 'gold' in line 1 changes when it is used again in line 8. What does this convey about the speaker's view of life?

- "Whatever happens in nature can make you feel happy or sad or … ." Discuss this by referring to the three poems on this page.
- Read all four poems again. Which of them do you like best? Why?

[1] dust *Staub* [2] crow [krəʊ] *Krähe* [3] hemlock tree ['hemlɒk] *Hemlocktanne* [4] rue [ru:] *bereuen, bedauern*
[5] hue [hju:] *(Farb-)Ton* [6] subside [səb'saɪd] *sich fallen lassen, sinken* [7] Eden ['i:dn] *(der Garten) Eden, das Paradies*
[8] sink to grief [gri:f] *zugrunde gehen* [9] dawn [dɔ:n] *(Morgen-)Dämmerung* [10] paradoxical [ˌpærə'dɒksɪkl] *paradox*
[11] queer [kwɪə] *seltsam, sonderbar* [12] harness ['hɑ:nɪs] *(Pferde-)Geschirr* [13] sweep *(Dahin-)Fegen, Stürmen*
[14] downy ['daʊnɪ] *flaumig* [15] flake [fleɪk] *Flocke* [16] connotation [ˌkɒnə'teɪʃn] *Nebenbedeutung, Beiklang*
[17] pattern *Muster, Schema*

Whale Nation

Extracts from an epic poem[1]
by Heathcote[2] Williams

From space, the planet is blue.
From space, the planet is the territory
Not of humans, but of the whale.

Blue seas cover seven-tenths of the earth's surface[3],
And are the domain[4] of the largest brain[5] ever created,
With a fifty-million-year-old smile. [...]

Whales play
For three times as long as they
Spend searching for food. [...]

They can go for eight months without food;
And they do not work to eat.
They play to eat.

[1] epic poem ['epɪk] *Epos, Heldengedicht* (The complete 733-line poem *Whale Nation* was published in Britain in 1988. The book is richly illustrated with beautiful photos.) [2] Heathcote ['hi:θkət] [3] surface ['sɜ:fɪs] *Oberfläche*
[4] domain [də'meɪn] *Bereich, Sphäre* [5] brain [breɪn] *Gehirn*

The Humpback[1] catches its food by blowing bubbles.
Five-foot-wide bubbles, as large as weather-balloons:
When they burst[2], they make a circle of confusing mist[3].

The plankton […]
Is corralled[4] into the middle
By a bewildering[5] ring
Of hissing[6] bubble-bombs.

The whale then rises up
Into the centre of a round plate
Of brimming[7] water,
And eats.

… Imagine blowing soap-bubbles,
And food drops out of the sky.

After dinner, music:
Ethereal[8] music that carries for miles,
A siren's song,
Leading sailors to believe,
As the sounds infiltrated[9] through the wooden hull[10],
That their vessels were haunted[11]
By spirits of the deep. […]

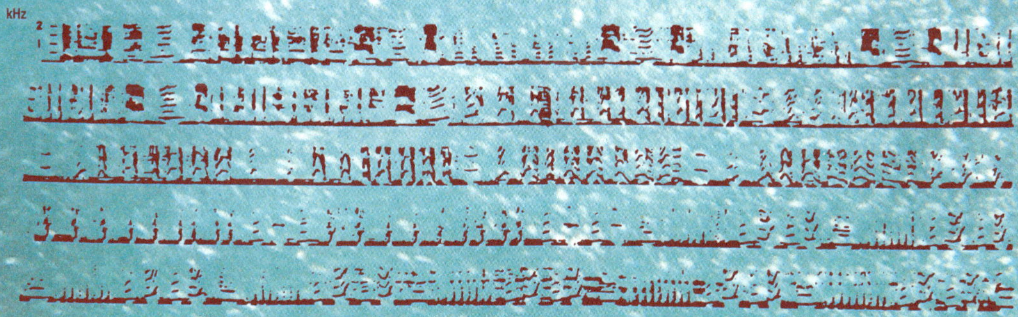

The Inuit[12] say:
"We like the way whales think." […]

The Nootka[13] claim that the whale allows his death
To spare[14] people from hunger,
And that therefore they must be worthy[15] of it.

[1] humpback ['hʌmpbæk] *Buckelwal* [2] burst [bɜːst] *platzen* [3] mist *(feiner) Nebel*
[4] corral (into) [kə'rɑːl], -ll- *einpferchen, einsperren (in)* [5] bewildering [bɪ'wɪldərɪŋ] *verwirrend* [6] hiss *zischen*
[7] brim, -mm- *überfließen, übersprudeln* [8] ethereal [ɪ'θɪərɪəl] *himmlisch* [9] infiltrate ['ɪnfɪltreɪt] *eindringen, einsickern*
[10] hull [hʌl] *Rumpf (eines Schiffes)* [11] their vessels were haunted ['vesl, 'hɔːntɪd] *in ihren Schiffen spukte es*
[12] Inuit ['ɪnʊɪt] *„Menschen" (Selbstbezeichung der Eskimos)*
[13] Nootka ['nʊtkə] *Indianerstamm an der Pazifikküste im Nordwesten Nordamerikas*
[14] spare sb (from) sth [speə] *jm etwas ersparen* [15] be worthy of sth ['wɜːðɪ] *einer Sache würdig sein*

But other men have elected to view[1] the whale
As an essential component[2] of an expanding economy …

When an underwater shape is detected on the submarine radar[3],
Catcher boats are despatched[4] from the factory-ship.
The harpoon on the raised foredeck[5] is manned[6]
And swivelled[7] in the direction of the whale. […]

With no enemies in the sea
The whale is loth[8] to believe in the attack,
As were the Indians, as were the aborigines. […]

Yet civilisation was built on the back of the whale:
Coastal settlements followed the presence of whales;
Shore-stations[9] near the whaling grounds became cities.

Boston, New York, Plymouth, […]
Philadelphia, Liverpool …
London, Hamburg …
Urban conglomerations[10] plugged[11] into the corpse[12] of the whale,
Growing larger and larger by its light. […]

Millions and millions and millions died in a marine holocaust. […]

The sullen[13] killing continues.
The killing of the largest creatures[14]
In the world. […]

Large creatures disappear;
Life becomes smaller …

Blind dwarves[15]
Crawl[16] on top of the corpses
Of slaughtered[17] giants. […]

[1] view *sehen, betrachten* [2] essential component [ɪˌsenʃl kəm'pəʊnənt] *wesentlicher/unerlässlicher (Bestand-)Teil*
[3] submarine radar [ˌsʌbməriːn 'reɪdɑː] *Unterwasserradargerät* [4] despatch [dɪ'spætʃ] *(ab)schicken, losschicken*
[5] foredeck *Vor(der)deck* [6] man, -nn- *bemannen* [7] swivel ['swɪvl], -ll- *drehen, schwenken*
[8] be loth to do sth [ləʊθ] (fml) *etwas (sehr) widerwillig tun* [9] shore-station ['ʃɔːˌsteɪʃn] *Küstenstützpunkt*
[10] urban conglomeration [ˌɜːbən kənˌglɒmə'reɪʃn] *Anhäufung von Städten*
[11] plug into [plʌg], -gg- *(ein elektrisches Gerät) einstecken in, (durch Steckkontakt) anschließen an*
[12] corpse [kɔːps] *Leichnam, Leiche* [13] sullen ['sʌlən] *düster* [14] creature ['kriːtʃə] *Geschöpf, Lebewesen*
[15] dwarf, *pl* dwarves [dwɔːf, -vz] *Zwerg* [16] crawl [krɔːl] *kriechen, krabbeln*
[17] slaughter ['slɔːtə] *(ab)schlachten, niedermetzeln*

In the water, whales have become the dominant species,
Without killing their own kind.

In the water, whales have become the dominant species,
Though they allow the resources they use to renew themselves.

In the water, whales have become the dominant species,
Though they use language to communicate, rather than to eliminate[1] rivals. [...]

In the water, whales have become the dominant species,
Though they acknowledge[2] minds[3] other than their own.

In the water, whales have become the dominant species,
Without allowing their population to reach plague proportions[4]. [...]

A marine intelligentsia[5],
With a knowledge of the deep.

From space, the planet is blue.
From space, the planet is the territory
Not of humans, but of the whale.

1. What general impression of the whale do you get from the poem?
   Find proof in the text to support your first impressions.
2. What impression of human beings does Heathcote Williams try to convey?
3. What attitude towards the whale does each of the two groups of human beings have?
   Find evidence in the poem to support your answer.
4. What is the effect on you of the repetition at the end of the poem?
5. If you see the whale as a symbol of nature, in what way might the relationship between human beings and the whale be considered symbolic?

[1] eliminate [ɪ'lɪmɪneɪt] *ausschalten, beseitigen*
[2] acknowledge [ək'nɒlɪdʒ] *anerkennen*
[3] mind *Verstand, Geist, Seele*
[4] plague proportions [ˌpleɪg prə'pɔːʃnz] *das Ausmaß einer Pest oder Seuche* [8] marine intelligentsia [məˌriːn‿ɪnˌtelɪ'dʒentsɪə] *Intelligenz des Meeres*

Explaining grammar in English

Check your knowledge of English grammatical terms

To explain grammar in English, you need to know the correct grammatical terms *(see the list on pages 186-187)*. You also need to know certain words and expressions which are often used in grammar rules. Here are some exercises to help you check your knowledge of this vocabulary.

→ Grammar review, pp. 120-134

1 Class differences

a A lot of English words belong to two (or even more) different word classes.
Say which word class (i.e. noun, adjective, question word, etc.) the underlined words belong to in the following sentences.

1. I'm looking forward to your reply. – Please reply soon. 2. Don't empty the whole bottle. – Take the empty bottles back to the shop. 3. Which coat is Bill's? Is this his? – I don't think this is his coat. 4. I haven't seen Jennifer since Friday. – I haven't seen Jennifer since she arrived. 5. I made the tea when I came home. – When did you come home? 6. Don't be too hard on the children. – The children didn't work hard enough. 7. Who did you ask? – I asked the man who followed me. 8. Mrs Evans has no right to treat me like that. – You're right.

b Most word classes can be divided into smaller classes. For example, verbs can be divided into main verbs and auxiliary verbs.
The following sentences each contain[1] one pronoun. Find it and say what kind of pronoun it is.

PRONOUNS

1. I'm from Germany.
2. That's Peter at the bus stop.
3. People who live in glass houses shouldn't throw stones.
4. Some people think only of themselves.
5. Your bike is faster than mine.
6. Ms Carlson spoke to the mayor himself.

2 Don't get tense over your tenses

The following rules are from an English grammar book. *Which tenses are described here?*

1. The ★★★ is used for an action happening now. 2. We use the ★★★ to talk about things that people have decided to do (often in the near future). 3. The ★★★ is used to say that something has happened but we do not know or want to say exactly when. 4. We use the ★★★ when we talk about an event that happened before another one in the past. 5. You use the ★★★ to describe an activity in progress in the past. 6. We use the ★★★ to refer to future events which we cannot influence or control. 7. The ★★★ is used to express the idea that something happened at a specific[2] time in the past. 8. We use the ★★★ with *since* or *for* to talk about an activity which began in the past and has continued up to the present. 9. The ★★★ is used for repeated actions in the present.

3 Put your word order in order

Complete the sentences with the correct phrases from the box on the right.

… adverbs of time.
… the main clause. … the verb.
… the direct object. … the subject.

1. An *if*-clause can come either before or after …
2. In questions we put the auxiliary verb before …
3. The indirect object with *to* comes after …
4. The subject must come before …
5. Adverbs of place normally come before …

[1] contain [kən'teɪn] *enthalten* [2] specific [spə'sɪfɪk] *bestimmt*

Applying your knowledge

1 Can you explain?

a *Look at the following sentences and answer the questions on the right. Explain your answers.*

1. Did you see Jill yesterday? Who said that?	How do you form questions in the simple past? Why is *did* not used in the second question?
2. I wonder how I can help you.	What is the word order in indirect questions? Is it the same as in direct questions?
3. The calculator which you gave me doesn't work.	Can you use *who* instead of *which*? Can *which* be left out here? What do you call a relative clause without a relative pronoun?
4. All the cakes have been eaten. Your life will be changed by this book.	How is the passive formed? What do you call a structure such as *be changed*?
5. Jim and Bill hurt each other.	How does the meaning of the sentence change if you replace *each other* with *themselves*?
6. If Mandy left now, she wouldn't have to run to the station.	Does the past tense in the *if*-clause refer to the past? What does *if* + past tense express?
7. Frank always looks sad.	Why isn't the adverb *sadly* used here?

b *Explain in English why the underlined grammatical forms have been used.*

1. Did you do well in your maths test? 2. I like reading about history. I'm particularly interested in the history of Britain in the Middle Ages. 3. Walking around the harbour, they saw lots and lots of boats. Anja had never seen so many in just one place. 4. I'm looking forward to seeing you. 5. Dad told me he was going to do the shopping later.

2 What's the difference?

Try to explain the difference in meaning between the verb forms in each of the following sentence pairs. Then translate the sentences into German.

1. What are you doing at the moment? – What are you doing tomorrow?
2. I saw Sandra yesterday. – If I saw Sandra tomorrow, I'd talk to her.
3. I couldn't get the tickets yesterday. – I couldn't possibly get the tickets tomorrow.
4. When Sue arrived, we were having lunch. – When Sue arrived, we had lunch.
5. I'm staying here for five weeks. – I've been staying here for five weeks.
6. "I've lived in London for four years." – "I lived in London for four years."

3 In English, please

Translate the following sentences into English and explain why the underlined forms are tricky for Germans to translate.

1. Ich habe dich gestern gesehen. 2. Mir ist eine Stelle angeboten worden. 3. Ich will, dass sie mir hilft. 4. Diese Informationen sind nützlich. 5. Sprichst du Deutsch? 6. Carl schlug vor, ins Kino zu gehen. 7. Warte, ich öffne dir die Tür. 8. Ich fühle mich nicht wohl. 9. Wenn du mit dem Zug fahren würdest, könntest du Geld sparen. 10. Mit wem spricht er?

Using a monolingual[1] dictionary

Do you know what 'chip' means? Well, see if you can understand the word in these sentences:

1. Take the other one – this plate has got a **chip** in it.
2. Sorry, can I quickly **chip** in? How much is this shirt, please?
3. Some of the Berliners were **chipping** pieces off the Wall and selling them as souvenirs.
4. Fish and **chips** for me, please!
5. Her firm produces **chips** for use in cameras.

Which meanings can you guess from the context or from similar German words? (Careful though: German 'Chips' are not necessarily English 'chips'.) Which words do you have to look up?

- Now look at the dictionary excerpt on the right and try to find the definitions that fit the 'chips' in the five sentences.
- Look at the two entries for the headword 'chip'. What is the difference? How does the dictionary show this difference?
- What do the numbers (1, 2, 3, …) in each entry tell you?
- Which of the definitions in the dictionary are illustrated?
- The dictionary uses **bold**[2], normal and *italic*[3] print[4]. Say what each type is mainly used for.

Which word is used in British English for what the Americans call 'chips'? (See the dictionary excerpt for help.)

chip¹ /tʃɪp/ *n* **1** a small or thin piece cut or broken off from wood, stone, glass, etc: ***a chip of wood*** ∘ ***chocolate chip cookies*** (ie biscuits containing small pieces of chocolate). **2** the place from which a small piece has been broken: *This mug has a chip in it.* ⇨ picture. **3** (*usu pl*) a long thin piece of potato fried in deep fat: *a plate of chips* ∘ *ˌfish and ˈchips* (ie fish in BATTER², fried and served with chips). ⇨ picture at POTATO. Compare FRENCH FRIES. **4** (*US*) = CRISP *n* 1. **5** a round flat piece of plastic used to represent money, esp in gambling: (*fig*) *The deal is being used as a* ***bargaining chip*** (ie offered in return for sth else). **6** = MICROCHIP. **7** (also **ˈchip shot**) (esp in golf and football) a shot or kick in which the ball goes high in the air and then lands within a short distance. **IDM a ˌchip off the old ˈblock** (*infml usu approv*) a person who is like her or his mother or father in character. **have a ˈchip on one's shoulder** (*infml*) to be bitter(3) and easily offended because one thinks that one has been unfairly treated or that one is regarded as inferior by other people: *She's got a chip on her shoulder about not having gone to university.* **have had one's ˈchips** (*Brit sl*) to be dead, dying or defeated. **when the chips are ˈdown** (*infml*) when one has reached a very important point in one's affairs and realizes what must be done: *When the chips were down he found the courage to carry on.*
■ **ˈchip shop** (also *sl* **chippy**, **chip·pie**) *n* (*Brit infml*) a shop selling fish and chips and certain other esp fried foods for people to take home and eat.

chip² /tʃɪp/ *v* **(-pp-) 1(a)** to break or cut sth at the edge or surface: [Vn] *a badly chipped saucer* ∘ *chip a tooth/a bone* ∘ *He chipped one of my best glasses.* ∘ *chipped nail varnish.* ⇨ picture at CHIP¹. **(b)** to break at the edge or surface: [V] *Be careful with these plates — they chip very easily.* ∘ *The paint is chipping badly.* **2(a) ~ sth from/off sth; ~ sth off** to break or cut a small piece from the edge or surface of sth: [Vnpr] *A piece was chipped off the piano when we moved house.* ∘ *We chipped the old plaster (away)* (ie removed it in small pieces) *from the wall.* [also Vnp]. **(b) ~ off (sth)** to be broken off in small pieces: [Vp] *The paint has chipped off where the table touches the wall.* [also Vpr]. **3** (esp in golf and football, etc) to hit or kick the ball so that it goes high in the air and then lands within a short distance: [Vp, Vnp] *He chipped (the ball) in* (ie into the hole) *from forty yards.* [also V, Vn]. **PHRV ˌchip aˈway at sth** to break off small pieces from sth continuously: *chipping away at a block of marble with a chisel* ∘ (*fig*) *He kept chipping away at the problem until he had finally solved it.* **ˌchip ˈin (with sth)** (*infml*) **1** to join in or interrupt a conversation: *She chipped in with some interesting remarks.* **2** to contribute money: *If everyone chips ˈin we'll be able to buy her a really nice present.*
▶ **chip·pings** *n* [pl] (*Brit*) small pieces of stone, etc used for making a road surface: *Danger! Loose chippings* (eg as a warning to drivers).

chip·board /ˈtʃɪpbɔːd/ *n* [U] a building material made of small pieces of wood pressed and stuck tightly together in flat sheets.

chip·munk /ˈtʃɪpmʌŋk/ *n* a small N American animal similar to a SQUIRREL but with black and white markings along its back.

chipo·lata /ˌtʃɪpəˈlɑːtə/ *n* (*esp Brit*) a small thin SAUSAGE.

chippy (also **chip·pie**) /ˈtʃɪpi/ *n* (*Brit sl*) = CHIP SHOP.

From the *Oxford Advanced Learner's Dictionary, 1995*

[1] monolingual [ˌmɒnəˈlɪŋgwəl] *einsprachig* [2] bold *fett* [3] italic [ɪˈtælɪk] *kursiv* [4] print *Druck*

Dictionary skills

1 As you know, a dictionary is in alphabetical order. So which word will come after which here?

rare receiver recognize rap real receive
reappear rearm RAM rebellion recorder

Write the words down in their correct order and underline the letter in each word which determines[1] where it belongs.

2 Why do **chipboard** and **chipmunk** come *after* **chippings** in the dictionary excerpt on page 94? Copy out from the excerpt
- new words formed on the basis[2] of **chip**,
- phrases and expressions with **chip**.

(The symbol ~, known as a tilde, stands for the headword.)

3 You learned above that not every word is listed as a separate headword. Decide where you would look up the following words and expressions. Then check in your dictionary to see if you were right.

to rain cats and dogs wavy monkey business to mess sth up
child's play head teacher privatization visiting-card

4 Combinations of words which regularly go together are called 'collocations'. See if you can find the correct collocation in the following sentences. (Choose one of the words in brackets.) But check in a dictionary, because often the collocations in English are quite different from the ones in German.

1. Since her accident she suffers (at/from/under) bad headaches.
2. Give me the money by Wednesday, please. I'll be away (into/during/in/on) holiday after that.
3. Excuse me, could you please (shoot/make/take/do) a photo of me and my friend in front of the palace?
4. After the accident Ann was in (big/great/huge/large) pain for two weeks.

Getting the most out of your dictionary

Your monolingual dictionary allows you to check spelling, and it explains meanings. But it can help you with much more than that, so it is worth finding out where and how your own dictionary can give you information on
- *pronunciation,*
- *grammar, including irregular forms, countable and uncountable nouns, comparative and superlative forms,*
- *what preposition a word takes,*
- *the context you can use a word in,*
- *alternatives to a word,*
- *British and American English,*
- *register[3] and usage[4].*

- *Which of this information can't you find in an English-German dictionary?*

Here is a dictionary game you can play. Working in pairs, you look for an interesting-looking word in the dictionary and copy out its meaning (or one of its meanings). Then you make up two false (but likely) definitions of that word. Finally, everybody writes their word on the board and reads out all three definitions. The others must guess which definition is right.

[1] determine [dɪ'tɜːmɪn] *bestimmen* [2] basis ['beɪsɪs] [3] register ['redʒɪstə] *Sprachebene, Stilebene, z.B. „infml"*
[4] usage ['juːsɪdʒ] *(korrekter) Sprachgebrauch*

Using a grammar

1 Getting to know your grammar

Before you can start working with a grammar book, you should ask yourself these questions:

- What kind of information is in the grammar?
- Where do I find the information I'm looking for?
- What do I need to know to understand all the information given?

To help you answer these questions, look up the following things in your own grammar.

The **table of contents**[1] tells you what sections the grammar contains[2] and in what order they come.

Contents

Thanks & key to symbols
Introduction
Main verb forms
1 Present continuous and present simple: **I am doing** and **I do**
2 Present continuous or simple? **I am doing** or **I do**?
3 State verb or action verb? **I think** or **I am thinking**?
4 The present perfect: **I have done**
5 The past simple: **I did**
6 Present perfect or past simple? **I have done** or **I did**?

At the end of the book you'll find an alphabetical **index**[3] of all the topics, grammatical structures and important words dealt with in the grammar.

Mengenbezeichnungen 59-64
~ als Bestimmungswort 2
mid-position 56-57
might(n't) 83, 88, 105
~ in der indir. Rede 228b
mine (Pron.) 67
modale Hilfsverben 80, 83-106
~ im Hauptsatz eines *if*-Satz-Gefüges 232-236
~ in der indir. Rede 228-229

N
Nachsilben 251
~ bei fem. Gattungsnamen 5
Namen von Wissenschaften auf *-ics* 16c
Nationalitätsbezeichnungen 11
near (Adj.), Steigerung 42a
~ */nearly* (Adv.) 50
~ (Präp.) 248
nearest/next 42

Cross-references[4] will lead you from one section to another which also contains relevant[5] information.

Das *present progressive* wird mit *am/are/is* + *-ing form* gebildet.

▷ Besonderheiten bei der Schreibung der *-ing form*: 113
▷ Verben, die üblicherweise nicht in der *progressive form* verwendet werden: 118

In some sections you'll see special **symbols**. These may highlight[6] important points or show that a point is for understanding rather than active use. As a rule[7] all the symbols are explained at the beginning of the book.

Erläuterung der Symbole

▷ verweist auf Abschnitte, die weitere Informationen zu dem behandelten Thema enthalten.

▲ macht auf Sachverhalte aufmerksam, die besonders zu beachten sind.

📖 weist darauf hin, dass sich weitere Beispiele in Wörterbüchern finden.

✱ bezeichnet Abschnitte, in denen grammatikalische Erscheinungen behandelt werden, die man nur zu verstehen, aber nicht selbst zu verwenden braucht.

Colour, bold print[8] and other means[9] are used to highlight parts of the examples, or to show where there are differences between sentences or structures.

77 **b) Verben mit zwei Objekten**

			Indirect object	Direct object
Active:	**The firm**	**pays**	**her**	**a lot of money.**
	Subject			Direct object
Passive:	**She**	**is paid**		**a lot of money.**

Grammatical terms are usually explained in an alphabetical list at the back of the book.

Verzeichnis grammatikalischer Begriffe (List of grammatical terms)

		Beispiele oder Erläuterung
abstract noun	Abstraktum	ability, education, knowledge, lie
active sentence	Aktiv(satz)	*Fred met her* at the station.
activity verb	Tätigkeitsverb	play, read, shine, work
adjective	Adjektiv	bad, good, nice, sweet
adverb of degree	Gradadverb	*extremely* important, *very* good
adverb of frequency	Häufigkeitsadverb	always, never, often, sometimes

[1] table of contents *Inhaltsverzeichnis* [2] contain [kən'teɪn] *enthalten* [3] index *Register*
[4] cross-reference [,-'--] *Querverweis* [5] relevant ['---] [6] highlight *hervorheben* [7] as a rule *in der Regel*
[8] bold print *Fettdruck* [9] means *Mittel*

2 Looking for answers

Look at the following text from a test. The grammatical mistakes have been corrected in the column on the right. How can a grammar help you find out what was wrong and why?

Dear Sir or Madam,
I am writing about a parking ticket[1] that me was given last Monday.
The fine was £12. I was very upset because I have left my moped on
the pavement outside a shop for less than five minutes.
Usually I leave not my moped on the pavement. But this was a very
special situation because I must buy a birthday present for my father
and I am having a broken leg at the moment and cannot walk very far.
I would not have had enough time if I would have parked my moped
somewhere else. And it was the fiftieth birthday of my father. I hope
you will now understand why I left my moped on the pavement.
I look forward to hear from you soon.

Yours faithfully,
John Brown

Corrections:
- I was given — a
- left
- do not leave — b
- had to
- have
- had parked
- my father's fiftieth birthday
- hearing

a The easiest and quickest way of finding a specific[2] point such as the form of the passive is to look in the **index** at the back of the grammar. (Notice that the numbers given after the entries usually refer to sections, not pages.) Many problems are indexed under several different names and there are usually cross-references to help you find the entry you want. You can also try looking up individual problem words, e.g. *give* if you want to know more about how this verb is used in the passive.

parts of speech 55
passive 37–41
  passive verb tenses 37
  passive with **get** 37C
  special patterns 39
  passive to-infinitive and ing-form 41
past

get
  the passive with **get** 37C
  get something done 40
give + objects 68
  passive patterns 39A
go on + to-infinitive or ing-form 43C

39 Special passive patterns

A I was given ...

In an active sentence, a verb of giving can have two different patterns after it.
The Queen gave ***a medal to the pilot.***
The Queen gave ***the pilot a medal.***

Either **a medal** or **the pilot** can be the subject of a passive sentence:
A medal *was given to the pilot.*
The pilot *was given a medal.*

It is quite normal in English for the person receiving something to be the subject in a passive sentence. Here are some more examples:
A government minister *was sent a letter bomb.*
The workers *are paid £200 a week.*
Verbs in this pattern are: **give, send, pay, lend, hand, sell, promise, show, offer, teach, owe, award, grant, allow, leave** (in a will) and **feed**.

b If you need help with a particular topic such as 'negative statements' or you want to revise all the aspects of a grammar topic such as 'the adverb', you can look up these topics in the **table of contents**. You should also go through the table of contents if you are unsure which grammatical term describes your grammar problem. The contents list gives you a general view of how the grammar book is organized.

Wortstellung

Verneinter Satz 45
Fragesatz 45
Die Stellung des indirekten und direkten Objekts 46
Inversion 47

45

76 Verneinter Satz (Negative sentence)

Subject	Auxiliary + "not"	Verb	Object
Mark	**can't**	speak	Italian.
The children	**aren't**	writing	letters.
The Jacksons	**don't**	like	Indian food.

Der verneinte Satz wird mit einem **Hilfsverb + not** gebildet. Ist kein anderes Hilfsverb vorhanden, muss eine Form von *do (do/does/did)* verwendet werden.

c Now try and clarify[3] the other mistakes in the above test with the help of your own grammar. Use the index and the table of contents.

[1] parking ticket *Strafzettel (für falsches Parken)* [2] specific [spəˈsɪfɪk] *bestimmt* [3] clarify [ˈklærɪfaɪ] *(er)klären*

Presenting a paper[1]

Prepare it

1

1. Collect all the material you can find about your topic. Check in a library, use an encyclopedia or the Internet, ask teachers, parents and friends.
2. Go through your material and decide which information is important. Write down useful excerpts or quotations[2].
3. Set an alarm clock[3] to ring after 10 minutes and make a list of what you now know about your topic. Don't stop before that.
4. Write down the key words from your list.

Structure it

2

A presentation[4] should be clearly structured in three parts. If you like, prepare index cards[5] with headings, key words and important excerpts or quotations.

Introduction

1. The first part of your presentation should make others feel you really have something important and interesting to say. A good way to start is by using short anecdotes[6], quotations, interesting statistics or jokes.
2. You need to tell your audience[7] at the beginning what you are aiming at. Explain the structure of your presentation in a few words.

Main part

1. The main part of your paper will present your main points. Your paper should go logically[8] from one point to the next.
2. Don't try to say everything you know about your topic. Decide what information is essential[9]. Give examples. Don't use specialized vocabulary. Try to use simple language or explain new words on the board.

Conclusion[10]

The conclusion should summarize your main points in a few words.

Organize it

3

1. Write down the complete text of your presentation. Read it aloud several times.
2. Write the introduction and conclusion on index cards. This will make you feel more sure of yourself.
3. Write down each point you want to make in note form on index cards. Number your cards.
4. Prepare a handout. Only use headings and leave lots of room for your listeners' notes.
5. Practise in front of a mirror, with a cassette-recorder or with friends.

[1] present a paper *ein Referat halten* [2] quotation [kwəʊ'teɪʃn] *Zitat* [3] set an alarm clock *einen Wecker stellen*
[4] presentation [ˌprezn'teɪʃn] *Vortrag, Referat* [5] index card ['ɪndeks kɑːd] *Karteikarte* [6] anecdote ['ænɪkdəʊt]
[7] audience ['ɔːdiːəns] *Zuhörer/innen, Publikum* [8] logical ['lɒdʒɪkl] *logisch* [9] essential [ɪ'senʃl] *wesentlich; unentbehrlich*
[10] conclusion [kən'kluːʒn] *Schluss*

Add colour

Now that you have got the 'bones'[1] of your talk, it is time to add the 'meat'. Keep your listeners' attention by making your presentation interesting.
For example, you can:

- write key words on the board or the overhead projector
- illustrate difficult concepts[2] with the help of transparencies[3]
- show pictures or objects
- use diagrams[4]
- use wall maps

These things will support your paper. Keep them short.

Present it

1. When you walk to the front of the classroom, concentrate on your body, breathe slowly and deeply, and keep your shoulders back.
2. Use your index cards and try to speak as freely as possible.
3. Link your sentences and paragraphs with expressions like *firstly, to start with*[5], *the next point I want to make is*.
4. Don't be afraid to repeat things. Summarize each point before you continue, e.g. *so, to summarize, in short*[6]. Show clearly with a pause when you move on to a new point.
5. Don't talk too fast or for too long. Keep eye contact. Watch your listeners' faces to see if they understand.
6. Be prepared to answer questions.
   Don't forget to thank your audience.

And remember:

– You are well prepared.
– You have your notes.
– You have something relevant[7] to say.

[1] bones [bəʊnz] *Knochen(gerüst)* [2] concept ['kɒnsept] *Begriff* [3] transparency [træns'pærənsɪ] *Folie*
[4] diagram ['daɪəgræm] *Diagramm, Schaubild* [5] to start with *zuerst, zunächst einmal*
[6] in short *kurz (zusammengefasst)* [7] relevant ['---]

Literary terms and their collocations

action *Handlung*
The ~ takes place in a small town / in 1989.
There is little / a lot of ~ in this novel.
In the course of the story the ~ develops dramatically[1].
The ~ covers the period of a day.

allusion [ə'lu:ʒn] *Anspielung*
When she says 'politics is a messy[2] business', this is an ~ to that episode when the crowd threw eggs at Mr Brooke.
This is a literary / historical / biblical ~ .
His/Her writing is full of ~*s* to …

author *Autor/in*
The ~ creates an atmosphere of sadness by using …
The ~*'s* intention is to show us what freedom might mean …
The ~ wants to make us aware of / make us think about …
He/She criticizes / blames[3] / encourages …
The ~ wants us to change our attitude towards …

character *Person, Figur; Charakter*
A is the main / an important / a minor[4] ~.
B is presented as a friendly ~.
The motive for C's behaviour / actions lies in his/her ~.
trait of character *Charakterzug*
Kindness is his/her dominant[5] ~.

characterize *beschreiben, charakterisieren*
The author ~*s* A implicitly[6] / explicitly.
B *is ~d* as an honest person / by his/her behaviour.

connotations *Nebenbedeutung(en), Beiklang*
This word / phrase has certain ~ for the reader.
It has ~ of love / closeness.

fable *Fabel*
The animals in the ~ behave as if they were human beings.
The moral of this ~ can be interpreted[7] in different ways.

image *sprachliches Bild*
A rose is the central / dominant ~ in the poem / story.
The ~ is well-chosen / powerful / hard to understand.
The ~ expresses / conveys the idea / feeling convincingly.
The function of the ~ is to make the reader realize / see that …
(→ metaphor, simile)

imagery ['ɪmɪdʒərɪ] *Bildersprache, Metaphorik*
The poem is full of the ~ of death.

metaphor ['metəfə] *Metapher, bildhafter Vergleich*
The author says Johnson is a 'tower of strength[8]'. This ~ is repeated in the next paragraph.
Her/His use of ~ is impressive[9].

narrator [nə'reɪtə] *Erzähler/in eines narrativen Textes / Prosatextes*
The ~ addresses the reader directly.
The ~ emphasizes / points out …

novel *Roman* (→ text, poem, short story)

play *(Theater-)Stück*
(→ text, poem, short story)

plot *Handlungsverlauf*
The ~ is very difficult to follow.
Tell me the ~ of the story.

poem *Gedicht*
The ~ is about / deals with / is concerned[10] with …
The ~ is easy / hard to understand.
It consists of six lines / stanzas / verses.
It arouses[11] people's emotions / pleasant feelings.
The words in line 4 are related to / associated with …
Through the ~ the poet makes us aware that …

poet *Dichter/in* (→ author)

[1] dramatic [drə'mætɪk] *dramatisch* [2] messy *schmutzig* [3] blame sb *jm die Schuld geben*
[4] minor ['maɪnə] *Neben(figur, -rolle)* [5] dominant ['---] *dominierend* [6] implicit [-'--] *indirekt* [7] interpret [ɪn'tɜ:prɪt]
[8] strength *Stärke, Kraft* [9] impressive *beeindruckend* [10] be concerned with *behandeln, handeln von*
[11] arouse [ə'raʊz] *wecken, erregen*

poetic[1] *dichterisch, poetisch*
The poet uses end rhyme / special stress patterns[2]/ repetition / a certain kind of rhythm as a ~ device[3].
The most obvious ~ device in this poem is the use of images / comparisons.

point of view *(Erzähl-)Standpunkt, (Erzähl-) Perspektive*
The story is told from the ~ of the narrator / the main character / a third person.
The author presents the events from the main character's / an observer's ~.

reader *Leser/in*
Most ~*s* might enjoy the story / poem / play because …
The ~ is puzzled[4] / confused / impressed by the title / ending / unfamiliar images.
The ~ can identify with the main character.
The ~ can understand why …
The ~ is deeply moved / misled by …

repetition *Wiederholung*
The passage / poem contains several ~*s*.
The ~ of the word '…' stresses / makes us see …
The author uses ~ to draw the reader's attention to …

rhyme *Reim; (sich) reimen*
The ~ scheme of the poem is a-b-a-b / (ir)regular.
The ~ scheme contributes to / adds to the atmosphere of the poem.
The author makes use of the ~ to emphasize that …
'Move' and 'love' *don't* ~.
'Cough' ~*s* with 'off'.

setting *Schauplatz*
The ~ of this story is (in) a village.
The ~ has a symbolic meaning.
The ~ reflects the main character's mood.

short story *Kurzgeschichte*
This text is typical of / contains the typical elements of / shows the typical structure of a ~.
The beginning / exposition[5] of this ~ ends in line X, the actual conflict / the climax is reached in line Y.
The ~ has a surprise ending / a happy ending / is open-ended[6].
The ~ is set[7] in a prison.

simile ['sɪməlɪ] *Vergleich mit den Wörtern 'like' oder 'as'*
The ~ 'he was as strong as a horse' is not very powerful in my opinion.

speaker (in a poem) *das „Ich" in einem Gedicht*
(→ narrator)

stanza *Strophe*
The first ~ begins with a description of …
In the second ~ the poet introduces / describes …
The first and the last ~*s* are quite simple / similar / different in structure.
The last ~ contains / conveys the message of the poem.

symbol *Symbol*
The bird is used as a ~ of freedom.
This ~ stands for …

symbolic [sɪm'bɒlɪk] *symbolisch*
The word '…' has ~ qualities / a ~ meaning.
The cross is ~ of Christian belief.

text *Text*
The ~ is an excerpt from / is based on …
The ~ deals with / is concerned with …
The ~ can be divided into four parts / passages.

theme *Thema*
The author treats his/her ~ with humour.
The ~ of this text is love.
The central / main ~ is introduced in lines 15 and 16.

tone *Ton; Stimmung*
The passage has a playful[8]/ humorous / sad ~.
The poet creates a serious ~ by using / choosing …

verse *Strophe, Vers* (→ stanza)

1 poetic [pəʊ'etɪk] 2 stress pattern *Betonungsmuster* 3 (poetic) device [dɪ'vaɪs] *(dichterisches) Stilmittel*
4 puzzled ['pʌzld] *verwirrt* 5 exposition [ˌekspə'zɪʃn] *Exposition, einführender Teil*
6 be open-ended *einen offenen Schluss haben* 7 be set in *spielen in* 8 playful *spielerisch, munter, ausgelassen*

Option 13

Indirect speech/Reported speech (Revision)

I met a wonderful boy at the disco yesterday. He's really good-looking. You'll probably see us at the baseball game next Friday.

Nancy

Tracey

When we report what someone has said, thought or written, certain changes are often necessary.

Look at how Tracey reports what Nancy has told her. Consider
a) tense changes,
b) pronoun changes,
c) vocabulary changes,
d) why one sentence hasn't been changed.

I talked to Nancy last Saturday. She told me she had met this great guy at the disco. She thinks that he's really good-looking. She said we would probably see them at the baseball game next Friday.

1 The main features of indirect speech

a If the introductory[1] verb is in the past tense (e.g. *she said, he told me*), there is usually a tense change (backshift of tenses). This tense change isn't always necessary, but it is never wrong.

Direct speech: (Tracey:) "I **haven't** met Nancy's boyfriend yet."
Indirect speech: Tracey **said** (that) she **hadn't** met Nancy's boyfriend yet.
…, sie **habe/hätte** Nancys Freund noch **nicht** getroffen.

present tense	→ past tense	*going to*-future	→ *was/were going to* + infinitive
past tense	↘	*will/won't*	→ *would/wouldn't*
present perfect	→ past perfect	*can, may*	→ *could, might*
past perfect	↗		

- *Would, could, should, ought to, might, must, needn't* don't change in indirect speech.
- The simple past (e.g. *I met*) often stays the same in indirect speech (i.e. *she said she met* rather than *she said she had met*).

b The tense needn't be changed if the statement is generally true (e.g. laws of nature like *The earth moves around the sun*), or if it is still true at the time of reporting.

Nancy **said** her boyfriend **is** eighteen.

c There is no tense change if the introductory verb is in the simple present *(she says)*, the present perfect *(she has said)*, or in the *will*-future *(she will say)*.

Nancy **says** we**'ll** probably **see** them at the baseball game.

⚠ In English there is no comma after the introductory verb.

2 Indirect questions

- The word order (S-V) in indirect questions is the same as in direct statements. *Do* is not used.
- The tense in indirect questions changes in the same way as in indirect statements.
- Yes/no questions are reported with *if* or *whether*.
- Question words (e.g. *when, where, why, how*) are used in the same way as in direct questions.

Direct speech: (Tracey:) "**Does** George **like** parties?"
Indirect speech: Tracey **asked** me **if/whether** George **liked** parties.

Direct speech: (Tracey:) "**What are** you **going to** wear at the party?"
Indirect speech: Tracey **asked** me **what** I **was going to** wear at the party.

[1] introductory [ˌɪntrəˈdʌktəri] *einleitend*

3 Commands[1], requests, suggestions and advice in indirect speech

Imperatives are reported with introductory verbs like *tell, ask, advise* or *suggest*:
- *Tell, ask, advise* are followed by an object + *to*-infinitive. (Negative imperatives are reported with *not to*.)
- *Suggest* is followed by an *-ing* form.

(*Tell, ask, advise* and *suggest* can be followed by a *that*-clause with or without *should*.)

Direct speech: (Teacher:) "**Don't buy** a little pocket dictionary. They don't have enough information in them. **Why don't you buy** a good monolingual[2] learner's dictionary?"

Indirect speech: My teacher **advised me not to buy** a pocket dictionary. She **suggested buying / (that) I (should) buy** a good monolingual learner's dictionary.

Ex 1 Women in politics

The following extracts are from a talk by the American politician Dianne Petonita about the changing role of women in politics.

Verbs to introduce indirect statements:

say, tell, mention, point out, think, be sure, agree, know, feel, explain, write, answer, hope, remember, complain, be sad, be sorry, be happy, stress the fact that, add, go on to say, predict[3]

Using indirect speech, write a short report of what Mrs Petonita said. Remember that in indirect speech people don't report everything exactly as it was said, just the most important points. So you needn't quote[4] *Mrs Petonita's exact words. It is more important to report what she meant rather than what she actually said.*

"... It doesn't matter what political beliefs a woman has. The question is whether she is interested in women's issues. ... As long as women have been able to vote, we have never been encouraged to enter politics. Women have always been told they have to have a family. ... What has now happened is that women, like myself, have started to get interested in politics at an earlier age. In other words, they can gain[5] political experience as early as men. ... Politics still is a male-dominated area. And a woman coming into politics can be seen as a threat. ... The important thing is to create respect. By doing this women create a position for themselves from which they cannot be pushed out. ..."

Ex 2 What did they want to know?

After the baseball game the other girls asked Nancy questions about her new boyfriend. *Say how Nancy reported the questions to her boyfriend later on.*

Verbs to introduce indirect questions:

ask, want to know, wonder

1. Why did he leave so early? 2. Did you first speak to him or did he first speak to you? 3. What does he plan to do after college? 4. Who did he go out with before? 5. Is there anything about him you don't like at all? 6. Did he give you the ring you're wearing? 7. Will you send him a Valentine[6] card? 8. How often have you seen him? 9. Can you give us his phone number? *Go on and make some more questions.*

Ex 3 Adults always know better!

Say what teenagers/you are often told to do/not to do by adults.

1. Don't leave your homework till the last minute. 2. You must work harder. 3. Don't sit around in your room all the time. 4. You can't stay longer than 10 o'clock. 5. Do as you're told. 6. Don't be late home. 7. Tidy up your room. 8. Wear a warm coat or you'll catch a cold[7]. *Go on.*

[1] command [kə'mɑ:nd] *Befehl* [2] monolingual [ˌmɒnə'lɪŋgwəl] *einsprachig* [3] predict [prɪ'dɪkt] *vorhersagen*
[4] quote [kwəʊt] *wörtlich anführen, zitieren* [5] gain [geɪn] *gewinnen, erwerben* [6] Valentine ['væləntaɪn]
[7] catch a cold *sich erkälten*

What to say in the UK

A quiz on British customs and manners[1]

**Decide if the following statements are true or false.
Discuss in class the reasons for your decisions.
As you work through the Option, check whether your decisions were correct or not.**

1 If somebody says to you, "How do you do?", he or she wants to hear about your problems or about your real feelings. It is quite normal to say that you have a terrible headache, you feel sick or you are in a bad mood[2].

2 The British **never** shake hands, except, of course, when they meet a German person.

3 The British think it is very rude if you just say "Yes" or "No" when they offer you something.

4 If you are staying with a British family, never start a meal before your host has said "Good appetite[3]" or "Mealtime".

5 If you ask for something in Britain, use the word 'please' as often as you can. Even small children are taught to say 'the magic[4] word' when they learn to speak.

6 Don't forget to say "Please" when somebody says "Thank you" to you.

7 If somebody offers you something and you don't really want to accept it, it is polite to say "No, thank you".

8 Young schoolchildren in Britain are taught to look right and then look left before they cross a road.

[1] manners ['mænəz] *Umgangsformen, Manieren* [2] be in a bad mood [mu:d] *schlechte Laune haben*
[3] appetite ['æpɪtaɪt] [4] magic ['mædʒɪk] *magisch, Zauber-*

When you go to Britain on holiday, on a class trip, or as part of an exchange with a British school, you don't need to worry. You have now learned enough English to get along very well in Britain. However, it might be helpful to practise the language again for some of the situations you might find yourselves in and to make your own *phrase book*[1]. This will make you more confident.

Meeting people

Two pupils from Munich, Lisa and Nadine, are taking part in an exchange with a British school. They have just arrived in Bath, a town in the southwest of England, and met the English family they are going to stay with: Mr and Mrs Wynne and their two children.

Listen to or read the following scene.

9

Mrs W.: Hallo, Lisa. Hallo, Nadine. It's nice to meet you. My name is Janice Wynne. And this is my husband, Tom.
Mr W.: How do you do? I'm pleased to meet you.
Lisa and Nadine: How do you do?
Mr W.: Well, did you have a good journey?
Lisa: Yes, thank you, but we're very tired. We left Munich yesterday afternoon, and we didn't sleep very much on the ferry.
Mrs W.: Well, we have a very comfortable room for you. I'm sure you'll feel at home. If you'd like[2] to come with us, we'll show you where we live. It's only 10 minutes in the car.
Lisa: Thank you.
Mr W.: Here, let me carry your luggage[3]. Our car is just over there.
Nadine: Thank you. That's very kind of you.
Mr W.: What was the crossing like?
Nadine: Terrible. The sea was rough and I felt seasick most of the time.

Some questions to help you find expressions for your phrase book:
1. How does Mrs Wynne introduce herself and her husband? 2. How does Mr Wynne greet[4] the girls? 3. How does Lisa answer Mr Wynne's question about their journey? 4. What does Nadine say when Mr Wynne offers to carry their luggage?

x 1 *Work in groups and practise how to introduce yourselves. Two of you are the English hosts, two are visitors.*

The British don't usually shake hands as often as the Germans. It is only usual when you meet somebody for the first time, or you haven't met somebody for a long time. Young people often just say "Hi" or "Hallo". "How do you do?" is not a question. It is a formal way to say "Hallo".

x 2 *Work in groups. Two of you are an English couple. Two others are tourists. Ask each other questions and develop a conversation about the journey: what the crossing or flight was like, how long it took, whether you have been to Britain before.*

When you meet people for the first time, it is important to talk. It is often an awkward[5] situation to meet somebody for the first time, and silence makes things worse. If somebody asks a question, don't just answer "Yes" or "No". Look again at how Lisa answers the question about their journey to Britain.

[1] phrase book *Sprachführer* [2] If you would like to … *(höfliche Formel für:) Sei(d)/Seien Sie bitte so freundlich und …*
[3] luggage ['lʌgɪdʒ] *Gepäck* [4] greet [gri:t] *(be)grüßen* [5] awkward ['ɔ:kwəd] *peinlich*

Mealtimes

If you stay with a family in Britain, you will certainly have some of your meals with them. You will not only find the food different, but also some of the customs.

Mrs W.: Good morning. If you'd like to sit down at the table, I'll get some breakfast for you. Would you like to start with fruit juice or cornflakes?
Lisa: Fruit juice, please.
Nadine: Can I have cornflakes, please?
Mr W.: Yes, of course. And would you prefer a full English breakfast with eggs and bacon or just toast and marmalade[1]?
Lisa: Just toast and marmalade for me, please. I don't usually eat a lot in the morning.
Nadine: I think I'll have eggs and bacon. I've always wanted to try that.
Mrs W.: Oh, and before I forget. Would you like tea or coffee?
Lisa: Tea for me, please.
Nadine: Could I have a glass of milk, please?
Mr W.: That's no trouble at all. Well, please start. The toast will be ready in a couple of seconds.

After the meal

Mr W.: Would you like some more toast or tea?
Lisa: No, thank you. I'm fine[2].
Nadine: That was delicious[3]. I really enjoyed it.
Mrs W.: Thank you. I'm glad you liked it. We'll be having an evening meal at about seven. Well, I hope you have a nice day.

Some questions to help you find expressions for your phrase book: How do the girls …
1. … say what they would like to eat? 2. … say what they would like to drink? 3. … explain that they have had enough to eat? 4. … compliment[4] Mr and Mrs Wynne on the meal?

Ex 1 *Work with a partner:*
- *Compliment the cook/your host after a meal, or after you have eaten some cakes or sandwiches.*
- *Imagine you are Lisa and you're still hungry. Ask politely for some more toast. Imagine you can't reach the salt or the sugar. How would you ask for them?*

Thank you. – No, thank you.
The British say "Thank you" to a compliment or when you give them something.
They say "No, thank you" to refuse an offer politely.

Please
The British use the word 'please' when they ask for something. They never say "Please" in reply to "Thank you" – they usually don't say anything at all. But if you want to be especially polite, you can say, "That's all right.", "Don't mention it."[5], "You're welcome." or "Not at all."[6]
The British have no expression for "Guten Appetit". They often say "Please start." or "Don't wait for us."

Ex 2 **Role play** *Write a dialogue, then role-play it.*

It's evening. Mrs Wynne asks Lisa and Nadine whether they had a nice day. She asks if they would like to eat dinner. Mr Wynne wants to know what kinds of things people eat in Germany.

[1] marmalade ['mɑːməleɪd] *Orangenmarmelade* [2] I'm fine. *Ich bin zufrieden/satt.* [3] delicious [dɪ'lɪʃəs] *köstlich*
[4] compliment (on) 1. *(v)* ['kɒmplɪment] *ein Kompliment machen (wegen, zu)*; 2. *(n)* ['kɒmplɪmənt] *Kompliment (zu)*
[5] Don't mention it. ['menʃn] *etwa: Nicht der Rede wert.* [6] Not at all. *Keine Ursache. Gern geschehen.*

Going into town

9

Lisa: Mrs Wynne, Nadine and I would like to change some money. Can you tell us where the nearest bank is?

Mrs W.: Yes, of course. It's a bit far to walk, though. Why don't you take the bus? The bus stop is only a couple of minutes away.

Nadine: Can you tell us how to get there?

Mrs W.: Go to the end of the road, turn right and go straight on until you come to the garage[1]. Turn right again and you'll see the bus stop. It's in front of a pub called *The King George*. Look for the number 27 bus. It'll say 'Town Centre' on the front.

Nadine: Do we have to change?

Mrs W.: No. Oh, and if you want to come back on the bus, they leave from the bus station every half hour at 7 and 37 minutes past the hour.

Lisa: I'm sorry, I didn't quite follow that. Could you say it again, please?

Mrs W.: Yes, of course. A bus leaves from the bus station at 7 minutes past the hour, and again at 37 minutes past.

Lisa: Oh, I see. Thank you. Can we bring anything back for you?

Mrs W.: It's very kind of you to ask, Lisa, but no thanks. I've got everything I need.

Nadine: Should we be back at any particular time?

Mrs W.: Well, we want to have dinner at seven o'clock. So try and be back by then, please.

Some questions to help you find expressions for your phrase book:
1. How do the girls ask for directions[2]? 2. How does Mrs Wynne give them directions to the bus stop? 3. How does Nadine ask if they have to take more than one bus? 4. How does Mrs Wynne tell the girls about the times of the buses back? 5. How does Lisa react when she doesn't quite understand what Mrs Wynne tells her? 6. What does Mrs Wynne say when Nadine offers to do some shopping for her?

x 1 *Work with a partner:*
- *Ask for and give directions to a bank, post office, the nearest telephone, the bus station. Use a map of your town or another town.*
- *Use timetables to explain when a bus or train leaves.*

People drive on the left in Britain, so be careful when you cross the road. You should look right first, then left before you cross the road. If you use a bike, wear a helmet and be particularly careful when you turn right.

x 2 **Role play**

Nadine and Cathy, the Wynnes' 14-year-old daughter, have decided to go into Bath by bus in the afternoon. Nadine wants to change some money at the bank. Then they would like to visit the old Roman baths and go on a boat trip along the river Avon. One trip leaves at 2.30, another at 3.30. The trips take an hour and a half. If the girls have time, they would also like to look at the shops. Most shops stay open till 5.30, so they could be back in time for dinner.
Role-play the dialogue as Nadine and Cathy plan the afternoon.

[1] garage *Reparaturwerkstatt mit Tankstelle*
[2] ask for/give directions [də'rekʃnz] *nach dem Weg fragen; den Weg erklären*

Option 14

Asking for permission and apologizing

Nadine: Mr Wynne, my parents would like to phone me while we are here. Could I call them quickly and give them your number?
Mr W.: Yes, of course. It's 01225 422778.
Nadine: That's very kind of you. I haven't seen a phone box near your house.
Mrs W.: No, I'm afraid there isn't one very near. Do you know the dialling code[1] for Germany?
Nadine: Yes, it's 0049, I think.

* * *

Lisa: We're going to a disco with some friends this evening. It could be quite late when we get back. I hope that's all right.
Mr W.: No problem, I'll give you a key. We don't go to bed before 11, but if you are coming home later than that, you'll need a key.
Mrs W.: The buses only run once an hour after 9 o'clock.
Mr W.: And the last bus is at 11 o'clock, I think.
Lisa: Oh, thank you.

* * *

Nadine: Excuse me, Mr Wynne. I think the chair is broken in our room. I sat down on it and it sort[2] of broke. I'm sorry if it was my fault.
Mr W.: Don't worry about it. It was an old one. I'll look at it later.

Some questions to help you find expressions for your phrase book:
1. How does Nadine ask for permission to use the phone? 2. How does she thank Mr and Mrs Wynne? 3. How does Lisa inform the Wynnes of the girls' plans for the evening? 4. How does Nadine explain about the chair? 5. How does Mr Wynne react?

Ex 1 *Work with a partner:*
– *Practise how to apologize because you are late, because you don't like a particular kind of food, because you are tired and would like to go to bed, or because you didn't understand what somebody said.*
– *Practise how to ask for permission to use the phone, to get a drink, to wash some clothes, to watch TV, or to stay out late because you want to go to a disco.*
– *Practise how to find out and say phone numbers in English.*

It is useful to have a phonecard in Britain, as many public telephones don't accept coins. You can buy a phonecard from a newsagent's[3] or a post office.

Ex 2 *Write a dialogue:*

It's time to leave Bath. Nadine and Lisa say goodbye to the Wynnes and thank them for their hospitality[4] and a wonderful stay. The Wynnes want to know if they enjoyed their stay.

[1] dialling code ['daɪəlɪŋ kəʊd] *Vorwahl(nummer)* [2] sort of (infml) *irgendwie*
[3] newsagent's ['nju:zeɪdʒənts] *Zeitungsladen* [4] hospitality [ˌhɒspɪ'tæləti] *Gastfreundschaft*

Varieties of English …

… around the world

There are many varieties of English, for example, British English, American English, Australian English or Indian English. These varieties of English are very similar, but there are some differences. The most important difference is pronunciation, but vocabulary and grammar can also vary[1].

Listen to the four people on the cassette. Make notes about them, the countries they come from and the variety of English they speak.

accent /'æksent, -sənt/ *n* a national, local or individual way of pronouncing words: *speak English with a foreign accent* ◦ *have an American accent* ◦ *a voice without (a trace of) accent.*

dialect /'daɪəlekt/ *n* the form of a language used in a part of a country or by a class of people with grammar, words and pronunciation that may be different from other forms of the same language: *the Yorkshire dialect* ◦ *a play written in dialect* ◦ *dialect words/ pronunciations.*

- In your own words, say what the difference is between a dialect and an accent.
- Why are learners of English usually taught 'standard British English' or 'standard American English'? What do you understand by these terms? Would you agree "that standard English is as much a dialect as any other variety"? Give reasons for your answer.

… in the UK

Different kinds of English can also be heard within the UK. Most native speakers speak English with a regional accent. This can often tell you where they are from, for example whether they are from the north or south of England, from Wales or from Scotland.

Listen now to these seven young people as they talk about themselves and where they live. Look at a map to see what parts of Britain they are from. What is special or interesting about their accents? Which accent do you find easiest and which most difficult to understand?

Fiona McKay, 16, Edinburgh

Kirsty McCall, 17, Belfast

Gwyneth Thomas, 16, Bangor

Oliver Weaver, 15, St Albans

Sudhamani Parekh, 18, Leeds

Jeff Turner, 21, Wigan

Vance Johnson, 17, London

… and according to social class and situation

The way people speak is not just a question of where they come from. Social class plays a role, too. What we say in a particular situation also depends on our topic and who we are communicating with. An informal conversation with a friend will contain different language from a letter of application[2] for a job.

[1] vary ['veəri] *variieren, sich unterscheiden* [2] letter of application [ˌæplɪ'keɪʃn] *Bewerbungsschreiben*

What to say in the USA

A quiz on American customs and manners[1]

Decide if the following statements are true or false. Discuss and explain the reasons for your decisions before you check the answers.

1 In the USA calling someone by their first name is like saying *du* to someone in German.

2 If you are invited to an American home for a meal, you should bring flowers for your host.

3 As a general rule Americans pay each other more compliments[2] than Germans do.

4 Americans usually wish each other "Good appetite[3]" before they begin a meal together.

5 It is considered polite in the US to leave a little bit of food on your plate when you have finished eating.

6 Because of the heating and air-conditioning[4] in most American homes and offices, it is important to keep doors closed.

7 Guests in an American home usually offer to help with household[5] work, including working in the kitchen.

8 When you need to use a toilet in the States, the polite thing to say is "May I use your toilet, please?" or "Where is your toilet?", or something similar.

9 Only very old-fashioned[6] people will be shocked[7] or surprised if you use so-called 'four-letter words'[8] in everyday[9] conversation (like the 's-word' and the 'f-word').

10 When Americans ask you "How do you like the US?", they usually expect a full and honest answer, including all the things you like and don't like about their country.

[1] manners ['mænəz] *Umgangsformen, Manieren* [2] pay sb a compliment ['kɒmplɪmənt] *jm ein Kompliment machen* [3] appetite ['æpɪtaɪt] [4] air-conditioning ['eə kənˌdɪʃnɪŋ] *Klimaanlage, Klimatisierung* [5] household ['--] *Haushalt(s-)* [6] old-fashioned *altmodisch* [7] shocked *schockiert* [8] four-letter word *etwa: unanständiges Wort* [9] everyday *Alltags-*

Answers

1 False.
American adults use first names with each other much more often than Germans. Neighbors, colleagues[1] at work (including the boss) as well as people you have met at a party or other social event are usually called by their first names. In banks, restaurants, stores, and other places where employees often wear name badges[2], either the first name only *(Tom)* or the first and last name *(Tom Brown)* will be printed[3] on the badge (very rarely *Mr. Brown*). Customers usually call the employees by their first names.
But there are some people who prefer to be called *Mr. Smith* or *Mrs. Riley* or *Ms. Stokey* by people they don't know well. Many people still expect and prefer children and young people to use the more formal expressions when they talk to adults. If you are a foreign visitor in the US, most people will probably say to you, "Please call me Bob (or Kathy or Bill)", but if you are in doubt[4], it's best to wait until they offer.
It's not impolite to greet people without using their name ("Hi!" or "Hello" is enough), but it's a little compliment to the person if you use their name when you speak to them.
Speaking of[5] names, as a foreigner you should be prepared to pronounce your name (both first and last) in an English way. People who don't know German will find it difficult to understand and say your name if you use the German sounds – especially if you have an 'r', 'ö' or 'ü' in your name.

2 False.
Although your host would probably be pleased to receive flowers (and enjoy the 'old European custom'), bringing flowers is not too common in the States and is certainly not something that is expected of a guest. However, it's never wrong to give a little present, like flowers, a box of chocolates[6], something you have made yourself, but it's not necessary.
When they are invited to an informal dinner, Americans very often ask their host, "What can I bring?", which means they would like to bring part of the meal. Among friends, it is common for one person to bring the salad and another the dessert[7], for example. The host then just prepares the main part of the meal.
If you stay overnight in someone's house, you should plan to give them a little present. As a foreigner, it's nice to bring something typical of your home country. It's a 'must' to write a thank-you note to your host a day or two after you have left.

What to say	
When you give someone a present, don't say "please" (German *bitte schön*). Instead you could say …	"This is for you." "I've brought you a little present." "Here's a little souvenir from Germany for you."
When someone gives you a present, you can say …	"Oh, thank you!" "Thank you, Brian, it's beautiful!" "How did you know I loved chocolates? These really look delicious[8]. Thanks!" "Oh, you really shouldn't have – but thank you very much."
When you leave someone's home …	"Thanks, Helen, I had a great time." "I'm sorry I have to leave already, but I have to be home by midnight. This was really a wonderful party. Thanks so much."
When a guest leaves your house, you can say …	"Thanks for coming." "I'm so glad you could come."

Note: Americans don't send greetings[9] to other people (*Schöne Grüße an deine Eltern*) as often as Germans do. If you wish to do this, however, you can say, "Please give my regards to your parents", or "Say 'Hi' to Bob for me".

[1] colleague ['kɒliːg] *Kollege, Kollegin* [2] name badge [bædʒ] *Namensschild* [3] print *drucken* [4] doubt [daʊt] *Zweifel*
[5] speaking of *apropos* [6] chocolates *Pralinen* [7] dessert [dɪ'zɜːt] *Nachtisch* [8] delicious [dɪ'lɪʃəs] *köstlich*
[9] greetings *Grüße*

3 True.
Most Americans are very generous[1] with compliments and very careful not to make comments that are too critical. The best reaction if someone pays you a compliment is to smile and say "Thank you" and accept the compliment.

4 False.
There is no similar expression. However, you should wait for some kind of signal[2] from your host before you begin to eat. Some families hold hands or say a prayer[3] before the meal. If you are the special guest, the host will probably give the bowls[4] of food to you first and say "Help yourself". It's polite to take at least a little bit of everything. The serving bowls are often sent around the table two or three times during a meal. Watch what the others are doing and keep passing them along.

5 False.
If you are a guest and don't eat everything, your host will probably be disappointed and think you didn't like the food. He or she will of course be pleased if you like the food – and if you say so. It's safest to take small portions[5] if you are not sure you'll like something. You will almost certainly be offered seconds[6] and then you can take more of the things you especially liked. If you are served something you really don't like and can hardly eat, you should never say "I don't like that". Try to be positive: take an extra portion of something you liked.
If you are in a restaurant and can't finish your meal, it's perfectly acceptable (even in an expensive restaurant) to ask for a 'doggy bag' so you can take home some of the food. Everyone knows that doggy bags aren't really for the dog.

What to say

If you are offered more food and would like to accept …	"Yes, please, it's really delicious." "Well, I'm getting quite full, but I'll have one more spoonful. It's so good." "Thanks. Everything tastes so good."

Note: A simple 'Thanks' or 'Thank you' by itself (without 'no' in front of it) means 'yes' in English, unlike in German, where a simple *Danke* usually means 'no': "Would you like some more coffee?" – "Thanks." (= "Yes, I would.")

And if you don't want any more …	"No, thank you." "I'm sorry. It's delicious, but I really couldn't eat any more, thank you."

6 False.
In American offices, schools, and private homes, room doors are usually left open. A closed door is a very clear sign that the person or persons inside want to be left alone. If you are given a room of your own in an American home, don't close the door unless you really want to be left alone. (Of course you can close it when you want to change clothes.) American families who often host[7] foreign students sometimes complain that their guests 'disappear' too much into their rooms and close the doors behind them. If the family is sitting together in the living-room or kitchen, they expect their guest to be there too, at least most of the time. Bathroom doors are also left open unless someone is using the room. In fact, a closed door is such a strong signal that the room is occupied, that if you close the bathroom door behind you when you leave the room, the other members of the household may think someone is still in there – and wait impatiently for a long time.

[1] generous ['dʒenərəs] *großzügig* [2] signal ['sɪgnəl] [3] prayer ['preə] *(Tisch-)Gebet* [4] bowl [bəʊl] *Schüssel* [5] portion ['pɔːʃn] [6] seconds *(pl) Nachschlag* [7] host sb [həʊst] *jn zu Gast haben*

7 True.
Unless you are invited to a very formal dinner, it's polite to ask if there is anything you can do to help. After an informal meal, the guests often help with the dishes.
If you are staying in an American home for a few days or longer, you should always ask what you can do to help around the house. You should at least make your own bed in the morning and keep your room as tidy as possible. Your host will probably tell you to help yourself to anything you want from the refrigerator[1]. But don't forget to put things away. Don't leave a mess[2] in the kitchen!

What to say	
If you want to help someone …	"Can I help you with something?" "Is there anything I can do to help?"
If someone offers to help you …	"No thanks, just enjoy yourself." "Thanks for offering. That would really be a big help."

8 False.
The word 'toilet' in American English is not exactly taboo[3], but it is not used very often. In private homes it's always the 'bathroom'. The question to ask is "May I use your bathroom?" – nobody thinks you plan to take a bath in there. (*Ich muss mal* is "I have to go to the bathroom".)
In a public place, e.g. a hotel or restaurant, the most common word is 'restroom', and the question to ask is "Where's the restroom?", but many people call public restrooms bathrooms too, at least informally. Other possible names are 'men's room' or 'ladies' room'.
In schools, toilets are usually called the 'boys' bathroom' and the 'girls' bathroom' even though it is not possible to take a bath in them!

9 False.
Although these words are not as taboo as they used to be and you will probably hear them often in the States, there are still a lot of people who would not be pleased to hear them, especially from a foreigner. The English 's-word' has a lot stronger shock-effect than the German '*Sch*-word'. Schoolteachers are often very strict about these words and punish any student who uses them in class. Be careful.

10 False.
This is a question you will probably hear very often as a guest in the USA. Most Americans expect a short, positive answer. "I'm having a great time!" or "There are so many new things to see and do here – it's really interesting".
In American newspapers and on TV you will probably read and hear lots of reports on the negative aspects of American life (drug problems, crime, homeless people, race problems, etc.) – but if an American family is kind enough to take you as a guest, they do not want to hear about all those negative things from you, the foreign guest. Americans are almost fanatical about wanting other people to like them – both as individuals and as a country. Be very careful with criticism and try to stress the positive.
You will probably find that most Americans are not too well-informed about Europe and most are not as interested in world politics as many Europeans are. On the other hand, Americans are usually open and friendly and interested in hearing about your home town and your lifestyle in Germany.

Now try to make up a similar quiz for American students who are planning to come and stay with a German family. How many 'tricky' points can you think of?

[1] refrigerator [rɪ'frɪdʒəreɪtə] *Kühlschrank* [2] mess *Unordnung, Durcheinander* [3] taboo [tə'buː] *tabu*

The passive (Revision)

"Excuse me, Mr Moneybags? It seems our computer was hacked[1] into by a young schoolboy last night. All our money has been transferred[2] to a Swiss bank. Your reputation will be seriously damaged if this story is made public ..."

Find all the passive forms.
Say what tense they are and how they are formed.

1 Use

a We use the passive to draw attention to what is done or happens to people or things. In most cases the 'doer' is unimportant, not worth mentioning, or unknown.

b If we want to say who the 'doer' is, we use *by*:
The loss of all the firm's money was discovered **by Mr Moneybags' secretary**.

2 Form

We form the passive in all tenses with a form of be + past participle, e.g. *is/are made*, *was/were made*, *has/have been made*, *had been made*, *will/can/must be made*. (In the present and past, progressive forms can also be used, e.g. *is/are being made*, *was/were being made*.)

3 The passive with different types of verbs

a Verbs with one object

Active: [subject: A boy] has transferred [object: the money] to Switzerland. According to our information, ...

Passive: ... [subject: it (the money)] **has been transferred** to a bank in Zurich[3].

b Verbs with two objects

With verbs with two objects (e.g. *tell, give, show, offer, send sb sth*), the indirect object is usually used as the subject of the passive sentence ('personal passive').

Active: The police gave [indirect object: Mr Moneybags] [direct object: some more information about the young hacker.]

Passive: [subject: He (Mr Moneybags) / Ihm (Herrn Moneybags)] **was given** details about the boy's family background.
wurden ... gegeben./Man gab ihm ...

c Prepositional verbs

Verbs connected with a preposition (e.g. *laugh at, ask/call for, think of, break into, look after*) can also be used in passive constructions. The preposition remains with the verb.

Active: A young schoolboy **broke into** the firm's computer system.
Passive: The computer system **was broken into** for the first time.

[1] hack into *mithilfe eines Personalcomputers unerlaubt in fremde Computersysteme eindringen*
[2] transfer [træns'fɜː], -rr- *überweisen* [3] Zurich ['zʊərɪk]

Ex 1 **Slaves and the slave trade** *Complete the text with the correct passive forms.*

Most slaves who (bring) to the New World to work on farms and plantations came from the 'Slave Coast' in West Africa. To make as much money as possible, slaves (pack) into ships like goods. It (estimate[1]) that one third of all slaves died before reaching America. The Atlantic crossing (describe) by a former slave in this way:
"We (catch) like animals and (take) to the coast, where a ship was waiting for us. There we (soon put) below deck. I (offer) food by some white men and then I (beat) because I refused to eat it. It was impossible to escape because we (watch) closely by the crew[2]. When we finally reached America, we (examine) by different people. We had to jump up and down, we (look at) closely and we (even laugh at). Then we (order) to leave the ship. Many of us thought we (eat) by the white men. We (finally tell) by some old slaves that we (not eat) but that we (force) to work in the fields. Later we (sell)."

Ex 2 **An earthquake report**
Some years ago a large earthquake hit Northern California. *Complete the following report with the correct active and passive forms.*

Earthquake shakes Northern California

At 5.04 pm local time the earth (begin) to shake. The quake's centre (be) 75 miles south of San Francisco, near Santa Cruz, where the downtown area (destroy) completely. The quake (last) for about 15 seconds and (feel) far beyond the Bay[3] Area. More than 60 people (die) and hundreds (injure). Lots of people (lose) their homes. The total damage which (cause) by the earthquake (estimate) at $10 billion[4].
The San Francisco region is known to be a major earthquake area, and a strong quake (expect) for a long time. This earthquake, however, (come) without warning. The worst damage (do) when a mile-long part of the top level[5] of a two-level highway in Oakland, a city on the east side of San Francisco Bay, (fall) onto the lower level. Many cars (crush[6]) and 42 people (die). A few miles away, cars and passengers (also trap[7]) when a 50-foot piece of the Bay Bridge, which

(connect) San Francisco and Oakland, suddenly (fall down).
People (now ask) how these highways (can fall down) although they (design) to survive even more powerful quakes.

Ex 3 **In English, please** *Translate the following text using the passive. Sometimes different passive constructions are possible.*

Gute Neuigkeiten! Man hat mir endlich eine Stelle angeboten. Aber meine Geduld ist wirklich auf eine harte Probe gestellt worden *(put to the test)*. Zuerst musste ich eine Bewerbung *(application)* an die Firma schicken. Außer mir wurden etwa zwanzig andere Bewerber *(applicants* ['æplɪkənts]*)* gebeten, einen Test zu machen. Einige Wochen später wurden zehn der Bewerber zu einem Interview eingeladen. Man befragte uns nacheinander, stellte viele Fragen über Zeugnisse *(qualifications)*, darüber, was man uns in der Schule beigebracht hatte, und über unsere Interessen im Allgemeinen. Nach den Interviews sagte man dreien von uns, dass wir im nächsten Monat mit der Arbeit beginnen könnten. Dann führte uns jemand in der Firma herum *(show around the company)* und gab uns weitere Informationen über unsere zukünftige Arbeit. Man zahlt uns 30 000 Dollar pro Jahr. Und man versprach uns sogar eine Sonderzahlung *(bonus)* an Weihnachten. Nicht schlecht, oder?

[1] estimate ['estɪmeɪt] *schätzen* [2] crew [kruː] *Mannschaft, Besatzung* [3] bay *Bucht* [4] billion ['bɪljən] *Milliarde*
[5] top level *hier: obere Fahrbahn einer doppelstöckigen Autobahn* [6] crush [krʌʃ] *zerquetschen*
[7] trap, -pp- *(wie in einer Falle) fangen, einschließen*

Option 18

Conditional sentences (Revision)

In these sentences the speakers state[1] conditions and talk about their possible consequences.
Say – in which part of the sentences the conditions/their consequences are expressed,
– what verb forms are used,
– which conditions can/cannot be fulfilled[2].

⚠ The *if*-clause can come before or after the main clause. A comma is often used when the *if*-clause comes first. There is usually no comma when the *if*-clause follows the main clause.

Conditional sentences I

If you **see** Professor Clever,	he**'ll talk** about his latest invention.
(this is possible and will probably happen)	you **must ask** him about his new magic drink.
	don't drink any of his magic drink.
if + present tense	*will*-future
	modal auxiliary + infinitive
	imperative

If + present tense is used if the speaker thinks that there is a real possibility that the condition will be fulfilled (it is a 'real condition').

⚠ Don't use *will* in the *if*-clause (even if the condition refers to the future)!

Instead of the simple present, other tenses or a modal auxiliary may be used in the *if*-clause, according to the context:

If Prof Clever **is** still **working** on his invention,	don't go into his room.
If he **hasn't invented** anything useful yet,	he ought to give up trying.
If you **should drink** any of his magic drink,	you'll certainly feel it soon.
(this is possible, but not very probable)	

The simple present is used in the *if*-clause and the main clause to talk about things that are always true:

If the temperature **falls** below zero,	water **freezes**.
(if = whenever)	

[1] state *nennen, angeben* [2] fulfil [fʊlˈfɪl] *erfüllen*

1. SPLASH bubble bath[1] – feel like a new-born baby

2. WIZARD vacuum cleaner[2] – spend less time on the housework

3. SOFT shampoo – shiny[3] hair

4. GENTLE[4] soap – softer[5] skin

5. HURRICANE toothpaste – fresh all day long

6. PIRATE, the new camera – fantastic pictures

Ex 1 Adverts

a *Make adverts for the products above and on the right.*

Example: WHIRL washing powder[6] – cleaner clothes
If you wash with WHIRL washing powder, your clothes will be cleaner.
or: If you want cleaner clothes, use WHIRL washing powder.

b *Make up some adverts yourself. Choose real products or invent your own.*

Conditional sentences II

a) If I **invented** a magic drink, (this is possible, but <u>improbable</u>)	I **would be** happy and I **could make** a lot of money.
b) If I **was** twenty years younger, (this is <u>impossible</u>)	I **might marry** the young woman.
if + past tense	*would/could/might* + infinitive

If + past tense is used if the speaker thinks that
a) it is improbable that the condition will be fulfilled, or
b) it is impossible that the condition can be fulfilled (this is an 'unreal condition').
The past tense in the *if*-clause does not refer to the past, but to the present or future.

⚠ Don't use *would* ('würde') in the *if*-clause!

In more formal English you can use *were* instead of *was* after *I/he/she/it:* If I **was/were** rich, I would …
Were is always used in the expression *if I were you*: If I **were** you, I would …

Ex 2 If pigs could fly …

a wing

Do you think pigs (fly) if they (have) wings?
– I don't think so. If pigs (want) to fly, they (need) huge wings. But I'm sure pigs are far too heavy, no matter how big their wings are.
I suppose if they (have) wings, it (not make) them much happier. They (probably be) locked up most of the time because they (fly away) from the farm if they (not be locked up). And if they (fly away), there (be) no chops[7] for dinner. There (really be) more disadvantages than advantages if pigs (have) wings. But a flying pig is a funny idea, don't you think?
– It certainly is. But I think I (prefer) it if I (have) wings myself. Because if I (have), I (fly) to a sunny island right now and I (not have to) do my homework.
Yes, 'If wishes (be) horses, beggars (ride)'.

Ex 3 I often wish I was a king, and then I could do anything

Say what you would or could do
– if you were a king/queen, a politician, a famous sportsman/sportswoman, James Bond, the head teacher of your school, a bird, …
– if you had a million dollars, a motorbike, magic powers, a time machine, …
Write a short text.

Ex 4 Life without cars

How would our lives be different if we didn't have cars?
Think of advantages and disadvantages.

[1] bubble bath *Schaumbad* [2] vacuum cleaner ['vækjʊəm] *Staubsauger* [3] shiny *glänzend* [4] gentle ['dʒentl] *zart, sanft*
[5] soft *weich* [6] washing powder ['wɒʃɪŋ ˌpaʊdə] *Waschpulver, -mittel* [7] chop [tʃɒp] *Kotelett*

Conditional sentences III

If Prof Clever **hadn't** later **lost** the formula[1],	he **would have become** famous.
If the young woman **had drunk** the new drink,	she **might have stayed** young for ever and
(this is no longer possible)	she **might** still **be** as beautiful as she was.
if + past perfect	*would/could/might* + *have* + past participle
	would/could/might + infinitive

If + past perfect is used if the condition can no longer be fulfilled (this is an 'unreal condition' referring to the past). The speaker speculates[2] about possible consequences of things that did not happen in the past.

Ex 5 If history had been different, ...

Just imagine some of the consequences – then and now. You needn't be too serious!

1. If the Romans had had planes, ...
2. If Columbus hadn't had a compass[3], ...
3. If Guy Fawkes hadn't been caught, ...
4. If Britain hadn't had so many colonies, ...
5. If the wheel hadn't been invented, ...
6. If I had been on the moon on July 21st, 1969, ...

Example: If William the Conqueror hadn't invaded Britain, he would never have seen the beautiful British Isles. He wouldn't have been called 'the Conqueror'. The Angles and Saxons could have lived in peace. British history and the English language would be totally different. We couldn't visit the castles the Normans built. Pupils wouldn't have to remember the date '1066'.

Ex 6 If I had lived a hundred years ago, ...

If you had lived a hundred or even more years ago, what would your life have been like?

Conditional sentences without *if*

If you **should wish** to complain, **Should** you **wish** to complain,	speak to the head teacher.
If the young woman **had drunk** the magic drink, **Had** the young woman **drunk** the magic drink,	she might have stayed young for ever.

In *if*-clauses with *should* or *had* the *if* can be left out in formal English. The subordinate clause must then begin with *should* or *had* + subject.

Ex 7 What have you learnt about *if*-clauses?

Put in the correct tense of the verbs. Be careful, sometimes there is more than one solution.

1. If I (be) you, I (accept) this offer. 2. If you (learn) your words well, you (not have to) be afraid of the vocabulary test. 3. I (meet) Mary this morning. I'm sure she (come) to your party last night if you (invite) her. 4. If you (enjoy) the party, (not go) home yet. 5. If your brother (drive) more carefully, the accident (not happen). 6. I (tell) Alan everything yesterday. (you/tell) him the truth if he (ask) you? 7. If air (get) warmer, it (rise). 8. I think life (be) very boring if we (have) nothing to do. 9. I (not suppose) Jack (call) while I (be) away, but if he (do), tell him I (ring) him back later. 10. If you (not forget) the map, we (not lose) our way. 11. If I (live) in Australia, I (probably be) a sheep farmer. 12. Take my advice! If you (give up) smoking, you (feel) a lot better.

[1] formula ['fɔːmjələ] *Formel* [2] speculate ['spekjʊleɪt] *nachdenken, Vermutungen anstellen*
[3] compass ['kʌmpəs] *Kompass*

Grammar for recognition[1]*: special* that*-clauses*

When you read English texts, you will sometimes come across[2] new structures. You should understand what they mean, but you don't necessarily have to use them in your own English. Often there are other ways of saying the same thing.

a *Look at the following sentence pairs and say what difference in structure there is between 1 and 2.*

1. – It is important that Carl realizes what we expect of him.
   – I suggest that we don't invite Ann.

2. – It is important that Carl should realize what we expect of him.
   – I suggest that we shouldn't invite Ann.

There is no difference in meaning between sentences 1 and 2. So how would you translate them into German?

that-clauses with *should* + infinitive

The doctor recommended[3] **that** Sonia **should stay** in bed for two more days.
It is desirable[4] **that** pupils **should not stay** out too late during term[5].
(= It is desirable for pupils not to stay out too late during term.)

A *that*-clause with *should* can be used to express the idea that something must or should be done.
Such a clause can be used after verbs like *advise, ask, recommend, request* or *suggest*, and after adjectives like *crucial*[6], *desirable, essential*[7], *important, vital*[8]. (We can also use *for* + *to*-infinitive to express the same idea.)

b *Here is another alternative with the same meaning as sentences 1 and 2 above. What is strange about the verbs in the* that*-clause?*

3. – It is important that Carl realize what we expect of him.
   – I suggest that we not invite Ann.

that-clauses with the subjunctive[9]

The doctor recommended **that** Sonia **stay** in bed for two more days.
It is desirable **that** pupils **not stay** out too late during term.

The subjunctive is a special form of the English verb: it is identical[10] with the infinitive. There is no *-s* in the third person singular, and no *do* in negative sentences. It is the same whether the sentence is present or past.

The subjunctive is mainly used in writing, and it is more common in American English than British English.
In British English, use of the subjunctive is restricted[11] to rather formal contexts.

⚠ The English subjunctive and the German 'Konjunktiv' are not used in the same way. The English subjunctive is not, for example, used in conditional sentences or to mark indirect speech.

Ex *Translate these sentences into German.*

1. It is important that inner-city areas with large black populations not be allowed to decay *(verfallen)* further. 2. Politicians of all parties are demanding that the Government spend more money on education. 3. It is desirable that children from all racial backgrounds should integrate. 4. A head teacher in Germany recommended that Turkish children and German children spend an evening with a family of the other nationality. 5. It is essential that everybody remember Martin Luther King's message. 6. We suggest that all students should be made to study Dr. King's famous speech 'I have a dream'.

[1] grammar for recognition [ˌrekəg'nɪʃn] *grammatische Erscheinungen, die man erkennen und verstehen sollte, aber nicht selbst zu verwenden braucht* [2] come across *begegnen* [3] recommend [ˌrekə'mend] *empfehlen*
[4] desirable [dɪ'zaɪərəbl] *wünschenswert* [5] term *Schulzeit (im Gegensatz zur Ferienzeit)* [6] crucial ['kruːʃl] *entscheidend*
[7] essential [ɪ'senʃl] *unbedingt notwendig, unerlässlich* [8] vital ['vaɪtl] *unbedingt notwendig, lebenswichtig*
[9] subjunctive [səb'dʒʌŋktɪv] *Konjunktiv* [10] identical [aɪ'dentɪkl] *identisch* [11] restrict (to) [rɪ'strɪkt] *beschränken (auf)*

Grammar review[1]

The main verb

1 Finite and non-finite verb forms . . . 121
2 Use of tenses: present and past time . . . 121
3 Use of tenses: future time . . . 122
4 The progressive aspect of the verb . . . 123

Be, *have* and *do*

5 ***Be***, ***have*** **and** ***do*** used as auxiliary verbs . . . 124
6 The main verb *be* . . . 124
7 The main verb *have* . . . 125
8 The main verb *do* . . . 125

Modal auxiliaries

9 Forms . . . 126
10 Time reference . . . 126
11 Meanings . . . 126

The infinitive

12 Forms . . . 128
13 The infinitive with *to* . . . 128
14 The infinitive without *to* after *let/make* + object . . . 129

The gerund

15 Forms . . . 129
16 The gerund as subject . . . 129
17 The gerund as object after certain verbs . . . 129
18 The gerund after prepositions . . . 130
19 The gerund after certain words and phrases . . . 130
20 The gerund with its own subject . . . 131

The participle

21 Forms . . . 131
22 Participles used with nouns . . . 131
23 (Adverbial) participle clauses . . . 131
24 Participles after verbs of perception + object . . . 132
25 Participles after verbs of rest and movement . . . 132

Subordinate clauses

26 Adverbial clauses . . . 132
27 Relative clauses . . . 134
28 *That*-clauses and indirect questions . . . 134

→ Option 8: Explaining grammar in English
→ Grammatical terms, pp. 186-187

[1] review [rɪ'vjuː] *Rückblick; Übersicht; (Stoff-)Wiederholung*

The main verb

1 Finite and non-finite verb forms

a I **live** in London now. I **lived** in Manchester before.
Mike often **goes** to the cinema, but his parents usually **go** to the theatre.
I **am** first, you **are** second and Sonia **is** third. OK?

The finite forms of the verb show contrasts of tense *(I live – I lived)*. They can also show contrasts of number *(he goes – they go)* and person *(I am – you are – she is)*. Finite verb forms can be the main verb in a simple sentence.

b I am happy **to live** in London, but I wasn't quite so happy **to live** in Manchester.
Mike likes **going** to the cinema, but his parents prefer **going** to the theatre.
Asked to leave, I/he/we/they protested.

The non-finite verb forms do not show contrasts of tense, number or grammatical person. There are three forms: the infinitive (e.g. *to live*), the gerund (e.g. *going*) and the participle (e.g. *asked*).

→ The infinitive 12-14 → The gerund 15-20 → The participle 21-25

2 Use of tenses: present and past time

a Simple present

Active: **ask/asks** Passive: **am/is/are asked**

I usually **go** to bed late.	– a regular action or habit
My parents **hate** discos.	– a (present) state
Food **gives** you energy.	– a permanent fact

b Present progressive

Active: **am/is/are asking** Passive: **am/is/are being asked**

It**'s raining** now, look.	– an action that is in progress at the moment
I**'m going** to school by bus this week.	– a temporary routine[1] or situation

Simple present and present progressive in contrast

Simple present:
repeated actions and habits

I often **write** letters to my friends.
We usually **have** lunch at home.

Present progressive:
actions at the moment; temporary routines

I**'m writing** postcards at the moment.
This week we**'re having** lunch at school.

c Present perfect

Active: **has/have asked** Passive: **has/have been asked**

Someone **has taken** my bike.	– an action in the period up to the present
I **have known** Jane since 1991.	– a state that began in the past and has continued up to the present

d Present perfect progressive

Active: **has/have been asking**

They **have been walking** for hours.	– an action that has been going on continuously[2] up to the present
We **have been discussing** the problem for years now.	– an action that has gone on repeatedly up to the present

[1] routine [ruːˈtiːn] *Routine, gewohnheitsmäßige Ausführung einer Tätigkeit*
[2] continuous [kənˈtɪnjʊəs] fortlaufend, ununterbrochen

Grammar review

e **Simple past**

Active: **asked**	Passive: **was/were asked**

The plane **arrived** at 10.50.
The police **caught** the thief last night.
– an action that happened at a point of time in the past, or during a period of time that finished in the past

I **was** ill last week.
– a past state

f **Past progressive**

Active: **was/were asking**	Passive: **was/were being asked**

It **was raining** when we got off the bus.
– an action that was in progress at a particular point or period of time in the past

Present perfect and simple past in contrast

Present perfect:	**Simple past:**
actions in the period up to the present; states in the period up to the present	actions in the past; past states
Have you **seen** John? I **have lived** here since 1994.	I **saw** John yesterday. I **lived** in London from 1980 to 1994.

g **Past perfect**

Active: **had asked**	Passive: **had been asked**

When I looked at her photo, I knew that I **had seen** her before.
– an action before a point of time in the past

They **had been** friends for a long time before they got married.
– a state before a point of time in the past

h **Past perfect progressive**

Active: **had been asking**

She **had been waiting** a long time when Tom finally came.
– an action that had been going on up to a point of time in the past

3 Use of tenses: future time

a ***Will*-future**

Active: **will ask**	Passive: **will be asked**

The weather **will be** fine.
– a future event which cannot be influenced or controlled

I expect Tim **will get** the job.
– a prediction[1] of future events

Wait a minute. I**'ll help** you.
– a spontaneous[2] reaction, a promise, an offer

b **Future progressive**

Active: **will be asking**

What **will** they **be doing** this time tomorrow?
– an action that will be in progress at a point of time in the future

I**'ll be seeing** Carl at the disco tonight. He's usually there.
– a future action which is expected to happen anyway (as the result of a routine)

[1] prediction [prɪ'dɪkʃn] *Voraus-, Vorhersage* [2] spontaneous [spɒn'teɪnɪəs] *spontan*

c **Future perfect**

Active: **will have asked**	Passive: **will have been asked**

We**'ll have finished** this job in an hour or two. – something that will be over at a point of time in the future

d ***Going to*-future**

Active: **am/is/are going to ask**	Passive: **am/is/are going to be asked**

We**'re going to visit** my sister next week. – a plan, an intention

It's already ten. You**'re going to miss** the bus. – a future event based on present evidence

e **Present progressive**

Active: **am/is/are asking**	Passive: **am/is/are being asked**

We**'re playing** tennis tomorrow. – something that has been arranged for the future

f **Simple present**

Active: **ask/asks**	Passive: **am/is/are asked**

The next train **leaves** at six. – a future event which is part of a timetable or calendar

4 The progressive aspect of the verb

a Laurie **is working** in the garden.
We **have been watching** TV since lunch.
I **was having** a bath when you phoned.
What **will** our friends **be doing** when we get home?

The progressive form of the verb is used to say that an action is, was or will be in progress at a particular point of time. The action is, was or will be not complete or not permanent.

Compare:	Progressive form:	I**'m reading** the newspaper.	(not complete)
		The tourists **were lying** on the beach.	(not complete)
	Simple form:	I**'ve read** the newspaper.	(complete)
		London **lies** on the Thames.	(permanent)

b Most English verbs can be used in the simple form and the progressive form. They are called **activity verbs**.
Examples: *ask, catch, give, help, make, rain, talk, work.*

c Some verbs cannot normally be used in the progressive form. These verbs are called **state verbs**.
The most common state verbs are:

– *be, belong to, consist of, contain, cost, depend on, have* (besitzen), *look* (aussehen), *mean, need, own, seem, smell (of)* (riechen nach), *sound, taste (of)* (schmecken nach), *weigh* (wiegen/Gewicht haben)*;*
– verbs expressing mental[1] or emotional[2] states: *agree, believe, disagree, imagine, know, realize, recognize, remember, see* (verstehen, einsehen), *suppose, think* (meinen, glauben), *understand, wonder;*
– verbs of liking and disliking: *dislike, hate, like, love, mind, prefer, want, wish;*
– verbs of perception: *feel, hear, notice, see, smell, taste.*

[1] mental ['mentl] *geistig* [2] emotional [ɪ'məʊʃənl] *Gefühls-, seelisch*

d Some verbs have different meanings. They can describe activities or states. As activity verbs they can be used in the simple and the progressive form. As state verbs they are normally used in the simple form only. Examples:

Activity verbs	State verbs
I'**m looking** at the castle. Ich schaue mir das Schloss an.	This castle **looks** very old. Dieses Schloss sieht sehr alt aus.
What **are** you **thinking** about? Worüber denkst du nach?	**Do** you **think** we should go? Meinst du, wir sollten gehen?
I'**m having** a shower. Ich dusche gerade.	Our friends **have** a caravan. Unsere Freunde haben einen Wohnwagen.
The cook **is tasting** the soup. Der Koch/Die Köchin probiert die Suppe.	The soup **tastes** wonderful. Die Suppe schmeckt wunderbar.

Be, have and *do*

Be, have and *do* can be auxiliary verbs or main verbs.

5 *Be, have* and *do* used as auxiliary verbs

Jane **is repairing** her motorbike.
This church **was built** in the 16th century.

be: – Progressive: form of *be* + *-ing* form
– Passive: form of *be* + past participle

Sandra **has broken** her leg.
I remembered that I **had seen** her before.

have: – Present perfect: *have/has* + past participle
– Past perfect: *had* + past participle

I **don't know** that girl.
Does she **live** here?
You **didn't phone**, **did** you?
Don't smoke in here.

do: – Simple present/past: negative statements
– Simple present/past: questions
– Simple present/past: question tags
– Negative imperatives

The auxiliary verbs *be, have* and *do* are used with main verbs to form the progressive, the passive, the perfect and some negative and question forms.

6 The main verb *be*

a My sister **is** a pilot.
We**'re** lucky.
I **was** in London last week.

The main verb *be* is used as a linking verb between the subject and a complement (noun, adjective) or adverbial.

b Sita **is** always kind. (permanent state)
Sita **is being** very kind today. (temporary behaviour)

Be is a state verb and is most often used in simple tenses. But the progressive form (e.g. *is being*) can be used for temporary behaviour.

c **There are** a lot of people in the waiting-room.
Im Wartezimmer sind viele Leute.

There's a good film on TV tonight.
Heute Abend gibt es einen guten Film im Fernsehen.

Were there any phone calls for me?
Gab es Anrufe für mich?

There was no doubt. She was quite sure.
Es gab keinen Zweifel.

There + *be* is used to say that something exists somewhere. This structure is normally used with 'indefinite subjects', e.g. nouns with *a/an/some/any/a lot of/no*.

7 The main verb *have*

a *Have* as a state verb

We aren't allowed **to have** pets in our flat.
My friends **have (got)** a large garden.
Tom **has had** a cold for a week now.
We **had** a dog when I was ten.

When it expresses possession[1] and other related meanings, *have (got)* is a state verb. It is not used in the progressive form. *Got*-forms of *have* are informal, and are mostly used in the present.

Sally **hasn't got** a sister.	=	Sally **doesn't have** a sister.
Has she **got** a brother? – Yes, she **has**.	=	**Does** she **have** a brother? – Yes, she **does**.
		We **didn't have** a dog when I was twelve.

Negatives and questions with *have got* are formed without *do/does*.
Negatives and questions with *have* in the simple present and simple past are formed with *do/does/did*.

b *Have* as an activity verb

I'd like **to have** a cup of tea. (= to drink)
Peter **is** just **having** a wash. (= is washing himself)
We **don't have** breakfast before seven. (= don't eat)

Have + object is often used to express actions. Here *have* is an activity verb and can be used in the progressive form. Negatives and questions in the simple present and the simple past are formed with *do/does/did*.

Common expressions:

have breakfast/lunch/tea/a drink/a meal
have a bath/a shower/a wash
have a walk/a run/a ride/a swim/a dance
have a good time/a nice morning/a holiday/fun
have a sleep/a dream
have a talk/a conversation/an argument
have a look/a guess/a try

8 The main verb *do*

What **are** you **doing**?
We **didn't do** much yesterday.
They **will do** what they can to help you.
Have you **done** the shopping?
Did you **do** the translation yesterday?

The main verb *do* is used to talk about actions. It is an activity verb and can be used in the progressive form. Negatives and questions are formed in the same way as with other main verbs.

[1] possession [pəˈzeʃn] *Besitz*

Grammar review

Modal auxiliaries

9 Forms

a I/You/He/She/We/They **can** speak English.
She **shouldn't** drive so fast, **should** she?
What **shall** we do?

The modal auxiliaries are *can, could, may, might, will, would, shall, should, must, ought to, needn't.* They always have the same form. They do not have *-s* in the third person singular. They are followed by an infinitive without *to.* *Do/does/did* is not used with a modal auxiliary.

b I **can't** go to discos this year. But I**'ll be allowed to** go next year.

Modal auxiliaries cannot form every tense. But there are substitutes[1] for some modal auxiliaries: *be able to, be allowed to, have to.*

10 Time reference[2]

a That **must** be Tom. I know his voice.
Das muss Tom sein.

I **might** go to London tomorrow.
Ich fahre vielleicht morgen nach London.

Modal auxiliaries normally refer to the present or the future.

b My brother **could** walk when he was eleven months old. (past)
Mein Bruder konnte laufen, …

Tom asked what they **should** do. (indirect speech)
Tom fragte, was sie machen sollten.

Could, would, should, might can sometimes be used as past forms of *can, will, shall, may,* especially in indirect speech after a past reporting verb.

c What **can have happened** to Jonathan?
Was kann nur mit Jonathan passiert sein?

You **should have asked** me before you accepted their offer.
Du hättest mich fragen sollen, …

Modal auxiliaries + perfect infinitive (*have* + past participle) can refer to the past.

11 Meanings

Modal auxiliaries fulfil the following functions:
- They express meanings such as ability, permission, prohibition[3], necessity[4] or obligation. → 11a-c
- They can be used to give advice, make requests and offers, invitations and suggestions. → 11d-g
- They can be used to express various degrees of certainty[5], probability[6] and possibility. → 11h

a **Ability: *can, could* (substitute: *be able to*)**

My sister **can** stand on her head.
Could you swim when you were five?

We **were able to** get a taxi, so we arrived in time.
My leg is better now. Next week I**'ll be able to** move it again.

[1] substitute ['sʌbstɪtjuːt] *Ersatz, Stellvertreter* [2] reference ['refərəns] *Bezug* [3] prohibition [ˌprəʊɪ'bɪʃn] *Verbot* [4] necessity [nə'sesətɪ] *Notwendigkeit* [5] certainty ['sɜːtntɪ] *Gewissheit* [6] probability [ˌprɒbə'bɪlətɪ] *Wahrscheinlichkeit*

b Permission: *can, may, Could …?* – Prohibition: *can't, may not, mustn't* (substitute: *be allowed to*)

You **can** ask/**are allowed to** ask questions if you need help.
Every citizen **may** vote in elections.
May/Can/Could we use your telephone, please?

I'm sorry but you **can't/may not** swim/**aren't allowed to** swim here.
Teacher: You **can't/mustn't** use a dictionary in the test.

c Necessity, strong obligation: *must, needn't* (substitutes: *have to, need to*)

I **must** go home. I don't feel well.
Sorry, I **have to** go. The last bus leaves in a few minutes.
We **needn't** work/**don't have to** work/**don't need to** work today.
Luckily I**'ve** never **had to** go/I**'ve** never **needed to** go into hospital.

d Advice, obligation: *should, ought to; had better*

You **should** apologize/**ought to** apologize for what you said.
Your sister **shouldn't** have done that.

You **had better**[1] be home by 11 o'clock.

Had better (not) is stronger than *should* or *ought to* and can express a threat or warning.

e Requests: *Can/Could you …?, Will/Would you …?*

Can/Could you tell us more about the pupil exchange programme?
Will/Would you post this letter for me, please?

f Offers, invitations: *I'll/We'll …, Shall/Can/Could I …?, Will/Won't you …?, Would you like (to) …?*

I'll carry your bag for you.
Shall/Can/Could I help you carry your bag?

Will/Won't you join us?
Would you **like to** have dinner with us on Sunday?

g Suggestions: *can/could, might, Shall I/we …?, Can't/Couldn't …?*

We **can/could** eat in a restaurant if you like.
You **might** ask Bill; he'd know.

Shall we meet at two?
Can't/Couldn't we take the car?

h Degrees of certainty: *might, could, may, should/ought to, must, can't be*

She **might** be at home.
Sie könnte eventuell zu Hause sein.

She **could** be at home.
Sie könnte zu Hause sein.

She **may** be at home.
Sie ist vielleicht zu Hause.

She **should** be/**ought to** be at home.
Sie sollte/müsste/dürfte zu Hause sein.

She **must/can't** be at home.
Sie muss/kann nicht zu Hause sein.

possibility
↓
probability
↓
certainty

[1] had better do *lieber tun sollen*

Grammar review

The infinitive

12 Forms

	Active	Passive
Present infinitive	**(to) ask**	**(to) be asked**
Perfect infinitive	**(to) have asked**	**(to) have been asked**
Progressive form	**(to) be asking**	

→ Modal auxiliaries + infinitive without *to* 9a

13 The infinitive with *to*

a The *to*-infinitive after certain verbs, adjectives and nouns

They didn't **expect to be** home before ten.
Sue was very **happy to see** her American friends.
Your **decision to go** to Cuba surprised us all.

→ *to*-infinitive or gerund after certain verbs 17b/c

b The *to*-infinitive after certain verbs + object

Pete **wants Anne to go** to the party with him.
Pete möchte, dass Anne mit ihm zur Party geht.
They **told us not to forget** our passports.
Man sagte uns, dass wir unsere Pässe nicht vergessen sollten.

After certain verbs + object the *to*-infinitive can be used. They are mainly verbs of request and wanting (e.g. *advise, ask, expect, invite, remind, teach, tell, want, wish, would like*). The object of the verb (e.g. *Anne, us*) is the 'subject' of the *to*-infinitive.

c The *to*-infinitive to express purpose

We left early **(in order) to avoid** the traffic.
My brother is studying in the USA **to improve** his English.

d The *to*-infinitive to express result

It's **too windy to sit** in the garden today.
Tom isn't **confident enough to win** the match.

After *too* + adjective/adverb and after adjective/adverb + *enough*, the *to*-infinitive can be used to express result.

e The *to*-infinitive after question words and 'whether'

We didn't know **who to ask**.
The question is **whether to go** by car or by bus.

→ Indirect questions 28b

f The *to*-infinitive after *for* + noun/pronoun

Here's a magazine **for Terry to read** on the journey.
That's too difficult **for a young person to understand**.
The earth is too dry **for plants to grow**.
Tom is waiting **for his wife to phone**.

g **The *to*-infinitive after certain nouns, *someone, something* etc., and after adjectives**

Miss Jones is **the woman to organize** the show.
We need **someone to help** us.
Tim is always **the last to come**.
The youngest girl to play the trumpet is six.

The *to*-infinitive can be used after *man, woman, person* etc., after *someone, something, anybody* etc., after *the first/last/next/only* or after a superlative (+ noun).

→ Relative clauses 27c

14 The infinitive without *to* after *let/make* + object

My mother **lets me watch** TV every evening.
Meine Mutter lässt mich jeden Abend fernsehen.

Mr Connor never **makes Kevin clean** his room.
Mr Connor zwingt Kevin nie, sein Zimmer sauber zu machen.

The infinitive without *to* is used after *let* (German 'zulassen, erlauben') and *make* (German 'veranlassen, zwingen, dazu bringen') + object.

→ The infinitive without *to* after verbs of perception 24

The gerund

15 Forms

	Active	Passive
Present	**asking**	**being asked**
Perfect	**having asked**	**having been asked**

16 The gerund as subject

Flying is great fun.

The gerund can be used as the subject of the sentence.

17 The gerund as object after certain verbs

a My father **dislikes doing** the housework.
Could you **imagine living** in Hong Kong?

The gerund is used after certain verbs, e.g. *admit, avoid, consider, dislike, enjoy, finish, give up, imagine, keep (on), mention, mind, miss, practise, risk, suggest.*

"Excuse me, but would you mind scratching[1] my nose?"

b I **hate** | **flying**. / **to fly**.

The children **like** | **watching** TV. / **to watch** TV.

Some verbs, e.g. *begin/start, continue, hate, like, love* and *prefer* may be followed by a gerund <u>or</u> a *to*-infinitive without a difference of meaning.

[1] scratch [skrætʃ] *kratzen*

c I'll never **forget climbing** in the Rocky Mountains.
Ich werde nie vergessen, wie ich in den Rocky Mountains geklettert bin.

Don't **forget to phone** your father.
Vergiss nicht, deinen Vater anzurufen!

I still **remember skiing** for the first time.
Ich erinnere mich noch, wie ich zum ersten Mal Ski gefahren bin.

You must **remember to post** the letter tomorrow.
Du musst daran denken, morgen den Brief einzustecken.

She **went on talking** as if nothing had happened.
Sie sprach weiter, als ob nichts geschehen sei.

After discussing the economy, the president **went on to talk** about foreign policy.
…, sprach er als Nächstes über die Außenpolitik.

You should **stop smoking**.
Du solltest mit dem Rauchen aufhören.

After three hours we **stopped to have** a drink.
Nach drei Stunden hielten wir an, um etwas zu trinken.

The bus has gone. That **means taking** a taxi.
… Das bedeutet, dass wir ein Taxi nehmen müssen.

Sorry, I didn't **mean to interrupt** you.
Es tut mir Leid, ich wollte dich nicht unterbrechen.

Try going to work by public transport.
Versuch mal, mit öffentlichen Verkehrsmitteln zur Arbeit zu fahren.

Try to be here by seven.
Versuch, bis um sieben hier zu sein!

With the verbs *forget, remember, go on, stop, mean* and *try*, there is a difference of meaning between 'verb + gerund' and 'verb + *to*-infinitive'.

18 The gerund after prepositions

a Are you **interested in working** for us?
I hate the **idea of getting** old.
My little sister often **dreams of becoming** a pilot.

The gerund is used after prepositions which are closely linked with an adjective, noun or verb.

b Why don't you do some work **instead of sitting** in front of the television?
Before talking to your boss, think about your arguments.

The gerund is used after prepositions which are not linked with a certain word, e.g. *after, before, by, for, instead of, in spite of, without.*

→ Adverbial clauses 26g

19 The gerund after certain words and phrases

It's not much **fun spending** the evening alone.
How about having a cup of coffee?

The gerund is used after certain expressions, e.g. *it's no use*[1], *it's no good*[2], *it's worth*[3], *it's fun, can't/couldn't help*[4], *how/what about …?*

[1] it's no use *es hat keinen Zweck* [2] it's no good *es hat keinen Zweck* [3] it's worth *es lohnt sich*
[4] can't help doing *nicht umhin können zu tun, einfach tun müssen*

20 The gerund with its own subject

We hate **our neighbours playing** their cassette-recorder in the garden.
Do you mind **me sitting** next to you?

A noun or personal pronoun can be the 'subject' of the gerund.
When a personal pronoun is the subject of the gerund, it usually has the object form: *me, him, her, …*

Compare: **John** loves **going** to discos.
But John's father doesn't like **him going** so often.

The participle

21 Forms

A participle can be an *-ing* form like *asking* (present participle), or a form like *asked, kept, gone* (past participle).
In participle clauses, there are also progressive, passive and perfect forms:

	Active	Passive
Present participle	**asking**	**being asked**
Past participle		**asked**
Perfect participle	**having asked**	**having been asked**

22 Participles used with nouns

a The exchange was a **fascinating experience**.
… eine faszinierende Erfahrung.

Have they found the **stolen car**?
… das gestohlene Auto?

Participles can be used before nouns. Compounds are often formed with them: *a good-looking teacher, a well-organized party, a time-saving invention.*

b **Machines produced** in Germany are exported to many countries.
Maschinen, die in Deutschland produziert werden, werden in viele Länder exportiert.

Do you know any of **the people taking part** in the exchange programme?
Kennst du jemanden von den Leuten, die am Austausch teilnehmen?

In certain cases, participle clauses can be used in the same way as relative clauses.

‣ Relative clauses 27d

23 (Adverbial) participle clauses

a I cut my hand **opening** a can of coke.
Ich schnitt mir in die Hand, als ich eine Dose Cola öffnete.

Warned not to walk the streets at night, the reporter took a taxi.
Da der Reporter davor gewarnt worden war, nachts allein auf die Straße zu gehen, nahm er ein Taxi.

Participle clauses can often be used in the same way as adverbial clauses of time and reason. The subject of the participle clause is usually understood to be the same as the subject of the main clause. Adverbial participle clauses are mainly used in formal English.

‣ Adverbial clauses 26g

b **If posted** first class, a letter should arrive the following day.
Wenn ein Brief als Eilbrief aufgegeben wird, sollte er am folgenden Tag ankommen.

Although feeling better, the patient was advised to remain in hospital.
Obwohl sich die Patientin besser fühlte, wurde ihr empfohlen, noch im Krankenhaus zu bleiben.

Participle clauses can be used after conjunctions such as *after, before, when, while, until, since, (al)though, if.* *Because* and *as* cannot be used before a participle.

‣ Adverbial clauses 26g

c **With the children making** such a noise, **I** can hardly work.
Wenn die Kinder solchen Lärm machen,/Bei dem Lärm der Kinder kann ich kaum arbeiten.

You can't go to school **with your hair looking** like that.
Du kannst nicht zur Schule gehen, wenn deine Haare so aussehen/mit diesen Haaren.

A participle clause can sometimes have a subject which is different from the subject of the main clause. In that case *with* is often used to introduce the participle clause.

24 Participles after verbs of perception + object

We **saw a lot of people waiting** at the entrance.
Wir sahen viele Leute am Eingang warten.

Couldn't you **hear us shouting**?
Konntest du uns nicht rufen hören?

After verbs of perception such as *feel, hear, notice, see, watch, smell* an object + present participle can be used.

Verbs of perception (except *smell*) can also take an object + infinitive without *to*. Compare:

I **watched the men building** a new house.
The present participle is used to say that the action is or was seen in progress.

I **watched the children build** a castle in the sand.
The infinitive is used to say that the complete action is meant.

25 Participles after verbs of rest and movement

I can't just **stand** here **talking**.
Ich kann hier nicht einfach rumstehen und reden.

Some children **came running** towards us.
Einige Kinder kamen auf uns zugerannt.

After verbs of rest (e.g. *lie, remain, sit, stand*) and after some verbs of movement (e.g. *come, go*), a present participle can be used.

Subordinate clauses

26 Adverbial clauses

We arrived at the cinema | **after eight**. (adverbial phrase)
| **after the film had started**. (adverbial clause)

Though David played well, he lost the game.

An adverbial clause has the same function in a sentence as other adverbials. It is always introduced by a conjunction such as *after, because* or *though*.
When the adverbial clause comes at the beginning of the sentence, it is often separated off by a comma.

a Adverbial clauses of time

We arrived **after** our friends had left the party.
Close the windows **before** you leave.
When we're in town, we usually have lunch in a restaurant.

Conjunctions: *after* (nachdem), *as* (als), *as long as* (solange wie), *as soon as* (sobald), *before* (bevor, ehe), *by the time* (bis), *once* (sobald, wenn), *since* (seit, seitdem), *till/until* (bis), *when* (wenn; als), *whenever* (wann auch immer; jedes Mal, wenn) *while* (während, solange)

b Adverbial clauses of place

I can't remember **where** I put the new CD.
I'll find you **wherever** you are.

Conjunctions: *where* (wo, wohin), *wherever* (wo auch immer; überall, wo; wohin auch immer)

c Adverbial clauses of reason

As it is raining today, I'll take my coat.
The teacher was angry **because** so many pupils were late.

Conjunctions: *as* (da, weil), *since* (da, weil), *because* (da, weil)

d Adverbial clauses of contrast

Although/Though the women were very tired, they went on working.
I like him **even if** he can be boring at times.
My wife prefers tea **while** I love coffee.

Conjunctions: *although/though* (obwohl, obgleich), *even if/even though* (auch wenn), *whereas/while* (während)

e Adverbial clauses of purpose

I gave him a map **so that** he could find my house.

Conjunction: *so that* (damit, sodass)

f Adverbial clauses of condition

If you eat all that, you'll be ill.
We'll miss the last bus **if** we don't hurry/**unless** we hurry.
Pack a pullover **in case** it's cool in the evening.

Conjunctions: *if* (falls, wenn), *even if* (sogar wenn), *unless* (falls nicht, wenn nicht), *in case* (falls; für den Fall, dass), *as long as* (sofern; vorausgesetzt, dass)

g Participle clauses and gerund clauses

When I sat down,
Sitting down, | I felt a little better.

As Sandra is unemployed, she
Being unemployed, Sandra | can't afford to go by taxi.

Though Monique spoke little English, she
Though speaking little English, Monique | tried to translate for her guests.

Mr Fox was still very tired | although he had slept ten hours.
in spite of having slept ten hours.

In certain cases, participle and gerund clauses can be used in the same way as adverbial clauses of time, reason, contrast or condition. Participle and gerund clauses are usually rather formal.

→ (Adverbial) participle clauses 23 → The gerund after prepositions 18b

Grammar review

27 Relative clauses

a Defining relative clauses

The man **who was injured in the accident** was my father.
Where's the nearest shop **that sells cameras**?

A defining relative clause identifies or classifies[1] a noun. (The clauses here tell us which man and what kind of shop we are talking about.) Without the relative clause, the main clause would make no sense.
A defining relative clause does not have commas. The relative pronouns used in a defining clause are *who/that* and *whose* for people, and *which/that* and *whose* for things.

Where is the CD **that I bought**?	Do you know the woman **who Mr Ross is talking to**?
Where is the CD **I bought**?	Do you know the woman **Mr Ross is talking to**?

When the relative pronoun is the object of the relative clause, it can be left out. A preposition comes in the same place as in the main clause, i.e. after the verb.

b Non-defining relative clauses

We spent our last holidays in Edinburgh, **which is the capital of Scotland**.

A non-defining relative clause gives additional information about a noun. Even without the relative clause, the main clause still makes sense.
A non-defining relative clause is usually separated from the main clause by commas. The relative pronouns used in a non-defining clause are *who, whose* and *whom* for people, and *which* for things.

It has been raining for hours now, **which** means we can't play tennis today.

The relative pronoun *which* can relate to the whole of the previous[2] clause.

c Infinitive clauses

Margaret was the only one | who helped me.
| **to help me**.

In certain cases, infinitive clauses can be used in the same way as relative clauses.

› The *to*-infinitive after certain nouns 13g

d Participle clauses

The girl | who is wearing white jeans | is the camp leader.
| **wearing white jeans** |

In certain cases, participle clauses can be used in the same way as relative clauses.

› Participles used with nouns 22b

28 *That*-clauses and indirect questions

a When we came back, we discovered **that our car had been stolen**.
You'd never guess **how old he is**.
I don't know **if/whether I'll be able to get there by ten**.

That-clauses usually begin with the conjunction *that*, but *that* can be left out in informal English.
Indirect questions are introduced by a question word or *if/whether*.

b Can you tell me | how I can get to the library?
| **how to get to the library**?

In certain cases, infinitive clauses can be used in the same way as indirect questions.

› The *to*-infinitive after question words 13e

 [1] classify ['klæsɪfaɪ] *klassifizieren, einordnen* [2] previous ['priːvɪəs] *vorangehend*

Vocabulary

Im folgenden Wörterverzeichnis *(Vocabulary)* sind die **neuen Wörter jeder Unit** aufgeführt. **Eingerückte Wörter** sollen mit dem vorausgehenden Wort mitgelernt werden, obwohl sie nicht an der betreffenden Stelle der Unit vorkommen. **Eigennamen** stehen nach dem *Mini-dictionary* auf der Seite 185. Eine Übersicht aller in den Bänden A1 bis A6 benutzten **grammatischen Fachausdrücke** steht auf den Seiten 186-187. Die neuen Wörter aus den *Options* sind im *Vocabulary* nicht aufgeführt, weil nur eine Auswahl an *Options* bearbeitet wird und der darin enthaltene neue Wortschatz später nicht als bekannt vorausgesetzt werden kann.

Die **fett gedruckten Wörter** gehören zum Grundwortschatz.

Die wenigen **normal gedruckten Wörter** gehören zum so genannten „Situationswortschatz". Es sind Wörter, die zwar zum Thema einer bestimmten Unit gehören, aber weniger gebräuchlich sind und daher in den folgenden Units nicht als bekannt vorausgesetzt werden.

Die **Tilde** (~) in der dritten Spalte steht anstelle des Wortes oder der Wendung aus der ersten Spalte. Pro Tilde muss ein Wort eingesetzt werden.

sb = somebody, sth = something; jd = jemand, jm = jemandem, jn = jemanden
adj = adjective, adv = adverb, conj = conjunction, n = noun, prep = preposition, v = verb;
sing = singular, pl = plural
AE = American English, BE = British English
fml = formal (förmlich), infml = informal (umgangssprachlich)

Unit 1: Education in Britain and the USA

p. 5	**caption** ['kæpʃn]	Bildunterschrift	the text under a photo
	graduation [ˌgrædʒʊ'eɪʃən]	(US) (Schul-)Abschluss(feier)	
	(to) salute [sə'lu:t]	grüßen, salutieren	
	(morning) assembly [ə'semblɪ]	Versammlung; (GB *auch:*) Morgenandacht *(aller Lehrer und Schüler vor Unterrichtsbeginn)*	*Morning* ~ is at 9 o'clock in most British schools.
	pledge of allegiance [ˌpledʒ‿əv‿ə'li:dʒəns]	(US) *amerikanischer Treueeid*	
	(to) pledge allegiance	Treue geloben	
	republic [rɪ'pʌblɪk]	Republik *(hier: Staatsform, bei der alle gleich sind)*	
	indivisible [ˌɪndɪ'vɪzəbl]	unteilbar	

1 A American high schools

p. 6	**airline** ['eəlaɪn]	Fluggesellschaft	I'm flying to Boston. – What ~ are you flying with?
	soft drink [ˌsɒft 'drɪŋk]	alkoholfreies Getränk	"No alcohol for me, I'm driving," the man said. "I'll have a ~~."
	ad [æd] (infml)	Annonce, Anzeige, Inserat	advert
	(to) **be tired of** sth	etwas satt haben	to be fed up with something
	(to) **regret** [rɪ'gret], **-tt-**	bedauern, bereuen	to wish that one had not done something
	cheerleader ['tʃɪəˌli:də]	*jd, der die Zuschauer bei Sportveranstaltungen zum Beifall anfeuert*	

Unit 1

(p. 6)	**editor** ['edɪtə]	Herausgeber/in; Redakteur/in	the person responsible for the content of a newspaper or a part of it

p. 7

Cognates[1] – but not quite

⚠ *Pronunciation, stress, spelling*

association [əˌsəʊsɪ'eɪʃn]	Assoziation; Vereinigung, Verband	**mathematics** [ˌmæθə'mætɪks]	Mathematik
category ['kætəgrɪ]	Kategorie	**parallel** ['pærəlel]	Parallele
certificate [sə'tɪfɪkət]	Zertifikat, Zeugnis	**perfect** ['pɜːfɪkt]	perfekt, vollkommen
conventional [kən'venʃnəl]	konventionell	**section** ['sekʃn]	Sektion, Abschnitt, Stück, Teil
literature ['lɪtrətʃə]	Literatur	**type** [taɪp]	Typ, Art, Sorte

[1] cognates ['kɒgneɪts] *verwandte Wörter;* hier: *englische Wörter, die ähnliche Entsprechungen im Deutschen haben*

extracurricular activity [ˌekstrə kəˌrɪkjʊlər_æk'tɪvɪtɪ]	außerunterrichtliche Aktivität, Arbeitsgemeinschaft	something you do at school which is not a subject like math or English
cheerleading ['tʃɪəˌliːdɪŋ]	(das) Anfeuern von Zuschauern/-innen	
senior ['siːnjə]	(US) *Schüler/in der 12. Klasse der High School; Student/in im 4. Studienjahr*	
sophomore ['sɒfəmɔː]	(US) *Schüler/in der 10. Klasse; Student/in im 2. Studienjahr*	
freshman ['freʃmən]	(US) *Schüler/in der 9. Klasse; Student/in im 1. Studienjahr*	
elementary school [ˌelɪ'mentərɪ]	(US) *(meist sechsjährige)* Grundschule	(GB) primary school
schedule [BE: 'ʃedjuːl, AE: 'skedʒuːl]	Zeitplan; (AE *auch:*) Stundenplan	(BE) timetable
requirement [rɪ'kwaɪəmənt]	(An-)Forderung; (AE *auch:*) Pflichtfach	What are the ~*s* for this job? – Well, one ~ is that you speak good English.
elective [ɪ'lektɪv] (AE)	Wahlfach	
shop (AE)	Werkunterricht	
throughout [θruː'aʊt] *(prep)*	während des/der ganzen; überall in	It rained ~ the night. = It rained all night. ~ the country = all over the country
cross-country [ˌkrɒs'kʌntrɪ]	Querfeldein*(lauf)*	
soccer ['sɒkə]	Fußball	
track and field [ˌtræk_ən 'fiːld]	Leichtathletik	
lacrosse [lə'krɒs]	Lacrosse *(Hockey-ähnliches Spiel, bei dem ein Ball mit Schlägern in ein Tor geschleudert wird)*	

1 A A German pupil at a British school

p. 8	**term** [tɜːm]	Trimester	The autumn ~ finishes a few days before Christmas.
	(to) **stream** [striːm]	in Leistungsgruppen einteilen	*S~ing* is the opposite of having mixed-ability classes.
	(to) **run** sth	etwas (durch)führen, veranstalten, betreiben, leiten	The youth club and the youth club show *are* both ~ by the members.

. 8)	**charity** ['tʃærətɪ]	wohltätige Zwecke; Wohltätigkeit(sorganisation); Wohltätigkeits-	a good cause At Christmas we usually give some money to ~. 'Brot für die Welt' is a German ~.
	(to) **set up**	einrichten, errichten	to establish
	(to) broadcast ['brɔːdkɑːst] – broadcast – broadcast	*(Radio-, Fernsehsendung)* senden	
	(to) tune in [tjuːn]	*(Radio, Fernsehen)* einschalten	
	community service	Sozialdienst	
	(to) **slice** [slaɪs]	in Scheiben schneiden	Shall I ~ the cheese, or do you want it in one piece?

1 A Focus on WORDS

. 9	**broad** [brɔːd]	breit, weit, ausgedehnt	The choice of colours is very ~; there are nineteen different ones. ⚠ Der Tisch ist 1m *breit.* = The table is 1m *wide.*
	compulsory [kəm'pʌlsərɪ]	obligatorisch	If something is ~, you have to do it.
	range [reɪndʒ]	Palette, Auswahl	choice
	instruction [ɪn'strʌkʃn]	Unterricht	teaching, education
	(to) **award** [ə'wɔːd]	verleihen, zuerkennen, zusprechen	Janet won the competition and *was ~ed* the prize.
	(to) **entitle** (to) [ɪn'taɪtl]	berechtigen (zu)	The weekend ticket *~s* you to free travel on all public transport in the city.
	cone [kəʊn]	(Schul-, Eis-)Tüte	
	vocational [və'keɪʃnl]	beruflich, Berufs-, berufsbezogen	*V~* training in Germany is offered, for example, at the 'Berufsschule'.
Ex 1	**gap** [gæp]	Lücke	a hole or space
	bubble ['bʌbl]	(Sprech-, Luft-, Gas-, Seifen-)Blase	In a cartoon what the characters say is usually written in speech *~s*.
	pouring rain ['pɔːrɪŋ]	strömender Regen	
	(to) **postpone** [pə'spəʊn]	aufschieben, verschieben	The football match had to *be ~d* till next week because of the snow.
2	(to) **apply** (to) [ə'plaɪ]	gelten (für), sich anwenden lassen (auf); anwenden (auf)	The school rules ~ to you too, Paul. You can ~ reading skills to any new language you learn.
3	**in particular** [pə'tɪkjʊlə]	insbesondere	especially
	loose [luːs]	frei; lose	A tiger is ~; it escaped from the zoo this morning. ⚠ *lose* [luːz] = verlieren – *loose* [luːs] = lose
	mad (at sb) [mæd] (*meist* AE, infml)	böse, sauer, wütend (auf jn)	another word for 'angry', especially in the USA
	(to) **take**	haben, gebraucht werden mit	*Does* the verb 'suggest' ~ the gerund or an infinitive?
6	**I spy with my little eye.** [spaɪ]	Ich sehe was, was du nicht siehst.	
	event [ɪ'vent]	Wettkampf, Disziplin	Which ~ are you going to run in, the 100 metres or the 200 metres?

Ex English-German translation

13	(to) **focus on** sth ['fəʊkəs]	sich auf etwas konzentrieren	to concentrate on something, to look closely at something

Unit 1

(p. 13)	(to) **demonstrate** ['demənstreɪt]	zeigen, nachweisen	to show
	(to) **convey** [kən'veɪ]	wiedergeben, vermitteln	This poem ~*s* a feeling of happiness.
	(to) **contain** [kən'teɪn]	enthalten	Coke ~*s* a lot of sugar.
	(to) **pay attention** (to sth) [ə'tenʃn]	aufpassen (auf etwas), (etwas) beachten	to take notice (of), to remember
p. 14	**fluent** ['flu:ənt]	fließend, flüssig *(Sprache, Vortrag)*	I'd like to speak English ~*ly*.

1 T The truancy officer's visit

p. 15	truancy ['trʊənsɪ]	(Schule-)Schwänzen	
	officer ['ɒfɪsə]	Beamte(r)/in; Polizist/in; Offizier/in	usually a state employee with some authority Ask those soldiers where their ~ is.
	multiple choice ['mʌltɪpl]	Multiple-Choice(-Verfahren) *(Testverfahren mit Mehrfachwahl-Antworten)*	
	(to) **justify** ['dʒʌstɪfaɪ]	rechtfertigen	How can anyone ~ spending £3000 on a pair of glasses? It's scandalous!

(p.15-p.17)

Text dictionary

accounts *(pl)* [ə'kaʊnts] Buchführung
ahead of sb [ə'hed] jm voraus
appeal [ə'pi:l] Einspruch einlegen
attendance [ə'tendəns] Besuch, Anwesenheit
behind im Rückstand
bet [bet] wetten
big deal große Sache
board Ausschuss, Kommission
buck [bʌk] (AE, infml) = dollar
butt [bʌt]: work one's butt off (infml) sich auf den Hintern setzen
casting vote ['kɑ:stɪŋ ˌvəʊt] ausschlaggebende Stimme
chairman ['tʃeəmən] Vorsitzende(r)
chalk dust ['tʃɔ:k dʌst] Kreidestaub
chapter ['tʃæptə] Kapitel
check out sich entfernen, sich abmelden
considerable [kən'sɪdrəbl] beträchtlich
dismiss [dɪs'mɪs] entlassen
equation [ɪ'kweɪʒn] Gleichung
exemption [ɪg'zempʃn] Befreiung
favor ['feɪvə(r)] (AE): in favor of sth für etwas
fuss [fʌs]: make a fuss over sth einen Wirbel um etwas machen
get: let sb get on with it jn machen lassen
get sth wrong etwas falsch machen
grant [grɑ:nt] gewähren
handle ['hændl] umgehen mit
irrelevant [ɪ'reləvənt]
key point entscheidender Punkt
kinda ['kaɪndə] (infml) = kind of
loan [ləʊn] Darlehen
maintenance ['meɪntənəns] Instandhaltung, Wartung
manual ['mænjʊəl] Handbuch
naval ['neɪvl] Marine-
neat [ni:t] (AE, infml) toll, geil
pause [pɔ:z] Pause
pretty *(adv)* ziemlich
pretty near (infml) so ziemlich
reckon ['rekən] schätzen
sale: for sale zum Verkauf, zu verkaufen
sew [səʊ] nähen
shipyard ['ʃɪpjɑ:d] Werft
smart [smɑ:t] frech
social studies Gemeinschaftskunde
statement Kontoauszug
straight away sofort
textbook Schulbuch
tote bag ['təʊt ˌbæg] (AE) Einkaufstasche
trust [trʌst] (ver)trauen
unimpressed [ˌʌnɪm'prest] unbeeindruckt
unlocked nicht abgeschlossen
way *(adv,* infml) weit
weirdo ['wɪədəʊ] Freak
while you're about it während du dabei bist
whole: on the whole im Großen und Ganzen

p. 17	**case** [keɪs]	Fall; Argumente	Will the committee give us the money, do you think? Have we got a good ~?

Unit 2: Great Britain – a multicultural society

18	mosque [mɒsk]	Moschee	

2A Who are the British?

19	(to) understand **by**	verstehen unter	Tell me, what do you *understand* ~ the term 'streaming'? – Doesn't it have something to do with the grouping of pupils in schools?
	by (ethnic group)	nach (ethnischer Gruppenzugehörigkeit)	according to The groups were organized ~ age.
	(to) **make up**	ausmachen, bilden	to form Ethnic minorities ~ ~ about 5% of Britain's population.

2A Different roles for Britain: from Empire to Commonwealth

20	**nature**	Beschaffenheit	the basic features or characteristics
	(to) **exploit** [ɪk'splɔɪt]	ausbeuten, verwerten	to make use of Several companies started to ~ the recently discovered oil fields.
	territory ['terətrɪ]	Territorium, (Hoheits-, Staats-)Gebiet	

Cognates – but not quite

⚠ *Pronunciation, stress, spelling*

athletics [æθ'letɪks]	(Leicht-)Athletik	(to) **fast**	fasten
biography [baɪ'ɒgrəfɪ]	Biografie	**flame** [fleɪm]	Flamme
blasphemy ['blæsfəmɪ]	Blasphemie, Gotteslästerung	**horror** ['hɒrə]	Horror, Entsetzen
civilization [ˌsɪvəlaɪ'zeɪʃn]	(die) Zivilisation	**ignorant** ['ɪgnərənt]	unwissend, ungebildet, ignorant
(to) **colonize** ['kɒlənaɪz]	kolonisieren	**nationalist** ['næʃənəlɪst]	Nationalist/in
(to) **confront** [kən'frʌnt]	konfrontieren	**patriotic** [BE: ˌpætrɪ'ɒtɪk; AE: ˌpeɪtrɪ'ɑ:tɪk]	patriotisch
cooperation [kəʊˌɒpə'reɪʃn]	Kooperation	**potential** [pə'tenʃl]	potenziell
cross-cultural [ˌkrɒs'kʌltʃərəl]	interkulturell	**racism** ['reɪsɪzm]	Rassismus
enormous [ɪ'nɔ:məs]	enorm, riesig	**racist** ['reɪsɪst]	Rassist/in
enthusiastic [ɪnˌθju:zɪ'æstɪk]	enthusiastisch, begeistert	**symbolic** [sɪm'bɒlɪk]	symbolisch

(to) **take over**	an sich reißen, Besitz ergreifen von; übernehmen	to take control of Colonists *took* ~ land that originally belonged to the native population.
Rule Britannia [ˌru:l brɪ'tænjə]	Es herrsche Britannien! *(Titel einer patriotischen Hymne)*	
law	Recht	Under British ~ it is illegal to discriminate against people at work because of their colour.
shipping	Schiffe; Schifffahrt, Schiffsverkehr	ships or traffic by sea
(to) **set – set – set**	untergehen *(Sonne, Mond)*	The sun rises in the east and ~*s* in the west.

Unit 2

p. 21	**inhabitant** [ɪn'hæbɪtənt]	Einwohner/in	The biggest cities, the ones with the most ~*s*, are in the Third World.
	(to) **go/be on strike**	in den Streik treten / streiken	There will be no trains tomorrow because the train-drivers *are going* ~ ~.
	non-violent [ˌnɒn 'vaɪələnt]	gewaltfrei	without violence Last night's protests were ~-~ and nobody was arrested.
	civil disobedience [ˌsɪvl ˌdɪsə'bi:djəns]	ziviler Ungehorsam	a protest by a lot of people breaking the law
	oppression [ə'preʃn]	Unterdrückung	In dictatorships people live in a state of ~.
	occasion [ə'keɪʒn]	Gelegenheit, Anlass	I've been stopped by American tourists in the street on several ~*s*. Ann only wears a dress on special ~*s*.
	wave [weɪv]	Welle	I couldn't swim in the sea today. The ~*s* were too big.
	literal ['lɪtərəl]	wörtlich	The ~ meaning of a word is its basic or original meaning.

2A Immigration after the war

p. 22	**social security** [ˌsəʊʃl sɪ'kjʊərətɪ]	soziale Sicherheit; Sozialhilfe	The ~ ~ system is the welfare system.
	housing ['haʊzɪŋ]	Wohnungen; Wohnungs-	The population is growing and more ~ is needed.
	(to) **speak out**	seine Meinung sagen, seine Stimme erheben	to say what you think in public, often in protest
	(to) **relieve** [rɪ'li:v]	ablösen; erleichtern, lindern, verringern	I work from 10 till 2, then I'*m* ~*d* by someone else. This cream *will* ~ the pain.
	supervisor ['su:pəvaɪzə]	Vorgesetzte(r), Abteilungsleiter/in; Aufseher/in	the boss or person somebody works under
	till	Kasse	
	satisfaction [ˌsætɪs'fækʃn]	Befriedigung, Genugtuung; Zufriedenheit	When Sue admitted she was wrong, it gave me great ~. Tim enjoys his job. It gives him a lot of ~.
	(to) **take action**	etwas/Schritte unternehmen, Maßnahmen ergreifen	We shouldn't just sit here complaining. We should ~ *action.*
	(to) **combat** ['kɒmbæt]	bekämpfen	to fight against

2A Keeping the faith

p. 23	(to) **get used to** ['ju:stə]	sich angewöhnen	I can't ~ *used* ~ these early mornings. I hate getting up so early.

used to + infinitive ↔ (to) be/get used to + *-ing* form (gerund)

Jim **used to go** to work by car, but now he goes by bike.	**Früher** ist Jim **(immer)** mit dem Auto zur Arbeit **gefahren,** …
At first he found it strange, but now he**'s used to going** to work by bike.	…, aber jetzt **ist** er **daran gewöhnt**, mit dem Fahrrad zur Arbeit **zu fahren**.
He soon **got used to going** to work by bike.	Er **hatte sich** bald **daran gewöhnt**, mit dem Fahrrad zur Arbeit **zu fahren**.

⚠ I **used to do** it.
Ich habe es früher immer getan.

I'm **used to doing** it./I'll get **used to doing** it.
Ich bin daran gewöhnt/Ich werde mich daran gewöhnen, es zu tun.

⚠ *pronunciation:*

I **used to** ['ju:stə] walk. — I'm **used to** ['ju:stə] walking.
Did you **use to** ['ju:stə] walk? — I'll get **used to** ['ju:stə] walking.

I **used** [ju:zd] petrol. — Ich habe Benzin benutzt.
The **use** [ju:s] of petrol … — Der Gebrauch von Benzin …

23)	**though** [ðəʊ] *(adv)*	jedoch, (aber) doch	Rod promised to phone yesterday. He didn't, ~. (= But he didn't.) ⚠ The adverb *though* can't be used at the beginning of a sentence, and there is usually a comma before it.

Conjunctions and linking adverbs of concession and contrast

We decided to go for a walk **although/even though** it was raining.	…, **obwohl** es regnete.
John said he'd help me with the dishes. He didn't, **though**.	… **Aber** dann hat er es **doch** nicht getan.
We had thought about going to the cinema. **Yet** we decided to stay at home. *or:* But we decided to stay at home **after all**.	… **Aber** wir haben dann **doch** beschlossen, zu Hause zu bleiben.
I went to bed early last night. **However**, I still feel tired. *or:* I still feel tired, **however**.	… **Aber** ich bin **doch** noch müde./ **Trotzdem** bin ich noch müde.
The water didn't look very clean, but we went swimming **anyway**.	…, aber wir gingen **trotzdem** schwimmen.
It was raining, but I didn't want to go out **anyway**.	…, aber ich wollte **sowieso** nicht rausgehen.

	(to) **pray** [preɪ]	beten	to speak to your God
	fuss [fʌs]	Theater, Getue	
	afterwards ['ɑːftəwədz]	nachher, hinterher, später	The film finishes at eight, so we could go for a meal ~.
	in case	falls; für den Fall, dass	Pack a pullover *in ~* it's cool in the evenings.
	(to) **let** sb **off** sth (infml)	jn von etwas befreien, jm etwas erlassen	to allow somebody not to do something
	(to) **feel like doing** sth (infml)	Lust haben etwas zu tun; (jm) danach sein, etwas zu tun	to want to do something It's so hot. I *feel ~* go*ing* for a swim.
	(to) **cheat** [tʃiːt]	mogeln, betrügen	Kai got a '6' in his maths test because he *~ed*.
	supplement ['sʌplɪmənt]	Beilage *(einer Zeitung)*	
Ex 1	**in hiding**	versteckt, untergetaucht	The freedom fighters lived ~ ~ so that the dictator's men couldn't find them.
	(to) **sentence** sb (to)	jn verurteilen (zu)	In many countries of the world, people who commit murder *are ~d* to death.
	absence ['æbsəns]	Abwesenheit	You weren't at school yesterday. Will you please explain your ~.
	cover	Umschlag, Einband	What does the photo on the front ~ of this book show?
2	**profile** ['prəʊfaɪl]	Kurzbiografie, -porträt; Profil	There's a ~ of Naomi Campbell in this week's magazine. the side view of something, especially a person's head
3	**census** ['sensəs]	Volkszählung	when the whole population of an area, usually a country, is counted
	proportion [prə'pɔːʃn]	Verhältnis; (An-)Teil	The ~ of girls to boys in this class is two to one.
4	(to) **be certain/sure to** do	bestimmt/sicherlich tun	They want to buy a gold ring? That*'s ~ to* be too expensive for them.
	(to) **be known to** do	bekanntlich tun	Everyone knows Don hates cats. = Don *is ~ to* hate cats.
	(to) **happen to** do	zufällig(erweise) tun	*Do* you *~ to* know what's on TV tonight? I didn't plan to meet Mike last night, we just *~ed to* be at the same party.
	oral ['ɔːrəl]	mündlich	opposite of 'written'
5	**bucket** ['bʌkɪt]	Eimer	a ~ 
	trolley ['trɒlɪ]	(Servier-, Einkaufs-)Wagen	 *~s*

Unit 2

2 Ex (5)	**humiliation** [hjuːˌmɪlɪ'eɪʃn]	Demütigung	It was a real ~, having to ask my much younger brother for help with my maths homework.
6	**marriage** ['mærɪdʒ]	Heirat; Ehe	Where did the ~ (= wedding) take place? – In Cairo. It was a happy ~. They lived together 53 years.
	task [tɑːsk]	Aufgabe	an exercise or a job
	(to) **bring** sb **up**	jn erziehen, aufziehen, großziehen	Celia *was brought* ~ by an aunt after her parents died. ⚠ Parents *bring up* children. Children *are educated* at schools etc.
8	(to) **rent; rent** [rent]	mieten; Miete	In Britain it's more common to buy than ~ a house. How much ~ do you pay per month for this flat? ⚠ In BE you *rent* things for a longer period of time, and you *hire* things for a short period.
	term of abuse [ə'bjuːs]	Schimpfwort	offensive expression
9	(to) **predict** [prɪ'dɪkt]	vorhersagen	to say what will happen in the future
	involuntary [ɪn'vɒləntrɪ]	unbeabsichtigt	When he saw all the money, he made an ~ movement with his hand.
	non-returnable [ˌnɒn rɪ'tɜːnəbl]	Einweg-, Wegwerf- *(-flasche, ...)*	A ~-~ bottle is one that is thrown away and not used again when it is empty.
	non-standard [ˌnɒn'stændəd]	*etwa:* nicht der Sprachnorm entsprechend	Slang expressions are ~-~.

2 T An eye for an eye

p. 30	an eye for an eye	Auge um Auge	
	Paki ['pækɪ] (BE, slang)	*(Schimpfwort für)* Pakistaner/in	
	yob [jɒb] (BE, slang)	Rowdy	
	(to) **ruin** ['ruːɪn]	zerstören, ruinieren	to destroy, to spoil
	fear (of) [fɪə]	Furcht, Angst (vor)	Because of his ~ of flying, Ed refuses to go by plane. ⚠ Angst haben vor = *(to) be afraid/frightened of*
	blanket ['blæŋkɪt]	(Woll-)Decke	In winter I sleep with at least two ~*s*.
	(to) **do something about** sb/sth	etwas gegen jn/etwas unternehmen	Can you *do something* ~ this door? It doesn't shut properly.
	tailor ['teɪlə]	Schneider/in	a person whose job it is to make clothes, especially for men
	(to) **send** sb **to sleep**	jn einschläfern, zum Schlafen bringen	The film was so boring that it *sent* everybody ~ ~.
	(to) **go on**	im Gange sein, vorgehen	to happen; to take place There's a party ~*ing on* next door.
p. 31	**bandage** ['bændɪdʒ]	Verband, Binde	something you put round a part of the body that has been injured 
	headmaster [ˌhed'mɑːstə]	(Schul-)Direktor	a man who is a head teacher
	proof (of) [pruːf]	Beweis(e), Nachweis(e) (für)	Do you have any ~ (= evidence) that you were at home on the night of the murder? I want ~ of your love. Lend me some money. ⚠ Both *proof* and *evidence* are uncountable nouns. They have no plurals and can't be used with 'a/an'.
	cloth [klɒθ]	Stoff; Tuch, Lappen	a piece of material that you might use to make a dress, for example something used to clean furniture, windows etc. ⚠ *cloth*, pl *cloths* [klɒθ, klɒθs] *clothes* (pl) [kləʊðz] = Kleidung
	match	Streichholz	a box of ~*es* 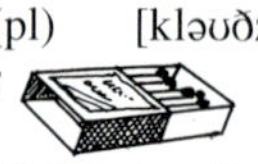
	row [rəʊ]	Reihe	a number of things in a line, e.g. a ~ of chairs

32	(to) **retell** [ˌriː'tel]	nacherzählen	to tell a story again in different words
	(to) **affect** [ə'fekt]	betreffen; sich auswirken auf; beeinträchtigen	*Are* you *~ed* by the new tax laws? – No, I don't pay any tax. Alcohol *~s* your driving.
	final ['faɪnl]	letzte(r, s), Abschluss-; endgültige(r, s)	last; coming at the end Saturday is the ~ day of the film festival. I refuse to pay more. £25 is my ~ offer.
	in the face of	im Angesicht von, angesichts (von), gegenüber	We are powerless *in the ~ of* such a threat.

Unit 3: The United States – years of growth

33	**on the move**	unterwegs, in Bewegung	They always seem to be ~ ~ ~. = They always seem to be going somewhere.
	in search of [sɜːtʃ]	auf der Suche nach	looking for
	painting	Gemälde, Bild	a picture painted by somebody
	stagecoach ['steɪdʒkəʊtʃ]	Postkutsche	
	buffalo, *pl* **buffalo(e)s** *or* **buffalo** ['bʌfələʊ]	Büffel	a herd of ~ 

Cognates – but not quite

⚠ *Pronunciation, stress, spelling*

best-seller [ˌ-'--]	Bestseller	**material** [mə'tɪərɪəl]	materiell
cable ['keɪbl]	Kabel	**naive** [naɪ'iːv]	naiv
cholera ['kɒlərə]	Cholera	**ox**, *pl* **oxen** [ɒks, 'ɒksn]	Ochse
confederate [ˌkən'fedərət]	konföderiert, verbündet	**plantation** [plæn'teɪʃn]	Plantage
contact ['kɒntækt]	Kontakt	**principle** ['prɪnsəpl]	Prinzip, Grundsatz
discipline ['dɪsɪplɪn]	Disziplin	**proclamation** [ˌprɒklə'meɪʃn]	Proklamation, Verkündung
disciplined ['dɪsɪplɪnd]	diszipliniert	(to) **provoke** [prə'vəʊk]	provozieren
element ['elɪmənt]	Element	**reservation** [ˌrezə'veɪʃn]	Reservat(ion)
emancipation [ɪˌmænsɪ'peɪʃn]	Emanzipation; Befreiung	**resource** [rɪ'sɔːs, rɪ'zɔːs]	Ressource, (Boden-) Schatz
experimental [ɪkˌsperɪ'mentl]	experimentell, Versuchs-	**routine** [ruː'tiːn]	Routine
fanatic [fə'nætɪk]	fanatisch; Fantiker/in	**specific** [spə'sɪfɪk]	spezifisch
harmony ['hɑːmənɪ]	Harmonie	**stereotype** ['sterɪətaɪp]	Stereotyp, Klischee
herd [hɜːd]	Herde	**transcontinental** [ˌtrænzˌkɒntɪ'nentl]	transkontinental
individuality [ˌɪndɪˌvɪdʒʊ'ælətɪ]	Individualität	**union** ['juːnjən]	Union, Einigkeit, Vereinigung
lieutenant [BE: lef'tenənt, AE: luː'tenənt]	Leutnant	**version** ['vɜːʃn, 'vɜːʒn]	Version, Fassung

telegraph pole ['telɪgrɑːf ˌpəʊl]	Telegrafenmast	

3A The frontier – westward ho!

34	**frontier** [BE: 'frʌntɪə, frʌn'tɪə; AE: frʌn'tɪər]	Grenze, Grenzland	where white settlement stopped in the USA

Unit 3

(p. 34)	westward ho! [ˌ-- ˈ-]	auf nach Westen!	
	(to) **cover**	*(eine Strecke)* zurücklegen	to travel
	disease [dɪ'zi:z]	Krankheit	illness
	popular	verbreitet; allgemein	A ~ view is a view held by a lot of people.
	manifest destiny [ˌmænɪfəst 'destɪnɪ]	nationale (*wörtlich:* offensichtliche) Bestimmung	
	boundary ['baʊndərɪ]	Grenze	another word for border
	spirit ['spɪrɪt]	Geist	the beliefs and aims of a person, movement or period in history
p. 35	**therefore** ['ðeəfɔ:]	deshalb, deswegen	so, for this reason
	railroad ['reɪlrəʊd] (AE)	Eisenbahn(strecke)	(BE) railway
	rail	Schiene	the piece of metal a train wheel runs on
	(to) **lay** [leɪ] – **laid** [leɪd] – **laid**	legen	to put *L*~ the dress on the table. ⚠ *lie (lying) – lay – lain* = liegen *lie (lying) – lied – lied* = lügen *lay (laying) – laid – laid* = legen
	official [ə'fɪʃl]	Beamte(r)/Beamtin	Mrs Black works for the government. She's a government ~. ⚠ *official* = 1. *(adj)* offiziell, amtlich = 2. *(n)* Beamte(r)/Beamtin
	chief [tʃi:f] *(adj)*	Chef-	most important ⚠ the *chief (adj)* engineer = der/die Chefingenieur/in the Indian *chief (n)* = der Indianerhäuptling unser *Chef (n)* Herr Lex = our *boss* Mr Lex
	spike [spaɪk]	Schienennagel	
	(to) **spread** [spred] – **spread – spread**	(sich) ausbreiten	The fire ~ quickly to all parts of the building.
	rancher ['ræntʃə]	Viehzüchter/in, Farmer/in	
	(to) **hire** sb	jn einstellen	to employ somebody, to give somebody a job
	(to) fatten up ['fætn]	(sich) mästen	
	exhausting [ɪg'zɔ:stɪŋ]	anstrengend	Something that makes you very tired is ~.
	poor	mangelhaft, schlecht	bad, not good at all
	even so *(adv)*	dennoch, trotzdem	in spite of this

Linking adverbs

additionally	zusätzlich, außerdem	**in spite of this/that**	trotzdem
in addition	zusätzlich, außerdem	**even so**	dennoch, trotzdem
furthermore	außerdem, überdies	**still**	trotzdem, dennoch
besides	außerdem	**yet**	doch, dennoch
		but	aber, sondern
above all	vor allem	**however**	jedoch, aber
so	deshalb, darum; also	**…, though**	jedoch, (aber) doch
that is why	deshalb, darum	**on the one hand**	einerseits, auf der einen Seite
therefore	deshalb, deswegen	**on the other hand**	andererseits, auf der anderen Seite
for this/that reason	aus diesem Grund, deshalb		
because of this/that	deshalb	**by/in contrast**	im Gegensatz dazu
consequently	folglich, daher	**alternatively**	andererseits, als Alternative
as a result	folglich; die Folge war, dass	**otherwise**	sonst, andernfalls
accordingly	(dem)entsprechend	**instead**	stattdessen, dafür

3 A American Indians

36	**brick** [brɪk]	Ziegelstein	a ~ 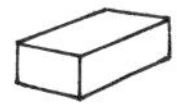
	deer, *pl* **deer** [dɪə]	Hirsch, Reh	two ~ 
	(to) **gather** ['gæðə]	sammeln, pflücken; sich versammeln	to collect
	nut [nʌt]	Nuss	*~s* 
	berry ['berɪ]	Beere	a small juicy fruit
	(in)fertile [BE: ɪn'fɜːtaɪl, AE: ɪn'fɜːrtl]	(un)fruchtbar	*F~* land is land where plants grow well.
	tear [tɪə]	Träne	His eyes filled with *~s* and he started to cry.

3 A Focus on WORDS

37	**immediate** [ɪ'miːdɪət]	nächste(r, s); engste(r, s); unmittelbar	close Will's grandad wants to celebrate his 80th birthday with just his ~ family – his children and grandchildren, but not any other relatives.
	extended family [ɪkˌstendɪd 'fæməlɪ]	Großfamilie	a family that includes not just parents and children, but other relatives too
	wealth [welθ]	Reichtum, Wohlstand	Only families with ~ can afford to send their children to a public school.
	wealthy ['welθɪ]	wohlhabend, reich	rich
	elderly ['eldəlɪ] *(adj)*	ältere(r, s)	a polite word to describe old people, often used in official language She is very active for an ~ woman.
	achievement [ə'tʃiːvmənt]	Leistung, Errungenschaft	Getting accepted at the best university in the country is a great ~. Well done!
	(to) **achieve** [ə'tʃiːv]	erreichen, zustande bringen	The team *has ~d* a lot this year. It has won over 10 competitions.
	(to) **value**	(hoch) schätzen	to think somebody or something is very important and worth a lot I always listen to what he has to say. I ~ his advice.
	classmate ['klɑːsmeɪt]	Klassenkamerad/in	The other pupils in your class are your *~s*.

3 A The American Civil War

38	**cotton** ['kɒtn]	Baumwolle	This pullover is made of ~, not of wool.
	whereas [ˌweər'æz]	wohingegen, während	while Sue likes Chinese food, ~ Mike likes Italian food.
	determined [dɪ'tɜːmɪnd]	fest entschlossen	I really want to win and I'm sure I can. I'm ~ to win.
	victory ['vɪktərɪ]	Sieg	success in a competition, election or war
	acre ['eɪkə]	*Flächenmaß (etwa 4047 m^2)*	
39	(to) **surrender** (to sb) [sə'rendə]	sich (jm) ergeben, kapitulieren	The army realized they had lost the battle, so they *~ed*.
	illiterate [ɪ'lɪtərət]	des Lesens und Schreibens unkundig; Analphabeten-; primitiv	Someone who can't read or write is ~.
	attorney [ə'tɜːnɪ] (AE)	(Rechts-)Anwalt/Anwältin	(BE) lawyer
	address	Ansprache, Rede	

Unit 3

3 Ex 1	**quotation** (by sb/from a book, play etc.) [kwəʊ'teɪʃn]	Zitat, Ausspruch (von jm/aus einem Buch, Stück usw.)	'Time is money' is a famous ~ by Benjamin Franklin. 'God is love' is a ~ from the Bible.
	(to) **sum** sth **up**, **-mm-** [sʌm]	etwas zusammenfassen	to summarize
	(to) **creep** [kri:p] – **crept** [krept] – **crept**	kriechen; schleichen	to move very slowly or carefully
	soaking wet [ˌsəʊkɪŋ 'wet]	völlig durchnässt, klatschnass	It's been raining for days and the tent is ~ *wet*.
	comfortless ['kʌmfətləs]	trostlos	
	vast [vɑ:st]	weit, gewaltig, riesig	huge
2	**copy**	Exemplar (eines Buchs usw.); Kopie	I've seen the film and now I'd like to read the book. Can you lend me your ~?
	miserable ['mɪzərəbl]	unglücklich, traurig; elend	very unhappy, poor
	judge [dʒʌdʒ]	Richter/in	
	(to) **judge** (by/from)	beurteilen, einschätzen (nach)	You shouldn't ~ a person by the way they dress.
	(to) **shake** [ʃeɪk] – **shook** [ʃʊk] – **shaken** ['ʃeɪkən]	schütteln; erschüttern; zittern	He didn't reply, but just *shook* his head. Nothing can ~ her belief that she was right. The whole building ~*s* when a train goes past.
	proposal [prə'pəʊzl]	Antrag, Vorschlag	He asked her to marry him. = He made her a ~ of marriage. The opposition is against the government's ~ to reform the prison system. ⚠ *Proposal* is more formal than *suggestion* and mainly used in business and official contexts.
3	**innocent** ['ɪnəsnt]	unschuldig	A person who hasn't done anything wrong is ~.
4	(to) **cry with joy** [dʒɔɪ]	vor Freude weinen	The woman *cried* ~ ~ when her son returned from the war.
6	**criticism** ['krɪtɪsɪzm]	Kritik	When you criticize something, you make a ~. ⚠ *a critic* = ein/e Kritiker/in eine Kritik = *a criticism*
	(to) **be to**	(tun) sollen	The coach will leave at 7.45. Pupils *are to* meet outside the school at 7.30.
	(to) **be in authority** [ɔ:'θɒrətɪ]	verantwortlich sein, das Sagen haben	If you *are in* ~, you can tell other people what to do.
	(to) **turn out**	ausfallen, werden; sich herausstellen, sich erweisen	How *did* things ~ *out*? Was the meeting a success?
	(to) **be supposed to** [sə'pəʊst tə]	sollen (angeblich); (tun) sollen	The castle *is* ~ *to* be the oldest in the country, but nobody really knows. We*'re* ~ *to* learn all the vocabulary before the next lesson. That's what the teacher said.
	(to) **be said to**	sollen (angeblich)	People say Mr Cox is very rich. = Mr Cox *is* ~ *to* be very rich.
	(to) **be believed to**	sollen (angeblich)	People believe Mr Cox is very rich. = Mr Cox *is* ~ *to* be very rich.
	(to) **be thought to**	sollen (angeblich)	People think Mr Cox is very rich. = Mr Cox *is* ~ *to* be very rich.
	(to) **be meant to**	sollen *(Angabe des Zwecks)*	The questions are here in order to guide you. = The questions *are meant to* guide you.
	(to) **be intended to** (to) **be designed to**	sollen *(Angabe des Zwecks)* sollen *(Angabe des Zwecks)*	They want to improve the traffic situation in the town centre. The new system *is intended/designed to* reduce the amount of traffic.
7	(to) **fail**	versagen, scheitern	the opposite of 'to succeed' I tried to finish my essay last night, but ~*ed*.
8	**monolingual** [ˌmɒnəʊ'lɪŋgwəl]	einsprachig	A ~ dictionary is one without translations. All the words and explanations are in one language.

3 T "Such is prairie life"

p. 45	**strenuous** ['strenjʊəs]	anstrengend	very tiring, hard, exhausting
	(to) **detect** [dɪ'tekt]	entdecken, bemerken, feststellen	to discover, to find out
	overall *(adj)* ['əʊvərɔ:l]	Gesamt-, allgemein	general or total Some teachers are not so happy, but the ~ impression is that the class has worked very hard. The ~ cost of the vacation – including tickets, hotel, food, spending money – will be about $900.
	mood [mu:d]	Stimmung, Laune	how you feel at a particular time
p. 47	(to) **be penniless** ['penɪləs]	keinen Pfennig Geld haben	to be completely without money
	attempt [ə'tempt]	Versuch	She tried to lift the piano. = She made an ~ to lift the piano.
	everyday ['evrɪdeɪ]	alltäglich, Alltags-	You don't need to wear anything special – just your ~ clothes. ⚠ *every day* = jeden Tag *everyday* (adj) = alltäglich, Alltags-
	artist ['ɑ:tɪst]	Künstler/in	the person who, for example, paints a picture

Unit 4: Blacks in the USA

p. 48	nigger ['nɪgə]	Nigger	a black person ⚠ This word is considered highly offensive by black people.
	Negro, *pl* **Negroes** ['ni:grəʊ]	Neger/in	⚠ The term *Negro* is now considered offensive by many people and should be avoided except in special historical contexts like 'Negro spiritual'.
	spiritual ['spɪrɪtʃʊəl]	Spiritual, geistliches Volkslied	

Cognates – but not quite

⚠ *Pronunciation, stress, spelling*

abrupt [ə'brʌpt]	abrupt
(al)mighty [ɔ:l'maɪtɪ]	(all)mächtig
(to) **appeal** (to) [ə'pi:l]	appellieren (an), ersuchen; gefallen
authentic [ɔ:'θentɪk]	authentisch, echt
basis, *pl* **bases** ['beɪsɪs, 'beɪsi:z]	Basis, Grundlage, Fundament
(to) **define** [dɪ'faɪn]	definieren, festlegen
emotion [ɪ'məʊʃn]	Gefühl, Emotion
frustrated [BE: frʌ'streɪtɪd, AE: '---]	frustriert
geographical [dʒɪə'græfɪkl]	geographisch
household ['haʊshəʊld]	Haushalt
(to) **integrate** ['ɪntɪgreɪt]	integrieren
intention [ɪn'tenʃn]	Intention, Absicht
Jesus ['dʒi:zəs]	Jesus
lip [lɪp]	Lippe
militant ['mɪlɪtənt]	militant
positive ['pɒzətɪv]	positiv
racial ['reɪʃl]	rassisch, Rassen-
rhythm ['rɪðm]	Rhythmus
(to) **sort**	sortieren
spiritual ['spɪrɪtʃʊəl]	Spiritual, geistliches Volkslied
talented ['tæləntɪd]	talentiert
thermometer [θə'mɒmɪtə]	Thermometer

Unit 4

(p. 48)	way down	= a long way down	
	yonder ['jɒndə]	*(veraltet für)* over there	
	graveyard ['greɪvjɑːd]	Friedhof, Kirchhof	area of land, sometimes near a church where there are graves 
	(to) **pass (by)**	vorbeigehen, -fahren (an)	to walk or drive past
	soul [səʊl]	Seele	Christians believe that a person's ~ never dies.
	fair [feə]	heiter, schön	We had a long period of ~ weather; it didn't rain for several weeks.
p. 49	**facilities** *(pl)* [fə'sɪlətɪz]	Einrichtungen, Anlage(n)	The school has excellent sports ~. It has its own swimming pool, for example.
	advancement [əd'vɑːnsmənt]	Förderung	
	moderate ['mɒdərət]	gemäßigt, mäßig; mittlere(r, s)	not extreme [ɪk'striːm]
	segregation [ˌsegrɪ'geɪʃn]	Rassentrennung, Absonderung	a system in which blacks are not allowed to use the same facilities as whites
	(to) **segregate** ['segrɪgeɪt]	trennen *(nach Rasse, Religion)*	the verb related to 'segregation'
	(to) **desegregate** [ˌdiː'segrɪgeɪt]	die Rassentrennung aufheben in	opposite of 'to segregate' In the US, laws were passed in the 1950s to ~ public facilities.
	climax ['klaɪmæks]	Höhepunkt	
	(to) **assassinate** [ə'sæsɪneɪt]	ermorden *(besonders aus politischen Gründen)*	to kill somebody, usually for political reasons

4 A Black America today

p. 50	**extremely** *(adv)*	extrem, äußerst	
	extreme [ɪk'striːm]	extrem, äußerste(r, s)	

Intensifying adverbs

completely normal	ganz normal	**particularly** good	besonders gut
deeply disappointed	tief enttäuscht	**really** happy	richtig froh
especially useful	besonders nützlich	I'm **terribly** sorry.	Es tut mir schrecklich Leid.
extremely hot	äußerst heiß	**thoroughly** confused	total verwirrt
highly unusual	höchst ungewöhnlich	**totally** wrong	völlig falsch

Ways of pronouncing "ex-"

betontes „ex-"		unbetontes „ex-" vor Konsonanten		unbetontes „ex-" vor Vokalen	
excerpt	['eksɜːpt]	extreme	[ɪk'striːm, ek'-]	examine	[ɪg'zæmɪn, eg'-]
exercise	['eksəsaɪz]	expand	[ɪk'spænd, ek'-]	example	[ɪg'zɑːmpl, eg'-]
expert	['ekspɜːt]	expensive	[ɪk'spensɪv, ek'-]	exist	[ɪg'zɪst, eg'-]
execute	['eksɪkjuːt]	exciting	[ɪk'saɪtɪŋ, ek'-]	exhausting	[ɪg'zɔːstɪŋ, eg'-]

(to) **make ends meet**	*(finanziell)* über die Runden kommen	Bill finds it difficult to ~ *ends* ~ on his pay.
department store [dɪ'pɑːtmənt stɔː]	Kaufhaus, Warenhaus	a very big shop 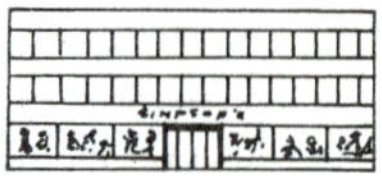
trap [træp]	Falle	We caught all the mice with this ~. → 
aged (2) [eɪdʒd]	im Alter von (2), (2-)jährig	She has a son ~ two. = Her son is two years old. ⚠ Always put *aged* after the noun: a boy ~ six.

. 51	**insult** ['ɪnsʌlt]	Beleidigung	John shouted ~*s* at Ed. He called him stupid and intolerant.
	on business	geschäftlich	My mother is going to London next week, ~ *business,* not on holiday.
	(to) **make it** (infml)	es schaffen, Erfolg haben, es zu etwas bringen	The train leaves at 3.30. You should ~ *it* if you hurry.
	bill [bɪl]	Rechnung	what you pay before you leave a hotel, restaurant etc.
	poverty line ['--- -]	Armutsgrenze	
	(to) **worry oneself sick** (about sb/sth)	vor Sorge (um jn/etwas) krank werden	to be so worried that you get ill ⚠ 'To worry' is usually not a reflexive verb.

Verbs that are reflexive in German but non-reflexive in English

(to) **afford**	sich leisten (können)	(to) **look forward to**	sich freuen auf
(to) **apologize**	sich entschuldigen	(to) **meet**	sich treffen
(to) **behave**	sich verhalten	(to) **move**	sich bewegen
(to) **calm down**	sich beruhigen	(to) **open**	sich öffnen
(to) **change**	sich verändern; sich umziehen	(to) **recover**	sich erholen
		(to) **refer to**	sich beziehen auf
(to) **complain**	sich beklagen	(to) **relax**	sich entspannen
(to) **concentrate**	sich konzentrieren	(to) **rely on**	sich verlassen auf
(to) **decide**	sich entscheiden	(to) **remember**	sich erinnern (an)
(to) **feel**	sich fühlen	(to) **sit down**	sich (hin)setzen
(to) **focus on**	sich konzentrieren auf	(to) **spread**	sich ausbreiten
(to) **imagine**	sich (etwas) vorstellen	(to) **surrender**	sich ergeben
(to) **improve**	sich (ver)bessern	(to) **turn round**	sich (um)drehen
(to) **lie down**	sich hinlegen	(to) **worry**	sich Sorgen machen

Examples:	I can't **concentrate**.	Ich kann **mich** nicht konzentrieren.
	I hope you'll **recover** soon.	Hoffentlich erholst du **dich** bald.
	We **remember** your aunt well.	Wir erinnern **uns** gut an deine Tante.
	They **worry** too much.	Sie machen **sich** zu viele Sorgen.

	gulf [gʌlf]	Kluft	
	skilled (in/at) [skɪld]	(hoch) qualifiziert, Fach-; geschickt (in)	It's usually easier for ~ workers to get a job than it is for un~ workers.
	appearance [ə'pɪərəns]	Erscheinen; Auftreten, Auftritt; Aussehen, äußere Erscheinung	A new type of electric car has been developed. Its ~ marks a new development in road travel. The ~ of the car is no different from that of traditional gas and diesel cars. It looks exactly the same from the outside.
	well-off [ˌwel'ɒf]	wohlhabend, reich	opposite of 'poor'; wealthy
	underclass ['ʌndəklɑːs]	Unterschicht	the group of 'poor', under-educated, underprivileged and often unemployed people in a society
	(to) **head**	anführen, leiten, *(einer Organisation)* vorstehen	Do you know who the president of this firm is? – Yes, the firm *is ~ed* by Pam Bond.
52	**chart** [tʃɑːt]	Schaubild, Diagramm, Tabelle	table or map that gives facts or information on a topic 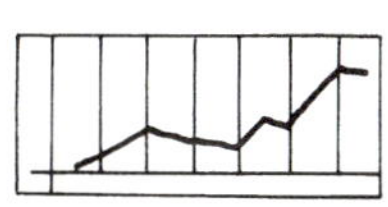
	graduate ['grædʒuət]	Hochschulabsolvent/in, Akademiker/in; (AE *auch:*) Schulabgänger/in	someone who has left university, having successfully passed their exams ⚠ In American English 'graduate' is also used for somebody who has completed high school.
	professional [prə'feʃənəl]	Angehörige(r) eines hoch qualifizierten Berufs	a person in a job needing very high qualifications, e.g. a doctor, architect etc.

Unit 4

(p. 52) **income** ['ɪnkʌm] Einkommen

Income

income – any money you receive regularly, not just money you get for your work
In most countries you pay tax on all your **income**, not just on your salary.

pay – the general word for the money that is paid for your work
I like the work, but the **pay** (= Bezahlung, Entgelt) is bad.

salary ['sælərɪ] – usually paid once a month and directly into your bank account[1]
We offer a **salary** (= Gehalt) of £18,000 a year.

wages *(pl)* ['weɪdʒɪz] – usually paid once a week and in cash[2], especially for manual[3] work
Your **wages** (= Lohn) will be £140 a week.

fee – what doctors, lawyers etc. get for their services
I had to pay a large **fee** (= Honorar) for my lawyer's advice.

[1]account *Konto* [2]in cash *bar* [3]manual ['mænjʊəl] *manuell*

decrease ['di:kri:s]	Rückgang	the opposite of 'increase' There has been a ~ in the number of unemployed from 720,000 to 695,000.
(to) **decrease** [dɪ'kri:s]	abnehmen	the opposite of 'to increase'
with regard to (fml) [rɪ'gɑ:d]	in/mit Bezug auf	The differences in grammar between British English and American English are not great. = The differences *with ~ to* grammar ... are not great.
largely ['lɑ:dʒlɪ] *(adv)*	weitgehend, größtenteils	mostly, mainly
finding *(usually pl)*	Ergebnis	result

4 A Focus on WORDS

p. 53	(to) **be fond of** sb/sth [fɒnd]	jn/etwas gern haben, mögen	to like somebody/something I'*m* very ~ *of* Simon, but I don't love him. I'*m* ~ *of* cycling. It's my favourite sport.
	affection (for) [ə'fekʃn]	Zuneigung (zu)	Louise must be very fond of her cousin; she always shows her a lot of ~.
	(to) **be terrified** (of) ['terɪfaɪd]	entsetzt sein, schreckliche Angst haben (vor)	to be very afraid (of)
	(to) **be scared** (of) [skeəd]	sich fürchten (vor)	to be frightened or afraid (of)
	anxiety [æŋ'zaɪətɪ]	Angst, Sorge	the feeling you have when you worry
	anger (at) ['æŋgə]	Ärger, Zorn (über)	Even if you're angry, try not to show your ~.
	rage [reɪdʒ]	Wut(anfall), Zorn, Rage	Why is Sandra in such a ~? – She's so angry because someone has stolen her new car.
	curious ['kjʊərɪəs]	neugierig, wissbegierig	I'm ~ to know what she told him. Do you know?
	robbery ['rɒbərɪ]	Raub(überfall)	There was a bank ~ this morning. The thieves got away with $780,000.

Adjectives and nouns (1)

angry	wütend	**colonial**	Kolonial-	**dead**	tot	**high**	hoch
anger	Ärger, Wut	**colony**	Kolonie	**death**	Tod	**height** [aɪ]	Höhe
attractive	anziehend	**dangerous**	gefährlich	**electric(al)**	elektrisch	**hot**	heiß
attraction	Attraktion	**danger**	Gefahr	**electricity**	Elektrizität	**heat**	Hitze

53)

Adjectives and nouns (2)

legal	gesetzlich, legal	**patient**	geduldig	**satisfactory**	befriedigend	**various**	verschieden (-artig)
law	Gesetz	**patience**	Geduld	**satisfaction**	Zufriedenheit	**variety**	Abwechslung; Vielfalt
long	lang	**poor** [ʊə, ɔː]	arm	**terrible**	schrecklich	**voluntary**	freiwillig
length	Länge	**poverty** [ɒ]	Armut	**terror**	Terror	**volunteer**	Freiwillige(r)
medical	medizinisch	**royal**	königlich	**tragic**	tragisch	**wide** [aɪ]	breit
medicine	Medizin	**king/queen**	König/Königin	**tragedy**	Tragödie	**width** [ɪ]	Breite
necessary	notwendig	**racial**	rassisch, Rassen-	**true**	wahr	**young** [ʌ]	jung
necessity [ˌ-ˈ---]	Notwendigkeit	**race**	Rasse	**truth**	Wahrheit	**youth** [uː]	Jugend(liche)

Ex 1	**(US) marshal** (AE) [ˈmɑːʃl]	*Gesetzeshüter/in einer US-Bundesbehörde; heute:* Polizeichef/in	
	former [ˈfɔːmə]	frühere(r, s), ehemalige(r, s)	the ~ owner of this car = the person who used to own it

German "früher"

Ms Hill's **previous** husband was Irish; her present husband is English. One of my **former** classmates now lives in Japan.	Ms Hills **früherer (= voriger, „letzter")** Ehemann … Eine meiner **früheren** Mitschülerinnen …	*Adjektiv „frühere(r, s)"*
We **used to** live abroad. My father **used to** go swimming every Sunday.	Wir haben **früher** (einmal) im Ausland gewohnt. Mein Vater ist **früher** jeden Sonntag schwimmen gegangen. (Heute geht er nicht mehr.)	*Adverb „früher"*
Can't you come a bit **earlier/sooner**? **Sooner** or later most thieves are caught.	Kannst du nicht etwas **früher** kommen? **Früher** oder später …	*Komparativ des Adverbs „früh" (= early)*

	anti-(slavery) [ˈæntɪ]	gegen (die Sklaverei); anti-	The newspaper was against slavery. It was an ~-slavery newspaper.
	(to) **rephrase** [ˌriːˈfreɪz]	neu formulieren, umformulieren	to express in different words
2	**depending on** [dɪˈpendɪŋ]	je nach	*D~ on* the weather, we'll either go swimming or visit a museum.
5	**circumstances** *(pl)* [ˈsɜːkəmstænsɪz]	Umstände, Verhältnisse	conditions
6	(to) **start**	anspringen *(Motor)*	In very cold weather the car sometimes won't ~.
7	(to) **release** [rɪˈliːs]	herausbringen, veröffentlichen *(Film, Buch, CD)*	to bring onto the market
8	(to) **mix** sth **up**	etwas verwechseln, durcheinander bringen	'Become' and 'get' are two words that Germans often ~ ~.
	murderer [ˈmɜːdərə]	Mörder/in	the person who commits a murder ⚠ *murderer* = Mörder/in *murder* = Mord

Unit 4

4 Ex (8)	**sensible** ['sensəbl]	vernünftig	opposite of 'silly' or 'stupid' ⚠ *sensible* = vernünftig *sensitive* ['sensətɪv] = 1. sensibel; 2. heikel Mark is a very *sensitive* child. He gets upset easily. AIDS is a *sensitive* issue. Some people don't like to talk about it.

4 T I have a dream

p. 59	**struggle** (with/for) ['strʌgl]	Kampf (mit/für, um); Bemühen (um)	a (long) fight or battle
	(to) **struggle**	kämpfen; sich abmühen, sich herumschlagen	to fight, or to try to do something that is difficult Markus ~*d* with his English homework. He found it very difficult.
	Baptist ['bæptɪst]	Baptist/in; Baptisten-	
	minister	Geistliche(r), Pfarrer/in	the usual word for a Protestant priest in American English
	(to) **deliver a speech** [dɪ'lɪvə]	eine Rede halten	another way of saying 'to give/make a speech'
	brief ['bri:f] *(adj)*	kurz	lasting only a short time; using few words Can you explain ~*ly* what we are to do?

(p. 59-p. 61)

Text dictionary

beacon ['bi:kən] Leucht-, Signalfeuer
brotherhood ['brʌðəhʊd] Brüderlichkeit
cash a check [kæʃ] (AE) einen Scheck einlösen
content ['kɒntent] Inhalt, Gehalt
daybreak ['deɪbreɪk] Tagesanbruch
decree [dɪ'kri:] Dekret, Erlass
flesh [fleʃ] *lebendiges* Fleisch
governor ['gʌvənə(r)] (US) Gouverneur/in *(eines US-Bundesstaates)*
heightening ['haɪtənɪŋ] *etwa:* aufragend
join hands sich die Hände reichen
joyous ['dʒɔɪəs] (fml) freudig
midst = middle
mountainside Berg(ab)hang
oasis [əʊ'eɪsɪs] Oase
pride [praɪd] Stolz
ring (er)schallen
shameful ['ʃeɪmfʊl] beschämend
skin [skɪn] Haut
snow-capped ['snəʊkæpt] schneegekrönt, schneebedeckt
speed up beschleunigen
stand up for Partei ergreifen, sich stark machen für
thee = an old word for 'you'

p. 61	**image** ['ɪmɪdʒ]	sprachliches Bild, bildlicher Ausdruck	a picture in words
	volume ['vɒlju:m]	Lautstärke; Volumen	I can't hear the music very well. Can you turn up the ~ a bit?
	repetition [ˌrepə'tɪʃn]	Wiederholung	noun from 'to repeat'
	imagery ['ɪmɪdʒərɪ]	Bildersprache, Metaphorik	the general term for 'images'
	metaphor ['metəfə]	Metapher, bildhafter Vergleich	'Jill flew out of the room' is an example of a ~ – unless Jill was a budgie.
	simile ['sɪməlɪ]	Vergleich *(mit den Wörtern „as" oder „like")*	'She's as brave as a lion' is an example of a ~.

Unit 5: The world of literature

Dreams and reality

63	(to) **address** [ə'dres]	sprechen zu, eine Ansprache halten vor	a formal way to say 'to speak to' Mr Clinton *~ed* a farmers' meeting.
	concrete ['kɒŋkri:t]	konkret	

Cognates – but not quite

⚠ *Pronunciation, stress, spelling*

alcohol ['ælkəhɒl]	Alkohol	**motive** ['məʊtɪv]	Motiv, Beweggrund
birth [bɜ:θ]	Geburt	**passage** ['pæsɪdʒ]	Passage, Textstelle
concrete ['kɒŋkri:t]	konkret	**relevant** ['reləvənt]	relevant
creative [kri:'eɪtɪv]	kreativ	**saga** ['sɑ:gə]	Saga; Geschichte; Heldenepos
explicit [ɪk'splɪsɪt]	explizit, ausdrücklich, deutlich, offen	**sardine** [sɑ:'di:n]	Sardine
fable ['feɪbl]	Fabel	**scheme** [ski:m]	Schema
function ['fʌŋkʃn]	Funktion	**sensational** [sen'seɪʃənl]	sensationell; Sensations-
humorous ['hju:mərəs]	humorvoll, lustig	**short story** [,- '--]	Kurzgeschichte
mass (of) [mæs]	Masse, Menge (von); Massen-	**speculation** [,spekjʊ'leɪʃn]	Spekulation, Vermutung
moral ['mɒrəl]	Moral, Lehre	**theme** [θi:m]	Thema, Leitgedanke
moth [mɒθ]	Motte, Nachtfalter	**tone** [təʊn]	Ton, Klang; Stimmung

	aloud [ə'laʊd] *(adv)*	laut	⚠ *aloud* = laut (für alle hörbar): Read the poem ~ so that we can all hear it. *loud* = laut (mit einer gewissen Lautstärke): You needn't speak so *loud*, we can all hear you.
	stanza ['stænzə]	Strophe *(eines Gedichtes)*	Anke, please read the first ~ of the poem aloud.
	verse [vɜ:s]	Strophe; Vers	Sing the first ~ again.
64	(to) **live by** the laws	nach den Gesetzen leben	to live according to the laws
	quality ['kwɒlətɪ]	Eigenschaft	Patience is a ~ that Jeremy just doesn't have.
	(to) **reveal** [rɪ'vi:l]	offenbaren, enthüllen	to make known Magicians never ~ their secrets.
70	**setting** ['setɪŋ]	Schauplatz	the place where the action of a film, story etc. takes place
	(to) **note** *(meist* fml*)*	beachten; bemerken, zur Kenntnis nehmen	to pay attention (to), to notice (and remember) *N~* how I solve the problem.
	(to) **infer** (from), **-rr-** [ɪn'fɜ:] (fml)	(er)schließen, folgern, ableiten (aus)	What can *be ~red* from these statistics? Although Mayor Michaels hasn't explicitly said what his position is, you can ~ from his comments that he'll vote for the bill. ⚠ Double 'r': inferred, preferred, referred
73	**currency** ['kʌrənsɪ]	Währung	The dollar is the ~ of the USA.
	(to) **take** sth **into consideration** [kən,sɪdə'reɪʃn]	etwas berücksichtigen, etwas bedenken	to consider something, to keep something in mind when making a decision When buying a new CD player, you have to ~ the sound quality *into ~*.

Unit 5

Playing with language

p. 74	**at first glance** [glɑ:ns]	auf den ersten Blick	when seen or examined for the first time *At* ~ ~ I thought it was Ann, but after I looked more closely I saw that it wasn't.
	audience ['ɔ:dɪəns]	Publikum, Zuschauer/innen, Zuhörer/innen	the people who watch or listen to, for example, a play or a concert 
	(to) **take** sb/sth **seriously**	jn/etwas ernst nehmen	You shouldn't *take* these comments ~; Joan was only joking. ⚠ *Never:* (to) take sb/sth ~~serious~~
p. 75	(to) **adopt** [ə'dɒpt]	*(einen Standpunkt)* einnehmen, annehmen; *(Kind)* adoptieren	In the US, the vice-president often ~*s* the president's opinions on many issues. Since the Connors had no children of their own, they decided to ~ one.
	human being [ˌhju:mən 'bi:ɪŋ]	Mensch	a person

Writing your own literature

p. 76	clerihew ['klerɪhju:]	*vierzeiliger humoristischer Vers*	
	characteristic (of) [ˌkærəktə'rɪstɪk]	(typisches) Merkmal; charakteristisch (für)	"What did the man look like?" asked the policeman. "Did he have any special ~*s*?" That style of church is ~ of the region.

The End Fredric Brown

Professor Jones had worked on the problem of time for many years.
"But at last I've found the answer," he said to his daughter. "This machine can take us into the past."
He pushed a button[1] on the machine.
"This ought to make time go backwards."
"Backwards go time make to ought this."
Machine the on button a pushed he.
"Past the into us take can machine this." Daughter his to said he, "Answer the found I've last at but."
Years many for time of problem the on worked had Jones Professor.

Brown Fredric **End The**

[1] button ['bʌtn] *Knopf*

Mini-dictionary

Alphabetical list of words (Books 1-6)

Die alphabetische Wortliste enthält den obligatorischen Wortschatz der Bände A1 bis A6. In der Regel wird nur die Schreibweise und Aussprache des britischen Englisch angegeben.
Da unbekannte Wörter aus den *Options* am Fuß der jeweiligen Seite erklärt werden und bei erneutem Vorkommen nicht als bekannt vorausgesetzt werden, sind diese Wörter nicht im *Mini-dictionary* enthalten.

sb = somebody, sth = something
adv = adverb, conj = conjunction, pl = plural, prep = preposition, sing = singular
AE = American English, BE = British English, fml = formal, infml = informal

A

a [ə] ein, eine; **50p a week** 50 Pence pro Woche
abbey ['æbɪ] Abtei, Kloster
abbreviation [əˌbri:vɪ'eɪʃn] Abkürzung
ability [ə'bɪlətɪ] Fähigkeit; **mixed-ability** gemischt, nicht leistungsdifferenziert
able ['eɪbl]: **be able to** können, fähig sein
abolish [ə'bɒlɪʃ] abschaffen; **abolition** [ˌæbə'lɪʃn] Abschaffung
Aborigine [ˌæbə'rɪdʒəni:] australische(r) Ureinwohner/in
about [ə'baʊt] **1.** über; **2.** ungefähr, etwa; **3.** wegen; **be about** handeln von; **like about** mögen an; **What about ...?** Wie stehts mit ...?, Wie wärs mit ...?
above [ə'bʌv] **1.** über, oberhalb (von); **2.** oben, darüber; **above all** vor allem
abroad [ə'brɔ:d] ins/im Ausland
abrupt [ə'brʌpt] abrupt
absence ['æbsəns] Abwesenheit
absorb [əb'sɔ:b] aufnehmen, absorbieren
absurd [əb'sɜ:d] absurd
academic [ˌækə'demɪk] akademisch, wissenschaftlich
accent ['æksənt] Akzent
accept [ək'sept] annehmen, akzeptieren; **acceptable** [ək'septəbl] akzeptierbar; **acceptance** [ək'septəns] Annahme; Akzeptierung; Zusage
access ['ækses] Zugang
accident ['æksɪdənt] **1.** Unfall; **2.** Versehen
accommodation [əˌkɒmə'deɪʃn] Unterkunft
according to [ə'kɔ:dɪŋ] entsprechend, gemäß, nach; **accordingly** (dem)entsprechend
accountant [ə'kaʊntənt] Buchhalter/in, Wirtschaftsprüfer/in
ache [eɪk] **1.** Schmerz; **(a) stomach ache** ['stʌmək͜eɪk] Magenschmerzen, Bauchschmerzen; **2.** wehtun, schmerzen
achievement [ə'tʃi:vmənt] Leistung, Errungenschaft
acid rain [ˌæsɪd 'reɪn] saurer Regen
acquire [ə'kwaɪə] erwerben, sich aneignen
across [ə'krɒs] (quer) über, durch
act [ækt] **1.** Tat, Werk, Akt; **2.** spielen, darstellen; **3.** handeln; **4.** Verordnung, Gesetz; **action** ['ækʃn] Handlung, Tat; Handeln; **active** ['æktɪv] rege, aktiv
activity [æk'tɪvətɪ] Projekt, Beschäftigung
actually ['æktʃʊəlɪ] wirklich, tatsächlich, eigentlich
AD [ˌeɪ'di:] n. Chr.
ad [æd] (infml) Annonce, Anzeige, Inserat
adapt [ə'dæpt] bearbeiten; **adapted from** eine Bearbeitung von, frei nach
add [æd] hinzufügen; **addition** [ə'dɪʃn] Hinzufügung, Zusatz, Ergänzung; **in addition** zusätzlich, außerdem; **additional** [ə'dɪʃnəl] zusätzliche(r, s); **additionally** zusätzlich, außerdem
address [ə'dres] **1.** Adresse, Anschrift; **2.** sprechen zu, eine Ansprache halten vor
administration [ədˌmɪnɪ'streɪʃn] Verwaltung
admiral ['ædmərəl] Admiral
admire [əd'maɪə] bewundern, verehren
admit [əd'mɪt] **1.** zugeben; **2.** zulassen, (hin)einlassen; **admittedly** [əd'mɪtɪdlɪ] zugegeben(ermaßen)
adopt [ə'dɒpt] einnehmen, annehmen; adoptieren
adult ['ædʌlt] Erwachsene(r)
advantage [əd'vɑ:ntɪdʒ] Vorteil
adventure [əd'ventʃə] Abenteuer
advert ['ædvɜ:t] Anzeige, Reklame; **advertise** ['ædvətaɪz] Reklame machen, werben; anzeigen; **advertising** ['ædvətaɪzɪŋ] Werbung; **advertising agency** ['ædvətaɪzɪŋ ˌeɪdʒənsɪ] Werbeagentur
advice [əd'vaɪs] Rat, Ratschläge
advise [əd'vaɪz] (be)raten; **adviser** [əd'vaɪzə] Berater/in
affairs [ə'feəz] Angelegenheiten; **foreign affairs** Außenpolitik
affect [ə'fekt] betreffen; sich auswirken auf; beeinträchtigen; **affection (for)** Zuneigung (zu)
afford [ə'fɔ:d] sich leisten
afraid [ə'freɪd]: **be afraid (of)** Angst haben, sich fürchten (vor); **I'm afraid** leider
Africa ['æfrɪkə] Afrika; **African-American** [ˌæfrɪkən͜ə'merɪkən] **1.** Afroamerikaner/in; **2.** afroamerikanisch; **African-Caribbean** [ˌæfrɪkənkærɪ'bi:ən] (Nachkomme der) Einwanderer aus Westindien; westindisch
after ['ɑ:ftə] **1.** nach; **2.** nachdem; **3.** hinter ... her; **after all** doch; **after that** danach; **afterwards** ['ɑ:ftəwədz] nachher, hinterher, später
afternoon [ˌɑ:ftə'nu:n] Nachmittag; **Good afternoon.** Guten Tag! **in the afternoon(s)** am Nachmittag; **on that afternoon** an jenem Nachmittag; **this afternoon** heute Nachmittag
again [ə'gen, ə'geɪn] wieder; noch (ein)mal
against [ə'genst] gegen
age [eɪdʒ] (Lebens-, Zeit-)Alter; **aged** im Alter von, -jährig
agency ['eɪdʒənsɪ] Agentur
ago [ə'gəʊ] vor; **not long ago** vor kurzem
agree (with) [ə'gri:] übereinstimmen (mit); zustimmen, sich einigen, beschließen; **agreement** [ə'gri:mənt] Vereinbarung, Abmachung, Übereinkunft
agricultural [ˌægrɪ'kʌltʃərəl] landwirtschaftlich, Landwirtschafts-
agriculture ['ægrɪkʌltʃə] Landwirtschaft
aid [eɪd] Hilfe, Unterstützung
aim [eɪm] Ziel
air [eə] Luft
airline ['eəlaɪn] Fluggesellschaft
airmail ['eəmeɪl] Luftpost
airport ['eəpɔ:t] Flughafen
alcohol ['ælkəhɒl] Alkohol
A-level ['eɪ ˌlevl] **= Advanced level exam** (BE) *etwa:* Abitur
alive [ə'laɪv] am Leben
all [ɔ:l] **1.** alle; alles; **2.** ganz; **all of you** ihr alle; **all over** überall in/auf; **all right** gut, in Ordnung; **all too clearly** nur zu deutlich, allzu deutlich; **I'm all right.** Mir gehts gut. **It's all right for Liz.** Liz ist gut dran. Liz hats gut. **If it's all right with Dad.** Wenn es Vati recht ist. **That's all right.** Schon gut. Nichts zu danken. **most of all** am allermeisten
alligator ['ælɪgeɪtə] Alligator

allow [ə'laʊ] erlauben; **be allowed to** dürfen

almighty [ɔ:l'maɪtɪ] allmächtig

almost ['ɔ:lməʊst] fast, beinahe

alone [ə'ləʊn] allein; **leave sb alone** jn in Ruhe lassen

along [ə'lɒŋ] entlang

aloud [ə'laʊd] laut

Alps [ælps] Alpen

already [ɔ:l'redɪ] schon, bereits

also ['ɔ:lsəʊ] auch; **not only ... but also** nicht nur ..., sondern auch

alternative [ɔ:l'tɜ:nətɪv] Alternative; Alternativ-; **alternatively** andererseits, als Alternative

although [ɔ:l'ðəʊ] obwohl, obgleich

altogether [ˌɔ:ltə'geðə] insgesamt, alles zusammen

aluminium [ˌælə'mɪnɪəm] Aluminium

always ['ɔ:lweɪz] immer

am [æm] bin

am [ˌeɪ‿'em] ... Uhr morgens/vormittags

amazed [ə'meɪzd] erstaunt; **amazing** [ə'meɪzɪŋ] erstaunlich

ambassador [æm'bæsədə] Botschafter/in

ambulance ['æmbjʊləns] Krankenwagen; **ambulance man/woman** Sanitäter/in

America [ə'merɪkə] Amerika; **American** [ə'merɪkən] amerikanisch; Amerikaner/in

among [ə'mʌŋ] (mitten) unter, zwischen

amount [ə'maʊnt] Menge; Summe; Betrag

an [æn, ən] ein, eine

ancestor ['ænsestə] Vorfahre

and [ænd, ən(d)] und

Angles ['æŋglz] Angeln; **Anglo-French** [ˌæŋgləʊ 'frentʃ] anglofranzösisch, englisch-französisch; **Anglo-Saxon** [ˌæŋgləʊ 'sæksn] **1.** angelsächsisch; **2.** das Angelsächsische

anger (at) ['æŋgə] Ärger, Zorn (über); **angry (with)** ['æŋgrɪ] wütend, böse, zornig (auf)

animal ['ænɪml] Tier

annoy [ə'nɔɪ] ärgern, belästigen; **annoying** ärgerlich, lästig; **be annoyed** verärgert sein, sich ärgern

anorak ['ænəræk] Anorak

another [ə'nʌðə] **1.** ein(e) andere(r, s); **2.** noch ein(e); **another 20 minutes** noch/weitere 20 Minuten; **another thing** noch etwas; **one ... after another** ein/e ... nach dem/der anderen

answer ['ɑ:nsə] **1.** Antwort; **2.** antworten, beantworten; **answer the (tele)phone** ans Telefon gehen

anti- ['æntɪ] anti-; gegen

anxiety [æŋ'zaɪətɪ] Angst, Sorge

any ['enɪ] (irgend)welche(r, s); jede(r, s) (beliebige); **not ... any** (gar) kein, keine; keins; **anybody/anyone** (irgend)jemand; jede/r (Beliebige); **not ... anybody** niemand; **anything** (irgend)etwas; irgendetwas (x-Beliebiges); **Anything else?** Sonst noch etwas? **not ... anything** nichts; **anyway** außerdem, überhaupt; sowieso; jedenfalls; trotzdem; **anywhere** irgendwo(hin); **not ... anywhere** nirgendwo(hin)

apartment [ə'pɑ:tmənt] (*meist* AE) Wohnung

appeal (to) [ə'pi:l] appellieren (an), ersuchen; gefallen

apologize [ə'pɒlədʒaɪz] sich entschuldigen; **apology** [ə'pɒlədʒɪ] Entschuldigung

apostrophe [ə'pɒstrəfɪ] Apostroph

appear [ə'pɪə] erscheinen, auftauchen; **appear (to be)** (zu sein) scheinen; **appearance** [ə'pɪərəns] Erscheinen, Auftreten, Auftritt; Aussehen, äußere Erscheinung

apple ['æpl] Apfel

appliance [ə'plaɪəns] (Haushalts-)Gerät

apply (for) [ə'plaɪ] sich bewerben (um), beantragen; **apply (to)** gelten für, sich anwenden lassen (auf); anwenden (auf)

appoint [ə'pɔɪnt] ernennen, machen zu

appreciate [ə'pri:ʃɪeɪt] schätzen, würdigen, zu schätzen wissen

April ['eɪprəl] April

aquarium [ə'kweərɪəm] Aquarium

archaeologist [ˌɑ:kɪ'ɒlədʒɪst] Archäologe/-in

archery ['ɑ:tʃərɪ] Bogenschießen

architect ['ɑ:kɪtekt] Architekt/in

architecture ['ɑ:kɪtektʃə] Architektur

are [ɑ:, ə] bist, sind, seid

area ['eərɪə] **1.** Gebiet, Gegend; **2.** Fläche

argue (about) ['ɑ:gju:] (sich) streiten, zanken (über/wegen); **argue for** eintreten für, sich aussprechen für; **argument** ['ɑ:gjʊmənt] **1.** Argument, Grund; **2.** Streit

ark [ɑ:k] Arche; **Noah's Ark** [ˌnəʊəz‿'ɑ:k] die Arche Noah

arm [ɑ:m] Arm

armchair [ˌɑ:m'tʃeə] Sessel

armed forces [ˌɑ:md 'fɔ:sɪz] Streitkräfte

army ['ɑ:mɪ] Armee, Heer

around [ə'raʊnd] um ... herum, im Gebiet um

arrange [ə'reɪndʒ] **1.** (an)ordnen; **arrange for** sorgen für; **arrangement** Vereinbarung, Abmachung; Vorkehrung

arrest [ə'rest] verhaften, festnehmen

arrival [ə'raɪvl] Ankunft; **on arrival** bei Ankunft; **arrivals lounge** Ankunftshalle; **arrive** [ə'raɪv] ankommen, eintreffen

art [ɑ:t] Kunst

article ['ɑ:tɪkl] Artikel

artificial [ɑ:tɪ'fɪʃl] künstlich

artist ['ɑ:tɪst] Künstler/in

as [æz, əz] **1.** als, während; **2.** da, weil; **3.** wie; **as a result** [rɪ'zʌlt] folglich; di Folge war, dass; **as if** als ob; **as late a ...** erst um ...; **as long as** solange, sofern; **(not) as fast as** (nicht) so schnell wie; **as soon as** sobald; **as well as** und auch, ebenso wie

Asia ['eɪʃə] Asien; **Asian** Asiat/in, asiatisch

ask [ɑ:sk] fragen; **ask about** fragen nach; **ask after sb/sth** nach jm/etwas fragen; **ask a question** eine Frage stellen; **ask for** bitten um; **ask sth of sb** von jm etwas verlangen, fordern, erbitten

asleep [ə'sli:p]**: be asleep** schlafen; **fall asleep** einschlafen

aspect ['æspekt] Aspekt, Gesichtspunkt

assassinate [ə'sæsɪneɪt] ermorden

assembly [ə'semblɪ] Versammlung; (BE *auch*) Morgenandacht; **assembly line** [ə'semblɪ ˌlaɪn] Fließband (-montage), Fertigungsstraße

assist [ə'sɪst] assistieren, unterstützen; **assistant** [ə'sɪstənt] **1.** Verkäufer/in; Assistent/in, Gehilfe/-in; **2.** stellvertretend

associate (with) [ə'səʊʃɪeɪt] assoziieren, (gedanklich) verbinden (mit); **association** [əˌsəʊsɪ'eɪʃn] Assoziation; Vereinigung, Verband

astronaut ['æstrənɔ:t] Astronaut/in

at [æt, ət] bei, an; **at breakfast** zur Frühstückszeit, beim Frühstück; **at Dave's/my house** bei Dave/mir (zu Hause); **at Easter** zu Ostern; **at first** zuerst, anfangs; **at home** zu Hause; **at last** endlich; schließlich; **at least** mindestens; wenigstens, zumindest; **at night** nachts, bei Nacht; **at once** sofort, (so)gleich; **at school** in der Schule; **at the end** am Ende, am Schluss; **at the moment** im Moment, im Augenblick; zurzeit; **at the side (of)** an der Seite (von); **at the weekend** am Wochenende; **at 3 o'clock** um 3 Uhr; **at 22 Albert Road** in der Albertstraße Nr. 22; **at work** bei der Arbeit; **good/bad at** gut/schlecht in; **look at** anschauen; **(not) at all** überhaupt (nicht)

athlete ['æθli:t] (Leicht-)Athlet/in, Sportler/in; **athletic** [æθ'letɪk] athletisch, sportlich; **athletics** (Leicht-)Athletik

Atlantic [ət'læntɪk] Atlantik; atlantisch

atmosphere ['ætməsfɪə] Atmosphäre; **atmospheric** [ˌætməs'ferɪk] atmosphärisch

attack [ə'tæk] **1.** angreifen; **2.** Angriff

attempt [ə'tempt] Versuch

attend [ə'tend] besuchen, teilnehmen an

attention [ə'tenʃn] Aufmerksamkeit; **pay attention (to sth)** aufpassen (auf etwas), (etwas) beachten
attitude ['ætɪtju:d] Haltung, Einstellung
attorney (AE) [ə'tɜ:nɪ] (Rechts-)Anwalt/Anwältin
attract [ə'trækt] anziehen, anlocken; **attraction** [ə'trækʃn] Attraktion, Anziehungspunkt; **attractive** anziehend, attraktiv, reizvoll
audience ['ɔ:dɪəns] Publikum, Zuschauer/innen, Zuhörer/innen
August ['ɔ:gəst] August
aunt [ɑ:nt] Tante
Australia [ɒs'treɪlɪə] Australien
Austria ['ɒstrɪə] Österreich
authentic [ɔ:'θentɪk] authentisch, echt
author ['ɔ:θə] Autor/in
authorities [ɔ:'θɒrətɪz] Behörde(n); **be in authority** verantwortlich sein, das Sagen haben
automatic(ally) [,ɔ:tə'mætɪklɪ] automatisch
auto(mobile) ['ɔ:təʊ, 'ɔ:təməbi:l] (AE) Auto, Wagen
autumn ['ɔ:təm] Herbst; **in (the) autumn** im Herbst
available [ə'veɪləbl] verfügbar, vorhanden; vorrätig
avenue ['ævənju:] Allee, Boulevard
average ['ævərɪdʒ] Durchschnitt; Durchschnitts-
avoid [ə'vɔɪd] (ver)meiden; ausweichen; **avoidable** vermeidbar
awake [ə'weɪk] wach
award [ə'wɔ:d] verleihen, zuerkennen, zusprechen
aware [ə'weə]: **be/become aware of** sich bewusst sein/werden
away [ə'weɪ] **1.** weg, fort; **2.** entfernt; **go away** verreisen; **throw away** wegwerfen

B

baby ['beɪbɪ] Baby
back [bæk] **1.** Rückseite, hinterer Teil; Rücken; **2.** hintere(r, s), Hinter-; **3.** zurück, wieder; **back down** nachgeben; **background** ['bækgraʊnd] Hintergrund; Herkunft; **in the back** hinten *(im Auto)*
bacon ['beɪkn] (Schinken-)Speck
bad [bæd] schlecht; schlimm; **a bad cold** ein starker Schnupfen; **bad at** schlecht in; **do badly** schlecht sein *(in einem Fach)*
bag [bæg] Tasche, Beutel, Tüte; **lunch bag** Tüte mit dem eingepackten Mittagessen; **mixed bag** bunte Mischung
baggage ['bægɪdʒ] Gepäck
baker ['beɪkə] Bäcker/in
balcony ['bælkənɪ] Balkon
ball [bɔ:l] Ball
banana [bə'nɑ:nə] Banane
band [bænd] Band, (Musik-)Gruppe
bandage ['bændɪdʒ] Verband, Binde
Bangladeshi [,bæŋlə'deʃɪ] aus Bangladesch
bank [bæŋk] Bank, Sparkasse; **banking** Bankwesen
barbarian [bɑ:'beərɪən] Barbar/in
barbecue ['bɑ:bɪkju:] Grillparty
bark [bɑ:k] bellen
baron ['bærən] Baron
barrel ['bærəl] Fass
baseball ['beɪsbɔ:l] Baseball
based [beɪst]: **be based on** basieren auf
basic ['beɪsɪk] **1.** Grund-; Haupt-; **2.** grundlegend; **basically** im Grunde; im Wesentlichen; **basis**, *pl* **bases** ['beɪsɪs, 'beɪsi:z] Basis, Grundlage, Fundament
basket ['bɑ:skɪt] Korb
basketball ['bɑ:skɪtbɔ:l] Basketball
bath [bɑ:θ] Bad; **have a bath** baden, ein Bad nehmen; **bathroom** ['bɑ:θrʊm] Bad(ezimmer)
battle ['bætl] Schlacht, Kampf
Bavaria [bə'veərɪə] Bayern
BC [,bi:'si:] v. Chr.
be [bi:] sein; stehen *(auf einem Schild usw.)*; **be about** handeln von; **be afraid** Angst haben; **be born** geboren sein/werden; **be certain to** bestimmt/sicherlich tun; **be descended from** abstammen von; **be early** zu früh kommen; **be frightened** Angst haben, sich fürchten; **be fun** Spaß machen; **be hungry** Hunger haben; **be known to** bekanntlich (tun); **be late** zu spät kommen; **be located** [lə'keɪtɪd] sich befinden, liegen; **be lucky** Glück haben; **be missing** fehlen; **be pleased (with)** sich freuen (über), zufrieden sein (mit); **be right** Recht haben; **be said to** sollen (angeblich); **be smelly** stinken; **be supposed to** [sə'pəʊst tə] sollen (angeblich); (tun) sollen; **be sure to** bestimmt/sicherlich tun; **be thirsty** Durst haben; **be to** (tun) sollen; **be wrong** Unrecht haben; **What do you want to be?** Was willst du werden?
beach [bi:tʃ] Strand; **on the beach** am Strand
bean [bi:n] Bohne
bear [beə] Bär
beat [bi:t] schlagen, besiegen
beautiful ['bju:tɪfəl] (wunder)schön; **beauty** ['bju:tɪ] Schönheit
because [bɪ'kɒz] weil; **because of** wegen
become [bɪ'kʌm] werden
bed [bed] Bett; **bed and breakfast** Übernachtung mit Frühstück; **go to bed** ins Bett gehen; **bedroom** Schlafzimmer
beef [bi:f] Rindfleisch; **roast beef** Rinderbraten, Roastbeef
before [bɪ'fɔ:] **1.** vor; **2.** bevor, ehe; **3.** vorher, schon einmal; **before that** davor, vorher
beggar ['begə] Bettler/in
begin [bɪ'gɪn] beginnen, anfangen; **beginning** Anfang, Beginn
behave [bɪ'heɪv] sich verhalten, sich benehmen; **behaviour** Verhalten, Benehmen
behind [bɪ'haɪnd] hinter
belief (in) [bɪ'li:f] Glaube (an), (religiöse) Überzeugung; **believe (in)** [bɪ'li:v] glauben (an); **be believed to** sollen (angeblich)
bell [bel] Klingel; Glocke
belong to [bɪ'lɒŋ] gehören
below [bɪ'ləʊ] unten; unter(halb von)
bend [bend] Kurve, Biegung
berry ['berɪ] Beere
besides [bɪ'saɪdz] *(prep)* außer, neben; *(adv)* außerdem
best [best] bester, beste, bestes; (das) Beste; **best-known** bekannteste(r, s); **best-seller** [,best'selə] Bestseller; **best wishes** mit den besten Wünschen; **like best** am liebsten mögen
better ['betə] besser; **like better** lieber mögen
between [bɪ'twi:n] zwischen
beyond [bɪ'jɒnd] über ... hinaus, jenseits (von)
Bible ['baɪbl] Bibel
bicycle ['baɪsɪkl] Fahrrad
big [bɪg] groß
bike [baɪk] Fahrrad, Rad; **by bike** mit dem Fahrrad
bill [bɪl] **1.** Gesetz(esvorlage, -entwurf); **2.** (AE) Geldschein; **3.** Rechnung
binoculars *(pl)* [bɪ'nɒkjʊləz] (ein) Fernglas
biography [baɪ'ɒgrəfɪ] Biografie
biology [baɪ'ɒlədʒɪ] Biologie
biotechnology [,baɪəʊtek'nɒlədʒɪ] Biotechnik
bird [bɜ:d] Vogel
biro ['baɪrəʊ] (BE) Kugelschreiber, Kuli
birth [bɜ:θ] Geburt; **birthday** ['bɜ:θdeɪ] Geburtstag; **for sb's birthday** zum Geburtstag; **Happy birthday (to you)!** Herzlichen Glückwunsch zum Geburtstag! **on your birthday** an deinem Geburtstag; **When's your birthday?** Wann hast du Geburtstag?
biscuit ['bɪskɪt] (BE) Keks
bit [bɪt]: **a bit** ein bisschen, etwas; **quite a bit of** einiges an
bitter ['bɪtə] bitter; verbittert; **bitterness** ['bɪtənɪs] Bitterkeit

black [blæk] **1.** schwarz; **2.** Schwarze(r); **blacken** schwärzen; verfinstern
blanket ['blæŋkɪt] (Woll-)Decke
blasphemy ['blæsfəmɪ] Blasphemie, Gotteslästerung
block [blɒk] **1.** Block, Klotz; **2.** Häuserblock; **block of flats** [ˌblɒk‿əv 'flæts] (BE) Mietshaus, Wohnblock; **3.** blockieren
blouse [blaʊz] Bluse
blow [bləʊ] wehen, blasen; **blow up** sprengen, in die Luft jagen; explodieren
blue [blu:] blau
blues [blu:z] Blues
board [bɔ:d] (Wand-)Tafel; Brett
boarding school ['bɔ:dɪŋ sku:l] Internat
boat [bəʊt] Boot; Schiff; **by boat** mit dem Schiff
body ['bɒdɪ] Körper
boil [bɔɪl] (ab)kochen, sieden
bonfire ['bɒnfaɪə] Feuer im Freien
boogie-woogie [ˌbu:gɪ 'wu:gɪ] Boogie-Woogie
book [bʊk] **1.** Buch; **2.** buchen, reservieren; **bookshelf** Bücherregal
boot [bu:t] Stiefel; BE *auch:* Kofferraum
border ['bɔ:də] Grenze, Grenzland
bored [bɔ:d] gelangweilt; **boring** langweilig
born [bɔ:n]**: be born** geboren sein/werden
borough ['bʌrə] Stadtbezirk, Stadtteil
borrow ['bɒrəʊ] sich (aus)leihen, entleihen
boss [bɒs] Chef/in, Boss
both [bəʊθ] beide, beides; **both ... and** sowohl ... als auch
bottle ['bɒtl] Flasche
bottom ['bɒtm] Boden, Fußende, unteres Ende
boundary ['baʊndrɪ] Grenze
box [bɒks] Kiste, Schachtel, Kästchen
Boxing Day ['bɒksɪŋ deɪ] (BE) der zweite Weihnachtsfeiertag
boy [bɔɪ] Junge; **boyfriend** ['bɔɪfrend] Freund *(eines Mädchens)*
boycott ['bɔɪkɒt] boykottieren
bracket ['brækɪt] Klammer
brake [breɪk] **1.** Bremse; **2.** bremsen
brave [breɪv] tapfer, mutig
bread [bred] Brot
break [breɪk] **1.** Pause; Bruch; **2.** (zer)brechen; kaputtmachen, kaputtgehen; unterbrechen; **break away (from)** brechen (mit), sich trennen (von); **break into** einbrechen; **break off** abbrechen; **break out** ausbrechen
breakfast ['brekfəst] Frühstück; **at breakfast** zur Frühstückszeit, beim Frühstück; **for breakfast** zum Frühstück; **have breakfast** frühstücken
breathe (in/out) [bri:ð] (ein-/aus)atmen
brick [brɪk] Ziegelstein
bridge [brɪdʒ] Brücke
brief(ly) ['bri:flɪ] kurz
bright [braɪt] hell, leuchtend; heiter
brilliant ['brɪljənt] toll, erstklassig
bring [brɪŋ] (mit-, her)bringen; **bring up** erziehen, aufziehen, großziehen
(Great) Britain ['brɪtn] Großbritannien; **British** britisch; Brite, Britin; **British-born** in Großbritannien geborene(r, s); **Briton** Britannier/in; Brite/-in
broad [brɔ:d] breit, weit, ausgedehnt
brochure ['brəʊʃə] Broschüre, Prospekt
broken ['brəʊkən] kaputt; zerbrochen, gebrochen
brother ['brʌðə] Bruder
brown [braʊn] braun
brush [brʌʃ] **1.** Bürste; Pinsel; **2.** bürsten
bubble ['bʌbl] Blase
bucket ['bʌkɪt] Eimer
budget ['bʌdʒɪt] Budget, Haushalt(splan)
budgie ['bʌdʒɪ] (BE) Wellensittich
buffalo, *pl* **buffaloes/buffalo** ['bʌfələʊ] Büffel
build [bɪld] (er)bauen; **builder** Baumeister; **building** Gebäude
bull [bʊl] Bulle, Stier
bungalow ['bʌŋgələʊ] Bungalow
bureau ['bjʊərəʊ] Amt
burn [bɜ:n] (ver)brennen
bus [bʌs] Bus; **bus stop** Bushaltestelle; **by bus** mit dem Bus
business ['bɪznɪs] Geschäft(e), Unternehmen; **business park** Gewerbegebiet; **do business with** Geschäfte machen mit; **on business** geschäftlich
busy ['bɪzɪ] **1.** beschäftigt; **2.** belebt, mit starkem Verkehr, hektisch
but [bʌt] aber, sondern; **not only ... but also** nicht nur ..., sondern auch
butcher ['bʊtʃə] Fleischer/in, Metzger/in
butter ['bʌtə] Butter
buy [baɪ] kaufen; **buyer** (Ein-)Käufer/in
by [baɪ] **1.** von; durch; **2.** (spätestens) bis, bis (zu); **by airmail** mit/per Luftpost; **by definition** per Definition; **by ethnic group** nach ethnischer Gruppenzugehörigkeit; **by (saying)** indem (er/sie/... sagte); **by the time** *(conj)* wenn, bis; **by the way** übrigens, nebenbei (bemerkt); **go by** vergehen, vorübergehen; **go by bike** mit dem Rad fahren; **live by the laws** nach den Gesetzen leben; **two by two** zu zweit, paarweise; **understand by** verstehen unter
Bye. [baɪ] Wiedersehen! Tschüs!

C

c. = circa ['sɜ:kə] ca. = circa
cab [kæb] Taxi
cabinet ['kæbɪnət] Kabinett
cable ['keɪbl] Kabel
café ['kæfeɪ] Café; kleines Restaurant; **cafeteria** [ˌkæfə'tɪərɪə] Restaurant mit Selbstbedienung, Cafeteria
cage [keɪdʒ] Käfig
cake [keɪk] Kuchen
calculator ['kælkjʊleɪtə] Taschenrechne
calendar ['kælɪndə] Kalender
calf, *pl* **calves** [kɑ:f, kɑ:vz] Kalb
call [kɔ:l] **1.** (An-)Ruf, Telefongespräch **2.** nennen; **What do you call ...?** Wie nennt man ...? **be called** heißen; **3.** (an)rufen
calm [kɑ:m] ruhig, still; gelassen; **calm down** (sich) beruhigen
camel ['kæml] Kamel
camera ['kæmrə] Fotoapparat, Kamera
camp [kæmp] **1.** (Zelt-)Lager; **2.** zelten, campen; **camp site** Campingplatz, Zeltplatz; **camper** Camper; **campground** (AE) Campingplatz, Zeltplatz; **camping** Camping, Zelten Zelt-
campaign [kæm'peɪn] Kampagne, (Werbe-)Feldzug; **campaigner** Kämpfer/in; (Umwelt-)Schützer/in
can [kæn] Dose
can [kæn, kən] kann, darf; **can't** [kɑ:nt] **= cannot** ['kænɒt] kann nicht
Canada ['kænədə] Kanada
canal [kə'næl] Kanal
candidate ['kændɪdət] Kandidat/in, Bewerber/in
canister ['kænɪstə] Kanister, Blechdose
canoe [kə'nu:] **1.** Paddelboot; Kanu; **2.** Kanu fahren, paddeln;
capital ['kæpɪtl] Hauptstadt; **capital (letter)** Großbuchstabe
capitalist ['kæpɪtəlɪst] **1.** Kapitalist; **2.** kapitalistisch
captain ['kæptɪn] Kapitän; Mannschaftskapitän
caption ['kæpʃn] Bildunterschrift
capture ['kæptʃə] erobern, erbeuten; gefangen nehmen
car [kɑ:] Auto, Wagen; **by car** mit dem Auto; **car park** (BE) (großer) Parkplatz; Parkhaus; **car pool** (*meist* AE) Fahrgemeinschaft
caravan ['kærəvæn] (BE) Wohnwagen
carbon dioxide [ˌkɑ:bən daɪ'ɒksaɪd] Kohlendioxid
card [kɑ:d] (Spiel-, Post-, Kartei-)Karte
care [keə] **1.** Sorgfalt; Pflege; **day care** Kinder-, Altenbetreuung; **2. care (about)** sich kümmern (um), wichtig nehmen; **careful** vorsichtig; sorgfältig; **careless** sorglos, nachlässig, unbekümmert

career [kəˈrɪə] Karriere
Caribbean [ˌkærɪˈbiːən] die Staaten in der Karibik
carnival [ˈkɑːnəvl] Karneval
carol [ˈkærəl]**: (Christmas) carol** Weihnachtslied
carpenter [ˈkɑːpɪntə] Tischler/in, Schreiner/in
carpet [ˈkɑːpɪt] Teppich
carrot [ˈkærət] Karotte, Möhre
carry [ˈkærɪ] tragen; befördern; **carry on** weitermachen, fortfahren; **carry out** aus-, durchführen
cartoon [kɑːˈtuːn] Cartoon, Karikatur
case [keɪs] Fall; Argumente; **in case** falls; für den Fall, dass
cassette [kəˈset] Cassette; **cassette-recorder** [kəˈset rɪˌkɔːdə] Cassettenrecorder
castle [ˈkɑːsl] Burg, Schloss
cat [kæt] Katze
catalogue [ˈkætəlɒg] Katalog
catch [kætʃ] fangen, erwischen; **catch a bus** einen Bus erreichen, nehmen
category [ˈkætəgrɪ] Kategorie
cathedral [kəˈθiːdrəl] Kathedrale, Dom
Catholic [ˈkæθlɪk] **1.** katholisch; **2.** Katholik/in
cattle *(pl)* [ˈkætl] (Rind-)Vieh
cause [kɔːz] **1.** Ursache; **2.** (gute) Sache; **3.** verursachen
cave [keɪv] Höhle
ceiling [ˈsiːlɪŋ] Zimmerdecke
celebrate [ˈselɪbreɪt] feiern
Celsius [ˈselsɪəs] Celsius
Celtic [ˈkeltɪk] **1.** keltisch; **2.** das Keltische; **the Celts** [kelts] die Kelten
census [ˈsensəs] Volkszählung
cent [sent] Cent *(US-Währung)*
centimetre [ˈsentɪˌmiːtə] Zentimeter
central [ˈsentrəl] Zentral-, Mittel-
centre [ˈsentə] Zentrum, *(Stadt-)*Mitte; **Information Centre** Auskunft, Verkehrsbüro
century [ˈsentʃərɪ] Jahrhundert; **a sixteenth-century house** ein Haus aus dem 16. Jahrhundert
ceremony [ˈserɪmənɪ] Zeremonie; Feier(-lichkeit)
certain [ˈsɜːtn] sicher, gewiss, bestimmt; **be certain to** bestimmt/sicherlich (tun); **certainly** gewiss, sicherlich
certificate [səˈtɪfɪkət] Zertifikat, Zeugnis
chain [tʃeɪn] Kette
chair [tʃeə] Stuhl
challenge [ˈtʃæləndʒ] Herausforderung, Aufgabe
chance [tʃɑːns] Gelegenheit, Chance; **take a chance** ein Risiko eingehen; es darauf ankommen lassen
chancellor [ˈtʃɑːnsələ] Kanzler/in; **Chancellor of the Exchequer** (brit.) Finanzminister/in
change [tʃeɪndʒ] **1.** (Ver-)Änderung, Wechsel, Umstellung; **(small) change** Wechselgeld; Kleingeld; **2.** (sich) verändern, umwandeln; (aus-)wechseln; **change into** sich verwandeln in; **change one's mind** seine Meinung ändern, sich anders besinnen; **3.** umsteigen
channel [ˈtʃænl] Kanal, Programm; **(English) Channel** Ärmelkanal
character [ˈkærəktə] Charakter; Figur (in einem Roman usw.); **characteristic** [ˌkærəktəˈrɪstɪk] **1.** (typisches) Merkmal; **2.** charakteristisch; **characterize** [ˈkærəktəraɪz] charakterisieren
charity [ˈtʃærətɪ] wohltätige Zwecke; Wohltätigkeit(sorganisation); Wohltätigkeits-
chart [tʃɑːt] Schaubild, Diagramm, Tabelle
charter flight [ˈtʃɑːtə flaɪt] Charterflug
chase [tʃeɪs] jagen, verfolgen
cheap [tʃiːp] billig
cheat [tʃiːt] mogeln, betrügen
check [tʃek] **1.** Kontrolle, Überprüfung, Nachprüfung; **2.** (über)prüfen, kontrollieren
cheer [tʃɪə] anfeuern, Beifall spenden
cheese [tʃiːz] Käse
chemical [ˈkemɪkl] **1.** Chemikalie; **2.** chemisch
chemist [ˈkemɪst] (BE) Apotheker/in
cheque [tʃek] (Bank-)Scheck
chess [tʃes] Schach
chewing gum [ˈtʃuːɪŋ gʌm] Kaugummi
chicken [ˈtʃɪkɪn] Huhn; (Brat-)Hähnchen
chief [tʃiːf] **1.** Oberhaupt; Häuptling; **2.** Chef-
child, *pl* **children** [tʃaɪld, ˈtʃɪldrən] Kind
chimney [ˈtʃɪmnɪ] Schornstein, Kamin
chimp [tʃɪmp] Schimpanse
Chinese [tʃaɪˈniːz] **1.** Chinesisch; **2.** Chinese, Chinesin; **3.** chinesisch
chips [tʃɪps] (BE) Pommes frites
chocolate [ˈtʃɒklət] Schokolade
choice (of) [tʃɔɪs] (Aus-)Wahl (an); **make a choice** eine Wahl treffen
choir [ˈkwaɪə] Chor
cholera [ˈkɒlərə] Cholera
choose [tʃuːz] (aus)wählen, aussuchen; **choose to do sth** es vorziehen, etwas zu tun; beschließen etwas zu tun
Christ [kraɪst] Christus; **Christian** [ˈkrɪstʃən] **1.** Christ/in; **2.** christlich; **Christianity** [ˌkrɪstɪˈænətɪ] (das) Christentum
Christmas [ˈkrɪsməs] Weihnachten, das Weihnachtsfest; **Christmas Day** der erste Weihnachtsfeiertag; **Christmas Eve** Heiligabend
church [tʃɜːtʃ] Kirche; **go to church** in die Kirche gehen
cinema [ˈsɪnəmə] (BE) Kino
circle [ˈsɜːkl] Kreis
circumstances *(pl)* [ˈsɜːkəmstænsɪz] Umstände, Verhältnisse
citizen (of) [ˈsɪtɪzn] Staatsbürger/in, Staatsangehörige(r)
city [ˈsɪtɪ] Stadt, Großstadt
civilization [ˌsɪvəlaɪˈzeɪʃn] (die) Zivilisation
civil disobedience [ˌsɪvl ˌdɪsəˈbiːdjəns] ziviler Ungehorsam
civil rights [ˌsɪvl ˈraɪts] Bürgerrechte; **civil war** Bürgerkrieg
civil servant [ˌsɪvl ˈsɜːvənt] (Staats-) Beamte(r); **civil service** [ˌsɪvl ˈsɜːvɪs] Staatsdienst; Beamtenschaft
claim [kleɪm] **1.** Behauptung; Forderung, Anspruch; **2.** behaupten; fordern, Anspruch erheben auf
class [klɑːs] Klasse; Unterricht(sstunde); **classmate** [ˈklɑːsmeɪt] Klassenkamerad/in
clean [kliːn] **1.** sauber; **2.** putzen, reinigen
clear [klɪə] klar, deutlich
clerk [klɑːk] Schalterbeamte(r)/-in
clever [ˈklevə] klug, schlau; geschickt; **cleverness** [ˈklevənəs] Klugheit
cliché [ˈkliːʃeɪ] Klischee
climate [ˈklaɪmɪt] Klima
climax [ˈklaɪmæks] Höhepunkt
climb [klaɪm] klettern, steigen; **climber** [ˈklaɪmə] Bergsteiger/in
clock [klɒk] *(Wand-, Stand-, Turm-)*Uhr; **o'clock** [əˈklɒk] ... Uhr
close [kləʊz] schließen, zumachen; **close down** *(eine Fabrik usw.)* zumachen, schließen; **closed** geschlossen, zu; **closing time** Ladenschlusszeit, Polizeistunde
close [kləʊs] **1.** genau, gründlich; **2.** knapp *(Sieg, Ergebnis)*; **3.** nahe, eng; nahebei
cloth [klɒθ] Stoff; Tuch, Lappen
clothes *(pl)* [kləʊðz] Kleidung(sstücke)
cloud [klaʊd] Wolke; **cloudy** [ˈklaʊdɪ] bewölkt, wolkig
club [klʌb] Verein, Klub
clue (to) [kluː] Anhaltspunkt (für), Hinweis (auf)
coach [kəʊtʃ] **1.** Trainer/in; **2.** (BE) Reisebus; **by coach** (BE) mit dem Reisebus
coal [kəʊl] Kohle
coalition [ˌkəʊəˈlɪʃn] Koalition
coast [kəʊst] Küste; **on the coast** an der Küste
coat [kəʊt] Mantel, Jacke
cocktail [ˈkɒkteɪl] Cocktail
cocoa [ˈkəʊkəʊ] Kakao
coffee [ˈkɒfɪ] Kaffee
coin [kɔɪn] Münze
coincidence [kəʊˈɪnsɪdəns] Zufall
coke [kəʊk] Cola

cold [kəʊld] **1.** kalt; **2.** Kälte; Unterkühlung; **3.** Schnupfen; **a bad cold** ein starker Schnupfen; **have a cold** Schnupfen haben, erkältet sein
collect [kə'lekt] **1.** (ein-, ver)sammeln; **2.** abholen; **collection** [kə'lekʃn] Sammlung
college ['kɒlɪdʒ] Hochschule; College
colon ['kəʊlən] Doppelpunkt
colonial [kə'ləʊnɪəl] kolonial, Kolonial-; **colonist** ['kɒlənɪst] Kolonist/in, Siedler/in; **colonize** ['kɒlənaɪz] kolonisieren; **colony** ['kɒlənɪ] Kolonie
colour ['kʌlə] Farbe; **What colour is/are ...?** Welche Farbe hat/haben ...? **coloured** ['kʌləd] farbig; bunt
column ['kɒləm] **1.** Spalte *(auf Buchseite);* **2.** Säule
comb [kəʊm] **1.** Kamm; **2.** kämmen
combat ['kɒmbæt] bekämpfen
combination exercise [ˌkɒmbɪ'neɪʃn] Kombinationsübung, Zuordnungsübung; **combine (with)** [kəm'baɪn] (sich) verbinden (mit), kombinieren (mit)
come [kʌm] kommen, mitkommen; **come and see** besuchen kommen; **come as a shock** ein Schock sein; **come from** von ... (her)stammen; **Come on.** Na, komm! Los, komm! **come out** herauskommen, hinauskommen; **come true** in Erfüllung gehen, wahr werden; **come up** aufkommen, sich ergeben
comedy ['kɒmədɪ] Komödie
comfortable ['kʌmftəbl] bequem, gemütlich
comic ['kɒmɪk] Comic-Heft
comma ['kɒmə] Komma
comment (about, on) ['kɒment] Kommentar, Bemerkung (über, zu); **make a comment (on)** einen Kommentar abgeben (zu); eine Bemerkung machen (über, zu); **comment (on)** kommentieren, sich (kritisch) äußern (zu)
Commerce Department ['kɒməs dɪˌpɑ:tmənt] (AE) (amerik.) Wirtschaftsministerium
commit [kə'mɪt] begehen, verüben
committee [kə'mɪtɪ] Ausschuss, Komitee, Kommission
common ['kɒmən] üblich; normal; häufig; **the common people** das einfache Volk; **the House of Commons, the Commons** (GB) das britische Unterhaus
the Commonwealth ['kɒmənwelθ] *Staatengemeinschaft aus ehemals zum britischen Weltreich gehörenden Ländern*
communicate (with) [kə'mju:nɪkeɪt] kommunizieren (mit), sich verständigen (mit); **communications** *(pl)* [kəˌmju:nɪ'keɪʃnz] Nachrichtentechnik, Telekommunikation
communism ['kɒmjʊnɪzm] Kommunismus; **communist** ['kɒmjʊnɪst] Kommunist/in
community [kə'mju:nətɪ] *(politische)* Gemeinde, Kommune; Gemeinschaft
commuter [kə'mju:tə] Pendler/in
company ['kʌmpənɪ] Gesellschaft; Firma; Begleitung
compare [kəm'peə] vergleichen; **comparison** [kəm'pærɪsn] Vergleich; **make comparisons** Vergleiche machen, vergleichen
competition [ˌkɒmpə'tɪʃn] **1.** Wettbewerb, Wettkampf; **2.** Konkurrenz
complain [kəm'pleɪn] sich beschweren, sich beklagen
complement ['kɒmpləmənt] ergänzen, vervollkommnen
complete [kəm'pli:t] **1.** vervollständigen; ergänzen; **2.** vollständig, völlig
compound (word) ['kɒmpaʊnd] Kompositum, zusammengesetztes Wort
comprehensive school [ˌkɒmprɪ'hensɪv sku:l] (BE) Gesamtschule
compromise ['kɒmprəmaɪz] Kompromiss
compulsory [kəm'pʌlsrɪ] obligatorisch
computer [kəm'pju:tə] Computer; **computer science** [kəmˌpju:tə 'saɪəns] Informatik
concentrate (on) ['kɒnsəntreɪt] sich konzentrieren (auf)
concern [kən'sɜ:n] **1.** Angelegenheit, Belang, Sache; **2. concern (for)** Sorge, Besorgnis (wegen); **3.** betreffen, angehen; **4.** beunruhigen, Sorge(n) bereiten
concert ['kɒnsət] Konzert
concrete ['kɒŋkri:t] konkret
conditions [kən'dɪʃnz] Verhältnisse, Umstände; Bedingungen
confederate [kən'fedərət] konföderiert, verbündet
conference ['kɒnfrəns] Konferenz, Besprechung
confident ['kɒnfɪdənt] (selbst)sicher, selbstbewusst, zuversichtlich
conflict ['kɒnflɪkt] Konflikt, Auseinandersetzung
conform [kən'fɔ:m] (sich) anpassen; (sich) einfügen
confront [kən'frʌnt] konfrontieren
confused [kən'fju:zd] verwirrt; **confusing** verwirrend
congestion *(sing)* [kən'dʒestʃn] Verstopfung, verstopfte Straßen
congratulations (on) [kənˌgrætʃʊ'leɪʃnz] (herzliche) Glückwünsche (zu); Gratuliere (zu)!
Congress ['kɒŋgres] der Kongress
connect (to, with) [kə'nekt] verbinden (mit); **connection** [kə'nekʃn] Verbindung, Zusammenhang; Anschluss
conquer ['kɒŋkə] erobern, besiegen; **conqueror** ['kɒŋkərə] Eroberer/in, Bezwinger/in
consequence ['kɒnsɪkwəns] Konsequenz, Folge; **consequently** folglich, daher
conserve [kən'sɜ:v] erhalten, bewahren; **conservation** [ˌkɒnsə'veɪʃn] Erhaltung; Naturschutz, Umweltschutz
consider [kən'sɪdə] **1.** über etwas nachdenken, etwas in Betracht ziehen; **2.** betrachten als, halten für; **take sth into consideration** [kənˌsɪdə'reɪʃn] etwas berücksichtigen, etwas bedenken
consist of [kən'sɪst] bestehen aus
consonant ['kɒnsənənt] Konsonant, Mitlaut
constitution [ˌkɒnstɪ'tju:ʃn] Verfassung
construction [kən'strʌkʃn] Konstruktion, (Auf-)Bau, Bauweise; Bau-
consult [kən'sʌlt] konsultieren
consumer [kən'sju:mə] Verbraucher/in; Konsument/in
contact ['kɒntækt] Kontakt, Verbindung
contain [kən'teɪn] enthalten
context ['kɒntekst] Zusammenhang, Kontext
continent ['kɒntɪnənt] Kontinent, Erdteil; **the Continent** das europäische Festland
continuation [kənˌtɪnjʊ'eɪʃn] Fortsetzung, Fortdauer; **continue** [kən'tɪnju:] fortsetzen, fortfahren (mit), weiter(hin) (tun); andauern
contract ['kɒntrækt] Vertrag
contrast ['kɒntrɑ:st] Gegensatz, Kontrast; **by/in contrast** im Gegensatz dazu
contribute (to) [kən'trɪbju:t] beitragen (zu), beisteuern; **contribution** [ˌkɒntrɪ'bju:ʃn] Beitrag
control [kən'trəʊl] **1.** Kontrolle, (Selbst-)Beherrschung; Aufsicht; **2.** beherrschen; die Kontrolle haben über; steuern; **be in control of** beherrschen, die Kontrolle haben über
conventional [kən'venʃnl] konventionell
conversation [ˌkɒnvə'seɪʃn] Gespräch, Unterhaltung
convey [kən'veɪ] wiedergeben, vermitteln
convince [kən'vɪns] überzeugen
cook [kʊk] **1.** Koch, Köchin; **2.** kochen, zubereiten; **cooker** (BE) Herd; **do the cooking** kochen
cool [ku:l] kühl
co-operate [kəʊ'ɒpəreɪt] zusammenarbeiten, kooperieren; **cooperation** [kəʊˌɒpə'reɪʃn] Kooperation
copy ['kɒpɪ] **1.** Exemplar; Kopie; **2.** abschreiben; kopieren
corn [kɔ:n] (AE) Mais; (BE) Korn, Getreide

corner ['kɔ:nə] Ecke
cornflakes ['kɔ:nfleɪks] Cornflakes
Cornish ['kɔ:nɪʃ] **1.** kornisch, aus Cornwall; **2.** die kornische Sprache; **Cornishman/Cornishwoman** Einwohner/in von Cornwall
correct [kə'rekt] **1.** richtig, korrekt; **2.** berichtigen, verbessern, korrigieren; **correction** [kə'rekʃn] Korrektur, Berichtigung
correspond (to) [ˌkɒrɪ'spɒnd] entsprechen; **correspondent** Korrespondent/in
corridor ['kɒrɪdɔ:] Korridor, Gang
corruption [kə'rʌpʃn] Korruption, Bestechung; Bestechlichkeit
cost [kɒst] **1.** Kosten; Preis; **2.** kosten
cottage ['kɒtɪdʒ] (kleines) Landhaus, Häuschen
cotton ['kɒtn] Baumwolle
cough [kɒf] Husten
could [kʊd] konnte(n); könnte(n)
council ['kaʊnsl] (Stadt-, Land-)Rat; **councillor** ['kaʊnsələ] Ratsmitglied, (Stadt-, Land-)Rat, Rätin
counselor (AE), **counsellor** (BE) ['kaʊnslə] Berater/in
count [kaʊnt] **1.** zählen; **2.** Zählung; **countable** ['kaʊntəbl] zählbar
country ['kʌntrɪ] Land, Staat; **in the country** auf dem Land; **countryside** (ländliche) Gegend, Landschaft
couple ['kʌpl] (Ehe-)Paar; **a couple of** (infml) ein paar, einige
courier ['kʊrɪə] Kurier
course [kɔ:s] Kurs, Lehrgang; **of course** natürlich
court [kɔ:t] Gericht(shof)
cousin ['kʌzn] Vetter, Kusine
cover ['kʌvə] **1.** bedecken, zudecken; **2.** abdecken; **3.** *(eine Strecke)* zurücklegen; **4.** Umschlag, Einband
cow [kaʊ] Kuh; **cowboy** ['kaʊbɔɪ] Cowboy; **cowshed** ['kaʊʃed] Kuhstall
coward ['kaʊəd] Feigling
crane [kreɪn] Kran
crash [kræʃ] **1.** Zusammenstoß, Absturz; **2. crash (into)** [kræʃ] zusammenstoßen (mit), hineinfahren (in); verunglücken
crazy ['kreɪzɪ] verrückt, wahnsinnig; **be crazy about** ganz verrückt sein auf; **go crazy** verrückt werden
cream [kri:m] **1.** Creme; **2.** Sahne
create [kri:'eɪt] (er)schaffen; **creative** [kri:'eɪtɪv] kreativ
credit card ['kredɪt kɑ:d] Kreditkarte
creep [kri:p] kriechen, schleichen
cricket ['krɪkɪt] Kricket
crime [kraɪm] Verbrechen; Kriminalität; **criminal** ['krɪmɪnl] **1.** verbrecherisch, kriminell; **2.** Verbrecher/in, Kriminelle(r)
crisps [krɪsps] (BE) Kartoffelchips
crisis ['kraɪsɪs] Krise
critical (of) ['krɪtɪkl] kritisch (gegenüber); **criticism** ['krɪtɪsɪzm] Kritik; **criticize (for)** ['krɪtɪsaɪz] kritisieren (wegen)
crop [krɒp] (Feld-)Frucht; Ernte
cross [krɒs] **1.** Kreuz; **2.** überqueren, kreuzen; **cross-cultural** [krɒs'kʌltʃrəl] interkulturell; **crossing** Überfahrt, Übergang; **(a) crossroads** ['krɒsrəʊdz] (BE) eine Kreuzung; **pedestrian crossing** [pɪˌdestrɪən 'krɒsɪŋ] Fußgängerüberweg
crossword ['krɒswɜ:d] Kreuzworträtsel
crowd [kraʊd] (Menschen-)Menge; **crowded** überfüllt, voll (gestopft)
crown [kraʊn] **1.** Krone; **2.** krönen
cruel ['kru:əl] grausam
cry [kraɪ] **1.** weinen; **2.** schreien
Cuba ['kju:bə] Kuba; **Cuban** **1.** Kubaner/in; **2.** kubanisch
culture ['kʌltʃə] Kultur; **cultural** ['kʌltʃrəl] kulturell
cup [kʌp] Tasse
cupboard ['kʌbəd] Schrank
curious ['kjʊərɪəs] neugierig, wissbegierig
currency ['kʌrənsɪ] Währung
curtain ['kɜ:tn] Vorhang, Gardine
custom ['kʌstəm] Brauch, Sitte, Gewohnheit
customer ['kʌstəmə] Kunde, Kundin
cut [kʌt] (ab)schneiden; **cut back** einschränken
cycle ['saɪkl] Rad fahren

D

dad [dæd], **Daddy** Vati, Papa, Papi
daily ['deɪlɪ] täglich
dairy farm ['deərɪ ˌfɑ:m] auf Milchwirtschaft spezialisierter Bauernhof
damage ['dæmɪdʒ] **1.** Schaden, Beschädigung; **do damage** Schaden anrichten; **2.** beschädigen
dance [dɑ:ns] **1.** Tanz, Ball; **2.** tanzen; **dancer** Tänzer/in
danger ['deɪndʒə] Gefahr; **dangerous** ['deɪndʒərəs] gefährlich
dark [dɑ:k] dunkel, finster; **after dark** nach Einbruch der Dunkelheit
dash [dæʃ] Gedankenstrich
date [deɪt] Datum; **What date is it (today)?** Der Wievielte ist heute?
daughter ['dɔ:tə] Tochter
day [deɪ] Tag; **the day after tomorrow** übermorgen; **the day before yesterday** vorgestern; **in those days** damals
dead [ded] tot; **deadly** tödlich, Tod-
deal with [di:l] sich beschäftigen mit, sich kümmern um, sich befassen mit; handeln von
dear [dɪə] **1.** Liebling, Schatz; **2.** liebe, lieber, liebes; **Dear Sir/Madam/Sir or Madam,** Sehr geehrter Herr/Sehr geehrte Dame/Sehr geehrte Damen und Herren
death [deθ] Tod; **deathbed** Totenbett, Sterbebett
debate (on) [dɪ'beɪt] Debatte, Diskussion (über)
debt [det] Schuld
December [dɪ'sembə] Dezember
decide [dɪ'saɪd] beschließen, (sich) entscheiden
decision [dɪ'sɪʒn] Entscheidung, Entschluss
make a decision eine Entscheidung treffen
deck [dek] Deck; **on deck** auf Deck, an Deck
declaration [ˌdeklə'reɪʃn] Erklärung, Verkündung, Bekanntgabe; **Declaration of Independence** Unabhängigkeitserklärung; **declare** [dɪ'kleə] erklären, verkünden
decline [dɪ'klaɪn] Niedergang, Verfall; Abnahme
decrease **1.** [dɪ'kri:s] abnehmen; **2.** ['di:kri:s] Rückgang
deep [di:p] tief; **deepen** vertiefen; tiefer machen; **deep mining** Tiefbergbau
deer, *pl* **deer** [dɪə] Hirsch, Reh
defeat [dɪ'fi:t] besiegen, schlagen
defence (BE), **defense** (AE) [dɪ'fens] Verteidigung; Verteidigungs-; **Defence Minister** Verteidigungsminister/in; **Defence** (BE), **Defense** (AE) **Secretary** (brit./amerik.) Verteidigungsminister/in; **Defense Department** (AE) (amerik.) Verteidigungsministerium; **defend** [dɪ'fend] verteidigen; **defender** Verteidiger/in, Schützer/in
define [dɪ'faɪn] definieren, festlegen
definite(ly) ['defɪnɪt, -lɪ] definitiv, sicher(lich), bestimmt
definition [defɪ'nɪʃn] Definition; **by definition** per Definition
degree [dɪ'gri:] Grad
delay [dɪ'leɪ] Verzögerung, Verspätung
delicate ['delɪkət] delikat, Fingerspitzengefühl erfordernd, heikel; zart
deliver [dɪ'lɪvə] *(Rede)* halten
demand [dɪ'mɑ:nd] **1.** verlangen, fordern; erfordern; **2.** Forderung, Nachfrage
demo ['deməʊ] Demo
democracy [dɪ'mɒkrəsɪ] Demokratie; **democrat** ['deməkræt] Demokrat/in; **democratic** [ˌdemə'krætɪk] demokratisch
demonstrate ['demənstreɪt] **1.** zeigen, nachweisen; **2.** demonstrieren;

demonstration [ˌdemənˈstreɪʃn] Demonstration
Denmark [ˈdenmɑːk] Dänemark
department [dɪˈpɑːtmənt] Ministerium; **Department of Commerce** (AE) [ˈkɒməs] (amerik.) Wirtschaftsministerium; **Department of Defense** (AE) (amerik.) Verteidigungsministerium; **Department of State** (AE) (amerik.) Außenministerium; **Department of the Interior** (AE) (amerik.) Innenministerium; **Department of the Treasury** (AE) [ˈtreʒərɪ] (amerik.) Finanzministerium; **Department of Trade and Industry** (brit.) Wirtschaftsministerium; **department store** Kaufhaus, Warenhaus
depend (on) [dɪˈpend] **1.** abhängig sein (von), abhängen (von); **2.** sich verlassen auf; **depending on** je nach
depressing [dɪˈpresɪŋ] deprimierend
descended: be descended from [dɪˈsendɪd] abstammen von
describe [dɪˈskraɪb] beschreiben; **description** [dɪˈskrɪpʃn] Beschreibung
desegregate [diːˈsegrɪgeɪt] die Rassentrennung aufheben in
design [dɪˈzaɪn] **1.** Design, Produktgestaltung, Konstruktion(slehre); Entwurf, Skizze; **2.** entwerfen, konstruieren; **be designed to** sollen; **designer** Designer/in, Konstrukteur/in
desk [desk] Schreibtisch, Schülertisch; **information desk** [ɪnfəˈmeɪʃn desk] Auskunftsschalter, Informationsschalter
destroy [dɪˈstrɔɪ] zerstören, vernichten
detached house [dɪˌtætʃt ˈhaʊs] frei stehendes Haus
detail [ˈdiːteɪl] Detail; Einzelheit; **detailed** detailliert
detect [dɪˈtekt] entdecken, bemerken, feststellen
detective [dɪˈtektɪv] Detektiv/in; **detective story** Detektivgeschichte, Krimi
determined [dɪˈtɜːmɪnd] fest entschlossen
develop [dɪˈveləp] (sich) entwickeln; **development** [dɪˈveləpmənt] Entwicklung; Erschließung; Verlauf
dial [ˈdaɪəl] wählen *(am Telefon)*
dialect [ˈdaɪəlekt] Dialekt, Mundart
dialogue [ˈdaɪəlɒg] Dialog
diary [ˈdaɪərɪ] Tagebuch; Taschenkalender, Notizbuch
dictate [dɪkˈteɪt] **1.** diktieren; **2.** vorschreiben, bestimmen; **dictator** [dɪkˈteɪtə] Diktator/in; **dictatorship** [dɪkˈteɪtəʃɪp] Diktatur
dictionary [ˈdɪkʃənrɪ] Wörterbuch
die (of) [daɪ] sterben (an); **die out** aussterben
differ [ˈdɪfə] sich unterscheiden; **difference** [ˈdɪfrəns] Unterschied; **different (from) 1.** verschieden, unterschiedlich; **2.** anders (als)
difficult [ˈdɪfɪkəlt] schwierig, schwer; **difficulty** Schwierigkeit
dig (up) [dɪg] (aus-, um)graben
dime [daɪm] (AE) 10¢-Münze
dining-room [ˈdaɪnɪŋ rʊm] Esszimmer
dinner [ˈdɪnə] (Festtags-, Mittags-, Abend-)Essen
dinosaur [ˈdaɪnəsɔː] Dinosaurier
diplomat [ˈdɪpləmæt] Diplomat/in; **diplomatic** [dɪpləˈmætɪk] diplomatisch
direct [dɪˈrekt, daɪˈrekt] direkt, unmittelbar; **direction** Richtung; **director** [dɪˈrektə] Direktor/in, Leiter/in
dirt [dɜːt] Schmutz; **dirty** schmutzig, dreckig
disabled [dɪsˈeɪbld] (körper)behindert
disadvantage [ˌdɪsədˈvɑːntɪdʒ] Nachteil
disagree (with) [ˌdɪsəˈgriː] nicht übereinstimmen (mit), anderer Meinung sein (als)
disappear [dɪsəˈpɪə] verschwinden
disappoint [ˌdɪsəˈpɔɪnt] enttäuschen; **disappointed** [ˌdɪsəˈpɔɪntɪd] enttäuscht; **disappointing** [ˌdɪsəˈpɔɪntɪŋ] enttäuschend; **disappointment** Enttäuschung
disaster [dɪˈzɑːstə] Katastrophe; Desaster, Fiasko
discipline [ˈdɪsəplɪn] Disziplin; **disciplined** diszipliniert
disco [ˈdɪskəʊ] Disco
discouraged [dɪˈskʌrɪdʒd] entmutigt
discover [dɪˈskʌvə] entdecken; feststellen; **discovery** Entdeckung
discrimination (against) [ˌdɪskrɪmɪˈneɪʃn] Diskriminierung (von)
discuss [dɪˈskʌs] besprechen, diskutieren über; **discussion** [dɪˈskʌʃn] Diskussion, Besprechung
disease [dɪˈziːz] Krankheit
dishes *(pl)* [ˈdɪʃɪz] Geschirr
dislike [dɪsˈlaɪk] **1.** Abneigung; **likes and dislikes** [ˈdɪsˌlaɪks] Vorlieben und Abneigungen; **2.** nicht mögen, nicht leiden können
dissatisfied [dɪˈsætɪsfaɪd] unzufrieden
distance [ˈdɪstəns] Entfernung; Ferne
district [ˈdɪstrɪkt] Gebiet, Bezirk
diver [ˈdaɪvə] Taucher/in
divide (into) [dɪˈvaɪd] (auf)teilen (in)
divorce [dɪˈvɔːs] Scheidung; **divorced** geschieden; **get divorced** sich scheiden lassen
DIY (BE) [ˌdiː‿aɪ ˈwaɪ] **(= Do-It-Yourself)** Heimwerken
do [duː] tun, machen; **do 50 metres** 50 Meter schaffen; **do a test/an exam** eine Arbeit schreiben/eine Prüfung machen; **do business (with)** Geschäfte machen (mit); **do damage** Schaden anrichten; **do one's homework** Hausaufgaben machen; **do magic** zaubern; **do sports** Sport treiben; **do something about sb/sth** etwas gegen jn/etwas unternehmen; **do the housework** die Haus(halts)arbeit machen; **do tricks** Kunststücke/Tricks vorführen; **do well/badly** gut/schlecht sein *(in einem Fach);* **do without** verzichten (auf), auskommen ohne
docklands [ˈdɒkləndz] Hafengebiet, -anlagen; **docks** [dɒks] Docks, Hafenanlagen
doctor [ˈdɒktə] Arzt, Ärztin
document [ˌdɒkjʊˈmənt] Dokument, Urkunde
dog [dɒg] Hund
dollar [ˈdɒlə] Dollar
domestic [dəˈmestɪk] häuslich, einheimisch
dominate [ˈdɒmɪneɪt] beherrschen
door [dɔː] Tür
dot [dɒt] Punkt, Pünktchen
double [ˈdʌbl] doppelt; Doppel-
down [daʊn] herunter, hinunter; herab, hinab; **down there** dort unten; **pull down** ab-, niederreißen; **sit down** sich setzen; **write down** aufschreiben; **downstairs** unten; nach unten; **downtown** (AE) in der/die Innenstadt, im/ins Zentrum
dozen [ˈdʌzn] Dutzend
Dr = Doctor [ˈdɒktə] Dr. = Doktor
dragon [ˈdrægən] Drache
drama [ˈdrɑːmə] Drama, Schauspiel
draw [drɔː] **1.** zeichnen; **2.** ziehen; **draw attention (to)** Aufmerksamkeit lenken (auf)
dream [driːm] **1.** Traum; **2.** träumen; **dreamer** Träumer/in
dress [dres] **1.** Kleid; **2.** sich (ver)kleiden; (sich) anziehen
drink [drɪŋk] **1.** Getränk; **2.** trinken; **drinkable** trinkbar; genießbar; **drinking water** Trinkwasser
drive [draɪv] **1.** (Auto) fahren; **2.** (an)treiben; **drive sb crazy** (infml) jn wahnsinnig, verrückt machen; **driver 1.** (Auto-)Fahrer/in; **2.** Lokführer/in; **driver's license** (AE) **driving licence** (BE) [ˈlaɪsəns] Führerschein
drop [drɒp] fallen lassen; fallen; **dropout** [ˈdrɒpaʊt] Abbrecher/in, Aussteiger/in; **drop out (of school)** (die Schule) abbrechen, vorzeitig verlassen
drown [draʊn] ertrinken, ertränken
drugs [drʌgz] Rauschgift
dry [draɪ] **1.** trocken; **2.** (ab)trocknen
dump [dʌmp] **1.** Halde, Kippe; **2.** abladen, auskippen, wegwerfen

during ['djʊərɪŋ] während
Dutch [dʌtʃ] **1.** holländisch, niederländisch; **2.** Holländisch, Niederländisch
duty ['dju:tɪ] Pflicht; **on/off duty** im/außer Dienst

E

each [i:tʃ] jeder, jede, jedes (einzelne); **each other** einander, sich (gegenseitig)
ear [ɪə] Ohr
early ['3:lɪ] früh, (früh)zeitig; **be early** zu früh kommen
earn [3:n] verdienen
earth [3:θ] Erde; **(earth)quake** ['3:θkweɪk] (Erd-)Beben
east (of) [i:st] **1.** östlich (von); **2.** Ost-; (nach) Osten; **eastern** östlich
Easter ['i:stə] Ostern, Oster-; **at Easter** zu Ostern
easy ['i:zɪ] leicht, einfach
eat [i:t] essen; **eat out** essen gehen; **eatable** essbar, genießbar
economic(ally) [ˌi:kə'nɒmɪklɪ] (volks)wirtschaftlich; Wirtschafts-; **economics** [ˌi:kə'nɒmɪks] (Volks-)Wirtschaftslehre; **economy** [ɪ'kɒnəmɪ] Wirtschaft
edge [edʒ] Rand, Kante
editor ['edɪtə] Herausgeber/in; Redakteur/in
educate ['edjʊkeɪt, 'edʒʊkeɪt] erziehen; (aus)bilden; **education** [ˌedjʊ'keɪʃn] (Aus-)Bildung, Erziehung; **educational** [ˌedjʊ'keɪʃənl] Bildungs-, Lehr-; pädagogisch; lehrreich
effect (on) [ɪ'fekt] Auswirkung (auf), Wirkung (auf); **effective** [ɪ'fektɪv] effektiv, wirkungsvoll, wirksam
efficient [ɪ'fɪʃnt] **1.** effizient, wirtschaftlich; **2.** leistungsfähig, tüchtig
e. g. [ˌi:'dʒi:] z. B. (= zum Beispiel)
egg [eg] Ei
Egypt ['i:dʒɪpt] Ägypten
either ... or ['aɪðə, 'i:ðə] entweder ... oder; **(not ...) either** auch nicht, auch kein
elderly ['eldəlɪ] ältere(r, s)
elect sb (sth) [ɪ'lekt] jm (zu etw) wählen
election [ɪ'lekʃn] (politische) Wahl
electric [ɪ'lektrɪk] elektrisch; **electrical** [ɪ'lektrɪkl] elektrisch; **electricity** [ˌɪlek'trɪsətɪ] Strom, Elektrizität
electronics [ɪˌlek'trɒnɪks] Elektronik
element ['eləmənt] Element
elementary school [ˌelə'mentrɪ] (US) Grundschule
elephant ['elɪfənt] Elefant
else [els] sonst; anders; **Anything else?** Sonst noch etwas?
e-mail ['i:meɪl] elektronische Post, E-Mail

emancipation [ɪˌmænsɪ'peɪʃn] Emanzipation; Befreiung
emigrate ['emɪgreɪt] auswandern, emigrieren
emotion [ɪ'məʊʃn] Gefühl, Emotion
emperor ['empərə] Kaiser
emphasis ['emfəsɪs] Emphase; Hervorhebung, Betonung; **emphasize** ['emfəsaɪz] betonen, hervorheben
empire ['empaɪə] Reich
employ [ɪm'plɔɪ] beschäftigen, anstellen; **employee** [ɪm'plɔɪi:, ˌemplɔɪ'i:] Arbeitnehmer/in, Angestellte(r); **employer** [ɪm'plɔɪə] Arbeitgeber/in; **employment** [ɪm'plɔɪmənt] Beschäftigung, Arbeit
emptiness ['emptɪnəs] Leere; **empty** ['emptɪ] leer
encourage [ɪn'kʌrɪdʒ] ermutigen, ermuntern; fördern
encyclopedia [ɪnˌsaɪklə'pi:dɪə] Enzyklopädie, Lexikon
end [end] **1.** Ende, Schluss; **at the end** am Ende, am Schluss; **2. end (in)** enden (auf, mit); beenden; **ending** Ende, (Ab-)Schluss; Endung; **endless** ['endləs] endlos; **come to an end** ein Ende finden, zu einem Ende kommen; **make ends meet** *(finanziell)* über die Runden kommen
enemy ['enəmɪ] Feind
energy ['enədʒɪ] Energie
engine ['endʒɪn] Motor, Maschine
engineer [ˌendʒɪ'nɪə] Ingenieur/in, Techniker/in; **engineering** Ingenieurwesen; Maschinenbau
England ['ɪŋglənd] England; **English** **1.** englisch; **2.** Englisch; **3.** Engländer/in; **in English** auf Englisch; **Englishman, Englishwoman** Engländer, Engländerin; **English-speaking** Englisch sprechend, englischsprachig
enjoy [ɪn'dʒɔɪ] genießen, Spaß haben an, gern haben/tun; **enjoy oneself** viel Spaß haben, sich amüsieren; **enjoyable** [ɪn'dʒɔɪəbl] nett; unterhaltsam
enormous [ɪ'nɔ:məs] enorm, riesig
enough [ɪ'nʌf] genug
ensemble [ɒn'sɒmbl] Ensemble
ensure [ɪn'ʃɔ:] sicherstellen, garantieren; sorgen für
enter ['entə] betreten, einreisen in
entertainment [ˌentə'teɪnmənt] Entertainment, Unterhaltung, Belustigung
enthusiastic [ɪnˌθju:zɪ'æstɪk] enthusiastisch, begeistert
entitle (to) [ɪn'taɪtl] berechtigen (zu)
entrance (to) ['entrəns] Eingang (zu); Eintritts-
entry ['entrɪ] **1.** Einsendung; **2.** Eintrag *(in Wörter-, Tagebuch)*

envelope ['envələʊp] Briefumschlag
environment [ɪn'vaɪrənmənt] Umwelt, Umgebung; **environmental** [ɪnˌvaɪrən'mentl] Umwelt-
episode ['epɪsəʊd] Fortsetzung, Folge *(einer Sendereihe)*; Episode, Begebenheit
equal ['i:kwəl] gleich; **equality** [ɪ'kwɒlətɪ] Gleichheit
equipment [ɪ'kwɪpmənt] Ausrüstung
equivalent [ɪ'kwɪvələnt] Entsprechung
escape [ɪ'skeɪp] **1.** Flucht; Entkommen; **2.** entkommen, entgehen; fliehen
Eskimo ['eskɪməʊ] **1.** Eskimo; **2.** Eskimo-
especially [ɪ'speʃlɪ] besonders; insbesondere
essay ['eseɪ] Aufsatz, Essay
establish [ɪ'stæblɪʃ] gründen, einrichten
estate [ɪ'steɪt] Siedlung, Gebiet
etc. [ɪt'setrə] usw. (und so weiter)
ethical ['eθɪkl] ethisch
ethnic ['eθnɪk] Volks-, ethnisch
Europe ['jʊərəp] Europa; **European** [ˌjʊərə'pi:ən] **1.** europäisch; **2.** Europäer/in; **European Union** ['ju:nɪən] Europäische Union
eve [i:v] Vorabend, Vortag; **New Year's Eve** Silvester(abend)
even ['i:vn] sogar, selbst; **even if** selbst wenn; **even so** *(adv)* dennoch, trotzdem; **even worse** (sogar) noch schlimmer; **not even** nicht einmal
evening ['i:vnɪŋ] Abend; **in the evening(s)** abends; **on a cold evening** an einem kalten Abend; **this evening** heute Abend
event [ɪ'vent] **1.** Ereignis; **2.** Wettkampf, Disziplin
ever ['evə] je(mals), schon mal; **for ever** für immer, ewig; **not ever** nie
every ['evrɪ] jeder, jede, jedes; **everybody/everyone** jeder(mann), alle; **everyday** ['evrɪdeɪ] alltäglich, Alltags-; **everything** alles; **everywhere** überall, überallhin
evidence (of) *(sing)* ['evɪdəns] Beweis(e) (für), Beleg(e) (für)
ex- [eks] Ex-, ehemalige(r/s), frühere(r/s)
exact [ɪg'zækt] genau
exam(ination) [ɪgˌzæmɪ'neɪʃn] Prüfung, Examen; **examine** [ɪg'zæmɪn] prüfen, untersuchen
example [ɪg'zɑ:mpl] Beispiel; **for example** zum Beispiel
excellent ['eksələnt] ausgezeichnet, hervorragend
except [ɪk'sept] außer, bis auf; **exception** [ɪk'sepʃn] Ausnahme
excerpt (from) ['eks3:pt] Auszug, Exzerpt (aus)
exchange [ɪks'tʃeɪndʒ] **1.** (Aus-, Um-)Tausch; (Geld-)Wechsel; **2.** austauschen, umtauschen; *(Geld)* wechseln

excited (about) [ɪk'saɪtɪd] aufgeregt, freudig erregt (wegen, über); **exciting** aufregend, spannend
exclamation mark [ˌekskləˈmeɪʃn mɑːk] Ausrufezeichen
exclusive [ɪk'skluːsɪv] exklusiv, vornehm
excuse [ɪk'skjuːs] Ausrede, Entschuldigung; **Excuse me.** [ɪk'skjuːz ˌmiː] Entschuldigen Sie.
execute ['eksɪkjuːt] hinrichten; **execution** [ˌeksɪ'kjuːʃn] Hinrichtung, Exekution
exercise ['eksəsaɪz] Übung(saufgabe); **exercise book** Heft, Schulheft
exhausting [ɪg'zɔːstɪŋ] anstrengend
exhibition [ˌeksɪ'bɪʃn] Ausstellung
exist [ɪg'zɪst] existieren, vorhanden sein
exit ['eksɪt] Ausgang; (Autobahn-)Ausfahrt
expand [ɪk'spænd] expandieren, (sich) vergrößern, (sich) ausdehnen
expect [ɪk'spekt] erwarten; annehmen, vermuten; **expectation** [ˌekspek'teɪʃn] Erwartung
expedition [ˌekspɪ'dɪʃn] Expedition
expensive [ɪk'spensɪv] teuer
experience [ɪk'spɪərɪəns] **1.** Erfahrung(en), Erlebnis; **2.** erfahren, erleben
experiment [ɪk'sperɪmənt] Experiment, Versuch (mit); **experimental** [ɪkˌsperɪ'mentl] experimentell
expert (at/in) ['ekspɜːt] **1.** Fachmann/-frau, Experte, Expertin (für); **2.** erfahren, geschickt
explain [ɪk'spleɪn] erklären, erläutern
explicit [ɪk'splɪsɪt] explizit, ausdrücklich, deutlich, offen
exploit [ɪk'splɔɪt] **1.** ausbeuten; **2.** verwerten
explore [ɪk'splɔː] erforschen; **explorer** Forscher/in
export 1. ['ekspɔːt] Ausfuhr, Export; **2.** [ɪk'spɔːt] exportieren
express [ɪk'spres] äußern, ausdrücken; **expression** [ɪk'spreʃn] Ausdruck, Äußerung
expressway (AE) Schnellstraße, Autobahn
extend (to) [ɪk'stend] ausdehnen (auf), erweitern (auf); verlängern, vergrößern; **extended family** Großfamilie
extra ['ekstrə] extra, zusätzlich; Extra-
extracurricular activity [ˌekstrəkə'rɪkjʊlə] außerunterrichtliche Aktivität, Arbeitsgemeinschaft
extract (from) ['ekstrækt] Auszug (aus)
extreme [ɪk'striːm] extrem; äußerste(r, s)
eye [aɪ] Auge; **keep an eye on** ein (wachsames) Auge haben auf

F

fable ['feɪbl] Fabel
face [feɪs] Gesicht; **face sb/sth** sich jm/einer Sache gegenübersehen, jm/einer Sache (mutig) ins Auge sehen; **in the face of** im Angesicht von, angesichts (von), gegenüber
facilities *(pl)* [fə'sɪlɪtɪz] Einrichtungen, Anlage(n)
fact [fækt] **1.** Tatsache, Information; **2.** Wirklichkeit; **in fact** eigentlich, genau gesagt, tatsächlich
factory ['fæktərɪ] Fabrik
fail [feɪl]**: fail (an exam)** (bei einer Prüfung) durchfallen, nicht bestehen; versagen, scheitern
fair [feə] **1.** fair, gerecht; **2.** heiter, schön
faith [feɪθ] Glaube(n)
faithfully ['feɪθfəlɪ]**: Yours faithfully** Mit freundlichen Grüßen; Hochachtungsvoll
fall [fɔːl] **1.** (AE) Herbst; **2.** fallen; **fall in love (with)** sich verlieben (in); **fall off** herunterfallen; **fall over** hinfallen, umfallen
falls [fɔːlz] (Wasser-)Fälle
false [fɔːls] falsch, unecht
familiar [fə'mɪlɪə] bekannt, vertraut, gewohnt
family ['fæmɪlɪ] Familie; **start a family** eine Familie gründen
famous ['feɪməs] berühmt
fan [fæn] Fan
fanatic [fə'nætɪk] **1.** fanatisch; **2.** Fanatiker/in
fantastic [fæn'tæstɪk] fantastisch, toll
far [fɑː] weit (entfernt); **so far** bis jetzt, bisher
fare [feə] Fahrpreis, Fahrgeld
farm [fɑːm] **1.** Bauernhof, Farm; **2.** (Land) bebauen; (Vieh) züchten, halten; **farmer** Bauer, Bäuerin; Farmer/in; **farmhouse** Bauernhaus; **farming** Landwirtschaft, Ackerbau; **farmland** Ackerland, landwirtschaftlich genutzte Fläche
farther ['fɑːðə] weiter (entfernt); **farthest** ['fɑːðɪst] am weitesten (entfernt)
fascinate ['fæsɪneɪt] faszinieren, begeistern
fast [fɑːst] **1.** schnell; **fast-food place** Fastfood-Laden; **2.** fasten
fat [fæt] dick
father ['fɑːðə] Vater; **Father Christmas** [ˌfɑːðə 'krɪsməs] (BE) der Weihnachtsmann
fault [fɔːlt] Schuld, Fehler
favour ['feɪvə] Gefallen; **do sb a favour** jm einen Gefallen tun; **in sb's favour** zu jemandes Gunsten, zugunsten von jm

favourite ['feɪvrɪt] Lieblings-
FBI [ˌefbiː'aɪ] **= Federal Bureau of Investigation** US-Bundeskriminalamt
fear (of) [fɪə] Angst (vor)
feature ['fiːtʃə] Merkmal, Eigenschaft
February ['februərɪ] Februar
fed: be fed up (with) [ˌfed‿'ʌp] satt haben, die Nase voll haben (von)
federal ['fedrəl] Bundes-
fee [fiː] Honorar
feeble ['fiːbl] schwach
feed [fiːd] füttern; ernähren; **feeding-time** Fütterungszeit
feel [fiːl] **1.** (sich) fühlen; **2.** meinen, glauben, halten für; **feel like doing sth** (infml) Lust haben etwas zu tun; (jm danach sein, etwas zu tun; **feel sorry (for)** bedauern, bereuen; **feeling** Gefühl
felt-tip ['felt tɪp] Filzstift
female ['fiːmeɪl] **1.** weiblich; **2.** weibliche Person, Weibchen
fence [fens] Zaun
ferry (boat) ['ferɪ] Fähre
fertile ['fɜːtaɪl] fruchtbar
festival ['festəvl] Festspiele, Festival; Fest(-tag)
fetch [fetʃ] **1.** holen; **2.** abholen
few [fjuː] wenige; **a few** ein paar, einige (wenige)
fiction ['fɪkʃn] Dichtung; Prosaliteratur; Fiktion
field [fiːld] **1.** Feld, Wiese, Weide; **2.** (Sport-)Platz; **3.** Gebiet; **in the field(s)** auf dem Feld
fierce [fɪəs] heftig; erbittert; wild
fifth [fɪfθ] Fünftel
fight [faɪt] **1.** Kampf; **2.** (be)kämpfen; **fighter** Kämpfer/in
figure ['fɪgə] **1.** Figur, Gestalt; **2.** Zahl, Ziffer
fill [fɪl] füllen, voll machen; **fill in** einsetzen; **filler** Füllwort
film [fɪlm] Film; **film star** Filmstar
final ['faɪnl] letzte(r, s), Abschluss-; endgültige(r, s); **finally** ['faɪnəlɪ] schließlich, endlich
financial [faɪ'nænʃl] finanziell
find [faɪnd] finden; **finding** Ergebnis; **find out** herausfinden, erfahren
fine [faɪn] **1.** Bußgeld, Geldstrafe; **2.** gut, fein, schön
finger ['fɪŋgə] Finger
finish ['fɪnɪʃ] (be)enden, aufhören (mit), fertig machen; ins Ziel kommen **I've finished.** Ich bin fertig. **finish line** Ziellinie
fire ['faɪə] Feuer, Brand; **fireworks** *(pl)* ['faɪəwɜːks] Feuerwerk(skörper)
firm [fɜːm] Firma
first [fɜːst] (zu)erst, zunächst; **firstly** erstens; **at first** zuerst, anfangs; **be first** der Erste sein, als Erster (an)kommen

fish [fɪʃ] Fisch, Fische; **fishing** 1. Fischen, Fischerei; 2. Fischer-; **go fishing** fischen, angeln (gehen)
fit [fɪt] 1. fit, gut in Form; 2. passen; **fitness** ['fɪtnəs] Fitness, Kondition
fix [fɪks] 1. bestimmen, festlegen; 2. befestigen, festmachen
flag [flæg] Fahne, Flagge
flame [fleɪm] Flamme
flat [flæt] 1. (BE) Wohnung; 2. flach, eben; **flatten** flach/glatt machen, ebnen
flight [flaɪt] Flug
floor [flɔː] 1. Fußboden; 2. Stockwerk; **first floor** (BE) erster Stock; (AE) Erdgeschoss; **ground floor** (BE) Erdgeschoss
flower ['flaʊə] Blume, Blüte
flu [fluː] Grippe
fluent ['fluːənt] fließend, flüssig *(Sprache, Vortrag)*
fly [flaɪ] fliegen; **flying time** Flugzeit
focus ['fəʊkəs] Blick-, Brennpunkt; **focus on** sich konzentrieren auf
fog [fɒg] (dicker) Nebel; **foggy** neblig
folk song ['fəʊk sɒŋ] Volkslied, Folksong
follow ['fɒləʊ] 1. folgen; 2. verfolgen, nachfolgen; **following** folgend
fond: be fond of [fɒnd] gern haben, mögen
food [fuːd] Essen, Lebensmittel, Nahrung; Futter
fool [fuːl] Dummkopf, Narr; **make a fool of sb** jn lächerlich machen
foot, *pl* **feet** [fʊt, fiːt] 1. Fuß; 2. *Längenmaß (= 30,5 cm)*; **football** ['fʊtbɔːl] Fußball
for [fɔː, fə] 1. für; 2. seit; **for about an hour** etwa eine Stunde lang; **for a long time** lange Zeit; **for breakfast, etc.** zum Frühstück usw.; **for ever** für immer, ewig; **for example** zum Beispiel; **for God's sake** um Gottes willen; **for hours** stundenlang; **for sb's birthday** zum Geburtstag; **for seven miles** sieben Meilen weit; **for the first time** zum ersten Mal; **good for** gut gegen
force [fɔːs] zwingen
forecast ['fɔːkɑːst] Vorhersage
foreign ['fɒrən] ausländisch, fremd; **foreign affairs** Außenpolitik; **foreign language** Fremdsprache; **Foreign Minister** Außenminister/in; **Foreign Office** (brit.) Außenministerium; **foreign policy** Außenpolitik; **Foreign Secretary** (brit.) Außenminister/in; **foreigner** Ausländer/in, Fremde(r)
forest ['fɒrɪst] Wald, Forst
forget [fə'get] vergessen
fork [fɔːk] Gabel
form [fɔːm] 1. Form; 2. (BE) Klasse, Jahrgangsstufe; 3. bilden, (sich) formen; **fifth former** Schüler/in des 5. Jahrgangs; **sixth form** Oberstufe, Sekundarstufe II; **sixth-former** (BE) Schüler/in der Oberstufe/Sekundarstufe II
formal ['fɔːml] formal; formell
former ['fɔːmə] frühere(r, s), ehemalige(r, s)
fortunately ['fɔːtʃnətlɪ] glücklicherweise
forward(s) ['fɔːwəd(z)] vorwärts
found [faʊnd] gründen, errichten; **foundation** Stiftung; Fundament, Grundlage
fountain ['faʊntɪn] Springbrunnen
France [frɑːns] Frankreich
Franconian [fræŋ'kəʊnɪən] 1. Franke, Fränkin; 2. Franken-; fränkisch
free [friː] 1. frei; 2. kostenlos; **free time** Freizeit; 3. freilassen; befreien; **freedom** Freiheit; **freedom of speech** Redefreiheit
freeze [friːz] (ge)frieren; erstarren; **freeze to death** erfrieren
French [frentʃ] 1. französisch; 2. Franzose, Französin; 3. Französisch; **Frenchman, Frenchwoman** Franzose, Französin
fresh [freʃ] frisch
Friday ['fraɪdɪ] Freitag
fridge [frɪdʒ] Kühlschrank
friend [frend] Freund/in; **make friends (with)** sich anfreunden (mit); Freunde finden; **friendliness** ['frendlɪnəs] Freundlichkeit; **friendly** freundlich; **friendship** Freundschaft
frightened ['fraɪtnd] erschrocken, verängstigt; **be frightened (of)** Angst haben (vor), sich fürchten (vor); **frightening** erschreckend, Schrecken erregend
from [frɒm, frəm] aus; von; **from now on** von jetzt an, ab jetzt; **come from** (her)stammen von; **I'm from ...** Ich bin/komme aus ...; **Where are you from?** Wo kommst du her?
front [frʌnt] Vorderseite; **front door** Haustür; **front garden** Vor(der)garten; **at the front** vorn, an der Vorderseite (vorn); **in front of** vor; **to the front** nach vorn, zur Vorderseite (vorn)
frontier [BE: 'frʌntɪə, frʌn'tɪə; AE: frʌn'tɪər] Grenze, Grenzland
fruit [fruːt] Obst, Früchte
frustrated [frʌ'streɪtɪd] frustriert
full (of), full up (with) [fʊl] voll (mit/von); **full stop** (BE) Punkt *(am Satzende)*
fun [fʌn] Spaß; **be fun** Spaß machen; **funny** ['fʌnɪ] lustig, komisch; seltsam
function ['fʌŋkʃn] Funktion
funeral ['fjuːnərəl] Beerdigung, Begräbnis
furniture *(sing)* ['fɜːnɪtʃə] Möbel
further ['fɜːðə] 1. weiter; 2. weitere(r, s), zusätzlich, noch; **further education** Weiterbildung; **furthermore** außerdem, überdies
future ['fjuːtʃə] 1. Zukunft; 2. (zu)künftig; **in future** künftig, ab jetzt

G

gallery ['gælərɪ] Galerie
game [geɪm] Spiel
gang [gæŋ] Bande, Gang
gap [gæp] Lücke
garage ['gærɑːdʒ] Garage
garden ['gɑːdn] Garten
gas [gæs] Gas; AE *auch:* Benzin; **gasoline** (AE) ['gæsəlɪːn] Benzin; **gas station** ['gæs ˌsteɪʃn] (AE) Tankstelle
gate [geɪt] Tor
gather ['gæðə] sammeln, pflücken; sich versammeln
GCSE [ˌdʒiː siː‿es‿'iː] = **General Certificate of Secondary Education** [ˌdʒenrəl sə'tɪfɪkət] (BE) *eine Art Hauptschulabschluss oder mittlere Reife*
general ['dʒenərəl] 1. General/in; 2. allgemein, generell; **general election** [ɪ'lekʃn] Parlamentswahlen (in GB); **generalize** verallgemeinern
generation [ˌdʒenə'reɪʃn] Generation
geographical [ˌdʒiːə'græfɪkl] geographisch; **geography** [dʒɪ'ɒgrəfɪ] Geographie, Erdkunde
German ['dʒɜːmən] 1. deutsch; 2. Deutsche, Deutscher; 3. Deutsch; **Germany** Deutschland
gesture ['dʒestʃə] Geste
get [get] 1. bekommen, kriegen; 2. werden; 3. holen, besorgen; 4. gelangen, (hin)kommen; **get along** zurechtkommen, sich zurechtfinden; **get better** sich erholen; **get divorced** sich scheiden lassen; **get in (the train)** (in den Zug) einsteigen; **get into trouble** in Schwierigkeiten geraten; **get lost** sich verlaufen; **get married** (sich ver)heiraten (mit); **get off** aussteigen (aus), absteigen (von); **get on** einsteigen (in), aufsteigen (auf); **get on sb's nerves** jm auf die Nerven gehen; **get out!** raus!; **get out (of the train)** (aus dem Zug) aussteigen; **get ready** sich fertig machen, bereitmachen; **get rid of sth/sb** etwas/jn loswerden; **get to know** kennen lernen; **get up** aufstehen; **get used to** sich angewöhnen
ghetto ['getəʊ] Getto
ghost [gəʊst] Geist, Gespenst
giant ['dʒaɪənt] 1. Riese, Riesin; 2. riesig
giraffe [dʒɪ'rɑːf] Giraffe

girl [gɜ:l] Mädchen; **girlfriend** ['gɜ:lfrend] Freundin *(eines Jungen)*; **Girl Scout** [ˌgɜ:l 'skaʊt] (AE) Pfadfinderin
give [gɪv] **1.** geben; **2.** schenken; **give in (to sb)** (jm) nachgeben; sich geschlagen geben; **give up** aufgeben
glad [glæd]: **be glad** froh sein, sich freuen
glamorous ['glæmərəs] aufregend, schön
glance [glɑ:ns] Blick; **at first glance** auf den ersten Blick
glass [glɑ:s] Glas; **glasses** *(pl)* (eine) Brille
global ['gləʊbl] global
glove [glʌv] Handschuh
go [gəʊ] **1.** gehen; **2.** fahren; **3. go** (grey, hard) werden; **Go!** Los! **go away** verreisen; **go back to** zurückgehen auf, zurückreichen bis; **go back to sleep** wieder einschlafen; **go by** vergehen, vorübergehen; **go fishing, etc.** fischen usw. gehen; **go for a ride** herumfahren, eine Spritztour machen; **go for a swim** schwimmen gehen; **go for a walk** spazieren gehen; **go home** nach Hause gehen; **go in** hineingehen; **go on 1.** weitermachen, weitergehen; **2.** im Gange sein, vorgehen; **go on a bus tour** eine Bus(rund)fahrt machen; **go on a guided tour** eine Führung (mit)machen; **go on a trip** eine Reise/Fahrt machen; **go out** ausgehen *(Licht)*; **go out (with)** ausgehen (mit); **go to bed** ins Bett gehen; **go to school** zur Schule gehen; **go without** verzichten (auf), auskommen ohne; **go wrong** schief gehen; **I'm going to ...** Ich werde/will ..., Ich habe vor/habe die Absicht zu ...
God, god [gɒd] Gott
gold [gəʊld] **1.** Gold; **gold-rich** reich an Gold; **gold rush** ['gəʊld rʌʃ] Goldrausch, Goldfieber; **2.** gold(en); **golden** ['gəʊldən] golden
gone [gɒn] weg
good [gʊd] gut; **good at** gut in, geschickt in; **good for** gut gegen; **Good afternoon.** Guten Tag! **good-looking** gut aussehend; **Good morning.** Guten Morgen!/Tag! **Goodbye.** [gʊd'baɪ] Auf Wiedersehen!
goods [gʊdz] Waren, Güter
gorilla [gə'rɪlə] Gorilla
gotten ['gɒtn] (AE) *Partizip Perfekt von „to get"*
govern ['gʌvn] regieren; **government** ['gʌvnmənt] Regierung
grade [greɪd] (Zeugnis-)Note, Zensur; AE *auch:* Klasse, Jahrgangsstufe
gradually ['grædʒʊəlɪ] allmählich
graduate ['grædʒʊət] Hochschulabsolvent/in, Akademiker/-in; (AE *auch*:) Schulabgänger/in
graffiti [grə'fi:ti:] Graffiti; Wandkritzeleien
gram [græm] Gramm
grammar ['græmə] Grammatik; **grammar school** (BE) Gymnasium
grandfather ['grænˌfɑ:ðə] Großvater; **grandma** ['grænmɑ:] Oma; **grandmother** ['grænˌmʌðə] Großmutter; **grandpa** ['grænpɑ:] Opa, Großvater; **grandparents** Großeltern; **grandson** ['grænsʌn] Enkel
graph [grɑ:f] Diagramm, Schaubild
grass [grɑ:s] Gras
grave [greɪv] Grab; **graveyard** ['greɪvjɑ:d] Friedhof, Kirchhof
great [greɪt] **1.** großartig, prima, toll; **2.** groß, beträchtlich; **3.** bedeutend, berühmt; **greatly** sehr, außerordentlich, höchst
Greece [gri:s] Griechenland; **Greek** [gri:k] **1.** griechisch; **2.** Grieche, Griechin; **3.** Griechisch
greedy ['gri:dɪ] (hab)gierig
green [gri:n] grün
Greenback ['gri:nbæk] Greenback *(US-Währung)*
greenhouse effect ['gri:nhaʊs‿ɹˌfekt] Treibhauseffekt
grey [greɪ] grau
ground [graʊnd] (Erd-)Boden; **ground floor** (BE) Erdgeschoss
group [gru:p] Gruppe
grow [grəʊ] **1.** wachsen; **grow up** aufwachsen, groß werden; sich entwickeln; **2.** anbauen, anpflanzen; **3. grow** (old) werden; **growth** Wachstum
guard [gɑ:d] Wächter/in, Wachmann, -frau
guess [ges] (er)raten
guest [gest] Gast; **guest house** Pension, Gästehaus
guidance counselor ['gaɪdns ˌkaʊnsələ] (AE) *Beratungslehrer/in an einer amerik. High School, berät Schüler/innen über Schullaufbahn und Beruf*
guide [gaɪd] **1.** (Fremden-)Führer/in; **2.** Reiseführer, Handbuch; **3.** führen, lenken, leiten; **go on a guided tour** eine Führung (mit-)machen
guitar [gɪ'tɑ:] Gitarre; **play the guitar** Gitarre spielen
gun [gʌn] (Schuss-)Waffe
guru ['gʊru:] Guru
guy [gaɪ] (infml) Kerl, Junge, Mann
gym [dʒɪm] Turnhalle, Sporthalle; **gymnastics** [dʒɪm'næstɪks] Turnen, Gymnastik

H

habit ['hæbɪt] (An-)Gewohnheit
hair [heə] Haar, Haare; **hairdresser** ['heəˌdresə] Friseur, Friseuse; **hairstyle** ['heəstaɪl] Frisur
half [hɑ:f] Hälfte; halb; **half a mile** eine halbe Meile; **half past ten** halb elf (= 10.30); **half-sister** Halbschwester; **halfway** auf halbem Weg
hall [hɔ:l] Flur, Diele; Halle, Saal
Hallo. [hə'ləʊ] = **Hello.**
ham [hæm] Schinken; **ham salad** Schinken mit Salat
hamburger ['hæmbɜ:gə] Hamburger
hammer ['hæmə] Hammer
hamster ['hæmstə] Hamster
hand [hænd] Hand; **on the one hand/on the other hand** einerseits/andererseits; **handball** ['hændbɔ:l] Handball; **handbook** ['hændbʊk] Handbuch; **handbrake** ['hændbreɪk] Handbremse
hang [hæŋ] **1.** hängen, aufhängen; **2.** erhängen
happen (to) ['hæpən] passieren, geschehen (mit); **happen to** zufällig(erweise) (tun)
happiness ['hæpɪnəs] Glück
happy ['hæpɪ] glücklich, froh; **Happy birthday (to you)!** Herzlichen Glückwunsch zum Geburtstag!
harbour ['hɑ:bə] Hafen
hard [hɑ:d] **1.** schwer; hart; **2.** heftig, mit aller Kraft; **harden** härten; hart werden; **hardship** Härte, Not, elend
hardly ['hɑ:dlɪ] kaum
harmony ['hɑ:mənɪ] Harmonie
harvest ['hɑ:vɪst] Ernte
hat [hæt] Hut
hate [heɪt] **1.** Hass; **2.** hassen, gar nicht mögen
have [hæv] **1.** haben; **2.** essen, trinken; **have a bath** baden, ein Bad nehmen; **Have a good time!** Viel Spaß! Viel Vergnügen! **have a nice time** eine schöne Zeit/viel Spaß haben; **have a picnic** ein Picknick machen; **have a race** ein Rennen veranstalten; **have a shower** (sich) duschen; **have a wash** sich waschen; **have a word with sb** (kurz) mit jm sprechen; **have breakfast** frühstücken; **have lunch** (zu) Mittag essen; **have sth done** etwas *(von jm)* tun/machen lassen; **have tea** Abendbrot essen, zu Abend essen; **have got** haben, besitzen; **have to** (tun) müssen
he [hi:] er
head [hed] **1.** Kopf; **2.** Oberhaupt; **3.** anführen, leiten; vorstehen; **headline** Schlagzeile; **head of state** Staatsoberhaupt; **headache** ['hedeɪk]

Kopfschmerzen, Kopfweh; **headmaster** [ˌhed'mɑːstə] (Schul-) Direktor; **headquarters** *(pl)* Hauptquartier; **head teacher** Schulleiter/in
headword ['hedwɜːd] Stichwort
health [helθ] Gesundheit; **health care** medizinische Versorgung; **healthy** gesund
hear [hɪə] hören; **hear of** hören von
heart [hɑːt] Herz; **heart attack** [ə'tæk] Herzanfall; **heartland** Kernland; **heartless** herzlos
heat [hiːt] **1.** Hitze; **2.** erhitzen; heizen; **heating** ['hiːtɪŋ] Heizung
heavy ['hevɪ] schwer; heftig
hectic ['hektɪk] hektisch
hedge [hedʒ] Hecke
height [haɪt] Höhe
helicopter ['helɪkɒptə] Hubschrauber, Helikopter
Hello. [hə'ləʊ] Hallo! (Guten) Tag! **say hello (to)** grüßen
helmet ['helmɪt] Helm
help [help] **1.** Hilfe; **2.** helfen; **help oneself** zugreifen, sich bedienen; **helpful** hilfreich, nützlich; **helpless** hilflos; **helplessness** Hilflosigkeit
her [hɜː] **1.** ihr, ihre; **2.** ihr, sie
herd [hɜːd] Herde
here [hɪə] hier; **Come here.** Komm(t) her! **Here you are.** Hier bitte. Bitte sehr. **here and there** hie und da
hero, *pl* **heroes** ['hɪərəʊ] Held; **heroine** ['herəʊɪn] Heldin
hers [hɜːz] ihre(r, s); **herself** [hɜː'self] sich (selbst)
Hi. [haɪ] (infml) Hallo!
hide [haɪd] (sich) verstecken; **in hiding** versteckt, untergetaucht
high [haɪ] hoch; **higher education** Hochschul(aus)bildung; **highly** höchst; **high school** ['haɪ skuːl] (AE) Oberschule *(in den USA)*; **high-tech** computergesteuert, hoch technisiert; **high time** höchste Zeit
hijack ['haɪdʒæk] entführen, überfallen
hill [hɪl] Hügel, (kleiner) Berg
him [hɪm] ihm, ihn; **himself** [hɪm'self] sich (selbst)
hippo ['hɪpəʊ] Flusspferd, Nilpferd
hire ['haɪə] *(Boot, Auto, Saal)* mieten, leihen; *(Person)* einstellen
his [hɪz] sein, seine(r, s)
Hispanic [hɪ'spænɪk] *Nachkomme der Einwanderer aus Lateinamerika*
historian [hɪ'stɔːrɪən] Historiker/in; **historical** [hɪ'stɒrɪkl] historisch, alt; **history** ['hɪstrɪ] Geschichte
hit [hɪt] schlagen, treffen
hobby ['hɒbɪ] Hobby
hockey ['hɒkɪ] Hockey
hold [həʊld] **1.** halten; **2.** veranstalten, abhalten; **hold out one's hand to sb** jm die Hand entgegenstrecken; **hold tight** [taɪt] festhalten; **hold up** aufhalten; **hold the line** am Apparat bleiben
hole [həʊl] Loch
holiday(s) ['hɒlɪdeɪ] **1.** Feiertag, freier Tag; **2.** (BE) Ferien, Urlaub; **go/be on holiday** (BE) in Urlaub fahren/sein, Ferien machen/haben
holy ['həʊlɪ] heilig
home [həʊm] **1.** Heim, Zuhause; **2.** Heimat-; **at home** zu Hause, daheim; **go home** nach Hause gehen; **homeless** obdachlos; **home-made** hausgemacht; **Home Office** (BE) (brit.) Innenministerium; **home-schooling** Unterricht zu Hause; **Home Secretary** (BE) (brit.) Innenminister/in; **homework** Hausaufgabe(n); **do one's homework** seine Hausaufgabe(n) machen
honest ['ɒnɪst] ehrlich
hooligan ['huːlɪgən] Rowdy, Schläger
hope [həʊp] **1.** Hoffnung; **2.** hoffen; **hopeful** hoffnungsvoll, voller Hoffnung; **hopeless** hoffungslos
horror ['hɒrə] Horror, Entsetzen
horse [hɔːs] Pferd; **horseman** Reiter
hospital ['hɒspɪtl] Krankenhaus, Klinik; **in/to hospital** (BE) im/ins Krankenhaus
host [həʊst] Gastgeber/in
hostel ['hɒstl]**: youth hostel** Jugendherberge
hot [hɒt] heiß, warm
hot dog [ˌhɒt 'dɒg] Hot Dog
hotel [həʊ'tel] Hotel
hour ['aʊə] Stunde; **for an hour** eine Stunde lang
house [haʊs] Haus; **at Dave's/my house** bei Dave/mir zu Hause; **housing** **1.** Wohnungen; **2.** Wohnungs-; **household** ['haʊshəʊld] Haushalt; **housework** Haus(halts)arbeit; **do the housework** die Haus(halts)arbeit machen
hovercraft ['hɒvəkrɑːft] Luftkissenfahrzeug(e)
how [haʊ] wie; **How are you?** Wie geht es dir? **How many?** Wie viele? **How much?** Wie viel? **How much is …?** Was kostet …? **How old are you?** Wie alt bist du? **this is how you do it** so, auf diese Weise macht man es;
however [haʊ'evə] **1.** jedoch, aber; **2.** wie (auch) immer
huge [hjuːdʒ] sehr groß, riesig
human ['hjuːmən] menschlich; **human being** [ˌhjuːmən 'biːɪŋ] Mensch
humiliation [hjuːˌmɪlɪ'eɪʃn] Demütigung
humor (AE)**/humour** (BE) ['hjuːmə] Humor; **humorous** ['hjuːmərəs] humorvoll, lustig
hunger ['hʌŋgə] Hunger; **hungry** ['hʌŋgrɪ] hungrig; **be hungry** Hunger haben; **be hungry for sth** nach etwas hungern
hunt [hʌnt] jagen; **hunting grounds** Jagdgründe
hurrah! [hʊ'rɑː] hurra!
hurry ['hʌrɪ] eilen; **be in a hurry** in Eile sein, es eilig haben; **hurry up** sich beeilen
hurt [hɜːt] wehtun, verletzen
husband ['hʌzbənd] (Ehe-)Mann
hut [hʌt] Hütte
hyphen ['haɪfn] Bindestrich

I

I [aɪ] ich
ice [aɪs] Eis; **ice-cream** [ˌaɪs'kriːm] (Speise-)Eis; **ice-cream parlor** ['pɑːlə] (AE) Eisdiele; **ice-skating** ['aɪsˌskeɪtɪŋ] Schlittschuhlaufen; **icy** eisig
idea [aɪ'dɪə] **1.** Idee, Einfall; **2.** Begriff, Vorstellung; Meinung; **no idea** keine Ahnung
ideal [aɪ'dɪəl] ideal
identify [aɪ'dentɪfaɪ] identifizieren, erkennen
idiomatic [ˌɪdɪə'mætɪk] idiomatisch
if [ɪf] **1.** wenn, falls; **2.** ob; **if I were you** (ich) an deiner Stelle; **if so** wenn ja
ignore [ɪg'nɔː] ignorieren; **ignorance** ['ɪgnərəns] Ignoranz, Unwissenheit, Unkenntnis; **ignorant** ['ɪgnərənt] unwissend, ungebildet, ignorant
ill [ɪl] krank; **illness** ['ɪlnəs] Krankheit
illegal [ɪ'liːgl] illegal
illiterate [ɪ'lɪtrət] des Lesens und Schreibens unkundig; Analphabeten-; primitiv
illustrate ['ɪləstreɪt] illustrieren, veranschaulichen; **illustration** [ˌɪlə'streɪʃn] Illustration, Bild, Abbildung
image ['ɪmɪdʒ] sprachliches Bild, bildlicher Ausdruck; **imagery** ['ɪmɪdʒərɪ] Bildersprache, Metaphorik
imagine [ɪ'mædʒɪn] sich vorstellen; sich einbilden; **Just imagine.** Denk dir nur! Stell dir mal vor!
immediate [ɪ'miːdɪət] nächste(r, s); engste(r, s); unmittelbar
immigrant ['ɪmɪgrənt] Einwanderer/-in **immigration** [ˌɪmɪ'greɪʃn] Einwanderung, Immigration
impatience [ɪm'peɪʃəns] Ungeduld; **impatient** [ɪm'peɪʃənt] ungeduldig
impersonal [ɪm'pɜːsənl] unpersönlich
impolite [ˌɪmpə'laɪt] unhöflich; **impoliteness** [ˌɪmpə'laɪtnəs] Unhöflichkeit
import 1. ['ɪmpɔːt] Einfuhr, Import; **2.** [ɪm'pɔːt] einführen, importieren
importance [ɪm'pɔːtəns] Wichtigkeit; **important** wichtig, bedeutend
impossible [ɪm'pɒsəbl] unmöglich
impractical [ɪm'præktɪkl] unpraktisch

impression [ɪm'preʃn] Eindruck
improve [ɪm'pru:v] (sich) (ver)bessern; besser machen/werden
in [ɪn] in; hinein; **go in** hineingehen; **in addition** [ə'dɪʃn] zusätzlich, außerdem; **in a hurry** in Eile; **in a minute** gleich, sofort; **in bed** im Bett; **in case** falls; für den Fall, dass; **in detail** im Detail; **in English** auf Englisch; **in front of** vor; **in future** künftig, ab jetzt; **in hiding** versteckt, untergetaucht; **in hospital** (BE) im Krankenhaus; **in January** im Januar; **in memory of** in Erinnerung an; **in my opinion** meiner Meinung nach; **in 1980** (im Jahre) 1980; **in ruins** zerstört; **in school** (*meist* AE) in der Schule; **in spite of** trotz; **in the back** hinten (im Auto); **in the country** auf dem Land; **in the field(s)** auf dem Feld; **in the morning(s)** am Morgen, morgens; **in the picture/photo** auf dem Bild/Foto; **in (the) spring** im Frühling/Frühjahr; **in the street** auf der Straße; **in those days** damals; **in town** in der (Innen-)Stadt; **interested in** interessiert an; **one in ten** eins von zehn
incident ['ɪnsɪdənt] Zwischenfall; Vorfall, Vorkommnis
include [ɪn'klu:d] (mit) einschließen, enthalten, beinhalten; **including** [ɪn'klu:dɪŋ] einschließlich
income ['ɪnkʌm] Einkommen
incorrect [,ɪnkə'rekt] inkorrekt, unrichtig
increase **1.** [ɪn'kri:s] ansteigen, zunehmen; erhöhen; **2.** ['ɪŋkri:s] Anstieg, Zunahme; Erhöhung
independence (from) [,ɪndɪ'pendəns] Unabhängigkeit (von); **independent (of)** [,ɪndɪ'pendənt] unabhängig (von)
India ['ɪndɪə] Indien; **Indian** ['ɪndɪən] **1.** Indianer/in; indianisch; **2.** Inder/in; indisch
indirect [,ɪndɪ'rekt] indirekt
individual [,ɪndɪ'vɪdʒʊəl] **1.** Einzelperson, Individium; **2.** individuell, Einzel-; einzeln; **individuality** [,ɪndɪ,vɪdʒʊ'ælətɪ] Individualität
indoors [,ɪn'dɔ:z] (nach) drinnen, im Haus
industrial [ɪn'dʌstrɪəl] Industrie-; industriell; **industrialist** [ɪn'dʌstrɪəlɪst] Industrielle(r); **industrialization** [ɪn,dʌstrɪəlaɪ'zeɪʃn] Industrialisierung **industry** ['ɪndəstrɪ] Industrie(zweig)
inedible [ɪn'edɪbl] nicht essbar, ungenießbar
inequality [,ɪnə'kwɒlətɪ] Ungleichheit
infer (from) [ɪn'fɜ:] (fml) (er)schließen, folgern, ableiten (aus)
infertile ['ɪn'fɜ:taɪl] unfruchtbar
influence ['ɪnflʊəns] **1.** Einfluss; **2.** beeinflussen
inform [ɪn'fɔ:m] informieren, benachrichtigen; **information** [,ɪnfə'meɪʃn] Information(en), Auskunft; **Information Centre** Auskunft, Verkehrsbüro; **information desk** Auskunftsschalter, Informationsschalter
informal [ɪn'fɔ:ml] informell, nicht förmlich
inhabitant [ɪn'hæbɪtənt] Einwohner/in
inhuman [ɪn'hju:mən] unmenschlich
initiate [ɪ'nɪʃɪeɪt] initiieren, einleiten
injured ['ɪndʒəd] verletzt
injustice [ɪn'dʒʌstɪs] Ungerechtigkeit
inner city [,ɪnə'sɪtɪ] problematisches Wohngebiet im Stadtkern
innocent ['ɪnəsənt] unschuldig
innovation [,ɪnə'veɪʃn] Innovation, Neuerung
inquiry [ɪn'kwaɪərɪ] Untersuchung
insect ['ɪnsekt] Insekt
inside [ɪn'saɪd] **1.** innen/drinnen; nach drinnen; **2.** *(prep)* innerhalb (von)
install [ɪn'stɔ:l] installieren
instead [ɪn'sted] stattdessen, dafür; **instead of** (an)statt, anstelle von
instinct ['ɪnstɪŋkt] Instinkt; Gefühl, Ahnung
institution [,ɪnstɪ'tju:ʃn] Institut(ion), (öffentliche) Einrichtung
instruction [ɪn'strʌkʃn] Anleitung; Anweisung, Vorschrift; Unterricht; **instructor** [ɪn'strʌktə] Betreuer/in, Lehrer/in
instrument ['ɪnstrəmənt] Instrument
insult ['ɪnsʌlt] Beleidigung
insurance [ɪn'ʃʊərəns] **1.** Versicherung; **2.** Versicherungs-
integrate ['ɪntɪgreɪt] integrieren
intelligent [ɪn'telɪdʒənt] klug, intelligent
intend [ɪn'tend] beabsichtigen, vorhaben; **be intended to** sollen; **intention** [ɪn'tenʃn] Intention, Absicht
intensive care [ɪn,tensɪv 'keə] Intensivstation
interactive [,ɪntər'æktɪv] interaktiv
intercultural [,ɪntə'kʌltʃərəl] interkulturell
interest ['ɪntrɪst] **1.** interessieren; **interested (in)** ['ɪntrɪstɪd] interessiert (an); **interesting** interessant; **2. interest (in)** Interesse (an)
interfere (with) [,ɪntə'fɪə] eingreifen (in), sich einmischen (in)
international [,ɪntə'næʃnl] international
interpret [ɪn'tɜ:prɪt] dolmetschen
interrupt [,ɪntə'rʌpt] unterbrechen
intersection ['ɪntə,sekʃn] (AE) (Straßen-) Kreuzung
Interstate ['ɪntəsteɪt] (AE) (staatenübergreifende Bundes-)Autobahn
interview ['ɪntəvju:] **1.** Interview; **2.** befragen, interviewen; **interviewer** ['ɪntəvju:ə] Interviewer/in
into ['ɪntʊ, 'ɪntə] in ... (hinein)
intolerance [,ɪn'tɒlərəns] Intoleranz; **intolerant** intolerant
introduce (to) [,ɪntrə'dju:s] **1.** vorstellen, bekannt machen (mit); **2.** einführen; **introduction** [,ɪntrə'dʌkʃn] Einführung
invade [ɪn'veɪd] einmarschieren, einfallen in; **invader** Invasor/in, Eindringling
invent [ɪn'vent] erfinden; **invention** [ɪn'venʃn] Erfindung; **inventor** [ɪn'ventə] Erfinder/in
invitation [,ɪnvɪ'teɪʃn] Einladung; **invite** [ɪn'vaɪt] einladen
involuntary [ɪn'vɒləntrɪ] unbeabsichtigt
involved [ɪn'vɒlvd]: **be involved (in)** etwas zu tun haben (mit), beteiligt sein (an); **become/get involved** verwickelt, hineingezogen werden; sich engagieren, beteiligen
Ireland ['aɪələnd] Irland; **Northern Ireland** Nordirland; **Irish 1.** Ire(n), Irin(nen); **2.** irisch
iron ['aɪən] Eisen; Bügeleisen
irregular [ɪ'regjʊlə] unregelmäßig
irresponsible [,ɪrɪ'spɒnsəbl] unverantwortlich
is [ɪz] ist
island ['aɪlənd] Insel; **isle** [aɪl]**: the British Isles** die Britischen Inseln
issue ['ɪʃu:] Sachverhalt, Angelegenheit; (Streit-)Frage
it [ɪt] es (er, sie; ihn, sie)
Italian [ɪ'tæljən] **1.** italienisch; **2.** Italienisch; **3.** Italiener/in; **Italy** ['ɪtəlɪ] Italien
item ['aɪtəm] (Programm-)Punkt; (Presse-)Notiz, Meldung; **vocabulary item** Vokabel
its [ɪts] sein, seine; ihr, ihre; **itself** [ɪt'self] sich (selbst)

J

jacket ['dʒækɪt] Jacke, Jackett
jam [dʒæm] Marmelade
January ['dʒænjʊərɪ] Januar
Japanese [,dʒæpə'ni:z] **1.** japanisch; **2.** Japanisch; **3.** Japaner/in
jazz [dʒæz] Jazz
jealous ['dʒeləs] eifersüchtig
jeans *(pl)* [dʒi:nz] Jeans
Jesus ['dʒi:zəs] Jesus
Jew [dʒu:] Jude, Jüdin; **Jewish** ['dʒu:ɪʃ] jüdisch
jewel(s) ['dʒu:əl(z)] Juwel(en)
jigsaw ['dʒɪgsɔ:] Puzzle
job [dʒɒb] Beruf, Arbeit, Job; Aufgabe
jog [dʒɒg] joggen
join [dʒɔɪn] sich anschließen; mitmachen; eintreten *(in einen Klub usw.)*
joke [dʒəʊk] Scherz, Spaß; Witz
journey ['dʒɜ:nɪ] Reise, Fahrt

joy [dʒɔɪ] Freude
judge [dʒʌdʒ] Richter/in
judo ['dʒu:dəʊ] Judo
juice [dʒu:s] Saft; **juicy** saftig
July [dʒu:'laɪ] Juli
jump [dʒʌmp] springen; **jump at** anspringen
June [dʒu:n] Juni
jungle ['dʒʌŋgl] Dschungel
junior ['dʒu:nɪə] Junioren-, Jugend-
just [dʒʌst] **1.** nur, bloß (mal); **2.** gerade (eben); **3.** einfach; **just (before)** gleich (vor); **just (like, as)** genau (wie)
justice ['dʒʌstɪs] Gerechtigkeit
justify ['dʒʌstɪfaɪ] rechtfertigen
Jutes [dʒu:ts] Jüten

K

kangaroo [ˌkæŋgə'ru:] Känguru
karate [kə'rɑ:tɪ] Karate
keep [ki:p] behalten; aufbewahren; halten; *(Gesetz, Vorschrift)* einhalten, befolgen; **keep a diary** (ein) Tagebuch führen; **keep alive** am Leben erhalten; **keep a promise** ein Versprechen halten **keep cattle** (sich) Rinder halten; **keep an eye on sb/sth** ein (wachsames) Auge auf jn/etwas haben; **keep ... ing** etwas weiter tun, weiter-; **keep (out)** (draußen) halten; **keep to** sich halten an; **keep up (with)** (sich) auf dem neuesten Stand/auf dem Laufenden halten (über); **keeper** Wärter/in, Wächter/in
key [ki:] Schlüssel
kick [kɪk] treten, mit dem Fuß stoßen
kid [kɪd] (infml) Kind; Jugendliche(r)
kill [kɪl] töten, umbringen
kilo ['ki:ləʊ] Kilo
kilometre ['kɪləˌmi:tə] Kilometer
kilt [kɪlt] Schottenrock
kind (of) [kaɪnd] Art; **kind (of you)** nett, freundlich (von dir)
kindergarten ['kɪndəgɑ:tn] Kindergarten
king [kɪŋ] König; **kingdom** ['kɪŋdəm] Königreich
kit [kɪt]: **repair kit** Flickzeug
kitchen ['kɪtʃɪn] Küche
knee [ni:] Knie
knife, ***pl*** **knives** [naɪf, naɪvz] Messer
knight [naɪt] Ritter
knock [nɒk] **1.** (an)klopfen; **2.** schlagen, stoßen
know [nəʊ] **1.** kennen; **2.** wissen; **you know** weißt du, nämlich; **known** bekannt; **be known to** bekanntlich (tun); **well-known** (wohl) bekannt
knowledge ['nɒlɪdʒ] Wissen; Kenntnis(se)
koala (bear) [kəʊ'ɑ:lə] Koala(bär)

L

Labour (Party) ['leɪbə] Labour-Partei (in GB)
lack (of) [læk] Mangel (an), Fehlen (von)
ladder ['lædə] Leiter
lady ['leɪdɪ] Lady, Dame
lake [leɪk] (ein) See
lamp [læmp] Lampe; **lamp-post** ['——] Laternenpfahl
land [lænd] **1.** (festes) Land, Boden; **landowner** ['lændˌəʊnə] Grundbesitzer; **landscape** ['lænskeɪp] Landschaft, Landschaftsbild **2.** landen *(Flugzeug)*; **3.** anlegen *(Schiff)*
lane [leɪn] (Fahr-)Spur
language ['læŋgwɪdʒ] Sprache; **foreign language** Fremdsprache; **official language** Amtssprache
large [lɑ:dʒ] groß, umfangreich; **largely** ['lɑ:dʒlɪ] weitgehend
last [lɑ:st] **1.** letzte(r, s); **last but not least** nicht zuletzt, nicht zu vergessen; **last night** gestern Abend; letzte Nacht; **last Saturday** (am) letzten Samstag; **at last** endlich, schließlich; **be last** der Letzte sein, als Letzter (an)kommen; **2.** (an-, fort)dauern; **3.** ausreichen
late [leɪt] spät; **be late** zu spät kommen; **latest** ['leɪtɪst] neueste(r, s)
Latin ['lætɪn] Latein, lateinisch
laugh [lɑ:f] lachen; **laugh at** lachen über; auslachen; **laughter** ['lɑ:ftə] Lachen, Gelächter
launching pad ['lɔ:ntʃɪŋ pæd] Abschussrampe
law [lɔ:] Gesetz, Recht; **law court** [kɔ:t] Gericht; **lawyer** ['lɔ:jə] Rechtsanwalt-/ -anwältin; Jurist/in
lay [leɪ] legen
layer ['leɪə] Schicht
laziness ['leɪzɪnəs] Faulheit; **lazy** faul, träge
lead [li:d] führen, leiten; **leader** ['li:də] (An-)Führer/in
leaf, ***pl*** **leaves** [li:f, li:vz] Blatt *(einer Pflanze)*
learn [lɜ:n] lernen; herausfinden, erfahren; **learner** ['lɜ:nə] Lernende(r), Anfänger/in
least [li:st] (der/die/das) wenigste, am wenigsten; **at least** mindestens; wenigstens, zumindest
leather ['leðə] Leder
leave [li:v] **1.** (ver-, zurück)lassen; **2.** stehen/liegen lassen; **3.** weggehen, abfahren; **leave alone** in Ruhe lassen; **leave out** auslassen; **leave school** von der Schule abgehen; **leave sth to sb** etwas jm überlassen
left [left] **1.** linke(r, s), nach links; **on the left** links, auf der linken Seite; **2. be left** übrig sein
leg [leg] Bein
legacy ['legəsɪ] Vermächtnis, Erbe
legal ['li:gl] legal; Rechts-, juristisch; **legalize** ['li:gəlaɪz] legalisieren
legend ['ledʒənd] Legende, Sage
lemonade [ˌlemə'neɪd] Limonade
lend [lend] (ver)leihen
length [leŋθ] Länge
less [les] weniger
lesson ['lesn] Unterrichtsstunde
let [let] (zu)lassen; **Let me see.** Warte mal! Lass mich mal überlegen! **let's = let us** lass(t) uns; **let sb off sth** (infml) jn von etwas befreien, jm etwas erlassen; **Let's see.** Wollen mal sehen.
letter ['letə] **1.** Brief; **2.** Buchstabe; **letter box** ['letə bɒks] *(meist* BE) Briefkasten
lettuce ['letɪs] Salat, Kopfsalat
level ['levl] Ebene; Höhe; Niveau
liberal ['lɪbrəl] **1.** Liberale(r); **2.** liberal; vorurteilslos
liberty ['lɪbətɪ] Freiheit
library ['laɪbrərɪ] Bibliothek, Bücherei
lid [lɪd] Deckel
lie [laɪ] **1.** Lüge; **2.** lügen; **3.** liegen; **lie down** sich hinlegen
lieutenant [BE: lef'tenənt; AE: lu:'tenənt] Leutnant
life, ***pl*** **lives** [laɪf, laɪvz] Leben; **lifeboat** ['laɪfbəʊt] Rettungsboot; **lifeline** ['laɪflaɪn] Rettungsleine
lift [lɪft] heben, hochheben
light [laɪt] **1.** Licht, Lampe; **traffic lights** *(pl)* ['træfɪk laɪts] (Verkehrs-)Ampel; **2.** leicht; hell; **3. light up** aufleuchten
like [laɪk] **1.** wie; **like this** so, auf diese Weise; folgendermaßen; **like that** so; **things like that** so etwas, solche Sachen; **What's it like?** Wie ist es? Wie sieht es aus?
2. mögen, gern haben/tun; **How do you like ...?** Wie gefällt dir ...? Wie findest du ...? **I'd like** ich möchte; **like better/best** lieber/am liebsten mögen
3. -like -ähnlich, -artig
4. likes and dislikes Vorlieben und Abneigungen
likely ['laɪklɪ] **be likely to do sth** etwas wahrscheinlich tun
limit ['lɪmɪt] **1.** (oberste) Grenze, Beschränkung; **2.** begrenzen, einschränken (auf)
line [laɪn] **1.** Zeile; Linie; **2.** *(meist* AE) Schlange *(wartender Menschen)*, Reihe

link [lɪŋk] sich verbinden; **be linked (by/with)** verbunden, verknüpft sein (durch/mit)
lion ['laɪən] Löwe
lip [lɪp] Lippe
list [lɪst] **1.** Liste; **2.** auflisten, aufführen, aufzählen
listen (to) ['lɪsn] zu-, anhören; **listener** Zuhörer/in; **listening comprehension** ['lɪsnɪŋ kɒmprɪˌhenʃn] Hörverstehen
literal ['lɪtrəl] wörtlich
literature ['lɪtrətʃə] Literatur
litre ['li:tə] Liter
litter ['lɪtə] Abfall, herumliegendes Papier
little ['lɪtl] **1.** klein, jung; **2.** wenig; **a little** ein wenig, ein bisschen
live [lɪv] wohnen, leben; **live on** leben von, sich ernähren von; **living-room** Wohnzimmer; **living thing** Lebewesen
live [laɪv] lebend, lebendig; live, direkt; **liveliness** Lebendigkeit; **lively** lebhaft
livestock *(sing)* ['laɪvstɒk] Vieh(bestand), Tiere
load [ləʊd] (auf)laden, (be)laden
loaf (of bread), *pl* **loaves** [ləʊf, ləʊvz] (Brot-)Laib, Brot
local ['ləʊkl] Orts-, Lokal-, örtlich
located [ləʊ'keɪtɪd]: **be located** sich befinden, liegen
lock [lɒk] ab-, zuschließen; **lock up** ein-/zusperren, ein-/zuschließen
locomotive [ˌləʊkə'məʊtɪv] Lokomotive
loneliness ['ləʊnlɪnəs] Einsamkeit; **lonely** einsam, verlassen
long [lɒŋ] lang; **long-distance** Langstrecken-, Fern-; **no longer** nicht mehr, nicht länger; **not long ago** vor kurzem
look [lʊk] **1.** sehen, schauen; **2.** aussehen; **look after** sich kümmern um, aufpassen auf; **look at** anschauen; **look for** suchen; **look forward to (doing) sth** sich auf etwas freuen; sich darauf freuen, etwas zu tun; **look up** *(ein Wort usw.)* nachschlagen; **3.** Blick
loose [lu:s] frei, lose
lord [lɔ:d] Herr, Adliger; Lord; **the House of Lords, the Lords** (GB) das britische Oberhaus
lorry ['lɒrɪ] (BE) Lastwagen
lose [lu:z] verlieren; **loser** ['lu:zə] Verlierer/in; **loss** [lɒs] Verlust
lost [lɒst]: **be lost** sich verlaufen haben; **get lost** sich verlaufen
lots [lɒts]**/a lot (of)** viele, viel, eine Menge
loud [laʊd] laut
lounge: arrivals lounge [ə'raɪvlz laʊndʒ] Ankunftshalle
love [lʌv] **1.** Liebe; **fall in love (with)** sich verlieben (in); **in love** verliebt; **Love** Viele liebe Grüße von; **2.** lieben, sehr mögen, sehr gern haben/tun; **I'd love** ich hätte (liebend) gern; **I'd love to** ich würde sehr gern; **lovely** schön, herrlich, hübsch
low [ləʊ] niedrig, tief
luckily ['lʌkɪlɪ] glücklicherweise; **be lucky** Glück haben; **lucky day** Glückstag
lunch [lʌntʃ] Mittagessen; **lunch bag** Tüte mit dem eingepackten Mittagessen; **at lunch time** zur Mittagszeit, mittags; **for lunch** zum Mittagessen; **have lunch** (zu) Mittag essen; **What's for lunch?** Was gibt's zum Mittagessen?

M

machine [mə'ʃi:n] Maschine; **machinery** *(sing.)* [mə'ʃi:nərɪ] Maschinerie, Maschinen
mad (at) [mæd] (*meist* AE, infml) böse, sauer, wütend (auf)
madam ['mædəm]**: Dear Madam** Sehr geehrte Dame; **Dear Sir or Madam,** Sehr geehrte Damen und Herren,
made of (paper) ['meɪd‿əv] aus (Papier)
magazine [ˌmægə'zi:n] Zeitschrift, Illustrierte
magic ['mædʒɪk] Zauberkunst, Magie; **do magic** zaubern; **magician** [mə'dʒɪʃn] Zauberer, Zauberin
mail [meɪl] (*meist* AE) Post(sendungen); **airmail** Luftpost
main [meɪn] Haupt-, wichtigste(r/s); **mainly** hauptsächlich
maintain [meɪn'teɪn] **1.** aufrechterhalten; **2.** (finanziell) unterstützen
majesty ['mædʒəstɪ] Majestät
major ['meɪdʒə] gewichtig, bedeutsam
majority [mə'dʒɒrətɪ] Mehrheit
make [meɪk] machen, bauen; **make a choice** eine Wahl treffen; **make a fool of sb** jn lächerlich machen; **make a phone call** ein Telefongespräch führen; **make a speech** eine Rede halten; **make it** (infml) es schaffen, Erfolg haben, es zu etwas bringen; **make sb do sth** jn veranlassen/zwingen etwas zu tun; jn etwas tun lassen; **make sb sth** jn zu etwas machen; **make sure** sich vergewissern; darauf achten, dafür sorgen (, dass); **make tea** Tee kochen; **make up** sich ausdenken; erfinden; ausmachen, bilden
male [meɪl] **1.** männlich; **2.** männliche Person; Männchen
man, *pl* **men** [mæn, men] Mann, Männer; **man-made** künstlich
manage ['mænɪdʒ] verwalten, leiten; **manager 1.** Geschäftsführer/in, Filialleiter/in; **2.** Führungskraft
manufacture [ˌmænjʊ'fæktʃə] herstellen, fertigen; **manufacturer** Hersteller; **manufacturing** Fertigung, Herstellung (von Waren)
many ['menɪ] viele
map [mæp] Landkarte, Stadtplan
marathon ['mærəθən] Marathon
march [mɑ:tʃ] **1.** marschieren; **2.** Marsch
March [mɑ:tʃ] März
mark [mɑ:k] **1.** (BE) Note, Zensur; **2.** kennzeichnen, bezeichnen
market ['mɑ:kɪt] Markt
marriage ['mærɪdʒ] Heirat; Ehe; **marry** ['mærɪ] heiraten; **get married** (sich ver)heiraten
marshal (AE) ['mɑ:ʃl] *Gesetzeshüter/in einer US-Bundesbehörde;* Polizeichef/in
mass [mæs] **1.** Masse, Menge; **2.** Massen-
Mass [mæs] (kath.) Gottesdienst, Messe
master ['mɑ:stə] meistern
match [mætʃ] **1.** Spiel, Wettkampf; **2.** passend zusammenfügen; zusammenpassen
match [mætʃ] Streichholz
material [mə'tɪərɪəl] **1.** Material, Stoff; **2.** materiell
math (AE)**/maths** (BE) [mæθ, mæθs] Mathe(matik); **mathematics** [ˌmæθə'mætɪks] Mathematik
matter ['mætə] **1.** eine Rolle spielen, von Bedeutung sein, darauf ankommen; **2. no matter (how/what/...)** egal, (wie/was/...)
may [meɪ] darf, kann; (kann) vielleicht
May [meɪ] Mai
maybe ['meɪbi:] vielleicht
mayor [meə] Bürgermeister/in
me [mi:] mir, mich; **(It wasn't) me.** Ich (wars nicht). **older than me** älter als ich
meal [mi:l] Mahlzeit, Essen
mean [mi:n] **1.** bedeuten; **meaning** Bedeutung; **2.** meinen; **mean by** verstehen unter, meinen mit; **mean to do sth** etwas absichtlich tun, etwas tun wollen; **be meant to** sollen; **I mean it.** Ich meine es ernst.
meat [mi:t] Fleisch
mechanic [mɪ'kænɪk] Mechaniker/in; **mechanization** [ˌmekənaɪ'zeɪʃn] Mechanisierung; **mechanize** ['mekənaɪz] mechanisieren
media ['mi:dɪə] Medien
medical ['medɪkl] medizinisch, Medizin-; ärztlich; **medical care** medizinische Betreuung/Versorgung; **medicine** ['medsn] Medizin, Arznei
medieval [ˌmedɪ'i:vl] mittelalterlich

meet [mi:t] **1.** (sich) treffen, kennen lernen; **2.** abholen; **meeting** ['mi:tɪŋ] Treffen, Versammlung; Veranstaltung
member (of) ['membə] Mitglied (in, von); **membership card** Mitgliedsausweis
memorial [mɪ'mɔ:rɪəl] Denkmal, Gedenkstätte: **memory** ['memərɪ] Gedächtnis; **in memory of** in Erinnerung an
mention ['menʃn] erwähnen
menu ['menju:] Speisekarte
merchant ['mɜ:tʃənt] Kaufmann
merry ['merɪ] froh, fröhlich
message ['mesɪdʒ] Nachricht, Botschaft; **(bike) messenger** ['mesɪndʒə] (Fahrrad-) Bote/-in
metal ['metl] Metall
metaphor ['metəfɔ:] Metapher, bildhafter Vergleich
method ['meθəd] Methode, Verfahren
metre ['mi:tə] Meter
metropolitan area [ˌmetrə'pɒlɪtən] städtischer Großraum, Ballungsraum
Mexican ['meksɪkən] **1.** Mexikaner/in; **2.** mexikanisch
micro-electronics [ˌmaɪkrəʊ‿ɪlek'trɒnɪks] Mikroelektronik
mid- [mɪd] mittlere(r/s), Mittel-
middle ['mɪdl] Mitte; **middle-aged** [ˌmɪdl‿'eɪdʒd] mittleren Alters; **Middle Ages** [ˌmɪdl‿'eɪdʒɪz] Mittelalter; **middle class** **1.** Mittelklasse; **2.** Mittelklasse-; **the Middle East** [ˌmɪdl 'i:st] der Mittlere Osten
the Midlands ['mɪdlənz] (GB) Mittelengland
midnight ['mɪdnaɪt] Mitternacht
the Midwest [ˌmɪd'west] (USA) der Mittlere Westen
might [maɪt] könnte(n) vielleicht
mighty ['maɪtɪ] mächtig
mild [maɪld] mild
mile [maɪl] Meile; **miles per hour = mph** [ˌmaɪlz pər‿'aʊə] Meilen pro Stunde
militant ['mɪlɪtənt] militant
military ['mɪlɪtrɪ] militärisch; Militär-
milk [mɪlk] **1.** Milch; **2.** melken
million ['mɪljən] Million
mind [maɪnd] **1.** Meinung; **change one's mind** seine Meinung ändern, sich anders besinnen; **make up one's mind** sich entschließen, sich entscheiden; **2.** etwas (einzuwenden) haben gegen; **Never mind.** Das macht doch nichts.
mine [maɪn] meine(r, s)
mine [maɪn] Bergwerk; **miner** Bergarbeiter, Bergmann
minerals ['mɪnərəlz] Mineralien, Bodenschätze
mini- ['mɪnɪ] Mini-
minimum ['mɪnɪməm] **1.** Minimum; **2.** Minimal-
minister ['mɪnɪstə] **1.** Minister/in; **Minister of Commerce** ['kɒməs] Wirtschaftsminister/in; **Minister of Defence** Verteidigungsminister/in; **Minister of Finance** ['faɪnæns] Finanzminister/in; **Minister of the Interior** [ɪn'tɪərɪə] Innenminister/in; **ministry** Ministerium; **2.** Geistliche(r), Pfarrer/in
minority [maɪ'nɒrətɪ] Minderheit
minus ['maɪnəs] minus
minute ['mɪnɪt] Minute; **in a minute** gleich, sofort; **Wait a minute.** Einen Augenblick! Moment mal!
mirror ['mɪrə] Spiegel
misbehave [ˌmɪsbɪ'heɪv] sich schlecht benehmen
miserable ['mɪzrəbl] unglücklich, traurig; elend
misinform [ˌmɪsɪn'fɔ:m] falsch informieren
mislead [ˌmɪs'li:d] irreführen
misplace [ˌmɪs'pleɪs] verlegen, falsch einordnen
Miss [mɪs] Fräulein/Frau; **miss** *häufige Anrede für eine Lehrerin in Großbritannien*
miss [mɪs] verpassen, verfehlen; vermissen; **missing** fehlend; **be missing** fehlen
misspell [mɪ'spel] falsch schreiben
mistake [mɪ'steɪk] Fehler, Irrtum
mistreat [ˌmɪs'tri:t] misshandeln, schlecht behandeln
misunderstand [ˌmɪsʌndə'stænd] missverstehen, nicht verstehen; **misunderstanding** Missverständnis
misuse [ˌmɪs'ju:z] missbrauchen, zweckentfremden
mix [mɪks]: **mix sth up** etwas verwechseln, durcheinander bringen; **mixed** ge-, vermischt; **mixed-ability** gemischt, nicht leistungsdifferenziert; **mixed bag** bunte Mischung; **mixture** ['mɪkstʃə] Mischung
moccassin ['mɒkəsɪn] Mokassin
model ['mɒdl] Modell, Modell-
moderate ['mɒdrət] gemäßigt, mäßig; mittlere(r, s)
modern ['mɒdn] modern; **modernize** ['mɒdənaɪz] modernisieren
mom [mɒm] (AE) Mutti, Mama, Mami
moment ['məʊmənt] Moment, Augenblick; **at the moment** im Moment, im Augenblick; zurzeit
monarch ['mɒnək] Monarch/in; **monarchy** ['mɒnəkɪ] Monarchie
monastery ['mɒnəstrɪ] Kloster
Monday ['mʌndɪ] Montag; **on Monday(s)** montags, am Montag
money ['mʌnɪ] Geld; **make money** Geld verdienen
monitor ['mɒnɪtə] überwachen
monkey ['mʌŋkɪ] Affe
monolingual [ˌmɒnə'lɪŋgwəl] einsprachig
monster ['mɒnstə] Ungeheuer
month [mʌnθ] Monat
monument ['mɒnjʊmənt] Denkmal
mood [mu:d] Stimmung, Laune
moon [mu:n] Mond
moped ['məʊped] Moped
moral ['mɒrəl] Moral, Lehre
more [mɔ:] mehr; **more and more** immer (mehr); **more exciting** aufregender; **no more** kein(e) mehr; **some more** noch einige/etwas
morning ['mɔ:nɪŋ] Morgen, Vormittag; **Good morning.** Guten Morgen!/Tag! **in the morning(s)** am Morgen, morgens; **on Monday morning(s)** am Montagmorgen; **this morning** heute Morgen; **tomorrow morning** morgen früh
most [məʊst] **1.** (der/die/das) meiste; **2.** am meisten; **3.** höchst; **most of all** am allermeisten; **(the) most exciting** (der/die/das) aufregendste; am aufregendsten; **mostly** meistens, hauptsächlich
moth [mɒθ] Motte, Nachtfalter
mother ['mʌðə] Mutter
motive ['məʊtɪv] Motiv, Beweggrund; **motivate** ['məʊtɪveɪt] motivieren
motorbike ['məʊtəbaɪk] BE: Motorrad, AE: Moped, Mofa; **motorcycle** ['məʊtəsaɪkl] AE: Motorrad; **motorhome** (AE) Wohnmobil, Campingbus; **motorway** (BE) Autobahn
mountain(s) ['maʊntən] Berg; Gebirge
mouse, ***pl*** **mice** [maʊs, maɪs] Maus
mouth [maʊθ] Mund
move [mu:v] **1.** (um)ziehen; **2.** (sich) bewegen; **Keep moving.** Mach(t) immer weiter! **moving** bewegend; **3.** Bewegung; Umzug; (Schach-)Zug, Schritt; **movement** Bewegung; **on the move** unterwegs, in Bewegung
movie ['mu:vɪ] (*meist* AE) Film; **go to the movies** (AE) ins Kino gehen; **movie theater** (AE) Kino(gebäude)
MP = Member of Parliament Mitglied des brit. Unterhauses
mph = miles per hour [ˌmaɪlz pər‿'aʊə] Meilen pro Stunde
Mr ['mɪstə] Herr; **Mrs** ['mɪsɪz] Frau; **Ms** [mɪz] Frau *(familienstandneutrale Anrede)*
much [mʌtʃ] viel; **(like) very much** sehr (gern mögen); **Thank you very much.** Vielen Dank.
mud [mʌd] Schlamm, Matsch
multinational [ˌmʌltɪ'næʃənl] multinational
mum [mʌm], **mummy** (BE) Mutti, Mama, Mami
Munich ['mju:nɪk] München
murder ['mɜ:də] Mord; **murderer** ['mɜ:dərə] Mörder/in

museum [mju:'zɪəm] Museum; **Museum of Natural History** Naturkundemuseum

music ['mju:zɪk] Musik; **musical** ['mju:zɪkl] Musical; **musician** [mju:'zɪʃn] Musiker/in

Muslim ['mʊzlɪm, 'mʌzlɪm] Moslem; moslemisch

must [mʌst, məst] muss; **mustn't** ['mʌsnt] darf nicht

my [maɪ] mein, meine; **myself** [maɪ'self] mir/mich (selbst)

mystery person ['mɪstərɪ ˌpɜ:sn] Rätselfigur

myth [mɪθ] Mythos, Märchen

N

nail [neɪl] Nagel

naive [naɪ'i:v] naiv

name [neɪm] **1.** Name; **2.** (be-, er-) nennen, taufen; **What's your name?** Wie ist dein Name? Wie heißt du?

narrow ['nærəʊ] eng, schmal

nasty ['nɑ:stɪ] gehässig, gemein; unangenehm, schlimm

nation ['neɪʃn] Nation, Volk; Stamm; **national** ['næʃnəl] national, National-; **nationalist** ['næʃnəlɪst] Nationalist/in; **nationality** [ˌnæʃə'nælətɪ] Staatsangehörigkeit, Nationalität; **nationalize** ['næʃnəlaɪz] verstaatlichen

native ['neɪtɪv] **1.** Eingeborene(r), Einheimische(r); **2.** einheimisch, gebürtig, Heimat*(land)*, Mutter*(sprache)*; **Native American** Indianer/in, amerikanische(r) Ureinwohner/in

natural ['nætʃrəl] natürlich, Natur-; **natural history** [ˌnætʃrəl 'hɪstrɪ] Naturkunde; **nature** ['neɪtʃə] Natur; Beschaffenheit

navy ['neɪvɪ] Marine

near [nɪə] in der Nähe von, nahe; **nearly** ['nɪəlɪ] fast, beinahe

necessary ['nesəsərɪ] notwendig, nötig; **necessarily** notwendigerweise; **necessity** [nɪ'sesətɪ] Notwendigkeit

neck [nek] Hals

need [ni:d] **1.** Notwendigkeit, Bedürfnis; **2.** brauchen, benötigen; **needn't** ['ni:dnt] braucht nicht, muss nicht

negative ['negətɪv] negativ

negotiations [nɪˌgəʊʃɪ'eɪʃnz] Verhandlungen

Negro, *pl* **Negroes** ['ni:grəʊ] Neger/in

neighbour ['neɪbə] Nachbar/in; **neighbourhood** ['neɪbəhʊd] Nachbarschaft; (Wohn-)Gegend

neither ['naɪðə, 'ni:ðə]: **neither do/will/am/... I** ich auch nicht

nerves [nɜ:vz]: **get on sb's nerves** jm auf die Nerven gehen; **nervous** ['nɜ:vəs] ängstlich, aufgeregt, nervös; **nervousness** ['nɜ:vəsnəs] Nervosität

nest [nest] Nest

net [net] Netz

network ['netwɜ:k] Netz(werk); Vernetzung

never ['nevə] nie, niemals

new [nju:] neu; **news** [nju:z] Nachricht(en), Neuigkeit(en); **newspaper** Zeitung

New Zealand [ˌnju: 'zi:lənd] Neuseeland

next [nekst] nächste(r, s); **next Monday** (am) nächsten Morgen; **the next house** das Haus nebenan; **next to** direkt neben

nice [naɪs] nett, schön, hübsch; **nice of you** nett von Ihnen

nickel ['nɪkl] (AE) 5¢-Münze

nickname ['nɪkneɪm] Spitzname

night [naɪt] Nacht, (später) Abend; **at night** nachts, bei Nacht; **last night** gestern Abend; letzte Nacht; **on the first night** in der ersten Nacht

no [nəʊ] **1.** nein; **2.** kein, keine; **no longer** nicht mehr, nicht länger; **no matter (how/what/...)** egal (wie/was/...); **no more** kein(e, n) mehr; **nobody/no one** niemand

no. = number ['nʌmbə] Nr. = Nummer

Noah's ark [ˌnəʊəz‿'ɑ:k] die Arche Noah

nod [nɒd] **1.** Kopfnicken; **2.** nicken (mit)

noise [nɔɪz] Lärm, Geräusch; **noisy** ['nɔɪzɪ] laut, lärmend

non- [nɒn] nicht-; Nicht-; **non-fiction** [ˌnɒn'fɪkʃn] **1.** nicht-fiktional; **2.** Sachbücher, -texte; **non-returnable** [ˌnɒnrɪ'tɜ:nəbl] Einweg-, Wegwerf- *(-flasche, ...)*; **non-standard** [ˌnɒn'stændəd] *etwa:* nicht der Sprachnorm entsprechend; **non-violent** [ˌnɒn'vaɪələnt] gewaltfrei

none (of) [nʌn] keine(r, s) (von)

nor [nɔ:]: **nor do/will/am/... I** ich auch nicht

normal ['nɔ:ml] normal

Norman ['nɔ:mən] **1.** normannisch; **2.** Normanne

north (of) [nɔ:θ] **1.** nördlich (von); **2.** Nord-; (nach) Norden; **northern** ['nɔ:ðən] Nord-, nördlich; **northwest** **1.** nordwestlich; **2.** Nordwest-; **3.** (nach) Nordwesten

nose [nəʊz] Nase

not [nɒt] nicht; **not ... any** (gar) kein, keine; keins; **not ... anybody** niemand; **not ... anything** nichts; **not ... anywhere** nirgends, nirgendwohin; **not at all** überhaupt nicht, ganz und gar nicht; **not (...) either** auch nicht, auch kein; **not ever** nie; **not till** erst um, nicht vor; **not yet** noch nicht

notable ['nəʊtəbl] beachtenswert, wichtig

note [nəʊt] **1.** (BE) (Geld-)Schein; **2.** Notiz; **3.** (*meist* fml) beachten; bemerken, zur Kenntnis nehmen; **note down** notieren, aufschreiben

nothing ['nʌθɪŋ] nichts

notice ['nəʊtɪs] **1.** Anschlag; Mitteilung, Hinweis(schild); **take notice** Notiz nehmen; **2.** (be)merken, beachten

novel ['nɒvl] Roman

November [nəʊ'vembə] November

now [naʊ] jetzt, nun; **nowadays** ['naʊədeɪz] heutzutage

nuclear ['nju:klɪə] Atom-

number ['nʌmbə] **1.** Zahl, Nummer; **2.** Anzahl; **a number of** mehrere; **3.** nummerieren

nun [nʌn] Nonne; **nunnery** ['nʌnərɪ] Nonnenkloster

nurse [nɜ:s] Krankenschwester, Krankenpfleger

nut [nʌt] Nuss

O

O [əʊ] null

object ['ɒbdʒɪkt] Gegenstand

obligation [ˌɒblɪ'geɪʃn] Verpflichtung, Pflich

observe [əb'zɜ:v] beobachten, betrachten; wahrnehmen

obvious ['ɒbvɪəs] offensichtlich

occasion [ə'keɪʒn] Gelegenheit, Anlass

occupy ['ɒkjʊpaɪ] besetzen

ocean ['əʊʃn] Ozean

o'clock [ə'klɒk] ... Uhr

October [ɒk'təʊbə] Oktober

Odd man out! [ˌɒd mæn‿'aʊt] Welches Wort passt hier nicht?

of [ɒv, əv] von; **of his own** sein eigene(r/s); **bottle of lemonade** Flasche Limonade; **both of them** sie beide, alle beide; **nice of you** nett von dir; **of course** [əv 'kɔ:s] natürlich; **the name of the street** der Name (von) der Straße; **the city/island of ...** die Stadt/Insel ...

off [ɒf] **1.** *(prep)* von ... herunter; **2.** weg( ); **march off** wegmarschieren; **off duty** außer Dienst; **off-road** Off-road-, Gelände-

offensive [ə'fensɪv] beleidigend, anstößig

offer ['ɒfə] **1.** Angebot; **2.** anbieten

office ['ɒfɪs] **1.** Büro; **2.** Amt; **officer** ['ɒfɪsə] Beamte(r)/-in; Polizist/in; Offizier/in; **official** [ə'fɪʃl] **1.** offiziell, amtlich; **2.** Beamte(r)/Beamtin; **official language** Amtssprache

often ['ɒfn, 'ɒftən] oft

oil [ɔɪl] Öl

OK = okay [əʊ'keɪ] gut, in Ordnung; **I'm OK.** Mir geht's gut.

old [əʊld] alt; **old age** (das) Alter

Olympic [ə'lɪmpɪk] olympisch

omelette ['ɒmlɪt] Omelett
on [ɒn] **1.** auf; an; **2.** weiter; **be on** an sein, laufen; **from now on** von jetzt an, ab jetzt; **on a bike** mit dem Fahrrad; **on a visit to ...** bei einem Besuch in ...; **on duty** im Dienst; **on holiday** (BE) auf Urlaub, in den Ferien; **on Monday(s)** montags, am Montag; **on Monday morning(s)** am Montagmorgen; **on my way to** auf dem Weg/unterwegs nach; **on October 12th** am 12. Oktober; **on the first night** in der ersten Nacht; **on the left/right** links/rechts; **on the one hand ... on the other hand** einerseits ... andererseits; **on the phone** am Telefon; **on the radio/on TV** im Radio/Fernseher; **on the River Thames** an der Themse; **on the train/bus/plane** im Zug/Bus/Flugzeug; **on your birthday** an deinem Geburtstag
once [wʌns] **1.** einmal; **2.** (früher) einmal, einst; **at once** sofort, (so)gleich; **3.** *(conj)* sobald, wenn (erst)
one/one's [wʌn, wʌnz] man/sein; **the blue one, the blue ones** der/die/das blaue, die blauen; **oneself** [wʌn'self] sich (selbst)
onion ['ʌnjən] Zwiebel
only ['əʊnlɪ] nur; **not only ... but also** nicht nur ..., sondern auch; **only one week old** erst eine Woche alt; **the only** der/die/das einzige, die einzigen
onto ['ɒntʊ, 'ɒntə] auf ... (hinauf)
open ['əʊpən] **1.** offen, geöffnet, auf **2.** öffnen, aufmachen; **opening times** Öffnungszeiten
opera ['ɒprə] Oper
operate ['ɒpəreɪt] (sich) betätigen; bedienen; **operation** [,ɒpə'reɪʃn] Operation
opinion [ə'pɪnjən] Meinung; **in my opinion** meiner Meinung nach
opportunity (of doing sth/to do sth) [,ɒpə'tju:nətɪ] Gelegenheit, Chance, Möglichkeit (etwas zu tun)
opposed [ə'pəʊzd]**: be opposed to sb/sth** gegen jn/etwas sein, jm/etwas ablehnend gegenüberstehen
opposite ['ɒpəzɪt] **1.** Gegenteil; **2.** gegenüberliegend; **3.** entgegengesetzt; gegenüber (von)
opposition (to) [,ɒpə'zɪʃn] Opposition, Widerstand (gegen)
oppression [ə'preʃn] Unterdrückung
or [ɔ:] oder
oral ['ɔ:rəl] mündlich
orange ['ɒrɪndʒ] **1.** orange(farben); **2.** Apfelsine, Orange
orchestra ['ɔ:kɪstrə] Orchester
order ['ɔ:də] **1.** Reihenfolge, (An-)Ordnung; **2.** Befehl; **3.** bestellen; **4. order sb to do sth** jm befehlen etwas zu tun; jn damit beauftragen, etwas zu tun; **in order to** um ... zu
ordinary ['ɔ:dənrɪ] einfach, gewöhnlich, normal
organization [,ɔ:gənaɪ'zeɪʃn] Organisation; **organize** ['ɔ:gənaɪz] organisieren, veranstalten
oriented ['ɔ:rɪentɪd]: **business-oriented** geschäftsorientiert
origin ['ɒrɪdʒɪn] Ursprung; Entstehung; Herkunft; **original** [ə'rɪdʒənl] **1.** Original; **2.** ursprünglich; Original-
orphan ['ɔ:fn] Waise, Waisenkind
other ['ʌðə] andere(r, s); **other than** *(prep)* außer; **otherwise** ['ʌðəwaɪz] sonst, andernfalls
ought to ['ɔ:tə] sollte eigentlich, müsste eigentlich
our ['aʊə] unser(e); **ours** ['aʊəz] unsere(r, s); **ourselves** [,aʊə'selvz] uns (selbst)
out [aʊt] **1.** hinaus, heraus; **2.** draußen; **come out** herauskommen, hinauskommen; **die out** aussterben; **find out** herausfinden, erfahren; **get out (of the train)** (aus dem Zug) aussteigen; **go out (with)** ausgehen (mit); **read out** vorlesen; **out of** aus (... heraus/hinaus); von; **out of work** arbeitslos
outdoor ['aʊtdɔ:] im Freien; **outdoors** [,aʊt'dɔ:z] (nach) draußen, im Freien
outlaw ['aʊtlɔ:] Geächtete(r)
outside [aʊt'saɪd] **1.** draußen; nach draußen; **2.** *(prep)* außerhalb (von)
outskirts ['aʊtskɜ:ts]: **on the outskirts** am Stadtrand, in den Außenbezirken
oval ['əʊvəl] oval
over ['əʊvə] über; vorüber; **be over** vorüber sein, zu Ende sein; **overall** [,əʊvər'ɔ:l, 'əʊvərɔ:l] Gesamt-, allgemein; **overpopulation** Überbevölkerung; **overreact** überreagieren; **over the years** im Laufe der Jahre; **over there** dort drüben, da drüben
overtake [,əʊvə'teɪk] überholen
owe [əʊ] schulden
own [əʊn] **1.** eigene(r, s); **I pay for my own clothes.** Ich bezahle meine Kleidung selbst. **of my own** mein eigene(r, s); **on their own** (für sich) allein; ohne Hilfe; **2.** besitzen; **owner** Besitzer/in
ox, *pl* **oxen** [ɒks] Ochse
Oxfam ['ɒksfæm] *brit. Hilfsorganisation zur Bekämpfung der Hungersnot*
ozone layer ['əʊzəʊn ,leɪə] Ozonschicht

P

p [pi:] **= pence** Pence
Pacific [pə'sɪfɪk] Pazifik; pazifisch
pack [pæk] (ein)packen
packet ['pækɪt] Paket, Päckchen; Packung
page [peɪdʒ] Seite *(im Buch)*
pain [peɪn] Schmerz
paint [peɪnt] **1.** Farbe *(zum Malen)*; **2.** streichen, anstreichen; **3.** malen; **painter** Maler/in, Anstreicher/in; **painting** Gemälde, Bild
pair [peə] Paar
Pakistan [,pɑ:kɪ'stɑ:n] Pakistan; **Pakistani** [,pɑ:kɪ'stɑ:nɪ] **1.** Pakistaner/in; **2.** pakistanisch
palace ['pælɪs] Palast, Schloss
pan [pæn] Pfanne, Topf
panic ['pænɪk] in Panik geraten
paper ['peɪpə] Papier; **paper = newspaper** Zeitung; **to have a paper route** (AE) Zeitungen austragen
parade [pə'reɪd] Umzug, Parade
paragraph ['pærəgrɑ:f] Absatz, Abschnitt
parallel ['pærəlel] Parallele
parenthesis, *pl* **parentheses** [pə'renθɪsɪs, pə'renθɪsi:z] Klammer
parents ['peərənts] Eltern; **parental** [pə'rentl] elterlich, der Eltern
park [pɑ:k] **1.** Park; **2.** parken; **parking lot** (AE) großer Parkplatz; Parkhaus **parking space** ['pɑ:kɪŋ speɪs] Parklücke, Parkplatz
parliament ['pɑ:ləmənt] Parlament
parrot ['pærət] Papagei
part [pɑ:t] **1.** Teil; **2.** Gegend; **3.** Rolle (eines Schauspielers); **part-time** Teilzeit-, halbtags; **take part (in)** teilnehmen (an), mitmachen (bei); **partly** zum Teil, teilweise
participant (in) [pɑ:'tɪsɪpənt] Teilnehmer/in (an)
particular [pə'tɪkjʊlə] bestimmte(r, s), spezielle(r, s); **particularly** besonders; **in particular** insbesondere
partner ['pɑ:tnə] Partner/in
party ['pɑ:tɪ] **1.** Party, Fest, Fete; **2.** Partei
pass [pɑ:s] **1.** vergehen, vorübergehen *(Zeit)*; **2.** *(eine Prüfung)* bestehen; **3.** (herüber)reichen; *(Ball)* abgeben, abspielen; **4.** *(ein Gesetz)* verabschieden; **5. pass (by)** vorbeigehen, -fahren (an)
passage ['pæsɪdʒ] **1.** Gang; **2.** Passage, Textstelle
passenger ['pæsɪndʒə] Fahrgast, Passagier
passport ['pɑ:spɔ:t] (Reise-)Pass
past [pɑ:st] **1.** Vergangenheit; **2.** vergangene(r, s); **3.** vorbei, vorüber (an); **half past ten** halb elf (= 10.30)
path [pɑ:θ] Pfad, Fußweg
patience ['peɪʃəns] Geduld; **patient** ['peɪʃnt] geduldig
patriotic [,pætrɪ'ɒtɪk] patriotisch
pavement ['peɪvmənt] (BE) Gehweg
pay (for) [peɪ] **1.** (be)zahlen; **2.** Bezahlung

peace [pi:s] Friede(n); **peaceful** ['pi:sfəl] friedlich, friedfertig

pedestrian [pɪ'destrɪən] Fußgänger/in; **pedestrian crossing** [pɪˌdestrɪən 'krɒsɪŋ] Fußgängerüberweg; **pedestrian precinct** [pɪˌdestrɪən 'pri:sɪŋkt] (BE) Fußgängerzone

pen [pen] Füller; Stift; **pen-friend** Brieffreund/in; **sheep pen** Schafhürde

pence [pens] Pence

pencil ['pensl] Bleistift; **pencil-case** ['penslkeɪs] Federtasche, Federmäppchen

penguin ['peŋgwɪn] Pinguin

peninsula [pə'nɪnsjʊlə] Halbinsel

penny ['penɪ] **1.** *kleinste britische Münze;* **2.** (AE) 1¢-Münze; **be penniless** keinen Pfennig Geld haben

pension ['penʃn] Altersrente, Pension

people ['pi:pl] **1.** Leute, Menschen; **2.** Volk

per cent [pə'sent] Prozent; **percentage** [pə'sentɪdʒ] Prozentsatz

perfect **1.** [pə'fekt] perfektionieren; **2.** ['pɜ:fɪkt] perfekt, vollkommen

perhaps [pə'hæps] vielleicht

period ['pɪərɪəd] **1.** Unterrichtsstunde; **2.** Zeitspanne, Zeitraum, Epoche; **3.** (AE) Punkt *(am Satzende)*

permanent ['pɜ:mənənt] dauerhaft, (be)ständig

permission [pə'mɪʃn] Erlaubnis, Genehmigung

persecute ['pɜ:sɪkju:t] verfolgen *(aus politischen oder religiösen Gründen)*; **persecution** [ˌpɜ:sɪ'kju:ʃn] Verfolgung

person ['pɜ:sn] Person, Mensch; **personal** ['pɜ:snl] persönlich, Personal-; **personality** [ˌpɜ:sə'nælɪtɪ] Persönlichkeit

pet [pet] Haustier, Tier; **pet shop** Tierhandlung

petition [pə'tɪʃn] Petition

petrol ['petrəl] (BE) Benzin; **petrol station** ['petrəl ˌsteɪʃn] (BE) Tankstelle

phone = telephone [fəʊn] **1.** Telefon; **2.** anrufen

phonetic [fə'netɪk] phonetisch

photo ['fəʊtəʊ] Foto, Bild; **in the photo** auf dem Foto; **take photos** fotografieren

phrase [freɪz] **1.** Redewendung; **2.** Wortgruppe

physiotherapist [ˌfɪzɪə'θerəpɪst] Physiotherapeut/in, Krankengymnast/in

piano [pɪ'ænəʊ] Klavier

pick [pɪk] pflücken; **pick up** aufheben; abholen, mitnehmen

picnic ['pɪknɪk] Picknick; **have a picnic** ein Picknick machen; **picnic area** Picknickplatz

picture ['pɪktʃə] Bild; Aufnahme, Foto; **in the picture** auf dem Bild; **take pictures** fotografieren, Fotos/Bilder machen

piece [pi:s] Stück

pig [pɪg] Schwein

pigeon ['pɪdʒən] Taube

pile [paɪl] Haufen

pilgrim ['pɪlgrɪm] Pilger/in

pilot ['paɪlət] Pilot/in

pink [pɪŋk] pink, rosa

pioneer [paɪə'nɪə] Pionier, Vorkämpfer/in

pirate ['paɪrət] Pirat, Seeräuber

pity ['pɪtɪ]: **It's a pity.** Das ist schade.

pizza ['pi:tsə] Pizza

place [pleɪs] **1.** Ort, Platz, Stelle; **2.** platzieren, lokalisieren

plain [pleɪn] **1.** einfach, klar; **2.** Ebene

plan [plæn] **1.** Plan, Vorhaben; **2.** planen; **planner** Planer/in

plane [pleɪn] Flugzeug; **by plane** mit dem Flugzeug

planet ['plænɪt] Planet

plant [pl:ɑnt] **1.** Pflanze; **2.** (ein)pflanzen, setzen; **plantation** [plæn'teɪʃn] Plantage

plastic ['plæstɪk] **1.** Plastik; **2.** Plastik-

plate [pleɪt] Teller

platform ['plætfɔ:m] **1.** Bahnsteig; **2.** Plattform

play [pleɪ] **1.** (Theater-)Stück; **2.** spielen; **play a trick (on)** einen Streich spielen; **player** Spieler/in; **playing field** (BE) Sportplatz

please [pli:z] bitte; **be pleased (with)** sich freuen (über); zufrieden sein (mit)

pliers *(pl)* ['plaɪəz] (eine) (Kombi-)Zange

plunder ['plʌndə] (aus)plündern, (aus)rauben

pm [ˌpi:‿'em] Uhr nachmittags/abends

pocket ['pɒkɪt] Tasche; **pocket-money** Taschengeld

poem ['pəʊɪm] Gedicht; **poet** Dichter/-in; **poetry** Dichtung, Dichtkunst

point [pɔɪnt] **1.** Punkt; Komma *(in Dezimalzahlen)*; **point of view** Standpunkt; (Erzähl-)Perspektive; **2.** **point (to/at)** zeigen (auf), deuten (auf); **point out** hinweisen auf

poison ['pɔɪzn] Gift

polar bear ['pəʊlə beə] Eisbär

police [pə'li:s] Polizei; **police officer** Polizist/in; **police station** Polizeiwache, Polizeirevier

policy ['pɒləsɪ] Politik

polio ['pəʊlɪəʊ] Kinderlähmung, Polio

Polish ['pəʊlɪʃ] **1.** polnisch; **2.** Polnisch

polite [pə'laɪt] höflich; **politeness** [pə'laɪtnəs] Höflichkeit

political [pə'lɪtɪkl] politisch; **politician** [ˌpɒlə'tɪʃn] Politiker/in; **politics** *(sing)* ['pɒlɪtɪks] Politik

poll [pəʊl] Umfrage; Abstimmung

pollute [pə'lu:t] verschmutzen; **pollution** [pə'lu:ʃn] (Umwelt-)Verschmutzung

pony ['pəʊnɪ] Pony; **pony-trekking** ['pəʊnɪ ˌtrekɪŋ] Ponyreiten

poor [pʊə, pɔ:] arm; mangelhaft, schlecht

popcorn ['pɒpkɔ:n] Popcorn

Pope [pəʊp] Papst

pop music ['pɒp ˌmju:zɪk] Popmusik; **pop song** Popsong

popular (with) ['pɒpjʊlə] beliebt (bei); verbreitet; allgemein

populate ['pɒpjʊleɪt] bevölkern; **population** [ˌpɒpjʊ'leɪʃn] Bevölkerung, Einwohner(zahl)

port [pɔ:t] Hafen; Hafenstadt

Portugal ['pɔ:tʃʊgl] Portugal

position [pə'zɪʃn] Lage; Position

positive ['pɒzətɪv] positiv

possibility [ˌpɒsə'bɪlətɪ] Möglichkeit; **possible** ['pɒsəbl] möglich; **possibly** möglicherweise, vielleicht; **I couldn't possibly** ich könnte unmöglich

post [pəʊst] **1.** (BE) Post(sendungen); **post office** Post(amt); **postcard** Postkarte; **postcode** ['pəʊstkəʊd] *britische Postleitzahl*; **2.** Posten

post-(industrial) [pəʊst] nach-(industriell)

poster ['pəʊstə] Poster, Plakat

postpone [pə'spəʊn] aufschieben, verschieben

potato [pə'teɪtəʊ], *pl* **potatoes** Kartoffel

potential [pə'tenʃl] potenziell

pottery ['pɒtərɪ] Keramik(herstellung)

pound [paʊnd] **1.** Pfund *(britische Währung)*; **2.** *engl./amerik.* Pfund (= 454 g)

poverty ['pɒvətɪ] Armut; **poverty line** Armutsgrenze

power ['paʊə] **1.** Macht, Kraft, Gewalt; **power station** Kraftwerk; **2.** Befugnis **powerful** ['paʊəfəl] mächtig, stark; **powerless** ['paʊələs] machtlos, kraftlos

practical ['præktɪkl] praktisch

practice ['præktɪs] **1.** Übung; Praxis; Training; **2.** (AE) üben, trainieren

practise ['præktɪs] (BE) üben, trainieren, ausüben

prairie ['preərɪ] Prärie, Grasebene

praise [preɪz] loben, rühmen, preisen

pray [preɪ] beten

precinct: pedestrian precinct [pɪˌdestrɪən 'pri:sɪŋkt] (BE) Fußgängerzone

predict [prɪ'dɪkt] vorhersagen

prefer (to) [prɪ'fɜ:] vorziehen, lieber haben (als)

prefix ['pri:fɪks] Vorsilbe, Präfix

prejudice ['predʒʊdɪs] Vorurteil, Voreingenommenheit; **prejudiced** voreingenommen

preparation [ˌprepə'reɪʃn] Vorbereitung; **prepare** [prɪ'peə] vorbereiten, zu-

bereiten; **be prepared (to do sth)** bereit sein, willens sein (etwas zu tun)
present ['preznt] **1.** Geschenk; **2.** Gegenwart; **3.** gegenwärtig, heutig, jetzige(r, s); **present-day** heutig, gegenwärtig; **4.** präsentieren, darlegen
president ['prezɪdənt] Präsident/in
press [pres] Presse
pressure ['preʃə] Druck, Zwang
prestige [pre'sti:ʒ] Ansehen, Prestige
pretend [prɪ'tend] so tun, als ob; vortäuschen
previous ['pri:vɪəs] vorige(r, s), vorhergehende(r, s)
price [praɪs] (Kauf-)Preis
priest [pri:st] Priester
primary school ['praɪmərɪ sku:l] (BE) Grundschule
prime minister [ˌpraɪm 'mɪnɪstə] Premierminister/in, Ministerpräsident/in
prince [prɪns] Prinz, Fürst; **princess** [prɪn'ses] Prinzessin, Fürstin
principal ['prɪnsəpl] (AE) Schulleiter/in, Direktor/in
principle ['prɪnsəpl] Prinzip, Grundsatz
prison ['prɪzn] Gefängnis; **prisoner** ['prɪznə] Gefangene(r)
private ['praɪvɪt] **1.** privat, Privat-; **2.** persönlich; **privatization** [ˌpraɪvətaɪ'zeɪʃn] Privatisierung; **privatize** ['praɪvətaɪz] privatisieren
privilege ['prɪvɪlɪdʒ] Privileg; **privileged** privilegiert, bevorzugt
prize [praɪz] Preis, Gewinn
probably ['prɒbəblɪ] wahrscheinlich
problem ['prɒbləm] Problem
process ['prəʊses] Prozess, Verfahren
proclamation [ˌprɒklə'meɪʃn] Proklamation, Verkündung
produce [prə'dju:s] produzieren, herstellen, erzeugen; **product** ['prɒdʌkt] Produkt, Erzeugnis; **production** [prə'dʌkʃn] Produktion
professional [prə'feʃnl] **1.** Berufs-, professionell, Fach-; **2.** Berufssportler/in, Profi; Angehörige(r) eines hoch qualifizierten Berufs
professor [prə'fesə] Professor/in
profile ['prəʊfaɪl] Kurzbiografie, -porträt; Profil
profit ['prɒfɪt] Profit, Gewinn
program ['prəʊgræm] (Computer-) Programm; AE *auch:* Sendung, Programm
programme ['prəʊgræm] (BE) Sendung, Programm
progress ['prəʊgres] *(sing)* Fortschritt(e); **in progress** im Gange
project ['prɒdʒekt] Projekt; Aufgabe
promise ['prɒmɪs] **1.** Versprechen; **2.** versprechen
pronounce [prə'naʊns] aussprechen; **pronunciation** [prəˌnʌnsɪ'eɪʃn] Aussprache
proof [pru:f] Beweis(e), Nachweis(e)
propaganda [ˌprɒpə'gændə] Propaganda
proper ['prɒpə] richtig, passend, geeignet
property ['prɒpətɪ] Eigentum, Besitz
proportion [prə'pɔ:ʃn] Verhältnis; (An-)Teil
proposal [prə'pəʊzl] Antrag, Vorschlag
protect [prə'tekt] (be)schützen; **protection** Schutz
protest **1.** ['prəʊtest] Protest; **2.** [prə'test] protestieren; **protester** [prə'testə] Protestierende(r), Demonstrant/in
Protestant ['prɒtɪstənt] **1.** Protestant/in; **2.** protestantisch, evangelisch
proud (of) [praʊd] stolz (auf)
provide [prə'vaɪd] zur Verfügung stellen, bereitstellen, schaffen; versorgen; (be)liefern
province ['prɒvɪns] Provinz
provoke [prə'vəʊk] provozieren
pub [pʌb] Kneipe, Lokal
public ['pʌblɪk] **1.** Öffentlichkeit; **2.** öffentlich; **public school** (BE) (teure) Privatschule *(meist mit Internat)*; **publicity** [pʌb'lɪsətɪ] Publicity, öffentliche Aufmerksamkeit; **public transportation** (AE) öffentliche Verkehrsmittel
publish ['pʌblɪʃ] veröffentlichen, verlegen; **publisher** Verleger/in
pull [pʊl] ziehen; **pull down** abreißen, niederreißen
pullover ['pʊlˌəʊvə] Pullover
pump [pʌmp] pumpen
punctuation mark [ˌpʌŋktʃʊ'eɪʃn mɑ:k] Satzzeichen
puncture ['pʌŋktʃə] (BE) Reifenpanne
punish ['pʌnɪʃ] bestrafen
pupil ['pju:pl] Schüler/in
purpose ['pɜ:pəs] Zweck
push [pʊʃ] stoßen, schieben; drängeln
put [pʊt] stellen, legen, setzen, *(an einen Platz)* tun; **put in** einsetzen; **put on** *(Kleidung)* anziehen; **put up** **1.** aufbauen, aufstellen; **2.** aufhängen, anbringen
puzzle ['pʌzl] Rätsel
pyjamas *(pl)* [pə'dʒɑ:məz] Schlafanzug, Pyjama

Q

qualification [ˌkwɒlɪfɪ'keɪʃn] Qualifikation
quality ['kwɒlətɪ] **1.** Qualität; **2.** Eigenschaft
quarter ['kwɔ:tə] **1.** Viertel; **2.** viertel; **quarter past/to ten** Viertel nach/vor zehn; **3.** (AE) 25¢-Münze
queen [kwi:n] Königin
question ['kwestʃən] Frage; **ask a question** eine Frage stellen; **question mark** Fragezeichen
queue [kju:] (BE) Schlange *(wartender Menschen)*, Reihe
quick [kwɪk] schnell
quiet ['kwaɪət] still, ruhig, leise
quit [kwɪt] aufhören; *(eine Stelle)* aufgeben
quite [kwaɪt] **1.** ziemlich; **2.** ganz; **quite a** ein(e) ziemlich(er, e, es); **quite a bit of** einiges an
quiz [kwɪz] Quiz
quotation (by/from) [kwəʊ'teɪʃn] Zitat, Ausspruch (von/aus); **quote** zitieren; **quotation mark** [kwəʊ'teɪʃn mɑ:k] Anführungszeichen

R

rabbit ['ræbɪt] Kaninchen
race [reɪs] **1.** Rennen, (Wett-)Lauf; **have a race** ein Rennen veranstalten; **racing driver** Rennfahrer/in; **2.** Rasse; **racial** ['reɪʃl] rassisch, Rassen-; **racism** ['reɪsɪzm] Rassismus; **racist** Rassist/in
radio ['reɪdɪəʊ] Radio, Rundfunk; **on the radio** im Radio
rage [reɪdʒ] Wut(anfall), Zorn, Rage
rail [reɪl] Schiene; **railroad** (AE) ['reɪlrəʊd] Eisenbahn(strecke); **railway** (BE) ['reɪlweɪ] Eisenbahn(strecke)
rain [reɪn] **1.** Regen; **2.** regnen; **raincoat** Regenmantel; **rainwater** Regenwasser; **rainy** regnerisch, verregnet
raise [reɪz] **1.** (hoch)heben; erhöhen; **2.** zur Sprache bringen
ranch [BE: rɑ:ntʃ; AE: ræntʃ] Ranch, große Farm; **rancher** Viehzüchter/in, Farmer/in
range [reɪndʒ] Palette, Auswahl
rape [reɪp] vergewaltigen
rapid ['ræpɪd] rapid, schnell
rare [reə] selten
rather ['rɑ:ðə] eher, lieber; **rather (a)** (ein/e) ziemlich
raw [rɔ:] roh; Roh-
reach [ri:tʃ] erreichen; reichen; **reach (for)** greifen (nach)
react (to) [ri:'ækt] reagieren auf; **reaction** Reaktion
read [ri:d] (vor)lesen; sich lesen; **read out** vorlesen; **readable** ['ri:dəbl] lesbar; **reader** Leser/in; **reading** Lesung, Lesen
ready ['redɪ] bereit, fertig; **Ready, steady, go!** Auf die Plätze, fertig, los!
real [rɪəl] echt, wirklich; **reality** [rɪ'ælətɪ] Realität, Wirklichkeit; **really** wirklich, tatsächlich, eigentlich

realize ['rɪəlaɪz] erkennen; sich klarmachen; einsehen; merken

reappear [ˌri:ə'pɪə] wieder auftauchen, wieder erscheinen

rearrange [ˌri:ə'reɪndʒ] neu ordnen, umstellen, ändern

reason ['ri:zn] Grund, Begründung; **for this reason** aus diesem Grund; **reasonable** ['ri:znəbl] vernünftig

rebel ['rebl] Rebell/in, Aufständische(r)

rebuild [ˌri:'bild] wieder aufbauen

receive [rɪ'si:v] erhalten, bekommen; empfangen

recent ['ri:snt] neueste(r, s), letzte(r, s); vor kurzem *(geschehen, entstanden usw.)*; **recently** neulich, vor kurzem

recognize ['rekəgnaɪz] **1.** erkennen; **2.** anerkennen

reconstruct [ˌri:kən'strʌkt] rekonstruieren

record **1.** ['rekɔ:d] Rekord; **2.** Schallplatte; **record-player** Plattenspieler; **record request** Plattenwunsch; **3.** schriftliche Überlieferung; **4.** [rɪ'kɔ:d] aufzeichnen, aufnehmen *(auf Band)*

recover [rɪ'kʌvə] sich erholen

recreation [ˌrekrɪ'eɪʃn] Erholung; Freizeitaktivität

rectangular [ˌrek'tæŋgʊlə] rechteckig

recyclable [ˌri:'saɪkləbl] wieder verwertbar; **recycle** wieder verwerten, wieder aufbereiten

red [red] rot

redevelop [ˌri:dɪ'veləp] sanieren

redo [ˌri:'du:] noch einmal machen, neu machen

reduce [rɪ'dju:s] verringern, vermindern, reduzieren

re-elect [ˌri:ɪ'lekt] wieder wählen

refer to [rɪ'fɜ:] sich beziehen auf

refill [ˌri:'fɪl] wieder füllen, nach-/auffüllen

reflect [rɪ'flekt] reflektieren, (wider)spiegeln

reform [rɪ'fɔ:m] **1.** Reform; **2.** reformieren

refuse [rɪ'fju:z] sich weigern; verweigern, ablehnen

regard: with regard to (fml) [rɪ'gɑ:d] in/mit Bezug auf

region ['ri:dʒn] Gegend, Gebiet, Region; **regional** regional, lokal

regret [rɪ'gret] bedauern, bereuen

regular ['regjʊlə] regelmäßig

regulation [ˌregjʊ'leɪʃn] Bestimmung, Vorschrift, Verordnung

reign [reɪn] Regierung(szeit)

reintroduce [ˌri:ɪntrə'dʒu:s] wieder einführen

reject [rɪ'dʒekt] ablehnen, zurückweisen

related [rɪ'leɪtɪd]: **be related (to)** verwandt sein (mit); sich beziehen (auf)

relations [rɪ'leɪʃnz] Beziehungen; **relationship** Beziehung

relative ['relətɪv] Verwandte(r)

relax [rɪ'læks] (sich) entspannen, sich ausruhen

release [rɪ'li:s] *(Film, Buch, CD)* herausbringen, veröffentlichen

relevant ['reləvənt] relevant

reliable [rɪ'laɪəbl] zuverlässig

relieve [rɪ'li:v] ablösen; erleichtern, lindern, verringern

religion [rɪ'lɪdʒn] Religion; **religious** [rɪ'lɪdʒəs] religiös

rely on [rɪ'laɪ] sich verlassen auf

remain [rɪ'meɪn] bleiben, übrig bleiben; **remains** (Über-)Reste

remember [rɪ'membə] **1.** sich erinnern (an); daran denken; **2.** sich merken

remind (of) [rɪ'maɪnd] erinnern (an)

rename [ˌri:'neɪm] umbenennen (in); neu benennen

renew [rɪ'nju:] erneuern; verlängern; **renewable** erneuerbar

rent [rent] **1.** Miete; **2.** mieten

reopen [ri:'əʊpən] wieder eröffnen

reorganize [ˌri:'ɔ:gənaɪz] umgestalten, neu organisieren

repair [rɪ'peə] **1.** Reparatur; **2.** reparieren; **repair kit** [rɪ'peə kɪt] Flickzeug; **repair shop** Reparaturwerkstatt für Fahrräder

repeat [rɪ'pi:t] wiederholen; **repetition** [ˌrepə'tɪʃn] Wiederholung

rephrase [ˌri:'freɪz] neu formulieren, umformulieren

replace (with/by) [rɪ'pleɪs] ersetzen (durch)

reply (to) [rɪ'plaɪ] **1.** Antwort, Erwiderung (auf); **2.** antworten (auf), beantworten; erwidern

report [rɪ'pɔ:t] **1.** Bericht; Zeugnis **2.** berichten; melden; *(bei der Polizei)* anzeigen; **reporter** Reporter/in

represent [ˌreprɪ'zent] repräsentieren, vertreten; darstellen; **representative: the House of Representatives** (USA) das Repräsentantenhaus

republic [rɪ'pʌblɪk] Republik; **republican** **1.** Republikaner/in; **2.** republikanisch

request [rɪ'kwest] Bitte

requirement [rɪ'kwaɪəmənt] (An-)Forderung; (AE *auch*) Pflichtfach

research [rɪ'sɜ:tʃ] Forschung(en)

reservation [ˌrezə'veɪʃn] Reservat(ion); **reserve** [rɪ'zɜ:v] reservieren (lassen); buchen

residential [ˌrezɪ'denʃl] Wohn-

resort [rɪ'zɔ:t] Ferienort, Urlaubsort

resource [rɪ'sɔ:s, rɪ'zɔ:s] Ressource; (Boden-)Schatz

respect [rɪ'spekt] **1.** Achtung, Respekt; **2.** achten, respektieren

responsibility [rɪˌspɒnsə'bɪlɪtɪ] Verantwortung; **responsible** [rɪ'spɒnsəbl] verantwortlich

rest [rest] Rest

restaurant ['restrɒnt] Restaurant, Gaststätte

restore [rɪ'stɔ:] wiederherstellen; restau rieren; neu aufbauen

result [rɪ'zʌlt] Ergebnis, Resultat

retell [ˌri:'tel] nacherzählen

return [rɪ'tɜ:n] zurückkommen, -gehen, -kehren; **returnable bottle** Mehrwegflasche, Pfandflasche; **return fare** Fahrpreis hin und zurück; **return flight** Rückflug

reveal [rɪ'vi:l] offenbaren, enthüllen

revise [rɪ'vaɪz] (BE) *(Lernstoff)* wiederholen

revolution [ˌrevə'lu:ʃn] Revolution

rewrite [ˌri:'raɪt] neu schreiben, noch ma schreiben

rhyme [raɪm] Reim, Vers; **rhyme schem** ['raɪm ski:m] Reimschema

rhythm ['rɪðm] Rhythmus

rich (in) [rɪtʃ] reich (an)

ride [raɪd] **1.** *(auf einem Pferd)* reiten; **2.** (Rad) fahren; **a one-minute ride by bus/car** eine Minute mit dem Bus/Auto; **go for a ride** herumfahren, ein Spritztour machen; **rider** ['raɪdə] (Rad-)Fahrer/in; Reiter/in

rig [rɪg] Bohrinsel

right [raɪt] **1.** richtig; **all right** gut, in Ordnung; **be right** Recht haben; **My watch is right** Meine Uhr geht richtig **That's right.** Richtig! Stimmt! **2.** rechte(r, s), nach rechts; **on the right** rechts, auf der rechten Seite; **to the right** nach rechts; **3.** direkt, genau; **4. rights** *(pl)* Rechte

ring [rɪŋ] **1.** Ring; **2.** klingeln, läuten; **3.** anrufen; **ring up** anrufen

riot ['raɪət] **1.** Krawall, Aufruhr; **2.** randalieren, an einem Krawall, einem Aufruhr teilnehmen

rise [raɪz] (an-, auf)steigen; aufgehen *(Sonne)*; aufstehen, sich erheben

risk [rɪsk] **1.** Risiko; **2.** riskieren, wagen

rival ['raɪvl] Rivale/-in, Konkurrent/in

river ['rɪvə] Fluss; **on the (River) Thames** an der Themse

road [rəʊd] (Land-)Straße; **road sign** Verkehrszeichen

roast beef [ˌrəʊst 'bi:f] Rinderbraten, Roastbeef

rob [rɒb] be-, ausrauben; **robber** Räuber; **robbery** ['rɒbərɪ] Raub(überfall)

robot ['rəʊbɒt] Roboter

rock [rɒk] Fels(en); **rock-climbing** ['rɒk ˌklaɪmɪŋ] Klettern (im Fels); **rocky** felsig

rocket ['rɒkɪt] Rakete

role [rəʊl] Rolle; **role-play** ['rəʊl pleɪ] Rollenspiel

roll [rəʊl] **1.** Brötchen, Semmel; **2.** rollen

Roman ['rəʊmən] römisch, Römer/in
romantic [rə'mæntɪk] romantisch
roof [ru:f] Dach
room [ru:m, rʊm] Zimmer, Raum
rough [rʌf] rau, stürmisch; grob, gewalttätig, hart
round [raʊnd] **1.** um (... herum); **2.** rund; **3.** Kanon
route [ru:t] Route, Strecke
routine [ru:'ti:n] Routine
row [rəʊ] rudern
row [rəʊ] Reihe
royal ['rɔɪəl] königlich
rub [rʌb] (ein)reiben
rubber ['rʌbə] **1.** (BE) Radiergummi; **2.** Gummi
rubbish ['rʌbɪʃ] **1.** Müll; **2.** Müll-; **rubbish tip** (BE) Müllhalde
rude [ru:d] unhöflich, grob; unanständig
ruin ['ru:ɪn] **1.** zerstören, ruinieren; **2.** Ruine; **in ruins** zerstört
rule [ru:l] **1.** Regel, Vorschrift; **2.** Herrschaft; **3.** (be)herrschen, regieren
ruler ['ru:lə] Lineal
run [rʌn] **1.** rennen, laufen; **2.** (durch)führen, veranstalten, betreiben, leiten; **runner** Läufer/in; **running water** fließendes Wasser; **2.** verkehren, fahren *(Zug, Bus)*; **run out** knapp werden, ausgehen; **run over** überfahren
rural ['rʊərəl] ländlich, Land-
Russia ['rʌʃə] Russland; **Russian** **1.** russisch; **2.** Russisch

S

sad [sæd] traurig; **sadness** ['sædnəs] Traurigkeit
safari park [sə'fɑ:rɪ pɑ:k] Safaripark
safe [seɪf] sicher, gefahrlos
saga ['sɑ:gə] Sage; Geschichte; Heldenepos
sail [seɪl] **1.** Segel; **2.** segeln, fahren; **sailor** Seemann, Matrose
saint [seɪnt] Heilige(r)
sake [seɪk]: **for God's sake** um Gottes willen
salad ['sæləd] (angemachter) Salat; **ham salad** Schinken mit Salat
salary ['sælərɪ] Gehalt
sale [seɪl] Verkauf
salt [sɔ:lt] Salz; **salty** salzig; versalzen
same [seɪm]: **the same** der-, die-, dasselbe
sand [sænd] Sand; **sandy** sandig
sandwich ['sænwɪdʒ] belegtes Butterbrot
Santa Claus ['sæntə klɔ:z] Weihnachtsmann
sapphire ['sæfaɪə] Saphir
sardine [sɑ:'di:n] Sardine
satisfaction [,sætɪs'fækʃn] Befriedigung, Genugtuung; Zufriedenheit; **satisfactory** [,sætɪs'fæktrɪ] befriedigend; **satisfied** ['sætɪsfaɪd] zufrieden; **satisfy** zufrieden stellen, befriedigen
Saturday ['sætədɪ] Samstag, Sonnabend
sauce [sɔ:s] Soße
saucer ['sɔ:sə] Untertasse
sausage ['sɒsɪdʒ] Wurst, Würstchen
save [seɪv] **1.** sparen; **2.** retten
saw [sɔ:] Säge
Saxon ['sæksn] Sachse, Sächsin
saxophone ['sæksəfəʊn] Saxophon
say [seɪ] sagen; **be said to** sollen (angeblich); **say hello (to)** grüßen; **The sign says ...** Auf dem Schild steht/heißt es ... ;
scared: be scared (of) [skeəd] sich fürchten (vor)
scene [si:n] Szene, Schauplatz, Ort-; **scenery** ['si:nərɪ] schöne Landschaft; **scenic** landschaftlich schön
schedule [BE: 'ʃedju:l; AE: 'skedʒu:l] Zeitplan; (AE *auch*) Stundenplan
scheme [ski:m] Schema
school [sku:l] Schule; **at school, in school** (*meist* AE) in der Schule; **go to school** zur Schule gehen; **leave school** von der Schule abgehen; **start school** eingeschult werden; **schoolchildren** Schüler und Schülerinnen, Schulkinder; **schoolgirl** Schülerin; **school-leaver** Schulabgänger/in; **school report** (BE) (Schul-)Zeugnis
science ['saɪəns] (Natur-)Wissenschaft; **scientific** [,saɪən'tɪfɪk] (natur)wissenschaftlich; **scientist** ['saɪəntɪst] (Natur-)Wissenschaftler/in
scissors *(pl)* ['sɪzəz] (eine) Schere
score [skɔ:] **1.** Spielstand; Ergebnis; **2.** *(einen Punkt/Treffer)* erzielen, *(ein Tor)* schießen
Scot [skɒt] Schotte, Schottin; **Scotland** Schottland; **Scotsman/Scotswoman** Schotte/Schottin; **Scottish** schottisch
scout [skaʊt]: **Girl Scout** (AE) Pfadfinderin
scream [skri:m] **1.** Schrei; Aufschrei; **2.** schreien, kreischen
screen [skri:n] Bildschirm; Leinwand
screw [skru:] Schraube; **screwdriver** ['skru:,draɪvə] Schraubenzieher
sea [si:] Meer; **sea lion** ['si:,laɪən] Seelöwe; **seasick** ['si:sɪk] seekrank; **seaside** ['si:saɪd] See-, Küsten-; Küste
search [sɜ:tʃ] Suche; **in search of** auf der Suche nach
season ['si:zn] Jahreszeit; Saison
seat [si:t] Sitzplatz; Sitz; **seatbelt** ['si:tbelt] Sicherheitsgurt
second ['sekənd] Sekunde
secondary ['sekəndrɪ]: **secondary education** höhere Schulbildung; höheres Schulwesen; **secondary modern school** (BE) *Mischung aus Haupt- und Realschule;* **secondary school** Oberschule
secondly zweitens
secret ['si:krət] **1.** Geheimnis; **2.** geheim; **secret service** Geheimdienst
secretary ['sekrətrɪ] Sekretär/in; **secretary (of state)** (US) Minister/in; **Secretary of Commerce** (AE) (amerik.) Wirtschaftsminister/in; **Secretary of State** (AE) (amerik.) Außenminister/in; **Secretary of the Interior** (AE) (amerik.) Innenminister/in; **Secretary of the Treasury** (AE) (amerik.) Finanzminister/in
section ['sekʃn] Sektion; Abschnitt, Stück, Teil
sector ['sektə] Sektor, Bereich
see [si:] sehen; zusehen; **I see.** Ich verstehe. Ach so! **Let me see, ...** Warte mal! Lass mich mal überlegen! **Let's see.** Wollen mal sehen. **See you soon.** Tschüs. Bis bald. **You see.** Verstehen Sie.
seem [si:m] scheinen
segregate ['segrɪgeɪt] trennen *(nach Rasse, Religion)*; **segregation** [,segrɪ'geɪʃn] Rassentrennung, Absonderung
self-employed [,self-ɪm'plɔɪd] selbstständig *(Geschäftsleute)*
self-study [self'stʌdɪ] Selbststudium
sell [sel] verkaufen
semi-colon [,semɪ'kəʊlən] Semikolon
semi-detached house [,semɪ dɪ,tætʃt 'haʊs] (BE) Doppelhaushälfte
seminar (on) ['semɪnɑ:] Seminar (über)
senate ['senɪt] Senat; **senator** ['senətə] Senator/in
send [send] schicken, senden; **send for** kommen lassen, holen; schicken nach; **send sb to sleep** jn einschläfern, zum Schlafen bringen
sensational [sen'seɪʃənl] sensationell; Sensations-
senior ['si:nɪə] (US) *Schüler/in der 12. Klasse der High School; Student/in im 4. Studienjahr*
sense [sens] Bedeutung, Sinn; **make sense** einen Sinn ergeben
sensible ['sensəbl] vernünftig
sensitive ['sensətɪv] sensibel, heikel
sentence ['sentəns] Satz
sentence ['sentəns] verurteilen
separate **1.** ['seprət] getrennt, selbstständig; **2.** ['sepəreɪt] trennen
September [sep'tembə] September
series ['sɪəri:z] Serie, Sendereihe; Reihe
serious ['sɪərɪəs] **1.** ernst(haft); **take sb/sth seriously** jn/etwas ernst nehmen; **2.** schlimm
serve [sɜ:v] (be)dienen, servieren; **servant** Diener/in, Dienstmädchen;

service [ˈsɜːvɪs] *(Zug-, Bus- usw.)* Verbindung; Dienst(leistung)
set [set] Satz
set [set] untergehen *(Sonne, Mond)*; **set off** aufbrechen; **set up** einrichten, errichten
setting [ˈsetɪŋ] Schauplatz
settle [ˈsetl] sich niederlassen, ansiedeln; besiedeln; **settlement** Siedlung; **settler** Siedler/in
several [ˈsevrəl] mehrere; verschiedene
sewage works [ˈsuːɪdʒ ˌwɜːks] (BE) Klärwerk(e)
sex [seks] Geschlecht; Sex; **sex appeal** Sexappeal
shabby [ˈʃæbɪ] schäbig
shadow [ˈʃædəʊ] Schatten
shake [ʃeɪk] schütteln; erschüttern; zittern; **(milk) shake** (Milch-)Shake, Mixgetränk
Shall I/we ... ? [ʃæl, ʃəl] Soll ich/Sollen wir ...? **I shall (= I will)** ich werde/will
shampoo [ʃæmˈpuː] Shampoo, Haarwaschmittel
shan't [ʃɑːnt]: **I shan't = I shall not**
shape [ʃeɪp] **1.** Gestalt, Form; **2.** gestalten, formen
share [ʃeə] **1.** Anteil; Aktie; **2. share (with)** [ʃeə] (sich) teilen (mit), gemeinsam benutzen
she [ʃiː] sie
sheep [ʃiːp] Schaf(e)
shelf, *pl* **shelves** [ʃelf, ʃelvz] Bord, Brett; Regal
shell [ʃel] Muschel(schale)
shine [ʃaɪn] **1.** scheinen *(Sonne)*; **2.** glänzen
ship [ʃɪp] Schiff; **shipping** Schiffe; Schifffahrt, Schiffsverkehr
shirt [ʃɜːt] (Ober-)Hemd
shock [ʃɒk] Schock
shoe [ʃuː] Schuh
shoot [ʃuːt] (er)schießen
shop [ʃɒp] Laden, Geschäft; **pet shop** Tierhandlung; **repair shop** Reparaturwerkstatt; **shop assistant** [ˈʃɒp‿əˌsɪstənt] (BE) Verkäufer/in; **shopping** Einkauf(en); BE *auch:* eingekaufte Sachen; **do the shopping** einkaufen, Einkäufe machen/erledigen; **shopping centre** Einkaufszentrum; **go shopping** einkaufen gehen
short [ʃɔːt] kurz; **shorts** *(pl)* Shorts, kurze Hose(n); **shorten** kürzen; **short story** [ˌʃɔːt ˈstɔːrɪ] Kurzgeschichte
should [ʃʊd, ʃəd] sollte(n), müsste(n)
shoulder [ˈʃəʊldə] Schulter
shout [ʃaʊt] (laut) rufen, schreien
show [ʃəʊ] **1.** Schau; Show; **2.** zeigen
showdown [ˈʃəʊdaʊn] Showdown, Entscheidungskampf
shower [ˈʃaʊə] Dusche, Brause; (Regen-)Schauer; **have a shower** (sich) duschen
shut [ʃʌt] schließen, zumachen
shy [ʃaɪ] scheu, zurückhaltend
sick [sɪk]: **be sick** (BE) sich übergeben (müssen); **feel sick** sich schlecht/übel fühlen; **sickness** [ˈsɪknəs] Krankheit
side [saɪd] Seite; Straßenrand; **take sides** Partei ergreifen
sidewalk [ˈsaɪdwɔːk] (AE) Gehweg
sigh (with) [saɪ] seufzen (vor)
sight [saɪt] Sehenswürdigkeit; Anblick; **see the sights** sich die Sehenswürdigkeiten ansehen; **sightseeing tour** Besichtigungstour, Rundfahrt
sign [saɪn] **1.** Zeichen; (Hinweis-)Schild; **road sign** Verkehrszeichen; **2.** unterschreiben; **signature** [ˈsɪgnətʃə] Unterschrift
silence [ˈsaɪləns] Stille; Schweigen; **silent** leise, still; schweigend, schweigsam
silly [ˈsɪlɪ] albern, dumm, doof, blöd; **silliness** [ˈsɪlɪnəs] Dummheit
silver [ˈsɪlvə] silbern; Silber
similar [ˈsɪmɪlə] ähnlich
simile [ˈsɪməlɪ] Vergleich
simple [ˈsɪmpl] einfach; einfältig, naiv; **simplify** vereinfachen
since [sɪns] seit; seitdem
sincerely [sɪnˈsɪəlɪ]: **Sincerely (yours)** (AE) Mit freundlichen/herzlichen Grüßen; **Yours sincerely** (BE) Mit freundlichen/herzlichen Grüßen
sing [sɪŋ] singen; **singer** [ˈsɪŋə] Sänger/in
single [ˈsɪŋgl] einzig, einzeln; Einzel-; ledig, unverheiratet; **single fare** (BE) einfacher Fahrpreis
sink [sɪŋk] **1.** sinken, untergehen; **2.** versenken
sir [sɜː] *höfliche Anrede für einen Mann;* **Dear Sir or Madam** Sehr geehrte Damen und Herren
sister [ˈsɪstə] Schwester
sit [sɪt] sitzen; **sit down** sich setzen; **sit still** still sitzen
site [saɪt] Gelände; Stätte, Stelle; **camp site** Campingplatz, Zeltplatz
situation [ˌsɪtjʊˈeɪʃn] Situation
sixth form [ˈsɪksθ fɔːm] (BE) Oberstufe, Sekundarstufe II
size [saɪz] Größe; **What size do you take?** Welche Größe hast du/haben Sie?
skateboard [ˈskeɪtbɔːd] Skateboard
ski [skiː] **1.** Ski; **2.** Ski laufen, fahren
skill [skɪl] Kenntnis, Fertigkeit; Geschicklichkeit; **skilled (in/at)** (hoch) qualifiziert, Fach-; geschickt (in)
skirt [skɜːt] Rock
sky [skaɪ] Himmel; **skyscraper** [ˈskaɪˌskreɪpə] Wolkenkratzer
slang [slæŋ] Slang
slave [sleɪv] Sklave/-in; **slavery** [ˈsleɪvərɪ] Sklaverei
sleep [sliːp] **1.** Schlaf; **go back to sleep** wieder einschlafen; **2.** schlafen; **sleep on** weiterschlafen; **sleepless** [ˈsliːpləs] schlaflos
slice [slaɪs] in Scheiben schneiden
slight(ly) [slaɪt, ˈslaɪtlɪ] leicht, gering(fügi
slow [sləʊ] langsam
small [smɔːl] klein
smell [smel] **1.** Geruch; **2.** riechen; **smelly** stinkend; **They're smelly.** Sie stinken.
smile (at) [smaɪl] (an)lächeln; Lächeln
smoke [sməʊk] **1.** Rauch, Dampf, Dunst **2.** rauchen
smuggler [ˈsmʌglə] Schmuggler/in
snow [snəʊ] Schnee; **snowy** verschneit
so [səʊ] **1.** darum, deshalb; **2.** also; **3.** so; **I don't think so.** Das glaube/finde ich nicht. **if so** wenn ja; **I think so.** Ich glaube (ja). **so-called** so genannte(r, s); **so do/will/am/... I** ich auch; **so far** bis jetzt, bisher; **so that** damit, sodass; **so to speak** sozusagen; **So what?** Na und?
soaking wet [ˌsəʊkɪŋ ˈwet] völlig durchnässt, klatschnass
soap [səʊp] Seife
social [ˈsəʊʃl] gesellschaftlich; sozial; Sozial-; gesellig; **socialism** [ˈsəʊʃəlɪzm] Sozialismus; **socialist** [ˈsəʊʃəlɪst] **1.** Sozialist/in; **2.** sozialistisch; **social science** Sozialwissenschaften; **social security** [ˌsəʊʃl sɪˈkjʊərətɪ] soziale Sicherheit; Sozialhilfe; **society** [səˈsaɪətɪ] Gesellschaft; Verein, Arbeitsgemeinschaft
sock [sɒk] Socke, Strumpf
soda [ˈsəʊdə] Limonade, Cola; Soda(wasser)
sofa [ˈsəʊfə] Sofa
soft drink [sɒft] alkoholfreies Getränk
soil [sɔɪl] (Mutter-)Boden, Erde
solar [ˈsəʊlə] Solar-
soldier [ˈsəʊldʒə] Soldat/in
solution (to) [səˈluːʃn] (Auf-)lösung (für
solve [sɒlv] *(Aufgabe, Problem)* lösen
some [sʌm, səm] **1.** einige, ein paar; **2.** etwas; **3.** irgendein(e); **some more** noch einige/etwas; **somebody/someone** jemand; **somehow** irgendwie; **something** etwas; **sometimes** manchmal; **somewhere** irgendwo(hi
son [sʌn] Sohn
song [sɒŋ] Lied
soon [suːn] bald; **sooner or later** frühe oder später
sore [sɔː] wund, rau, entzündet; **sore throat** Halsschmerzen, Halsweh
sorry [ˈsɒrɪ]: **(I'm) sorry.** Entschuldigung! Tut mir Leid! **Sorry?** Wie bitte? **Sorry I'm late.** Entschuldige Sie, dass ich zu spät komme. **feel sorr (for)** bedauern; bereuen

sort [sɔ:t] **1.** Sorte, Art; **2.** sortieren
soul [səʊl] Seele
sound [saʊnd] **1.** Laut, Ton; Klang; **2.** klingen, sich anhören
soup [su:p] Suppe
source [sɔ:s] Quelle
south (of) [saʊθ] **1.** südlich (von); **2.** Süd-; (nach) Süden; **southern** ['sʌðən] südlich, Süd-; **southerner** ['sʌðənə] Südstaatler/in; **southernmost** ['sʌðənməʊst] südlichste(r, s)
souvenir [ˌsu:və'nɪə] (Reise-)Andenken, Souvenir
space [speɪs] **1.** (Welt-)Raum; **2.** Platz
spaghetti [spə'getɪ] Spaghetti
Spain [speɪn] Spanien; **Spanish** **1.** spanisch; **2.** Spanisch; **the Spanish** die Spanier
spanner ['spænə] Schraubenschlüssel
speak (to) [spi:k] sprechen (mit); **speaker** Sprecher/in; **Amy Connor speaking.** (Hier) Amy Connor. *(am Telefon)*; **speak out** seine Meinung sagen, seine Stimme erheben
special ['speʃl] **1.** besondere(r, s); **2.** Sonder-; **specialist** ['speʃəlɪst] **1.** Spezialist/in; **2.** Spezial-
species ['spi:ʃi:z] Art, Spezies
specific [spə'sɪfɪk] spezifisch
spectacular [spek'tækjʊlə] sensationell, spektakulär
speculation [ˌspekjʊ'leɪʃn] Spekulation, Vermutung
speech [spi:tʃ] Rede
speed [spi:d] Geschwindigkeit
spell [spel] buchstabieren, schreiben; **spelling** Rechtschreibung, Orthographie
spend [spend] **1.** *(Geld)* ausgeben; **2.** *(Zeit)* verbringen
spider ['spaɪdə] Spinne
spirit ['spɪrɪt] Geist; **spiritual** ['spɪrɪtʃʊəl] Spiritual, geistliches Volkslied
spite: in spite of [ɪn 'spaɪt‿əv] trotz
spoil [spɔɪl] verderben, verschandeln; *(Kinder)* verwöhnen, verziehen
sponsored activity [ˌspɒnsəd‿æk'tɪvətɪ] *Aktivität um Geld für Wohltätigkeitszwecke zu sammeln*
spoon [spu:n] Löffel
sport [spɔ:t] Sport, Sportart; **do sport(s)** Sport treiben; **sporting grounds** (AE)/ **sports ground** (BE) Sportplatz
spray can ['spreɪ kæn] Sprühdose
spread [spred] (sich) ausbreiten
spring [sprɪŋ] Frühling, Frühjahr; **in (the) spring** im Frühling/Frühjahr
spy: I spy with my little eye. [spaɪ] Ich sehe was, was du nicht siehst.
square [skweə] **1.** Platz *(in einer Stadt)*; **2.** Quadrat; **3.** quadratisch, viereckig
squash [skwɒʃ] Squash
St. = Saint [snt] Sankt …
stadium ['steɪdɪəm] Stadion
stage [steɪdʒ] Bühne
stairs *(pl)* [steəz] Treppe(nstufen)
stamp [stæmp] (Brief-)Marke
stand [stænd] stehen; **stand up** **1.** aufstehen; **2.** aufrecht stehen; **stand still** still stehen
standard ['stændəd] **1.** Standard-, Normal-; **2.** Standard
stanza ['stænzə] Strophe *(eines Gedichts)*
star [stɑ:] **1.** Stern; **2.** Star
stare (at) [steə] (an)starren
start [stɑ:t] **1.** Anfang, Beginn, Start; **2.** anfangen, beginnen (mit); **3.** starten; **4.** anspringen *(Motor)*; **5.** gründen; **start school** eingeschult werden; **starter** ['stɑ:tə] Starter/in
state [steɪt] **1.** Staat; **2.** Zustand; **State Department** (AE) (amerik.) Außenministerium
statement ['steɪtmənt] Aussage, Feststellung; Erklärung
station ['steɪʃn] Bahnhof; **police station** Polizeiwache, Polizeirevier; **(TV/ radio) station** Sendestation, (Fernseh-/Rundfunk-)Sender
statistics *(pl)* [stə'tɪstɪks] Statistik
statue ['stætʃu:] Statue
status ['steɪtəs] Status
stay [steɪ] **1.** bleiben; **stay on (at school)** weiter die Schule besuchen; **2.** übernachten, wohnen; **3.** Aufenthalt
steak [steɪk] Steak
steal [sti:l] stehlen
steam [sti:m] Dampf
steel [sti:l] Stahl
steering wheel ['stɪərɪŋ wi:l] Steuer(rad), Lenkrad
stem [stem] (Wort-)Stamm
step [step] **1.** Schritt, Stufe; **2.** treten
stereo ['sterɪəʊ] Stereo, Stereo-; **stereotype** ['sterɪəʊtaɪp] Stereotyp, Klischee
stick [stɪk] Stock; (trockener, abgebrochener) Zweig
still [stɪl] **1.** (immer) noch; **2.** trotzdem, dennoch; **sit/stand still** still sitzen/ stehen
stomach ['stʌmək] Magen, Bauch; **stomach ache** ['stʌmək‿eɪk] Magenschmerzen, Bauchschmerzen
stone [stəʊn] Stein
stop [stɒp] **1.** Bushaltestelle; **2.** aufhören; anhalten, stoppen
store [stɔ:] (AE) Geschäft
storey (BE), **story** (AE) ['stɔ:rɪ] Stock(werk), Etage
storm [stɔ:m] Sturm; Gewitter; **stormy** ['stɔ:mɪ] stürmisch
story ['stɔ:rɪ] Geschichte, Erzählung; **storyteller** ['stɔ:rɪˌtelə] (Geschichten-) Erzähler/in
straight [streɪt] gerade(wegs), direkt
strange [streɪndʒ] seltsam, sonderbar; fremd; **stranger** ['streɪndʒə] Fremde(r)
stream [stri:m] in Leistungsgruppen einteilen
street [stri:t] Straße; **in Sandfield Street** in der Sandfieldstraße; **in the street** auf der Straße
strengthen ['streŋθn] (ver)stärken; stärker werden
strenuous ['strenjʊəs] anstrengend
stress [stres] **1.** Stress; **2.** Betonung; **3.** betonen
strict [strɪkt] streng
strike [straɪk] Streik; **go/be on strike** in den Streik treten/streiken
strike [straɪk] schlagen *(Uhr)*
strong [strɒŋ] **1.** stark; **2.** kräftig
structure ['strʌktʃə] Struktur
struggle (with/for) ['strʌgl] **1.** Kampf (mit/für, um); Bemühen (um); **2.** kämpfen, sich abmühen, sich herumschlagen
student ['stju:dənt] Student/in; AE *auch:* Schüler/in
studio ['stju:dɪəʊ] Studio, Senderaum
study (for an exam) ['stʌdɪ] (für eine Prüfung) lernen, sich vorbereiten; studieren
stuff [stʌf] (infml) Zeug, Kram
stupid ['stju:pɪd] dumm, blöd
style [staɪl] **1.** Stil, Mode; **2.** Art, Weise
subject ['sʌbdʒɪkt] (Schul-)Fach
submarine [ˌsʌbmə'ri:n] Unterseeboot
suburb ['sʌbɜ:b] Vorstadt, Vorort, Randbezirk
subway ['sʌbweɪ] (AE) U-Bahn
succeed (in) [sək'si:d] Erfolg haben (in, bei)
success [sək'ses] Erfolg; **successful** [sək'sesfəl] erfolgreich
such [sʌtʃ] solch, so (ein/e), so; **such as** (wie) zum Beispiel; **such is life** so ist das Leben
sudden(ly) ['sʌdn(lɪ)] plötzlich
suffer (from) ['sʌfə] ertragen; leiden
suffix ['sʌfɪks] Nachsilbe, Suffix
suffragette [ˌsʌfrə'dʒet] Stimmrechtlerin, Suffragette
sugar ['ʃʊgə] Zucker
suggest [sə'dʒest] vorschlagen; **suggestion** [sə'dʒestʃn] Vorschlag, Anregung
suit [su:t] *(jm)* stehen
suitable ['su:təbl] passend, geeignet
suitcase ['su:tkeɪs] Koffer
sum up [ˌsʌm‿'ʌp] zusammenfassen
summarize ['sʌməraɪz] zusammenfassen; **summary** ['sʌmərɪ] Zusammenfassung
summer ['sʌmə] Sommer; **in (the) summer** im Sommer
summit ['sʌmɪt] Gipfel
sun [sʌn] Sonne; **sunshine** Sonne(nschein); **sunny** sonnig
Sunday ['sʌndɪ] Sonntag
super ['su:pə] fantastisch, toll; Super-; **supermarket** ['su:pəˌmɑ:kɪt] Supermarkt

superstitious [ˌsu:pəˈstɪʃəs] abergläubisch
supervisor [ˈsu:pəvaɪzə] Vorgesetzte(r), Abteilungsleiter/in; Aufseher/in
supper [ˈsʌpə] Abendessen
supply [səˈplaɪ] **1.** Versorgung; Vorrat; Lieferung; **2.** (be)liefern, versorgen
support [səˈpɔ:t] **1.** Unterstützung; **2.** unterstützen; befürworten; ernähren; **supporter** Unterstützer/in, Befürworter/in; Anhänger/in *(eines Sportvereins usw.)*
suppose [səˈpəʊz] annehmen, vermuten; **be supposed to** [səˈpəʊst tə] sollen (angeblich); (tun) sollen
supreme [sʊˈpri:m] oberste(r/s)
sure [ʃʊə, ʃɔ:] sicher, gewiss; **be sure of oneself** selbstsicher sein; **be sure to** bestimmt/sicherlich (tun); **make sure** sich vergewissern; darauf achten, daür sorgen (dass); **Sure!** Sicher! Klar! Natürlich! **sure enough** tatsächlich; **surely** sicherlich
surge [sɜ:dʒ] Welle
surprise [səˈpraɪz] **1.** Überraschung; **2.** überraschen; **surprised** überrascht; **surprising** erstaunlich, überraschend; **surprisingly** überraschenderweise; **not surprisingly** wie zu erwarten war, wie erwartet
surrender (to sb) [səˈrendə] sich ergeben, kapitulieren
surround [səˈraʊnd] umgeben
survey [ˈsɜ:veɪ] Umfrage, Untersuchung
survive [səˈvaɪv] überleben
sweets [swi:ts] (BE) Süßigkeiten, Bonbons
swim [ˈswɪm] schwimmen; **go for a swim** schwimmen gehen; **swimming-pool** [ˈswɪmɪŋ pu:l] Schwimmbad; Schwimmbecken
switch [swɪtʃ] **1.** Schalter; **2.** (um)schalten; **switch on/off** ein-/ausschalten
sword [sɔ:d] Schwert
syllable [ˈsɪləbl] Silbe
symbol [ˈsɪmbl] Symbol, Zeichen; **symbolic** [sɪmˈbɒlɪk] symbolisch; **symbolize** [ˈsɪmbəlaɪz] symbolisieren
symphony [ˈsɪmfənɪ] Sinfonie
synonym [ˈsɪnənɪm] Synonym, bedeutungsähnliches Wort
system [ˈsɪstəm] System; Plan, Ordnung

T

table [ˈteɪbl] Tisch; Tabelle; **table-tennis** Tischtennis
tablet [ˈtæblɪt] Tablette
tailor [ˈteɪlə] Schneider/in
take [teɪk] **1.** (mit)nehmen; (hin)bringen; **2.** haben, gebraucht werden mit; **3.** dauern; **it takes** es dauert; man braucht; **it takes me (an hour)** ich brauche (eine Stunde); **take a chance** ein Risiko eingehen, es darauf ankommen lassen; **take action** etwas/Schritte unternehmen, Maßnahmen ergreifen; **take an exam** eine Prüfung ablegen, machen; **take off** *(Kleidung)* ausziehen; **take over** an sich reißen, Besitz ergreifen von; übernehmen; **take part (in)** teilnehmen (an), mitmachen (bei); **take photos/pictures** fotografieren, Fotos/Bilder machen; **take place** stattfinden; **take sides** Partei ergreifen; **take the dog for a walk** mit dem Hund rausgehen; **take time** Zeit kosten; **take to the streets** auf die Straße gehen; **What size do you take?** Welche Größe hast du/haben Sie?
talented [ˈtæləntɪd] talentiert
talk [tɔ:k] **1.** Vortrag, Referat, Rede; **2.** sprechen, reden; sich unterhalten
tall [tɔ:l] groß; hoch
tape [teɪp] (Ton-, Magnet-)Band; (Klebe-) Band
task [tɑ:sk] Aufgabe
taste (of) [teɪst] kosten; schmecken (nach)
tax [tæks] Steuer
taxi [ˈtæksɪ] Taxi
tea [ti:] Tee; **have tea** (BE) Abendbrot essen, zu Abend essen; **make tea** Tee kochen; **teabag** Teebeutel
teach [ti:tʃ] unterrichten, lehren, beibringen; **teacher** [ˈti:tʃə] Lehrer/in
team [ti:m] Team, Mannschaft, Gruppe
tear [tɪə] Träne
technology [tekˈnɒlədʒɪ] Technologie, Technik
teenager [ˈti:neɪdʒə] Teenager, Jugendliche(r)
telegraph pole [ˈtelɪgrɑ:f ˌpəʊl] Telegrafenmast
(tele)phone [ˈtelɪfəʊn] **1.** Telefon; **2.** anrufen; **answer the telephone** ans Telefon gehen; **be on the telephone** am Telefon sein, gerade telefonieren; **make a telephone call** einen Anruf machen, ein Telefongespräch führen
television [ˈtelɪˌvɪʒn, ˌtelɪˈvɪʒn] Fernsehen, Fernseher; **on television** im Fernsehen; **watch television** fernsehen
tell [tel] **1.** sagen, nennen; **2.** erzählen, berichten; **3.** erkennen; wissen; **tell the way** den Weg beschreiben
temperature [ˈtemprətʃə] Temperatur; Fieber
temple [ˈtempl] Tempel
temporary [ˈtempərərɪ] vorläufig, vorübergehend, (zeitlich) begrenzt
tennis [ˈtenɪs] Tennis
tense [tens] (an)gespannt, nervös; **tension** Spannung(en)
tent [tent] Zelt
term [tɜ:m] **1.** Ausdruck, Bezeichnung; **term of abuse** [ˌtɜ:m‿əv‿əˈbju:s] Schimpfwort; **2.** Trimester
terraced house [ˌterəst ˈhaʊs] (BE) Reihenhaus
terrible [ˈterəbl] schrecklich, furchtbar
terrified [ˈterɪfaɪd]: **be terrified (of)** entsetzt sein, schreckliche Angst haben (vor)
territory [ˈterətrɪ] Territorium, (Hoheits-, Staats-)Gebiet
terror [ˈterə] Terror; **terrorist** [ˈterərɪst] Terrorist/in; **terrorize** [ˈterəraɪz] terrorisieren, einschüchtern
test [test] Test, Prüfung, Klassenarbeit; **do a test** eine Arbeit schreiben, eine Prüfung machen
text [tekst] Text
textiles [ˈtekstaɪlz] Textilien
than [ðæn, ðən] als *(nach Komparativ)*
thank [θæŋk] danken, sich bedanken (bei); **Thank you.** Danke (schön). **Thank you very much.** Vielen Dank. **Thanks.** Danke (schön).
Thanksgiving Day [ˌθæŋksˈgɪvɪŋ] (AE) *Erntedankfeier/Familienfest im November*
that [ðæt, ðət] **1.** der/die/das (da), jene(r, s) (dort); **2.** dass; **3.** der/die/das *(Relativpronomen);* **(not) that bad** (nicht) so schlimm; **so that** damit, sodass; **that is (i.e.)** das heißt (d. h.)
the [ðə, ðɪ] der, die, das; die *(Plural)*; **the ..., the ...** je ..., umso/desto ...
theatre [ˈθɪətə] Theater
their [ðeə] ihr, ihre; **theirs** [ðeəz] ihre(r, s
them [ðem, ðəm] ihnen, sie; **themselves** [ðəmˈselvz] sich (selbst)
theme [θi:m] Thema, Leitgedanke
then [ðen] **1.** dann, danach; **2.** zu der Zeit, damals
there [ðeə] **1.** da, dort; **2.** dahin, dorthin; **here and there** hie und da; **over there** dort drüben, da drüben; **there is/are** da ist/sind, es gibt
therefore [ˈðeəfɔ:] deshalb, deswegen
thermometer [θəˈmɒmɪtə] Thermometer
these [ði:z] diese, die (hier)
they [ðeɪ] **1.** sie; **2.** man
thick [θɪk] **1.** dick; **2.** dicht
thief, *pl* **thieves** [θi:f, θi:vz] Dieb/in
thin [θɪn] dünn
thing [θɪŋ] Ding, Sache
think [θɪŋk] meinen, finden, glauben, denken; **be thought to** sollen (angeblich); **I don't think so.** Das finde/glaube ich nicht. **I think so.** Ich glaube (ja). **think about sth** über etwas nachdenken; **think of** denken an; halten von; **think up** (sich) ausdenken; **What do you think about ... ?** Was hältst du von ...? Wie findest du ...?

third [θɜ:d] Drittel
thirst [θɜ:st] Durst; **thirsty** ['θɜ:stɪ] durstig; **be thirsty** Durst haben
this [ðɪs] diese(r, s), der/die/das (hier); **This is how you do it.** So/Auf diese Weise macht man es; **this morning** heute Morgen
thoroughly ['θʌrəlɪ] total
those [ðəʊz] die/diese (da), jene (dort)
though [ðəʊ] **1.** *(conj)* obwohl; **2.** *(adv)* jedoch, (aber) doch
thought [θɔ:t] Gedanke; Einfall; **thoughtful** nachdenklich
threat [θret] (Be-)Drohung; **threaten** (be)drohen
throat [θrəʊt] Hals, Kehle; **a sore throat** Halsschmerzen, Halsweh
through [θru:] durch, hindurch; **throughout** [θru:'aʊt] während des/der ganzen; überall in
throw [θrəʊ] werfen; **throw away** wegwerfen
thumb [θʌm] Daumen
thunder ['θʌndə] Donner
Thursday ['θɜ:zdɪ] Donnerstag
ticket ['tɪkɪt] **1.** Eintrittskarte; Fahrkarte, Fahrschein; **ticket inspector** [ɪn'spektə] Kontrolleur/in; **2.** Strafmandat, -zettel
tidy ['taɪdɪ] ordentlich, aufgeräumt; **tidy up** aufräumen
tie [taɪ] Krawatte, Schlips
tiger ['taɪgə] Tiger
tight [taɪt] eng (anliegend), stramm
tilde ['tɪldə] Tilde
till [tɪl] bis; **not till six** erst um sechs, nicht vor sechs
time [taɪm] **1.** Zeit; **have a nice time** eine schöne Zeit/viel Spaß haben; **Have a good time.** Viel Spaß! Viel Vergnügen! **high time** höchste Zeit; **What time is it?** Wie spät ist es? **timeless** ['taɪmləs] zeitlos; **timetable** (BE) Fahrplan; Stundenplan; **2. time(s)** Mal; -mal; **for the first time** zum ersten Mal
tin [tɪn] (BE) Dose, Büchse
tin mine ['tɪn maɪn] Zinnmine, Zinnbergwerk
tired ['taɪəd] müde; **be tired of** satt haben
title ['taɪtl] Titel
to [tu:, tʊ, tə] **1.** zu, nach, in; **2.** um zu; **give to sb** jm geben; **happen to** passieren, geschehen mit; **I've been to ...** Ich bin in ... gewesen. **listen to** (sich) anhören; **next to** neben; **quarter to ten** Viertel vor zehn; **speak to** sprechen mit; **talk to** sprechen mit; **Try to come.** Versuche zu kommen. **write to** schreiben an
toast [təʊst] Toast
tobacco [tə'bækəʊ] Tabak
today [tə'deɪ] heute; **today's paper** die heutige Zeitung, die Zeitung von heute
together [tə'geðə] zusammen
toilet ['tɔɪlɪt] Toilette
tolerance ['tɒlərəns] Toleranz; **tolerant (towards)** ['tɒlərənt] tolerant (gegenüber)
tomato, *pl* **tomatoes** [tə'mɑ:təʊ] Tomate
tomorrow [tə'mɒrəʊ] morgen; **tomorrow morning** morgen früh; **tomorrow's paper** die morgige Zeitung, die Zeitung von morgen; **the day after tomorrow** übermorgen
tone [təʊn] Ton, Klang; Stimmung
tonight [tə'naɪt] heute Abend, heute Nacht
tonne [tʌn] Tonne *(Gewicht)*
too [tu:] auch; **too small** zu klein
tool [tu:l] Werkzeug
tooth, *pl* **teeth** [tu:θ, ti:θ] Zahn; **toothbrush** ['tu:θbrʌʃ] Zahnbürste; **toothpaste** ['tu:θpeɪst] Zahnpasta, Zahncreme
top [tɒp] **1.** Spitze; **2.** Kopfende, oberes Ende; **on top (of)** oben, zuoberst (auf); **top speed** [ˌtɒp 'spi:d] Höchstgeschwindigkeit; **top ten** Top Ten
topic ['tɒpɪk] Thema
total ['təʊtl] gesamt; völlig, total
touch [tʌtʃ] berühren, anfassen
tough [tʌf] zäh; stark; robust
tour [tʊə] (Rund-)Reise, (Rund-)Fahrt, Tour; **go on a bus tour** eine Bus(rund)fahrt machen; **go on a guided tour** eine Führung (mit)machen; **tourism** ['tʊərɪzm] Tourismus, Fremdenverkehr; **tourist** ['tʊərɪst] Tourist/in
toward (AE), **towards** (BE) [tə'wɔ:dz] auf ... zu, in Richtung auf; **towards sb** gegenüber jm
towel ['taʊəl] Handtuch
tower ['taʊə] Turm
town [taʊn] Stadt; **in town** in der (Innen-)Stadt
toy [tɔɪ] Spielzeug
track [træk] (Renn-)Bahn, Rennstrecke, Piste
trade (with) [treɪd] **1.** Handel (mit); **Trade (and Industry) Secretary** (brit) Wirtschaftsminister/in; **trade union** Gewerkschaft; **2. trade (with)** Geschäfte machen, handeln (mit); **trader** Händler/in
tradition [trə'dɪʃn] Tradition; **traditional** [trə'dɪʃnl] traditionell
traffic ['træfɪk] Verkehr; **traffic jam** ['træfɪk dʒæm] (Verkehrs-)Stau; **traffic lights** *(pl)* (Verkehrs-)Ampel
tragedy ['trædʒədɪ] Tragödie; **tragic** tragisch
trail [treɪl] Pfad; Weg; Wanderweg; Spur
train [treɪn] (Eisenbahn-)Zug; **by train** mit dem Zug; **on the train** im Zug
train [treɪn] trainieren, ausbilden; **trainee** [treɪ'ni:] Auszubildende(r); **training** Ausbildung, Schulung; Training
tram [træm] Straßenbahn
transcontinental [ˌtrænzˌkɒntɪ'nentl] transkontinental
transcription [træn'skrɪpʃn] (phonetische) Umschrift
transform [træns'fɔ:m] umwandeln, verwandeln; **transformation** [ˌtrænsfə'meɪʃn] Veränderung, Verwandlung
translate [trænz'leɪt] übersetzen; **translation** [trænz'leɪʃn] Übersetzung
transport ['trænspɔ:t] **1.** (BE) Transport, Verkehrsmittel; **(public) transportation** [ˌpʌblɪk ˌtrænspɔ:'teɪʃn] (AE) (öffentliche) Verkehrsmittel; **transportation center** (AE) Verkehrsknotenpunkt; **2.** befördern, transportieren
trap [træp] Falle
travel ['trævl] **1.** (das) Reisen; **2.** reisen, fahren; **travel agency** ['trævl‿eɪdʒənsɪ] Reisebüro; **space travel** ['speɪs ˌtrævl] Raumfahrt; **traveller** Reisende(r)
treasure ['treʒə] Schatz, Kostbarkeit
Treasury ['treʒərɪ] (BE) (brit.) Finanzministerium; **Treasury Department** (brit./amerik.) Finanzministerium
treat [tri:t] behandeln; **treatment** Behandlung
tree [tri:] Baum
trend [trend] Trend
trial ['traɪl] (Straf-)Prozess, Gerichtsverfahren
tribe [traɪb] (Volks-)Stamm
trick [trɪk] **1.** Kunststück; **2.** Trick; **play a trick** einen Streich spielen; **tricky** schwierig, heikel
trip [trɪp] Reise, Ausflug; **go on a trip; take a trip** (AE) eine Reise/Fahrt/einen Ausflug machen
trolley ['trɒlɪ] (Servier-, Einkaufs-) Wagen
trouble ['trʌbl] Schwierigkeiten; **get into trouble** in Schwierigkeiten geraten; Probleme bekommen; **give trouble** Schwierigkeiten machen, Probleme bereiten
trousers *(pl)* ['traʊzəz] (lange) Hose(n)
truck [trʌk] LKW
true [tru:] wahr; **come true** wahr werden; **truly** wahrhaftig, wirklich, tatsächlich
trumpet ['trʌmpɪt] Trompete
trunk [trʌŋk] (Baum-)Stamm
truth [tru:θ] Wahrheit
try [traɪ] versuchen, probieren; **try and do sth** versuchen etwas zu tun; **try on** anprobieren; **try-out** ['traɪaʊt] Probe(vorstellung)
T-shirt ['ti:ʃɜ:t] T-Shirt
tube [tju:b] (BE) *(Londoner)* U-Bahn

Tuesday [ˈtju:zdɪ] Dienstag
tunnel [ˈtʌnl] **1.** Tunnel; **2.** Bergwerksstollen
turkey [ˈtɜ:kɪ] Truthahn
Turkey [ˈtɜ:kɪ] Türkei
turn [tɜ:n] **1.** abbiegen, einbiegen; **2.** werden; **3.** drehen, wenden; **It's your turn.** Du bist an der Reihe. **turn down** herunterdrehen, leiser/kleiner stellen; **turn out** ausfallen, werden; sich herausstellen, sich erweisen; **turn round** (sich) (um)drehen; **turn to** sich wenden an, sich zuwenden
TV [ˌti:ˈvi:] = **television** Fernsehen, Fernseher; **on TV** im Fernsehen; **watch TV** fernsehen
twice [twaɪs] zweimal
type [taɪp] **1.** tippen, mit der Maschine schreiben; **typewriter** Schreibmaschine; **2.** Typ, Art, Sorte
typical (of) [ˈtɪpɪkl] typisch (für)

U

ugliness [ˈʌglɪnəs] Hässlichkeit; **ugly** [ˈʌglɪ] hässlich
unable [ʌnˈeɪbl] unfähig, untalentiert
unacceptable [ˌʌnəkˈseptəbl] inakzeptabel
unanswerable [ʌnˈɑ:nsərəbl] unbeantwortbar
unavoidable [ˌʌnəˈvɔɪdəbl] unvermeidbar
unbelievable [ˌʌnbɪˈli:vəbl] unglaublich
unborn [ˌʌnˈbɔ:n] ungeboren
unbreakable [ʌnˈbreɪkəbl] unzerbrechlich
uncle [ˈʌŋkl] Onkel
under [ˈʌndə] unter; **underclass** [ˈʌndəklɑ:s] Unterschicht; **Underground** [ˈʌndəgraʊnd] (BE) Untergrundbahn, U-Bahn; **by Underground** (BE) mit der U-Bahn
underline [ˌʌndəˈlaɪn] unterstreichen
underprivileged [ˌʌndəˈprɪvɪlɪdʒd] schlechter gestellt
understand (by) [ˌʌndəˈstænd] verstehen (unter), begreifen; **understandable** [ˌʌndəˈstændəbl] verständlich; **understanding** Verständnis
underwater [ˌʌndəˈwɔ:tə] **1.** Unterwasser-; **2.** unter Wasser
undress [ˌʌnˈdres] (sich) ausziehen
undrinkable [ˌʌnˈdrɪŋkəbl] nicht trinkbar, ungenießbar
uneatable [ˌʌnˈi:təbl] nicht essbar, ungenießbar
unemployable [ˌʌnɪmˈplɔɪəbl] nicht vermittelbar; **unemployed** [ˌʌnɪmˈplɔɪd] arbeitslos; **unemployment** Arbeitslosigkeit
unexplainable [ˌʌnɪkˈspleɪnəbl] unerklärlich, unerklärbar
unfair [ʌnˈfeə] unfair, ungerecht; **unfairness** [ʌnˈfeənəs] Ungerechtigkeit
unfamiliar [ˌʌnfəˈmɪlɪə] unbekannt, nicht vertraut, ungewohnt
unforgettable [ˌʌnfəˈgetəbl] unvergesslich
unfortunately [ʌnˈfɔ:tʃnətlɪ] leider, unglücklicherweise
unfriendliness [ʌnˈfrendlɪnəs] Unfreundlichkeit; **unfriendly** unfreundlich
unhappiness [ʌnˈhæpɪnəs] Unglück(seligkeit) **unhappy** [ʌnˈhæpɪ] unglücklich, traurig
unhealthy [ʌnˈhelθɪ] ungesund
uniform [ˈju:nɪfɔ:m] Uniform
unimaginable [ˌʌnɪˈmædʒɪnəbl] unvorstellbar
union [ˈju:nɪən] Gewerkschaft; Union, Einigkeit, Vereinigung
unit [ˈju:nɪt] **1.** Lektion; **2.** Einheit
united [ju:ˈnaɪtɪd] vereinigt; **United Kingdom** [ju:ˌnaɪtɪd ˈkɪŋdəm] Vereinigtes Königreich; **the United Nations** [ju:ˌnaɪtɪd ˈneɪʃnz] die Vereinten Nationen (UNO); **United States of America** Vereinigte Staaten von Amerika
universe [ˈju:nɪvɜ:s] Universum
university [ˌju:nɪˈvɜ:sətɪ] Universität, Hochschule
unknown [ˌʌnˈnəʊn] unbekannt
unless [ʌnˈles] wenn nicht, außer wenn, es sei denn (, dass)
unlike [ʌnˈlaɪk] anders als, im Gegensatz zu
unlikely [ʌnˈlaɪklɪ]: **be unlikely to do sth** etwas wahrscheinlich nicht tun
unload [ʌnˈləʊd] ausladen, abladen
unlucky day [ʌnˈlʌkɪ] Unglückstag
unnecessary [ʌnˈnesəsrɪ] unnötig
unpack [ˌʌnˈpæk] auspacken
unpronounceable [ˌʌnprəˈnaʊnsəbl] nicht aussprechbar
unsingable [ʌnˈsɪŋəbl] unsingbar, nicht singbar
unsinkable [ʌnˈsɪŋkəbl] unsinkbar
unskilled [ˌʌnˈskɪld] ungelernt, unerfahren; ungeschickt
unthinkable [ʌnˈθɪŋkəbl] undenkbar
untidy [ʌnˈtaɪdɪ] unordentlich, unaufgeräumt
until [ʌnˈtil, ənˈtɪl] bis; **not until (six)** erst um (sechs), nicht vor (sechs)
untouched [ʌnˈtʌtʃt] unberührt
unusual [ʌnˈju:ʒʊəl] un-, außergewöhnlich
up [ʌp] herauf, hinauf; **get up** aufstehen; **put up** aufbauen, aufstellen; aufhängen, anbringen; **stand up** aufstehen; aufrecht stehen; **up and down the country** landauf, landab; **up there** dort oben; **up to** bis (zu); **up-to-date** aktuell, zeitgemäß
upset (about) [ʌpˈset] **1.** durcheinander, aufgeregt, betrübt (wegen); **2. upset** aus der Fassung bringen, ärgern, beunruhigen
upside down [ˌʌpsaɪd ˈdaʊn] verkehrt (herum), mit dem Kopf nach unten
upstairs [ˌʌpˈsteəz] oben; nach oben
urban [ˈɜ:bən] städtisch, Stadt-
us [ʌs] uns
use **1.** [ju:s] Benutzung, Gebrauch; **2.** [ju:z] benutzen, verwenden; **get used to** sich angewöhnen; **I used to do** früher habe/bin ich immer ...; **useful** [ˈju:sfəl] nützlich, brauchbar; **useless** [ˈju:sləs] nutzlos, unnütz
usual [ˈju:ʒʊəl] üblich, gewöhnlich; **usually** [ˈju:ʒʊəlɪ] normalerweise, gewöhnlich

V

vacation [vəˈkeɪʃn] (AE) Ferien, Urlaub
vacuum [ˈvækjʊəm] Vakuum, luftleerer Raum
valley [ˈvælɪ] Tal
value [ˈvælju] **1.** Wert; **2.** (hoch) schätzen
variety [vəˈraɪətɪ] Vielfalt; Abwechslung; Sorte; Variante; **various** [ˈveərɪəs] verschieden(artig); verschiedene, mehrere
vast [vɑ:st] weit, gewaltig, riesig
vegetables [ˈvedʒtəblz] Gemüse; **vegetarian** [ˌvedʒəˈteərɪən] **1.** Vegetarier/in; **2.** vegetarisch
vehicle [ˈvi:ɪkl] Fahrzeug
verse [vɜ:s] Strophe; Vers
version [ˈvɜ:ʃn, ˈvɜ:ʒn] Version, Fassung
very [ˈverɪ] sehr; **(like) very much** sehr (gern mögen)
vet [vet] Tierarzt/-ärztin
veto [ˈvi:təʊ] Veto
via [ˈvaɪə] über, per, via
vice(-president) [ˌvaɪsˈprezɪdənt] Vize(präsident/in)
victim [ˈvɪktɪm] Opfer
victory [ˈvɪktrɪ] Sieg
video [ˈvɪdɪəʊ] Video
Vietnam [vɪetˈnæm] Vietnam; **Vietnamese** [vjetnəˈmi:z] **1.** Vietnamese/in; **2.** vietnamesisch
view [vju:] **1.** Aussicht, Blick **2.** Ansicht; **viewer** Zuschauer/in
Viking [ˈvaɪkɪŋ] Wikinger/in
village [ˈvɪlɪdʒ] Dorf
violence [ˈvaɪələns] Gewalt, Gewalttätigkeit; **violent** gewaltsam, gewalttätig; heftig
virus [ˈvaɪərəs] Virus, Krankheitserreger
visit [ˈvɪzɪt] **1.** Besuch; **on a visit** bei einem Besuch; **2.** besuchen, besichtigen; **visitor** [ˈvɪzɪtə] Besucher/in, Gast
vocabulary item [vəˈkæbjʊlərɪ‿aɪtəm] Vokabel
vocational [vəˈkeɪʃnl] beruflich, Berufs-, berufsbezogen
voice [vɔɪs] Stimme

volleyball ['vɒlɪbɔ:l] Volleyball
volume ['vɒlju:m] Lautstärke; Volumen
voluntary ['vɒləntrɪ] freiwillige(r/s); **volunteer** [ˌvɒlən'tɪə] sich freiwillig melden, freiwillig tun
vote [vəʊt] Abstimmung; Stimme *(bei Wahlen)*; Stimmrecht; Wahlrecht; **vote for** (ab)stimmen für, wählen; **voter** Wähler/in
vowel ['vaʊəl] Vokal, Selbstlaut

W

wages *(pl)* ['weɪdʒɪz] (Arbeits-)Lohn
wag(g)on ['wægən] Pferdewagen, Planwagen
wait (for) [weɪt] warten (auf); **Wait a minute.** Einen Augenblick! Moment mal!
waiter ['weɪtə] Kellner, Ober
wake (up) [weɪk] **1.** aufwachen; **2.** (auf-)wecken
Wales [weɪlz] Wales
walk [wɔ:k] **1.** Spaziergang; (Spazier-, Wander-)Weg; **go for a walk** spazieren gehen, einen Spaziergang machen; **take the dog for a walk** mit dem Hund rausgehen, mit dem Hund spazieren gehen; **2.** (zu Fuß) gehen, laufen; **go walking** wandern; **walk on** weitergehen
wall [wɔ:l] Wand; Mauer
wallet ['wɒlɪt] Brieftasche
want (to) [wɒnt] wollen, mögen
war [wɔ:] Krieg
warden ['wɔ:dn] (BE) Herbergsvater/-mutter
wardrobe ['wɔ:drəʊb] Kleiderschrank
warm [wɔ:m] warm; **global warming** [ˌgləʊbl 'wɔ:mɪŋ] globale Erwärmung
warn [wɔ:n] warnen, ermahnen; **warning** Warnung
wash [wɒʃ] (sich) waschen; **have a wash** sich waschen; **wash the dishes** (das Geschirr) spülen, abwaschen; **washable** ['wɒʃəbl] waschbar; **washing line** Wäscheleine; **washing machine** ['wɒʃɪŋ məʃi:n] Waschmaschine; **washroom** Waschraum
waste [weɪst] *(sing)* **1.** Verschwendung; **2.** Abfall, Abfälle; **waste disposal** [dɪs'pəʊzl] Abfallentsorgung; **waste management** Abfallwirtschaft, -beseitigung; **3.** verschwenden; **wasteland** Ödland, Einöde
watch [wɒtʃ] **1.** (Armband-)Uhr; **My watch is wrong.** Meine Uhr geht falsch. **watchmaker** ['wɒtʃˌmeɪkə] Uhrmacher/in; **2.** ansehen, beobachten; **3.** zuschauen; **watch TV** fernsehen
water ['wɔ:tə] **1.** Wasser; **2.** bewässern, gießen; tränken; **water colour** Wasserfarbe; **waterfall** Wasserfall; **watering can** Gießkanne; **water power** Wasserkraft; **waterway** Wasserstraße, -weg; **watery** wässerig
wave [weɪv] Welle
way [weɪ] **1.** Weg; **2.** Art und Weise; **3.** Eigenart; **a long way** ein weiter Weg; weit (entfernt); **by the way** übrigens, nebenbei (bemerkt); **in different ways** auf verschiedene Weise(n); **in the way** im Weg; **my way** in meine Richtung; **on my way (to)** unterwegs (nach); **tell the way** den Weg beschreiben; **the other way round** andersherum; **This is the way you do it.** So/Auf diese Weise macht man es. **way of life** [ˌweɪ‿əv 'laɪf] Lebensart, Lebensweise
we [wi:] wir
weak [wi:k] schwach; **weaken** (ab)schwächen; schwächer werden; **weakness** Schwäche
wealth [welθ] Reichtum, Wohlstand; **wealthy** wohlhabend, reich
weapon ['wepən] Waffe
wear [weə] tragen, anhaben; **wear out** sich abnutzen, verschleißen
weather ['weðə] Wetter; **weather forecast** Wettervorhersage
wedding ['wedɪŋ] Hochzeit
Wednesday ['wenzdɪ] Mittwoch
week [wi:k] Woche; **Weekday** ['wi:kdeɪ] Wochentag, Werktag; **weekend** [ˌwi:k'end, 'wi:kend] Wochenende; **at the weekend** am Wochenende
weigh [weɪ] wiegen; **weightlifting** Gewichtheben
welcome (to) ['welkəm] willkommen (in); **You're welcome.** Bitte (sehr). Nicht zu danken.
welfare ['welfeə] Wohlfahrts-; (AE) Sozialhilfe, Fürsorge
well [wel] **1.** gut; **2.** wohlauf, gesund; **3.** nun; also; **Well!** Na so was! Du meine Güte! Wirklich? **do well** gut sein *(in einem Fach)*; **well-known** (wohl) bekannt; **well-off** wohlhabend, reich
Welsh [welʃ] **1.** Waliser/in; **2.** walisisch; **3.** Walisisch
west (of) [west] **1.** westlich (von); **2.** West ; (nach) Westen, **western** ['westən] westlich, West-
West Indian [ˌwest 'ɪndɪən] **1.** Westinder/in; **2.** westindisch; **West Indies** [ˌwest‿'ɪndɪz] Westindische Inseln
wet [wet] nass; feucht
whale [weɪl] Wal
what [wɒt] was; was für ein(e); welche(r, s); **What a question!** Was für eine Frage! **What about ...?** Wie stehts/wärs mit ...? **What colour is ...?** Welche Farbe hat ...? **What date is it (today)?** Der Wievielte ist heute? **What do you call ...?** Wie nennt man ...? **What is it?** Was ist denn (los)? **What's it like?** Wie ist es? Wie sieht es aus? **What's wrong with Kevin?** Was fehlt/hat Kevin? **What time is it?** Wie spät ist es? **whatever** [wɒt'evə] was (auch) immer; **So what?** Na und?
wheat [wi:t] Weizen
wheel [wi:l] Rad; **steering wheel** Steuer(rad), Lenkrad; **wheelchair** Rollstuhl
when [wen] **1.** wann; **2.** wenn; **3.** als; **whenever** [wen'evə] immer wenn, wann (auch) immer
where [weə] wo, wohin; **Where are you from?** Wo kommst du her? **wherever** [ˌweər'evə] wo(hin) (auch) immer
whereas [ˌweə'ræz] wohingegen, während
whether ['weðə] ob
which [wɪtʃ] **1.** welche(r, s); **Which of you?** Wer von euch? **2.** der, die, das, was *(Relativpronomen)*; **whichever** [wɪtʃevə] welche(r, s) (auch) immer
while [waɪl] während
whisky, whiskey ['wɪskɪ] Whisky
white [waɪt] weiß
who [hu:] **1.** wer; wem, wen; **2.** der, die; dem, den *(Relativpronomen)*; **whoever** [hu:'evə] wer/wen (auch) immer
whole [həʊl] ganz, gesamt; **the whole of** ganz
whom [hu:m] den, die, das; dem, der, dem; wen; wem
whose [hu:z] **1.** wessen; **Whose is it?** Wem gehört es? **2.** dessen, deren *(Relativpronomen)*
why [waɪ] warum, weshalb; **Why not ...?** Warum nicht ...? Könnten wir nicht ...?
wide [waɪd] breit; **widen** (sich) erweitern, breiter machen/werden; **width** [wɪdθ] Breite
wife, *pl* **wives** [waɪf, waɪvz] (Ehe-)Frau
wild [waɪld] wild; ausgelassen; stürmisch
will [wɪl] wird (tun)
willingly ['wɪlɪŋlɪ] bereit(willig); **willingness** ['wɪlɪŋnəs] Bereitschaft
win [wɪn] **1.** gewinnen; **2.** erringen, erwerben
wind [wɪnd] Wind; **windsurfing** ['wɪndˌsɜ:fɪŋ] Windsurfen; **windy** windig
window ['wɪndəʊ] Fenster, Schaufenster
wine [waɪn] Wein
winter ['wɪntə] Winter; **in (the) winter** im Winter
wire ['waɪə] Draht, Leitung; **wired** verdrahtet
wise [waɪz] weise, klug
wish [wɪʃ] **1.** wünschen; **2.** Wunsch
witch [wɪtʃ] Hexe

with [wɪð] **1.** mit; **2.** bei; **within** [wɪ'ðɪn] innerhalb, in; **without** [wɪ'ðaʊt] ohne; **do/go without** verzichten (auf), auskommen ohne
wolf, *pl* **wolves** [wʊlf, wʊlvz] Wolf
woman, *pl* **women** ['wʊmən, 'wɪmɪn] Frau
wonder ['wʌndə] **1.** Wunder, Verwunderung; **2.** sich fragen, gern wissen wollen; **wonderful** ['wʌndəfəl] wunderbar
won't [wəʊnt] = **will not** wird/will nicht
wood [wʊd] **1.** Holz; **2.** Wald
wool [wʊl] Wolle
word [wɜ:d] Wort; **have a word with sb** (kurz) mit jm sprechen
work [wɜ:k] **1.** Arbeit; **2.** arbeiten; in Betrieb sein, funktionieren; **at work** bei der Arbeit; **go to work** zur Arbeit gehen; **out of work** arbeitslos; **working-class** **1.** Arbeiterklasse; **2.** zur Arbeiterklasse gehörig; **working clothes** Arbeitskleidung; **workman** Arbeiter, Handwerker; **work out** herausfinden, herausarbeiten; ausrechnen; **workshop** Werkstatt
world [wɜ:ld] Welt; **in the world** auf der Welt; **why in the world?** Warum in aller Welt?; **world-wide** weltweit
worry ['wʌrɪ] **1.** Sorge, Unruhe; **2.** sich Sorgen machen; **Don't worry.** Mach dir keine Sorgen! Ist schon gut! **worried (about)** besorgt (um), beunruhigt (wegen); **worry oneself sick (about sb/sth)** vor Sorge (um jn/etwas) krank werden
worse (than) [wɜ:s] schlechter (als); schlimmer als; **(the) worst** [wɜ:st] **1.** (der/die/das) schlechteste, schlimmste; **2.** am schlechtesten, schlimmsten
worship ['wɜ:ʃɪp] (an)beten; seine Andacht verrichten
worth [wɜ:θ] wert; **worthless** wertlos
would [wʊd, wəd] würde(n) (tun); **I'd like = I would like** ich möchte; **I'd love (to)** ich hätte (liebend) gern; ich würde sehr gern
wound [wu:nd] verwunden, veletzen
wreck [rek] Wrack; **wrecker** ['rekə] Strandräuber
wrench [rentʃ] (AE) Schraubenschlüssel
write (to) [raɪt] schreiben (an); **write down** aufschreiben; **writer** Schriftsteller/in, Verfasser/in
wrong [rɒŋ] falsch; **be wrong** Unrecht haben; **go wrong** schief gehen; **My watch is wrong.** Meine Uhr geht falsch. **What's wrong with Kevin?** Was fehlt Kevin? Was hat Kevin?

Y

yard [jɑ:d] Hof; (AE *auch:*) Garten
year [jɪə] Jahr; **yearbook** Jahrbuch
yellow ['jeləʊ] gelb
yes [jes] ja
yesterday ['jestədɪ] gestern; **the day before yesterday** vorgestern; **yesterday's lesson** die gestrige Stunde die Stunde gestern
yet [jet] **1.** schon; **not ... yet** noch nicht; **2.** doch, dennoch
yoghurt ['jɒgət] Joghurt
you [ju:, jʊ, jə] **1.** du, ihr, Sie; **2.** man; **you know** weißt du, nämlich
young [jʌŋ] jung
your [jɔ:] dein(e); Ihr(e); euer, eure; **yours** [jɔ:z] deine(r, s); Ihre(r, s); eure(r, s); **Yours** dein(e); Ihr(e); euer/eure *(am Briefende);* **yourself** [jɔ:'self] dir/dich (selbst); **yourselves** [jɔ:'selvz] euch (selbst)
youth [ju:θ] **1.** Jugend; **2.** Jugendliche(r); **youth club** ['ju:θ klʌb] Jubendklub, Jugendzentrum; **youthful** jugendlich; jung; **youthfulness** ['ju:θfəlnəs] Jugendlichkeit; **youth hostel** ['ju:θ ˌhɒstl] Jugendherberge

Z

zebra ['zebrə] Zebra
zero ['zɪərəʊ] null
zombie ['zɒmbɪ] Zombie
zone [zəʊn] Zone
zoo [zu:] Zoo

Names

Family names

Abbott ['æbət]
Allyn ['ælɪn]
Bentley ['bentlɪ]
Boyer ['bwaɪeɪ, 'bɔɪə]
Bradford ['brædfəd]
Bronski ['brɒnskɪ]
Brooks [brʊks]
Campbell ['kæmbl]
Clarke [klɑ:k]
Colt [kəʊlt, kɒlt]
Costner ['kɒstnə]
Crudup ['kru:dʌp]
Cummings ['kʌmɪŋz]
Dodge [dɒdʒ]
Douglass ['dʌgləs]
Dunbar ['dʌnbɑ:, dʌn'bɑ:]
Everett ['evrɪt]
Fuller ['fʊlə]
Grace [greɪs]
Hatcher ['hætʃə]
Holmes [həʊmz]
Hughes [hju:z]
Jackson ['dʒæksn]
Jenkins ['dʒeŋkɪnz]
Kay [keɪ]
Khanom ['kɑ:nɒm]
Knight [naɪt]
Kramer ['kreɪmə]
Lanigan ['lænɪgən]
Luchetti [lu:'tʃetɪ]
Manzaneque [ˌmænzə'ni:k]
McGough [mə'gɒf]
Milligan ['mɪlɪgən]
Monkton ['mʌŋktən]
Morris ['mɒrɪs]
Morrison ['mɒrɪsn]
Moseley-Braun
  [ˌməʊzlɪ'brɔ:n, -'braʊn]
Olwell ['ɒlwel]
Osborne ['ɒzbɔ:n]
Patel [pə'tel]
Poe [pəʊ]
Rand [rænd]
Revell ['revl]
Rigby ['rɪgbɪ]
Rosetti [rə'zetɪ]
Rushdie ['rʌʃdɪ, 'rʊʃdɪ]
Seaton ['si:tən]
Sedillo [se'dɪljəʊ]
Sheridan ['ʃerɪdən]
Spirropoulos [spɪ'rɒpəlɒs]
Stokes [stəʊks]
Swenson ['swensn]
Thurber ['θɜ:bə]
Wister ['wɪstə]

Female first names

Amelia [ə'mi:lɪə]
Angeles ['ændʒəlɪs]
Carole ['kærəl]
Cora ['kɔ:rə]
Felicity [fə'lɪsətɪ]
Gail [geɪl]
Kathryn ['kæθrɪn]
Leela ['li:lə]
Lydia ['lɪdɪə]
Mema ['meɪmə]
Miriam ['mɪrɪəm]
Molly ['mɒlɪ]
Naomi ['neɪəmɪ, neɪ'əʊmɪ]
Nazmin ['næzmɪn]
Rebecca [rɪ'bekə]
Rosa ['rəʊzə]
Sacajawea [ˌsækədʒə'wi:ə]
Seema ['si:mə]
Victoria [ˌvɪk'tɔ:rɪə]

Male first names

Allan, Allen ['ælən]
Craig [kreɪg]
Edgar ['edgə]
Edmund ['edmənd]
Edward ['edwəd]
Erin ['erɪn]
Floyd [flɔɪd]
Frederick ['fredrɪk]
Grenville ['grenvɪl]
Jesse ['dʒesɪ]
Leon ['li:ən]
Mohammed, Muhammad
  [mə'hæmɪd]
Owen ['əʊɪn]
Raymond ['reɪmənd]
Salman ['sælmən, 'sælmæn]
Spike [spaɪk]
Sumit ['sʊmɪt]
Toni ['təʊnɪ]
Willi ['wɪlɪ]

Place names

Alleghenies [ˌælə'geɪnɪz]
Bombay [ˌbɒm'beɪ]
Boonetown ['bu:ntaʊn]
Canyon de Chelly
  [ˌkænjən də 'ʃeɪ]
Falkland Islands
  ['fɔ:(l)klənd‿ˌaɪləndz]
Fresno ['freznəʊ]
Gary ['gærɪ]
Gettysburg ['getɪzbɜ:g]
Gibraltar [dzɪ'brɔ:ltə]
Merida ['merɪdə]
Morocco [mə'rɒkəʊ]
Promontory ['prɒməntərɪ]
Regina [rɪ'dʒaɪnə]
Roxbury ['rɒksbərɪ]
Saskatchewan
  [sə'skætʃəwən]
Trampas ['træmpəs]
Yucatan [ˌju:kə'tɑ:n]

Other names

Ayatollah Khomeini
  [ˌaɪə'tɒlə kə'meɪnɪ]
Calvin & Hobbes
  [ˌkælvɪn‿ənd 'hɒbz]
Cheney ['tʃeɪnɪ]
Cherokee ['tʃerəki:]
Chevy (= Chevrolet) ['ʃevɪ]
Comanche [kə'mæntʃɪ]
Hopi ['həʊpɪ]
Id al-Fitr [ˌɪd‿ʌl 'fi:tr]
Iroquois ['ɪrəkwɔɪ]
Langston Hughes
  [ˌlæŋstən 'hju:z]
Mahatma Gandhi
  [məˌhɑ:tmə 'gændɪ,
  'gɑ:ndɪ]
Monte Cristo
  [ˌmɒntɪ 'krɪstəʊ]
Navajo ['nævəhəʊ]
Pawnee [pɔ:'ni:]
Raffestry ['ræfəstrɪ]
Reader's Digest
  [ˌri:dəz 'daɪdʒest]
Sioux [su:]
Spectator [spek'teɪtə]
Vogue [vəʊg]

Grammatical terms (Books 1-6)

abstract noun ['æbstrækt] abstraktes Nomen, Abstraktum
active ['æktɪv] Aktiv
activity verb [æk'tɪvətɪ] Tätigkeits- oder Vorgangsverb
adjective ['ædʒɪktɪv] Adjektiv
adverb ['ædvɜ:b] **(of frequency** ['fri:kwənsɪ]**/ of manner** ['mænə]) Adverb (der Häufigkeit/ der Art und Weise)
adverbial (of place/of time) [əd'vɜ:bɪəl] adverbiale Bestimmung (des Ortes/der Zeit)
adverbial clause [klɔ:z] Adverbialsatz (= Nebensatz, der wie eine adverbiale Bestimmung einen Zeitpunkt, einen Grund, eine Bedingung u.a. angibt)
article ['ɑ:tɪkl] Artikel
aspect ['æspekt] Aspekt (= Wahl zwischen *simple* und *progressive* form)
auxiliary (verb) [ɔ:g'zɪljərɪ] Hilfsverb
backshift of tenses ['bækʃɪft] Verschiebung der Zeitformen (in der indirekten Rede)
clause [klɔ:z] Gliedsatz, Teilsatz
clause of concession [kən'seʃn]**/of reason/of time** Nebensatz der Einräumung/des Grundes/der Zeit
collective noun [kə'lektɪv] Gruppenbezeichnung, Sammelname
collocation [ˌkɒlə'keɪʃn] (häufige) Wortverbindung, Kollokation
command [kə'mɑ:nd] Aufforderung(ssatz)
common noun ['kɒmən] Gattungsname
comparative [kəm'pærətɪv] Komparativ, erste Steigerungsform
comparison (of adjectives/of adverbs) [kəm'pærɪsn] Steigerung (der Adjektive/der Adverbien)
complement ['kɒmplɪmənt] prädikative Ergänzung (zum Subjekt)
compound (word) ['kɒmpaʊnd] Kompositum, zusammengesetztes Wort
conditional sentence [kən'dɪʃnəl] Bedingungssatz
conjunction [kən'dʒʌŋkʃn] Konjunktion
consonant ['kɒnsənənt] Konsonant, Mitlaut
contact clause ['kɒntækt klɔ:z] Relativsatz ohne Relativpronomen
contrastive emphasis [kən'trɑ:stɪv] kontrastive Betonung
coordinating conjunction [kəʊ'ɔ:dɪneɪtɪŋ] nebenordnende Konjunktion
countable noun ['kaʊntəbl] zählbares Nomen
defining relative clause [dɪ'faɪnɪŋ ˌrelətɪv ˌklɔ:z] bestimmender Relativsatz
definite article ['defɪnɪt] bestimmter Artikel
demonstrative pronoun [dɪ'mɒnstrətɪv] Demonstrativpronomen
direct object ['daɪrekt] direktes Objekt, „Sachobjekt"
direct speech direkte Rede
dynamic verb [daɪ'næmɪk] Tätigkeits- oder Vorgangsverb
emotive emphasis [ɪ'məʊtɪv] Betonung zum Gefühlsausdruck
emphasis ['emfəsɪs] Emphase, Hervorhebung, Betonung
emphasizing pronoun ['emfəsaɪzɪŋ] verstärkendes Pronomen
filler ['fɪlə] Füllwort
finite verb form ['faɪnaɪt] finite Verbform (= veränderbare Verbform, im Unterschied zum Infinitiv, Partizip und Gerundium)
future ['fju:tʃə] Futur, Zukunft
future perfect [ˌfju:tʃə 'pɜ:fɪkt] vollendete Zukunft, Futur II („Futur des Perfekts")
gerund ['dʒerənd] Gerundium (= *-ing*-Form des Verbs in der Funktion eines Nomens)
***going to*-future** Futur mit *going to*
***if*-clause** Nebensatz mit *if*, *if*-Satz
imperative [ɪm'perətɪv] Imperativ
indefinite article [ɪn'defɪnɪt] unbestimmter Artikel
indirect object ['ɪndɪrekt] indirektes Objekt, „Personenobjekt"
indirect/reported speech ['ɪndɪrekt/rɪ'pɔ:tɪd] indirekte Rede
infinitive [ɪn'fɪnɪtɪv] Infinitiv
***-ing* form** *-ing*-Form
intensifying adverb [ɪn'tensɪfaɪɪŋ] verstärkendes Adverb
intransitive verb [ɪn'trænsətɪv] intransitives Verb
introductory verb [ˌɪntrə'dʌktərɪ] (die indirekte Rede) einleitendes Verb
inversion [ɪn'vɜ:ʃn, ɪn'vɜ:ʒn] Inversion (= Wortstellung Hilfsverb – Subjekt)
irregular verb [ɪ'regjʊlə] unregelmäßiges Verb
linking adverb ['lɪŋkɪŋ] satzverbindendes Adverb
linking verb Verb, das die Verbindung zwischen Subjekt und prädikativer Ergänzung herstellt, z.B. *be, become*
long form Langform (des Verbs)
main clause ['meɪn klɔ:z] Hauptsatz
main verb Vollverb (= Teil des Prädikats)
material noun [mə'tɪərɪəl] Stoffname
modal (auxiliary) [ˌməʊdl‿ɔ:g'zɪljərɪ] modales Hilfsverb
negative statement ['negətɪv] verneinter Aussagesatz
non-defining relative clause ['nɒndɪˌfaɪnɪŋ ˌrelətɪv ˌklɔ:z] nicht bestimmender Relativsatz
non-finite verb form [ˌnɒn'faɪnaɪt] infinite Verbform (= nicht veränderbare Verbform: Infinitiv, Partizip, Gerundium)
noun [naʊn] Nomen, Substantiv

number ['nʌmbə] grammatische Zahl, Numerus (= Singular oder Plural)
object ['ɒbdʒɪkt] Objekt
object form Objektform (eines Personalpronomens)
***of*-phrase** [freɪz] *of*-Fügung
pair noun [peə] „Paarwort"
part of speech [ˌ- - '-] Wortart
participle ['pɑːtɪsɪpl] Partizip
participle construction [kən'strʌkʃn] Partizipialkonstruktion
passive ['pæsɪv] Passiv
passive infinitive [ɪn'fɪnɪtɪv] Infinitiv Passiv
past participle [ˌpɑːst 'pɑːtɪsɪpl] Partizip Perfekt
past perfect [ˌ- '--] Plusquamperfekt
past perfect progressive [ˌ- ˌ-- -'--] Verlaufsform des *past perfect*
past progressive [ˌ- -'--] Verlaufsform der Vergangenheit
perfect infinitive [ɪn'fɪnɪtɪv] Infinitiv Perfekt
perfect participle ['pɑːtɪsɪpl] *having* + Partizip Perfekt, z.B. *having waited*
personal pronoun ['pɜːsənl] Personalpronomen
phrasal verb ['freɪzl] feste Verb-Adverb-Verbindung
plural ['plʊərəl] Plural
plural noun Nomen, das nur im Plural steht
positive statement ['pɒzɪtɪv] bejahter Aussagesatz
possessive adjective [pə'zesɪv] adjektivisch gebrauchtes Possessivpronomen
possessive form „besitzanzeigende Form", *s*-Genitiv
possessive pronoun nominal gebrauchtes Possessivpronomen
prefix ['priːfɪks] Vorsilbe, Präfix
preposition [ˌprepə'zɪʃn] Präposition
prepositional verb Verbindung aus Verb + Präposition
present participle [ˌpreznt 'pɑːtɪsɪpl] Partizip Präsens
present perfect [ˌ-- '--] *present perfect* (Perfekt)
present perfect progressive [ˌ-- ˌ-- -'--] Verlaufsform des *present perfect*
present progressive [ˌ-- -'--] Verlaufsform des Präsens
progressive form [prəʊ'gresɪv] Verlaufsform (des Verbs)
pronoun ['prəʊnaʊn] Pronomen
proper name/proper noun ['prɒpə] Eigenname
prop-word ['prɒpwɜːd] Stützwort *one*
question ['kwestʃn] Frage(satz)
question tag [tæg] Frageanhängsel
question word Fragewort, Interrogativpronomen
reflexive pronoun [rɪ'fleksɪv] Reflexivpronomen
regular verb ['regjʊlə] regelmäßiges Verb
relative clause ['relətɪv] Relativsatz
relative pronoun Relativpronomen
reported/indirect speech [rɪ'pɔːtɪd/'ɪndɪrekt] indirekte Rede
reporting verb [rɪ'pɔːtɪŋ] die indirekte Rede einleitendes Verb, „berichtendes Verb"
sentence ['sentəns] Satz, Satzgefüge
sentence adverb Satzadverb, kommentierendes Adverb
short answer Kurzantwort
short form Kurzform (des Verbs)
simple form einfache Form (des Verbs)
simple past [ˌ-- '-] einfache Form der Vergangenheit
simple present [ˌ-- '--] einfache Form des Präsens
singular ['sɪŋgjʊlə] Singular
state/stative verb [steɪt/'steɪtɪv] Zustandsverb
statement ['steɪtmənt] Aussagesatz
stem [stem] (Wort-)Stamm
stress [stres] Betonung
subject ['sʌbdʒɪkt] Subjekt
subordinate clause [sə'bɔːdnət] Nebensatz
subordinating conjunction [sə'bɔːdɪneɪtɪŋ] unterordnende Konjunktion, nebensatzeinleitende Konjunktion
substitute (verb) ['sʌbstɪtjuːt] Ersatzverb (für modale Hilfsverben)
suffix ['sʌfɪks] Nachsilbe, Suffix
superlative [suː'pɜːlətɪv] Superlativ, zweite Steigerungsform
tense [tens] Tempus, Zeitform
transitive verb ['trænsətɪv] transitives Verb, Verb mit direktem Objekt
uncountable noun [ʌn'kaʊntəbl] nicht zählbares Nomen
verb [vɜːb] Prädikat, Satzaussage
verb (of perception [pə'sepʃn]**/of rest/of movement** ['muːvmənt]) Verb (der Wahrnehmung/der Ruhe/der Bewegung)
vowel ['vaʊəl] Vokal, Selbstlaut
***will*-future** Futur mit *will*
***will*-future progressive** Verlaufsform des Futurs mit *will*
word class ['- -] Wortart, Wortklasse
word order ['- ˌ--] Wortstellung
word stress ['- -] Wortbetonung
***yes/no* question** ['kwestʃən] Entscheidungsfrage

Irregular verbs

Infinitive	Simple past	Past participle	
(to) be	(I) was, (you) were	(I've/she has) been	sein
beat	beat	beaten	schlagen, besiegen
become	became	become	werden
begin	began	begun	beginnen, anfangen
blow	blew [uː]	blown [əʊ]	blasen, wehen
break [eɪ]	broke [əʊ]	broken [əʊ]	(zer)brechen; kaputtmachen
bring	brought [ɔː]	brought [ɔː]	(mit)bringen, (her)bringen
build	built	built	(er)bauen
burn	burned, burnt	burned, burnt	(ver)brennen
buy	bought [ɔː]	bought [ɔː]	kaufen
catch	caught [ɔː]	caught [ɔː]	fangen, erwischen; erreichen
choose [uː]	chose [əʊ]	chosen [əʊ]	(aus)wählen, aussuchen
come	came	come	kommen
cost [ɒ]	cost [ɒ]	cost [ɒ]	kosten
creep	crept [e]	crept [e]	kriechen; schleichen
cut	cut	cut	schneiden
deal [iː]	dealt [e]	dealt [e]	sich befassen (mit); handeln (von)
dig	dug	dug	(aus-, um)graben
do	did	done [ʌ]	tun, machen
draw	drew	drawn	zeichnen; ziehen
dream	dreamed [iː], dreamt [e]	dreamed [iː], dreamt [e]	träumen
drink	drank	drunk	trinken
drive	drove	driven [ɪ]	(Auto) fahren; (an)treiben
eat	ate [eɪ, BE *also:* e]	eaten	essen
fall	fell	fallen	fallen
feed	fed	fed	füttern
feel	felt	felt	(sich) fühlen
fight	fought [ɔː]	fought [ɔː]	(be)kämpfen
find	found [aʊ]	found [aʊ]	finden
fly	flew [uː]	flown [əʊ]	fliegen
forget	forgot	forgotten	vergessen
freeze	froze	frozen	(ge)frieren; erstarren
get	got	BE: got, AE: gotten	bekommen; gelangen, (hin)kommen; holen, besorgen; werden
give	gave	given	geben; schenken
go	went	gone [ɒ]	gehen; fahren
grow	grew [uː]	grown [əʊ]	wachsen; anbauen, anpflanzen
hang	hung	hung	(auf)hängen;
	hanged	hanged	(er)hängen
have (got)	had	had	haben
hear [ɪə]	heard [ɜː]	heard [ɜː]	hören
hide [aɪ]	hid [ɪ]	hidden [ɪ]	(sich) verstecken
hit	hit	hit	schlagen, treffen
hold	held	held	halten
hurt [ɜː]	hurt	hurt	verletzen, wehtun
keep	kept	kept	(be)halten, aufbewahren; einhalten
know [əʊ]	knew [juː]	known [əʊ]	kennen; wissen
lay [eɪ]	laid [eɪ]	laid [eɪ]	legen
lead [iː]	led [e]	led [e]	führen, leiten
learn [ɜː]	learned, learnt	learned, learnt	lernen
leave	left	left	weggehen, verlassen; (zurück)lassen

Infinitive	**Simple past**	**Past participle**	
lend	lent	lent	(ver-, aus)leihen
let	let	let	(zu)lassen
lie	lay [eɪ]	lain [eɪ]	liegen
lose [u:]	lost [ɒ]	lost [ɒ]	verlieren
make	made	made	machen; (veran)lassen
mean [i:]	meant [e]	meant [e]	bedeuten; meinen
meet	met	met	(sich) treffen, kennen lernen
misunderstand	misunderstood [ʊ]	misunderstood [ʊ]	missverstehen, nicht verstehen
overtake	overtook [ʊ]	overtaken	überholen
pay [eɪ]	paid [eɪ]	paid [eɪ]	(be)zahlen
put [ʊ]	put [ʊ]	put [ʊ]	stellen, legen, setzen
quit	quit	quit	aufhören, aufgeben
read [i:]	read [e]	read [e]	(vor)lesen
ride [aɪ]	rode	ridden [ɪ]	reiten; (Rad) fahren
ring	rang	rung	klingeln, läuten; anrufen
rise [aɪ]	rose	risen [ɪ]	(an)steigen; aufgehen; sich erheben
run	ran	run	rennen, laufen; fahren *(Zug, Bus)*
say	said [e]	said [e]	sagen
see	saw	seen	sehen
sell	sold	sold	verkaufen
send	sent	sent	schicken, senden
set	set	set	untergehen *(Sonne, Mond)*
shake	shook [ʊ]	shaken	schütteln; erschüttern; zittern
shine	shone [BE: ɒ, AE: əʊ]	shone [BE: ɒ, AE: əʊ]	scheinen *(Sonne)*
shoot [u:]	shot [ɒ]	shot [ɒ]	(er)schießen
show [əʊ]	showed [əʊ]	shown [əʊ]	zeigen
shut [ʌ]	shut [ʌ]	shut [ʌ]	schließen, zumachen
sing	sang	sung	singen
sink	sank	sunk	sinken; versenken
sit	sat	sat	sitzen
sleep	slept [e]	slept [e]	schlafen
smell	smelt, smelled	smelt, smelled	riechen
speak	spoke	spoken	sprechen
spell	spelt, spelled	spelt, spelled	buchstabieren, schreiben
spend	spent	spent	*(Geld)* ausgeben; *(Zeit)* verbringen
spoil	spoilt, spoiled	spoilt, spoiled	verderben; verwöhnen, verziehen
spread [e]	spread [e]	spread [e]	(sich) ausbreiten
stand	stood [ʊ]	stood [ʊ]	stehen
steal	stole	stolen	stehlen
strike	struck	struck	schlagen *(Uhr)*
swim	swam	swum	schwimmen
take	took [ʊ]	taken	(mit)nehmen; (hin-, weg)bringen
teach	taught [ɔ:]	taught [ɔ:]	unterrichten, lehren
tell	told	told	sagen, nennen; erzählen, berichten
think	thought [ɔ:]	thought [ɔ:]	meinen, denken
throw [əʊ]	threw [u:]	thrown [əʊ]	werfen
understand	understood [ʊ]	understood [ʊ]	verstehen, begreifen
upset	upset	upset	verärgern
wake (up)	woke (up)	woken (up)	aufwachen; (auf)wecken
wear [eə]	wore [ɔ:]	worn [ɔ:]	*(Kleidung)* tragen, anhaben
win	won [ʌ]	won [ʌ]	gewinnen
write	wrote	written	schreiben

Bildquellen

AA Photo Library, Basingstoke (S. 18 Mitte links); Acaluso, Blumberg (S. 50 Kinder unten, S. 38); AP, Frankfurt a. M. (S. 14, S. 24 oben links, oben rechts); Anna Baker, York (S. 109 oben links, oben 2. von rechts, unten links, Mitte unten); Bavaria Bildagentur, Gauting (S. 39 oben, S. 88 oben); Picture Finders/Bavaria (S. 41 unten); BBC Enterprises, London (S. 30); John Birdsall, Nottingham (S. 18 oben rechts, S. 22 Mitte rechts, S. 24 unten); Torsten Brinkmann, Cambridge (S. 20 oben links); David W. Bygott/Bygott Photos (S. 8 oben rechts); J. Allan Cash, London (S. 18 oben links, S. 78 Landschaft unten); Columbia University, New York (S. 83 oben); Corbis-Bettmann, New York (S. 35 oben); UPI/Corbis-Bettmann (S. 49 unten links); Cornelsen-Archiv, Berlin (S. 5 oben links); P. W. Oldham/Cornelsen-Archiv (S. 55); Paul Dames, Berlin (S. 8 oben links); dpa, Frankfurt a. M. (S. 9, S. 21 Mitte rechts, S. 115); Bildarchiv Engelmeier, München (S. 35 unten); Elisa Lionelli/Focus, Hamburg (S. 50 Mitte); Magnum/Focus (S. 49 oben); Henning Christoph/Das Fotoarchiv, Essen (S. 5 unten rechts); Hulton Getty, London (S. 21 oben rechts, S. 22 oben links, oben rechts, S. 60, S. 83 unten); IFA-Bilderteam, München-Taufkirchen (S. 89); Held/IFA-Bilderteam (S. 18 unten rechts); Elyse Lewin/Image Bank, Berlin (S. 5 Mitte links); Martin Black/Impact Photos, London (S. 5 Mitte rechts); Piers Cavendish/Impact Photos (S. 5 oben rechts); Howard Sochurek/LIFE Magazine © TIME Inc./inter-TOPICS, Hamburg (S. 86); Kenji Kawano, Window Rock (S. 78 oben, Familie unten); Keystone, Hamburg (S. 57 oben links, S. 84 unten); Ute Klaphake, London (S. 28); John Lally, York (S. 11); Gary Larson, The Far Side, Copyright © 1987 Universal Press Syndicate (S. 12 unten); Library of Congress, Washing-ton, D.C. (S. 33); Orde Eliason/Link, London (S. 18 unten links); Richard A. Long (S. 54); Mirror Syndication International, London (S. 18 Mitte rechts); Tom Murray, Pittsfield (S. 7 oben links, oben rechts); Peter Newark's American Pictures, Bath (S. 39 unten, S. 45); Nottinghamshire County Library, Nottingham (S. 72); Nas D. Guravich/Okapia, Frankfurt a. M. (S. 90 unten); N. Rosing/Okapia (S. 71 Baum); Lewis Parker, The Warpath (S. 37); Bildarchiv Paysan, Stuttgart (S. 84 oben); Giles Bernard/Photofusion, London (S. 109 oben 2. von links, unten rechts); Julia Martin/Photofusion (S. 5 unten links); Bob Watkins/Photofusion (S. 109 oben rechts); David Graham/Picturefile, London (S. 6, S. 62-63, S. 71 Fenster, S. 79); Henrik Pohl, Berlin (S. 20 Münzen); Punch Ltd., London (S. 129 reproduced with permission of Punch Ltd.); Royal Mint, Wales (S. 73); Peter Sanders, Chesham (S. 23, S. 27); Rex/Marion Schweitzer, München (S. 42); Alasdair Smith, Aber-deen (S. 12 oben); Stuart Kendall/Sportsphoto Ltd., Scarborough (S. 21 unten links); Sygma, Paris (S. 48); Transglobe, Hamburg (S. 50 oben, Frau unten, S. 53); USIS, Bonn (S. 49 Mitte rechts); Ullstein-amw Pressedienst GmbH, Berlin (S. 59); D. J. Cox/Wildlife, Hamburg (S. 88 unten); St. Morello/Wildlife (S. 91); S. Morgan/Wildlife (S. 90 oben); ZEFA, Düsseldorf (S. 7 unten)

Textquellen

The German school system: based on *Facts about Germany* © Societäts-Verlag, Frankfurt a. Main (S. 9). Cartoon: from *The Authoritative Calvin and Hobbes* by Bill Watterson, Copyright © 1990 by Bill Watterson, distributed by Universal Press Syndicate (S. 10). *The truancy officer's visit:* from *Multiple Choice* by Roger Hall, © Roger Hall 1985 (S. 15). *A victim of racism speaks out:* from *Let's Beat Racism/MIZZ magazine* (S. 22). Newspaper article: from *The Times Educational Supplement*, 19.1.1996 (S. 23). *New hope for bullied boy:* adapted from an article in *The Guardian*, 14.1.1997 (S. 28). *An eye for an eye:* based on the BBC television programme *The Diary of Rita Patel*, produced by Carole Boyer and broadcast on 14.9.1988, © BBC Enterprises (S. 30-31). *East and West united* © 1996 Cornelsen & Oxford University Press (S. 35). *The plight of the naive American Indian* by Graham Rawle. Reproduced by permission of The Agency (London) Ltd. © 1991 Graham Rawle. First published by Fourth Estate. All rights reserved and enquiries to The Agency (London) Ltd., 24 Pottery Lane, London W11 4LZ (S. 41). *Dances with Wolves* © 1996 Cornelsen & Oxford University Press (S. 42). *Such is prairie life:* based on an extract from *Women of the West* Copyright © 1982 by Cathy Luchetti and Carol Olwell. Reprinted by permission of Anne Edelstein Literary Agency (S. 45-47). *Dreams:* from *The Dream Keeper and Other Poems* by Langston Hughes, © 1932 by Alfred A. Knopf, Inc. and renewed 1960 by Langston Hughes. Reprinted by permission of the publisher (S. 62). *Dream:* adapted from the *Oxford Advanced Learner's Dictionary,* fifth edition 1995, Cornelsen & Oxford (S. 62). *Dreams:* adapted from *New Webster's Universal Encyclopedia* (S. 62). *Daydreams:* adapted from *Psychology* by Charles G. Morris (S. 62). *The moth and the star* © 1940 James Thurber, © 1968 Rosemary A. Thurber. From *Fables For Our Time*, published by Harper Collins (S. 64). *The winner* by Donald E. Westlake, © Donald E. Westlake. Reprinted by permission of Andrew Nurnberg Associates (S. 65-70). *Dreampoem* by Roger McGough. Reprinted by permission of Peters, Fraser & Dunlop Group Ltd. (S. 71). *Hidden worlds:* extract from *Key to the Door* by Alan Sillitoe, © Alan Sillitoe 1961 and 1989 (S. 72-73). *Sardines* by Spike Milligan, © Spike Milligan Productions Ltd. (S. 74). *applaws):* from the *Complete Poems 1904-1962* by E. E. Cummings, edited by George J. Firmage, by permission of W. W. Norton & Company Ltd., Copyright © 1991 by the Trustees for the E. E. Cummings Trust and George James Firmage (S. 74). *Southbound on the freeway* by May Swenson. Reprinted with the permission of Simon & Schuster Books for Young Readers, an imprint of Simon & Schuster Children's Publishing Division from THE COMPLETE POEMS OF MAY SWENSON by May Swenson. Copyright © 1993 by The Literary Estate of May Swenson. First appeared in *The New Yorker, February 1963* (S. 75). *A story with a number of given words:* adapted from the winning entry of *The Jaspistos Competition* by O. Smith, © The Spectator, London (S. 76). *Just one of many stories in a park* by Angeles Manzaneque and *Out of the mouths of babes?* by Kathryn Clarke, © The Telegraph plc, London, 1994 (S. 77). *A question of identity:* based on 'Lynn, a Navajo' from *To live in two worlds* by Brent Ashabranner, © Dodd, Mead & Company, Inc., New York (S. 78-80). *It is Not!:* from *The Way*, edited by Shirley Hill Witt and Stan Steiner, Vintage Books (S. 80). *The rabbits who caused all the trouble* by James Thurber, © 1940 James Thurber, © 1968 Rosemary A. Thurber. From *Fables For Our Time*, published by Harper Collins (S. 81). *The telephone, Dust of snow, Nothing gold can stay* and *Stopping by woods on a snowy evening:* from *The Poetry of Robert Frost,* edited by Edward Connery Lathem. Copyright 1923, 1928, 1936, 1951 by Robert Frost, © 1964, 1975 by Lesley Frost Ballantine, Copyright 1923, © 1969 by Henry Holt & Co., Inc. Reprinted by permission of Henry Holt & Co., Inc. (S. 86-87). Extracts from *Whale Nation* by Heathcote Williams. Reprinted by permission of Jonathan Cape Ltd. (S. 88-91). Extracts from the *Oxford Advanced Learner's Dictionary,* fifth edition 1995, Cornelsen & Oxford (S. 94, S. 109). *The End* by Fredric Brown, © Fredric Brown and the publisher (S. 154).

Many thanks to the Centre for Research in Ethnic Relations, University of Warwick, for their kind support during the development of Unit 2.
Wir danken dem Amerika Haus, Berlin, für die freundliche Unterstützung bei der Recherche für die amerikakundlichen Teile des Buches.

Useful classroom phrases

Talking about texts

Giving your first impressions

I think the text/story/play/poem/song/excerpt/… is interesting/funny/exciting/boring/sad/(un)realistic/ … because …	Ich finde, der Text/die Geschichte/das Theaterstück/das Gedicht/das Lied/der Auszug/… ist interessant/lustig/ spannend/langweilig/traurig/(un)realistisch/…, weil …
The text made me feel sad/angry/concerned/confused/ happy/…	Der Text hat mich traurig/ärgerlich/besorgt/verwirrt/ glücklich/… gemacht.
I found the ending surprising/disappointing/annoying/confusing/predictable/…	Ich fand das Ende/den Schluss überraschend/enttäuschend/ärgerlich/verwirrend/vorhersagbar/…
I enjoyed/didn't enjoy reading this text because it reminded me/made me think of …	Ich habe diesen Text (nicht) gern gelesen, weil er mich an … erinnert hat.
The text deals with/presents a humorous/serious/ current/… theme.	In dem Text wird ein heiteres/ernstes/aktuelles/… Thema behandelt/dargestellt.
I can/can't identify with the main character because …	Ich kann mich mit der Hauptperson (nicht) identifizieren, weil …

Taking a closer look

• The author deals with the question why/criticizes/ analyses/comments on/compares/…	Der Autor/Die Autorin behandelt die Frage, wieso/ kritisiert/analysiert/kommentiert/vergleicht/…
At the beginning the author introduces the main character(s) … . Later on …	Am Anfang führt der Autor/die Autorin die Hauptperson(en) ein … . Später …
In the first paragraph the narrator describes the setting.	Im ersten Abschnitt beschreibt der Erzähler/die Erzählerin den Ort/Schauplatz des Geschehens.
The action takes place at/in/during …	Die Handlung spielt in/während …
• A is /is characterized as/seems to be a strong/weak/ aggressive/ambitious/thoughtful/thoughtless/ careful/brave/violent/creative/difficult/… (sort of) person/character.	A ist/wird dargestellt als/scheint … zu sein eine starke/schwache/aggressive/ehrgeizige/rücksichtsvolle/rücksichtslose/vorsichtige/mutige/ gewalttätige/kreative/schwierige/… Person.
A's behaviour/reaction shows that/is a result of …	A's Verhalten/Reaktion zeigt, dass/ergibt sich aus …
• To give an example, in line X the text says …	Um ein Beispiel zu nennen: In Zeile X steht im Text …
Another example of … is to be found in line X, where …	Ein anderes Beispiel von/für … findet man in Zeile X, wo …
This example/sentence shows/illustrates/suggests that/explains why …	Dieses Beispiel/Dieser Satz zeigt/veranschaulicht/legt nahe, dass/erklärt, warum …
• In comparison with A, B is/seems to be …	Im Vergleich zu A ist B …/scheint B … zu sein.
A is (very) similar to/(completely) different from/can(not) be compared to …	A ist … (sehr) ähnlich/(völlig) anders als/kann (nicht) verglichen werden mit …

Discussing different views

In my opinion/It seems to me that/As far as I can see …	Meiner Meinung nach/Mir scheint/Soweit ich sehe, …
I think it is important to consider …	Ich finde, es ist wichtig zu bedenken, …
I'm of the same opinion/also think that …	Ich bin der gleichen Meinung/finde auch, dass …
I agree with A's view that …	Ich stimme mit A's Ansicht überein, dass …
I can't agree/don't agree/disagree with A's view that … because …	Ich kann A's Ansicht, dass …, nicht zustimmen/stimme A's Ansicht, dass …, nicht zu, weil …
I'm not sure if/not convinced that …	Ich bin nicht sicher, ob/nicht überzeugt, dass …
I don't understand why/find it hard to believe that …	Ich verstehe nicht, wieso/finde es schwer, zu glauben, dass …
In contrast to A, I believe/would say that …	Im Gegensatz zu A glaube ich/würde ich sagen, dass …

→ Option 12: Literary terms and their collocations

The United St